Strangers in African Societies

EDITED BY WILLIAM A. SHACK

Strangers in

Contributions by Herschelle Sullivan Challenor,

Donald N. Levine, Ali A. Mazrui,

Christine Obbo, Margaret Peil,

Elliott P. Skinner, Aidan Southall,

SPONSORED BY THE JOINT COMMITTEE
SOCIAL SCIENCE RESEARCH COUNCIL AND THE

UNIVERSITY OF CALIFORNIA PRESS

AND ELLIOTT P. SKINNER

African Societies

Jeremy S. Eades, Jessica Kuper, Neil O. Leighton,
Ruth Schachter Morgenthau,
Enid Schildkrout, William A. Shack,
Niara Sudarkasa, Monica Wilson

ON AFRICAN STUDIES OF THE
AMERICAN COUNCIL OF LEARNED SOCIETIES

BERKELEY • LOS ANGELES • LONDON

University of California Press
Berkeley and Los Angeles, California
University of California Press, Ltd.
London, England
Copyright © 1979 by
The Regents of the University of California
ISBN 0-520-03458-9
Library of Congress Catalog Card Number: 77-73501
Printed in the United States of America

1 2 3 4 5 6 7 8 9

Contents

The Contributors

Herschelle Sullivan Challenor, formerly Assistant Professor of Political Science, Hunter College, New York City, is with the Committee on International Relations, United States Congress.

Jeremy S. Eades is Lecturer in Anthropology at Darwin College, University of Kent, Canterbury, England.

Jessica Kuper is resident in Leiden, the Netherlands.

Neil O. Leighton is Associate Professor of Political Science at the University of Michigan, Flint.

Donald N. Levine, Professor of Sociology, is at the University of Chicago.

Ali A. Mazrui is Professor of Political Science at the University of Michigan.

Ruth Schachter Morgenthau, Professor of Political Science, Brandeis University, is with the United States Mission to the United Nations.

Christine Obbo is in the Department of Anthropology, University of Wisconsin.

Margaret Peil, Reader in Sociology, is at the Center of West African Studies, University of Birmingham, England.

Enid Schildkrout is Associate Curator for Africa, American Museum of Natural History.

William A. Shack is Professor of Anthropology, University of California at Berkeley.

Elliott P. Skinner is Franz Boas Professor of Anthropology, Columbia University.

Aidan Southall is Professor of Anthropology at the University of Wisconsin.

Niara Sudarkasa is Professor of Anthropology, University of Michigan.

Monica Wilson is Emeritus Professor of Social Anthropology, University of Cape Town.

Preface

The essays in this book were first presented at an interdisciplinary symposium sponsored by the Joint Committee on Africa of the Social Science Research Council and the American Council of Learned Societies, at the Smithsonian Conference Center, Belmont, Maryland, 16–19 October 1974. William Shack, then a member of the Committee, proposed the theme of the symposium and invited as cochairman Elliott Skinner, who, a decade earlier, had addressed the problem of the position of strangers in West Africa.

By 1974, many new African states had taken legal steps to alter the privileged social and economic positions that African and non-African strangers still enjoyed in their societies, mainly a legacy of the colonial era. Where new legislation was promulgated, strangers often were mandated for expatriation to their homelands. Public interest in the plight of strangers in Africa was attracted mainly by the expulsion of Asians from Uganda. But worldwide publicity surrounding the forceful exodus of Ugandan Asians overshadowed similar events of far greater magnitude in other parts of the continent that preceded the East African situation by several years. What now is often seen as a contemporary human problem is, in matter of fact, rooted in antiquity, perhaps dating to the origins of city-states. In twentieth-century Africa the social and legal position of strangers has become increasingly precarious, straining political relations between African states and governments outside the continent of Africa. How African governments nowadays and in the past have addressed the question "who is a stranger?" provoked in the Committee considerable interest in seeing the problem aired in as broad an interdisciplinary forum as possible.

The absence of literary scholars from discussion of a symposium subject whose theme can be traced to early Greek and Roman literature might be considered a serious weakness in a book on strangers, in Africa or elsewhere. Social and political sciences can only benefit from intellectual insights cast on the study of society by scholars in humanistic traditions. We recognize this obvious lack of representation by humanists in the contributions published here, and we regret that invitations to participate in the symposium were necessarily restricted, with first priority assigned to scholars whose contributions would be primarily ethnographic in orientation and who had firsthand field experience in Africa. It also would have been of social science interest to broaden the comparative scope of enquiry to include studies of strangers in African societies not represented in this collection, most strikingly the Republic of South Africa. Here the white-dominated government's implementation of the Bantustan policy has legally designated black Africans as "strangers" in their own homeland. These and other apparent shortcomings inevitably arise when scholars motivated by different disciplinary persuasions come together to address problems of common interest. Nonetheless, the symposium at Belmont not only made possible lively intellectual debate between political scientists, economists, sociologists and social anthropologists. Of equal, if not more, importance, this symposium was, we think, the first scholarly undertaking to examine in historical and cross-cultural perspective the social and political conditions which have affected the position of strangers in African societies in the post independence era, as well as in past times. And for this opportunity we owe thanks to many.

Thanks first to the Joint Committee on Africa for their enthusiastic reception of the proposal by Shack for the conference; for without their scholarly and financial support, that prospectus would have become a matter of historical record in the Committee's minutes. Committee members participated in all conference sessions, lending to the discussions their expertise derived from research on related problems in Africa, thereby clarifying a range of theoretical issues raised in the preliminary papers of the contributors. We are most grateful to Dr. Alice Morton, then Social Science Research Council staff member to the Committee, for the invaluable service rendered in arranging the conference and tending to matters of detail at Belmont, and for serving as *rapporteur* for the sessions, the careful record of which aided considerably in writing the Introduction. Professor Elizabeth Colson kindly read an earlier draft of the Introduction, and we hope the final version does justice to her several critical comments, which have been incorporated in the revisions. The secretarial staff of the Institute of International Studies at the University of California, Berkeley, assisted in preparing the manuscript in form for the printer, with their usual diligence and dispatch. Mr. Gene Tanke's editorial assistance was indispensable in shaping the collection of essays into an integrated volume, and to him we are especially indebted. A grant-in-aid awarded by the Joint Committee on Africa underwrote much of the editorial cost of publication.

Finally, we thank the contributors to this book for interrupting their professional schedules to graciously accept our invitation to the conference. And we are especially grateful to Professor Monica Wilson, Dr. Jeremy Eades and Dr. Margaret Peil, who traveled great distances to lend their knowledge and experience in Africa toward making the conference a success.

WILLIAM A. SHACK   **ELLIOTT P. SKINNER**
University of California   *Columbia University*
at Berkeley

20 February 1978

Introduction

William A. Shack

S trangers in African societies, like strangers everywhere, are as socially ambiguous as the word "stranger" implies. Alien, intruder, interloper, foreigner, *novus homo*, newcomer, immigrant, guest, outsider, outlander, and so on—all are convenient labels that social groups habitually apply to persons who, by reasons of custom, language, or social role, stand on the margin of society. Literary men, taking advantage of this ambiguity, have often used the word "stranger" as a metaphorical device, casting characters in their novels and dramas in shadowy, ill-defined social roles. Shakespeare's stranger appeared variously as a woman in *Henry VI*, Part I, a Jew in *The Merchant of Venice*, a Moor in *Othello*, and a New World "savage" in *The Tempest*.[1] Ralph Ellison, in *The Invisible Man*, created an archetypal stranger, who by his words and deeds articulated the social boundaries artificially separating black and white Americans. Words such as "stranger," which are capable of being understood in two or more senses, are potentially misleading even in everyday conversation. And when they are raised to the level of social science concepts, it becomes a difficult task to define precise social units of analysis and the actors in them.

Ambiguity abounds in Georg Simmel's brief essay entitled "Der Fremde" ("The Stranger," 1908), which provides the sociological framework for the collection of papers in this volume.[2] The stranger, Simmel wrote, "is fixed within a particular spatial circle, or within a group whose boundaries are similar to spatial boundaries. But his position in this group is determined, essentially, by the fact that he has not belonged to it from the beginning, that he imports qualities into it which do not, and cannot, stem from the group itself." He says also that "the stranger . . . is an element of the group itself. His position as a full-fledged member involves both being outside it and confronting it." And so, "in spite of being inorganically appended to it, the stranger is yet an organic member of the group." Thus the characteristic unity of the stranger's position is that "it is composed of certain measures of nearness and distance."[3]

1. L. A. Fiedler, *The Stranger in Shakespeare.*
2. G. Simmel, *Soziologie*, pp. 685–691; trans. by R. E. Park and E. W. Burgess, *Introduction to the Science of Society*, pp. 322–327. See also K. Wolff, *The Sociology of Georg Simmel*, pp. 402–408; D. Levine, *On Individuality and Social Forms*, pp. 143–149.
3. Wolff, pp. 402, 403, 408.

Betwixt and between, though, is only one kind of ambiguity in Simmel's concept of the stranger. Another ambiguity is reflected in the different ways he uses the concept to analyze the individuality and the social form of the stranger. In certain passages of "Der Fremde" Simmel refers explicitly to the stranger as an individual, a member of a social aggregate; in other passages the implicit suggestion is that strangers constitute a social group. According to Donald Levine (in Chapter One), the assertion that strangers constitute a "category of persons" or "members of a collectivity" is only one of several "sprawling and confusing assortments of statements" by sociologists who have taken Simmel's formulations as a point of departure for analyzing social roles and social distance in stranger-host interactions. In Chapter One, which deals with the history and systematics of the sociology of the stranger, Levine points out that the confusion about what Simmel actually meant began among sociologists in the United States with Robert Park, who produced the first English translation of "Der Fremde."[4] In a later essay, Park altered Simmel's concept, which had pertained specifically to a social type, to explain the urban-cultural experiences of European immigrants in the United States.[5] What Simmel had conceived as a social phenomenon, Park and his students, notably E. W. Burgess and Everett Stonequist, translated into a cultural phenomenon. Stonequist's now classic study, *The Marginal Man*, set the tone for numerous sociological studies which borrowed what was originally Park's misreading of Simmel's stranger as a social type, shaping the concept to become synonymous to a racial and cultural type. Following these early misconceptions, latter-day followers of Simmel have taken the concept of the stranger as a category of persons and shifted it to apply to a collectivity.[6] This alteration in meaning has carried over to the level of structural analysis, and has become thoroughly entrenched in sociological studies of strangers and their hosts.

Although "stranger" is an ambiguous word, in sociological as well as literary usage, and although social scientists have often exhibited naiveté in their transmutation of Simmel's idea of *der Fremde*, the concept of the stranger remains one of the most powerful sociological tools for analyzing the social processes of individuals and groups confronting new social orders. Naiveté after all, is not without sociological value. Max Gluckman once argued persuasively in favor of the assumption of a certain naiveté in limiting the boundaries of analysis, thereby highlighting those social phenomena for which a deeper understanding is sought.[7]

4. Translated in Park and Burgess, pp. 322–327.
5. R. E. Park, "Human Migration and the Marginal Man," *American Journal of Sociology*, vol. 33, no. 6 (1928), pp. 881–893.
6. For example M. Twaddle, ed., *Expulsion of a Minority: Essays on Ugandan Asians.*
7. M. Gluckman, ed., *Closed Systems and Open Minds: The Limits of Naïvety in Social Anthropology.*

In the specific case of ambiguity in Simmel's concept of the stranger, the assumption of naiveté by Simmel's followers has, in fact, enriched their analyses of different types of social situations involving the interaction between hosts and strangers. In Africa or elsewhere, whether strangers are viewed as members of social aggregates or as constituting social groups depends largely upon the nature of the social situation and the character of their involvement with their hosts.

Sociological studies of strangers and their hosts outside the African continent, which is the geographical setting for the essays in this volume, for the most part have been set within the broader conceptual framework of race and ethnic relations. Assimilation or integration within the host society of racially and ethnically different strangers has been viewed as the end product of the social interaction process. One recent case in point is the collection of essays edited by Lloyd Fallers, describing the role and status of the overseas Chinese in Singapore and Madagascar, of the Lebanese in West Africa, and of the Ibo in the Calabar district of modern Nigeria. The principal concern of the contributors to Fallers' volume is with culturally alien communities produced by the migration of ethnic groups pursuing economic opportunities.[8] Invariably, as those studies make plain, immigrants form associations to further their own social and economic interests, and sometimes even their political interests. They pursue these interests whether settled in peaceful or in hostile social environments. And where immigrants are engaged as traders, middlemen, brokers, and entrepreneurs, and are thus cast in the role of economic go-betweens for competitive producing and consuming populations, the most natural response is for them to seek to protect their collective interests through some form of associational grouping, which provides a basis for common identity. None of the essays in Fallers' collection, however, address themselves to Simmel's concept of the stranger; indeed, Fallers himself makes only passing reference to Simmel's general proposition concerning the historical importance of strangers in human societies.[9]

With respect to Africa, Cohen and Middleton state that the concern of the collection of essays in *From Tribe to Nation* is "to analyze the ways in which existing political systems change in scale and/or take on new functions as a consequence of economic and other developments."[10] Integration theory, as understood in its widest sociological meaning, informs the types of analyses made of the African societies represented in their study. These range from relatively small-scale acephalous societies like the Tonga in Zambia and the Lugbara in Uganda, on the one hand, to the centralized states of the Bornu in Nigeria and the Mossi in the

---

8. L. A. Fallers, ed., *Immigrants and Associations*, p. 11.
9. *Ibid.*, pp. 7–9.
10. R. Cohen and J. Middleton, eds., *From Tribe to Nation in Africa: Studies in Incorporation Processes*, p. 5.

Upper Volta, on the other. The studies by Fallers and by Cohen and Middleton by no means exhaust the contemporary literature on variations of Simmel's idea of the stranger.[11] Nor do those essays, singularly or collectively, advance in any significant sociological sense the usefulness of Simmel's social type for the understanding of social processes in modern societies, in which strangers have played an increasingly important role under conditions of political and economic change. Rather, such studies have continued in the tradition set by Robert Park and his followers which, as already noted, transmuted Simmel's social type, the stranger, into a cultural model to explain processes of integration, assimilation, or incorporation of culturally diverse immigrant groups into larger societal wholes. Latter-day students of Park have demonstrated in their works that the process of change in the sociocultural status of Simmel's archetypal stranger has been in the direction of a more complete inclusion into the host society. The corresponding change in their legal status has been from "alien" to "citizen."

Alien and citizen define legal status, not social status. Legal status is regulated by the machinery of government at the level of nation-state, not at the level of local polities which have been incorporated into larger political systems. Alien and citizen also are at opposite ends of the legal-jural continuum, along which differential sets of rights, duties, and obligations obtain between social persons, social categories, and the state. This distinction between alien and citizen bears somewhat on Lewis Henry Morgan's famous dictum with respect to social organization (society) and political organization (state). As we know, Morgan termed the former *societas* and the latter *civitas*.[12] Aliens may belong to and become intricately involved in day-to-day activities of a *societas*, even to the extent of marrying among its members, accumulating property, and attaining superior social status. But ultimately it is the state (the *civitas*) that is empowered to exercise *jus in personam* and *jus in rem*, the epitome of which is the enfranchisement of its inhabitants by the bestowal of citizenship, or by disenfranchisement, as the case may be.

In the strict Simmelian sense of the term, strangers are not aliens. Strangers are not found at either end of the alien-citizen continuum; they are betwixt and between, as Simmel said. Through their involvement in sundry social, economic, and quasi-political activities, strangers symbolically mediate between society and the state. It is not surprising, therefore, that most studies of immigrant groups in Western societies have focused on the inclusion or enfranchisement of immigrants by the state, through legal processes such as "naturalization" in the United States, or

11. For a recent adaptation of Simmel's concept of the stranger to the African situation, see M. Fortes, "Strangers," in M. Fortes and S. Patterson, eds., *Studies in African Social Anthropology*, pp. 229–253.

12. L. H. Morgan, *Ancient Society*, pp. 6ff.

on their exclusion through denial of petitions for citizenship. Here it is important to note that the process of change in the legal status of strangers in many, though by no means all, African societies has been contrary to the historical experiences of most strangers (or immigrants) in Western societies. In the main, both before the imposition of colonial rule in Africa and during the dependency period, indigenous African and non-African strangers were left virtually free to move from one traditional African polity and temporarily resettle in another. They were true strangers in the sense that Simmel meant—immigrants, but not aliens. In the contemporary era of self-government, newly independent African nation-states have increasingly treated *jus in personam* and *jus in rem* as rights to be defined and enforced by the state within its legal and political boundaries. But exercising this privilege of sovereignty has reversed, as it were, the "normal" process of change in the status of strangers. In most Western societies, once strangers have been declared legal aliens, they have attained the status of citizen in their respective nation-states. On the contrary, strangers in several African societies have been declared legal aliens, denied petitions for citizenship, and mandated for repatriation to their homelands.

I

Elliott Skinner made the first systematic effort to adapt Simmel's concept of the stranger to African societies.[13] He called attention to the presence of permanent stranger communities in many West African societies as early as the eighteenth century—in Ghana, Malle, Gao, Djenne, and Timbuktu, for example. He also described how the changes in social role, spatial distance, and social status of West African strangers in relation to their hosts affects the socio-legal distinction between alien and citizen in the African context. In some areas in pre-colonial Africa, "chiefs and headmen represented their followers at the local courts; in other areas, the local ruler appointed one of his officials to deal with strangers and their chiefs. The common element here was that, with few exceptions, the African strangers were under the control of the local African political authorities, and stayed only at the sufferance of their hosts."[14]

Alterations of the status and the roles of African and non-African strangers were among the most profound results of the establishment of colonial governments in West Africa and elsewhere on the continent. Local African polities were thrust into the role of being involuntary hosts to uninvited guests. Migration encouraged by external authorities increased the numbers of African, European, and Asian strangers in commerce, mining, plantations, and urban centers outside their original

13. E. P. Skinner, "Strangers in West African Societies," *Africa*, vol. 33, no. 4 (1965), pp. 307–320.
14. *Ibid.*, p. 308.

homelands. In areas of resettlement, African strangers established their own permanent quarters under their own chiefs or headmen; in political relationships, strangers bypassed local African political authorities, especially in matters of dispute, and sought redress for grievances through the District Commissioners rather than the Native Courts; in economic relations, strangers became engaged in nontraditional activities controlled by Europeans, who were themselves strangers, competing with local people for employment and effectively eliminating their chances of economic mobility.[15] The economic aggressiveness of strangers, more than their political actions, inevitably engendered hostility, but local hosts were powerless to remedy the imbalance in the control and distribution of resources. Again, as Skinner writes: "in many countries the strangers even tried to oust local people from purely African economic pursuits. In the Ivory Coast, the fishing industry was almost entirely in the hands of Togolese and other strangers. In Ghana, Nigerians dominated the indigenous sector of the diamond-mining enterprise, the waterfront stores at Winneba, and the Fadama motor-parts market on the outskirts of Accra. About 40 percent of the female vendors in the Kumasi market were Yoruba, and the Gao men from Soudan accounted for 30 percent of the yam vendors there. So important were Gao men in this latter trade that the section of the market in which yams were sold was called 'the Gao market.'"[16]

After Ghana, the Ivory Coast, and Uganda, among other African nations, attained self-government, the nexus of socioeconomic relations between strangers and their hosts was again radically altered. The quasi-legal enfranchisement strangers had enjoyed outside their homelands during the long period of colonial rule, a status not unlike that of "honorary citizen," was eliminated. The former involuntary hosts, now having acquired the political privilege of drawing up their own "guest list," as it were, demanded the repatriation to their homelands of Dahomeyans, Togolese, and Nigeriens from the Ivory Coast, of Yoruba and other Nigerians from Ghana, and of Kenyan Luo and Asians from Uganda. These are but a few examples of what took place throughout the continent. Whatever humanistic and moral issues are raised by the forced exodus of masses of Africans, any subjective concern over unjust acts clashes with political reality. For on objective grounds, the compulsory repatriation of strangers to their homelands marked a significant stage in the political development of newly self-governing African states. It was the stage reached when African states could exercise sovereign control over their territorial boundaries, and could distinguish legally between aliens and citizens.[17]

15. *Ibid.*, pp. 309–310.
16. *Ibid.*, p. 310.
17. The historical background of the development of this legal distinction in the case of the Yoruba in Ghana is discussed by Sudarkasa in Chapter Eight.

That, in brief, is the broad conceptual framework for the theoretical and sociological discussion of the phenomenon of strangers in African societies. A social science approach to the problem gives rise to two different sets of guiding questions. The first set relates to the long-range economic and technological effects on the wider communities which have expelled strangers who have been an integral part of the fabric of their social and economic life.[18] But we do not yet know the real consequences of such policies on African nation-states; our factual information is scanty, and often unreliable. The second set of questions relates to the type of sociological inquiries that broaden the analysis of strangers in African societies, expanding it beyond the typically narrow concerns of ethnicity and occupational roles. In this respect, the essays in this volume have taken cognizance of the social-structural and political-economic variables that might help to explain why strangers have been tolerated at particular periods of historical time in some African societies and not in others. Of related sociological significance are the different levels of society in which analysis is made of stranger-host relations, a point to which reference has been made above. Toleration of strangers at the local level—in the village community, for instance—may not be endured at higher levels of the state and the political bureaucracy from which national policies affecting the status of strangers flow; the reverse may be the case also.

These general problems of analysis, though stated briefly, encompass four principal interrelated themes which emerged from the exchange of ideas between the participants in the symposium at which the essays published here were first presented. It will be useful, by way of introduction, to present the particulars of these themes in broad outline under the following headings: the characteristics of host response to strangers; the social-structural position of strangers in host societies; the nature of political and economic competition between strangers and hosts; and the scale of social and political complexity and the incorporation or expulsion of strangers.

II

Host Response to Strangers

Friendliness, ambivalence, indifference, fear, or antagonism represent the broad range of attitudes expressed by hosts toward strangers. Though always subject to change, in large measure such attitudes determine the initial and future roles strangers may assume within the larger society. Greifer was correct, up to a point at least, when he wrote that "the attitude towards the stranger by a group also characterizes the

18. An exception to the exclusive concentration on the expulsion of strangers is the collection of essays by Cohen and Middleton, which are devoted to a study of the incorporation of diverse ethnic groups within the political systems of developing nation-states in Africa.

future of the group, the stage of its development."[19] Greifer's assumption holds true only to the extent that host societies retain the political prerogative of permitting strangers to cross the threshold of their territorial-political boundaries voluntarily, and allowing them to engage in sundry activities. This was not the case during the colonial era in Africa. By and large, colonial rule stripped traditional African polities of their political sovereignty and denied them the right to control the movement of individuals and groups from one territorial-political boundary to the next. Whatever their scale of political complexity—whether kingdom-states like Buganda or chieftaincies such as the Ngoni—African polities were thrust into the role of being involuntary hosts to African and non-African strangers, both from within and from outside the continent. Even so, it would be romantic fantasy to suggest that prior to the colonial presence in Africa the receptivity to African strangers, let alone non-African strangers, by their African hosts was, in every situation, characteristically amicable and devoid of hostility. This was not so. Newcomers are seldom welcomed anywhere on the same social terms as indigenous members of the society.

Historical evidence concerning the receptivity to strangers in different pre-colonial African societies—societies of varying socio-demographic scale and political complexity, in various regions of the continent—is scanty. But there is just enough evidence to suggest that African strangers, and indeed strangers of other racial and ethnic origins, once moved with relative ease between indigenous African polities. Crossing the threshold of traditional political boundaries often required strangers to partake in rituals of the type van Gennep called "rites of incorporation," which legitimated the stranger's status and role and guaranteed him safe passage from one political community to the next. The role of ritual in the maintenance of social and spatial boundaries between hosts and strangers, a key aspect of Simmel's formulation on the stranger, is discussed in Chapter Two by William Shack. Following Victor Turner (*The Ritual Process*), Shack argues that strangers can be viewed as liminal *personae*, and that through "the ritual process" the status of liminality which strangers occupy is changed to that of *communitas*, a state enjoyed by their hosts. Often, the liminality of stranger communities was maintained by the imposition of tribute and taxation. The payment of these gave symbolic recognition to the superior social and political position of hosts, especially when stranger communities increased in demographic scale and assumed some form of organized leadership.

A case in point is the history of the Zonga communities, consisting of Yoruba strangers, who were expelled from Ghana in 1970. In Chapter

19. J. L. Greifer, "Attitudes to the Stranger: A Study of the Attitudes of Primitive Society and Early Hebrew Culture," *American Sociological Review*, vol. 10, no. 6 (1945), p. 739.

Eight Niara Sudarkasa presents a detailed historical account of the development of the Zongas over a period of seventy years, showing the process of change from a random collection of strangers to the formation of cohesive communities with elected spokesmen or "elders" who represented their constituents before the body politic of the host society. Periodic representations by spokesmen on behalf of their communities included the presentation of gifts, a ritual which symbolized the subordinate, liminal position of the strangers.

Similarly, in Chapter Twelve Christine Obbo describes how in the traditional Buganda kingdom in East Africa, strangers could attach themselves as clients to district chiefs or their subjects who, as patrons, received from strangers tribute in kind and in labor. Corporate presentation of tribute by strangers would seem to have had only a salutary effect on the attitudes held by their hosts toward them. Progressive changes in the attitudes which one group harbors toward another alter the character of their relations, and therefore bring about a rearrangement of the social structure. But the reverse can occur also: structural rearrangement can influence attitudes. An example of the latter can be drawn from the Zonga community founded by Hausa strangers and other savannah dwellers who settled in the Atebuba chiefdom of Akan people, known as Brong, in the last quarter of the nineteenth century. Traditionally, the payment of rent for land, and corporate presentation of tribute in the form of sheep and yams, distinguished strangers from subjects, who normally paid tax. Colonial intervention altered the structural arrangement between Brong and Zonga, and attitudes changed also. A once peaceful situation of accommodation changed to that of armed conflict. Finally, the imposition of external authority formally incorporated the Zonga through the political process into the Atebuba chiefdom.[20]

The cultural rather than the political process, including the adoption of language, customs, dress, mode of livelihood, fictive kinship, and religious practices, has been the most common and widespread method by which strangers have been completely incorporated into host societies. Monica Wilson describes in Chapter Three how strangers were so completely absorbed culturally into traditional Nyakyusa and Sotho local communities that all traces of their strangeness were eventually lost. Evidence of similar incorporation processes in Central Africa is seen in the pattern of stranger-host interaction among the Tonga, in Zambia.[21]

20. Kwame Arhin, "Strangers and Hosts: A Study in the Political Organization and History of Atebubu Town," *Transactions of the Historical Society of Ghana*, vol. 12 (1973), pp. 63–82.

21. For a discussion of the cultural methods used by Zambian Tonga to create an ethnically homogenous society in which immigrants lost their identity as strangers, see E. Colson, "The Assimilation of Aliens Among Zambian Tonga," in Cohen and Middleton, pp. 35–54.

The process was the same in East Africa and Ethiopia—for example, among the Alur in Uganda and the Abyssinians of classical times, respectively.[22] In Ethiopia, Syrians, Armenians, Greeks, and Arab merchants roamed the coastal areas of ancient Abyssinia during the early decades of the first millennium B.C. Many of these merchant strangers married local women and adopted their customs, including religious practices. European strangers became so completely absorbed culturally into ancient Abyssinian society that they never became a status group enjoying special political and economic privileges denied to the majority of the host population.

But incorporation of strangers through the cultural process took a decidedly different turn in the lower Zambesi valley of Mozambique, where the Portuguese government established several crown estates (prazos) between about 1650 and 1850.[23] Portuguese, Mestizos, and Indian colonists eventually acquired recognition as political chiefs and ruled subordinate African populations. Powerful estate owners took African names, lived like Africans, and, as the recognized legitimate royalty, retained monopoly power over commercial relations and the distribution of political power. Several parallel examples of the prazo phenomenon are to be found in the history of the incorporation by Africans of European strangers, and the strangers' rise to positions of superior political economic status. Not a few sailors shipwrecked around the coast of Madagascar became the consorts of queens, founded new ruling lines, and came to be revered almost as "divine kings."[24] The Europeanized former African slaves who were repatriated to Liberia and came to be known as Americo-Liberians, and the Creole in Sierra Leone, are two further cases in point.[25] Smallness of scale, rather than ethnicity or race, would appear to be a more decisive factor in defining the attitudes of receptivity by African hosts toward strangers.

The Structural Position of Strangers

A complicated set of interrelated socioeconomic and political factors affects the structural position of strangers in host societies. Contrary to Simmel's ideal type, the structural position of strangers is never static. As already noted, in pre-colonial Africa, stranger-host relations were expressed in terms of superordination-subordination, with the host occupying the superordinate status position. Colonial administrations created

22. See A. Southall, "Ethnic Incorporation Among the Alur," in Cohen and Middleton, pp. 71–92. The attitudes of ancient Abyssinians and modern Ethiopians toward strangers are briefly described by Shack in Chapter Two.

23. A. Isaacman, Mozambique.

24. Personal communication from Aidan Southall, who carried out field research in Madagascar.

25. It is to be noted that the demise of the Creoles' status as traders in Sierra Leone coincided with the arrival of Lebanese traders and merchants during the 1890s. See Leighton in Chapter Five.

social and economic conditions that placed strangers structurally on a lateral position with respect to the indigenous population. More often than not, colonial intervention produced the kind of situation that Herschelle Challenor describes for the Ivory Coast (Chapter Four), where Dahomeyan, Togolese, and Nigerien strangers came to occupy superior status positions in trade and commerce, and dominated the bureaucracy of public administration.[26] Yet as Neil Leighton points out in Chapter Five, the very economic success of the strangers, which in part is a function of their structural position, generates their opposition. Thus in Sierra Leone, Lebanese strangers successfully dislodged the fledgling African merchants and traders from commerce. But in pursuing their economic gains, the Lebanese created a class of rural farmers linked to a cash economy, which in turn drew the enmity of an emerging clerk class which was hostile to the Lebanese strangers' affluence. When the African middle class achieved political power, it sought to seize control of the most productive sector of the economy—the diamond mining industry, which the Lebanese controlled. In the long haul, the Lebanese found themselves hostage to the African elite, who exacted from them a regular "tribute" as a condition for conducting business.

The degree of rigidity in the social structure—that is, its ability to maintain fixed status positions—is in part a consequence of the role played by the indigenous population as voluntary or involuntary hosts to strangers. This feature of the social structure is exemplified by changes in the status position of Asian strangers in the former colonial protectorate of Uganda. After many years of indentured servitude, Asians eventually gained a superordinate status position over Ugandan Africans who, as a matter of sociological fact, were the involuntary hosts.[27] Jessica Kuper shows in Chapter Thirteen that Asian strangers in Uganda, both Goans and Indians, remained at the sufferance of the protectorate administration, not with the consent of Africans. Africans made no distinction between Hindu and Muslim Indians and Christian Goans, lumping all within the single category they called "Asian" or "Indian." Goans, however, distinguished themselves culturally from the Indians, whom they likened behaviorally to Africans. Cultural distinctions were reinforced by differences in structural position; Indians were structurally close to Africans because Indians were primarily engaged in low-status occupations, such as petty trading and small shopkeeping; Goans occupied most of the prestigious key civil service posts and thus were structurally close to the white British administrators. These structural positions of

26. The structural position of strangers in Francophone Africa and the economic and political factors underlying repatriation to their homelands is placed in historical perspective by Challenor in Chapter Four.

27. The first systematic sociological study of Asians in Uganda was carried out as recently as 1955. See H. S. Morris, *The Indians in Uganda*; Chapters 1, 2, 3, and 8 are especially relevant to the essays in this volume by Kuper (Chapter Thirteen) and Mazrui (Chapter Fourteen).

Africans, Asians, and whites remained firmly fixed until the withdrawal of British rule from Uganda in 1962. Assuming the role the British vacated, the post-independence African governments acted as if they had been the original "national hosts," subsequently expelling not only Asian strangers, but also the Luo and other Africans from Kenya and Tanganyika. Ali Mazrui argues in Chapter Fourteen that the expulsion from Uganda of Kenyan Africans in 1970 and Asians in 1972 during the regimes of Presidents Milton Obote and Idi Amin, respectively, can be understood in terms of an underdeveloped social class structure which lacks the capacity to accommodate outsiders, and is therefore characteristically inhospitable to strangers. This proposition is worth testing in other regions of Africa where evidence is available on the development of social class structure and the attitudes of hosts toward strangers. Simply put, the question is: was the expulsion of strangers, in every case, preceded by a radical alteration of their structural position in the host society?

The Power Structure

Power is here meant to refer to competition for and the exercise of control over political and economic resources. Differential access to power accentuates the structural position of strangers and hosts and the character of the competition between them. During the era of colonial administration of Anglophone and Francophone West Africa, for example, strangers often acquired greater relative political power than their hosts, a situation exemplified by the quasi-political positions of *fonctionnaire* occupied by Dahomeyans in the Ivory Coast. In East Africa, Goans and other Asians monopolized the civil service and commerce and trade at the expense of Ugandan Africans. Although absolute power over political and economic resources remained under the control of Whitehall or the Comité de l'Afrique Française, Africans, as involuntary hosts, were dispossessed of even the relative power that strangers enjoyed. Dispossession of the attributes of power can become internalized in a sense of relative deprivation, engendering in hosts deep feelings of hostility toward strangers (see Shack in Chapter Two). This brief characterization of the unequal distribution of power between strangers and hosts, with hosts being dispossessed of power, was generally true in the administration of African colonies, before new nation-states were created in the post-independence era. Dispossession of power was perhaps less widespread in local-level communities, or in small chieftaincies like the Nyakyusa, Nguni, and Sotho. Voluntary incorporation of hosts by strangers, who were usually few in number and easily regulated through the cultural process, enabled local populations and small political groups to retain control over their political and economic resources.

In the post-independence era, the locus of power in stranger-host relations at the nation-state level has shifted, thus altering the meaning of power itself. With African nations becoming involved increasingly in ever-widening international political and economic networks, the archetypal strangers engaged in petty trade and commerce have been replaced by strangers who are neither betwixt or between, nor here today and gone tomorrow. The new strangers in Africa are the multinational enterprises. They do not conform to Simmel's ideal type of stranger, and in their interaction with their African hosts they do not fit Levine's typology of stranger relationships. Although not visibly present and readily identifiable—and therefore not easily dislodged or mandated for repatriation to their overseas base—the new strangers in Africa exercise powerful control over the key economic sectors of African states and often engage overtly in manipulating the political machinery of government.

Paradoxically, in all too many cases it is only through the economic management of vital national resources provided by the new strangers that the gap has been narrowed between national expectations about raising overall standards of living and realistic goals of achievement. African indigenization measures, which were conceived to rectify the long history of economic injustices Africans endured under colonial rule, did not bring about the desired modification of the relationship of the national economy to the international market. National policies aimed toward Africanization of the economy barely touched the domains of overseas-based multinational enterprises. The new strangers in Africa, as Ruth Morgenthau states in Chapter Six, still manage to "sit on top of the cumulated wealth, technology and techniques of organization developed after hundreds of years of head start." Moreover, "the customary processes of acculturation and incorporation or 'Africanization' which have assured the integration of many layers of strangers into African society in the past, cannot be counted on to draw multinational enterprises closer to defined national objectives."

Scale and Stranger-Host Relations

Scale has already been mentioned as a significant factor in determining the character of receptivity exhibited by hosts toward strangers. Logically, the socio-demographic ratio between strangers and hosts is one in which strangers constitute a numerical minority, either at the level of the nation-state or of the local community. So also, it logically follows that if an inverse ratio obtained, that is, if strangers outnumbered their hosts, strangers would not be strangers. Before their expulsion from Ghana in 1970, Yoruba strangers numbered more than 100,000, yet they represented less than 1.2 percent of the total indigenous Ghanaian population which inhabits an area of about 92,000 square miles. Smaller in scale is the kingdom of Swaziland, in southern Africa. During the sixty-odd years in which administration of the kingdom was under the British High Commission, Zulu strangers moved northward from Natal Province in South Africa, some settling in the rural districts of Swaziland, others taking on civil service employment in Mbabane, the capital city, and the peripheral urban areas. Although they constituted less than 4 percent of the total Swaziland population in 1960, the Zulu are on the verge of being repatriated to their traditional homeland in Natal. "Nigerian" strangers in the Sudan, an ethnic label used to define as a category Muslim West Africans of various ethnic origins, who on pilgrimages to Mecca became stranded in Northern Sudan, face an uncertain future also, though their numbers are inconspicuous by comparison with Sudanese nationals. Other examples could be cited, including that of the Asians in Malawi and Tanzania, to stress the point: there would appear to be no direct correlation between the demographic ratio of strangers to hosts, on the one hand, and the territorial size of the host society, on the other, in determining a society's capacity to accommodate strangers within its political boundaries.

With the creation of new African nation-states, heretofore autonomous local polities have been incorporated into the national political organization which monopolizes decision-making powers with respect to the presence of strangers and the role they occupy at all levels of society. Now that local political autonomy has been usurped by the state, it is difficult if not impossible to determine the degree of correlation, if any, between the capacity of local-level host societies to accommodate strangers and the character of their political complexity. Meyer Fortes and the late Sir E. E. Evans-Pritchard alluded to this problem in their introduction to *African Political Systems*. "Centralized authority and an administrative organization seem necessary," they wrote, "to accommodate culturally diverse groups within a single political system, especially if they have different modes of livelihood."[28] In societies lacking "government"—that is, the so-called stateless societies—aliens or strangers are said to lose quickly their foreign identities, their strangeness, and become members of the host community. If the Fortes and Evans-Pritchard argument holds true, it might explain the relative ease by which strangers in Central Africa were absorbed into Nyakyusa, Nguni, and Sotho local communities (Wilson, Chapter Three), as well as the successful assimilation of aliens among the Zambian Tonga.[29]

Aidan Southall, in Chapter Eleven, sheds some light on the problem of scale and political complexity in his comparison of the successes and failures of white strangers and their religious activities on the coasts of Madagascar and East Africa in the nineteenth century. When white strangers tried to bring new religions to the smaller African societies consisting of a few thousand people—some with centralized political institutions, but others not—without any political umbrella (either their own, or one lent to them by local rulers), they failed. But when they worked

28. M. Fortes and E. E. Evans-Pritchard, eds., *African Political Systems*, pp. 9–10.
29. Colson, "The Assimilation of Aliens," in Cohen and Middleton, pp. 71–92.

under the political umbrella of the rulers of larger African societies, they achieved spectacular success. These nineteenth-century examples, although they enhance our understanding of the capacity of certain kinds of traditional political systems to accommodate strangers, are not so easily used as guides to the analysis of contemporary political events in Africa. For it has been at the nation-state level, where centralized authority and administrative organization are distributed laterally, that the lack of accommodation to culturally diverse groups is most manifestly expressed, as in Ghana, the Ivory Coast, and Uganda, to say nothing of the small kingdom of Swaziland.

Indeed, national decisions to distinguish clearly any ambiguity that might exist between aliens and citizens may often clash with local-level willingness to assimilate strangers. For example, in the early 1970s the Zambian government launched a national registration campaign as part of its effort to define its citizenship. Headmen were expected to identify their villagers and parents to identify their children as soon as they reached the age of 18. Instances occurred where headmen willingly vouched for Malawian and Rhodesian strangers who wanted to be accepted as Zambian citizens, thus avoiding their alien status.

Assuming that the Zambian example is not an isolated case, and that similar evidence exists for other regions of Africa, there is ample reason to suggest that the clash of ideologies between local communities and national government over the issue of the accommodation of strangers has little to do singularly with such factors as scale, social-structural arrangements, competition for power, or political complexity. It has a great deal to do with frailty of government. The social visibility of the archetypal strangers—being betwixt and between, neither alien nor citizen—makes them easily identifiable targets in periods of national political and economic crises; they become the significant "others" who, in some metaphysical sense, are deemed to be the root cause of social inequities. Like medieval *propheta*, strangers symbolically call into question the moral and ethical values underlying the local system of wants and needs; and as it has happened often enough in new African nation-states, that system can easily be thrown into disarray by periodic transformations of the social order.

III

The sociological perspective from which the essays in this volume are written attempts to take into account what Edward Tiryakian has called the dynamic aspect of the concept of the stranger—"the processual aspect of the relationship of stranger and host."[30]

The best-documented case exemplifying this dynamic process in Africa is presented in Chapters Seven through Ten, by Peil, Sudarkasa,

30. E. Tiryakian, "Sociological Perspectives on the Stranger," *Sounding* (1973). p. 56.

Eades, and Schildkrout, which analyze aspects of stranger-host relations in Ghana. After seventy years as strangers who came one day and stayed the next, the Nigerians were expelled from Ghana in 1970. The historical backdrop to the expulsion of Yoruba and other Nigerians, as outlined by Sudarkasa, also provides the social and political ground for Peil's analysis of the general decline in tolerance of Ghanaian citizens toward strangers, whatever their ethnic extraction. Peil's conclusion—that the concept of the stranger breaks down when new African nation-states come into being—places the stranger-host dichotomy squarely within the socio-political framework of *societas-civitas*. Contrary to Simmel's notion about the objectivity of the stranger, on the basis of the Ghana evidence Peil argues that Nigerian strangers, if not others, could not be "neutral" in an unstable or fluid political situation. Their political objectivity apart, the fact that strangers are most often engaged in entrepreneurial activities inevitably gives rise to the belief that their economic success is being achieved at the expense of members of the host society. So entrenched does this belief become that even the possibility of economic failure by strangers is seldom considered. Jeremy Eades' study of Yoruba traders in Tamale, Northern Ghana (Chapter Nine), should help dispel the myth that the entrepreneurial success of strangers is inevitable. By tracing the career of a Yoruba "family firm," Eades shows how kinship relations can be mobilized and manipulated to sustain a marginal trading enterprise through recurrent economic crises.

But stereotypes about strangers, like myths, die hard. Both are resilient, and are made even tougher when they are reinforced by marked socioeconomic discrepancies between hosts and strangers. Formal education also contributes by perpetuating various myths and stereotypes about strangers, which have their origin in traditional folktales and legends. Enid Schildkrout, in Chapter Ten, has examined the extent to which the traditional attitudes of superiority held by the southern Asante toward northern strangers have become inculcated through the formal educational system into the value systems of Asante children. In analyzing essays assigned to southern Asante children in order to elicit their ideological attitudes about northern strangers, she demonstrates that the ways in which Asante children perceive their own environment, and the environment of the strangers, becomes an important basis for the development of Asante stereotypes. Environmental perceptions, when transformed into stereotypical explanations, associate customs and behavior with ecological conditions. Southern Asante children perceive northern strangers as being like the environment from which they migrate, which is thought to be crude and inhospitable. The ideology of regional identity as a factor in understanding stranger-host interaction, of course, has relevance far beyond these Asante children in Ghana.

This collection of essays is not intended to exhaust all variations on the theme of the stranger in African societies. The essays are selective, representing the state of our knowledge about stranger-host interaction in a few specific African societies; these societies were selected because they offer sufficient historical and sociological evidence to warrant reexamining Simmel's concept of *der Fremde* in the context of the African experience. The fluid nature of political events in African states exerts an almost daily influence on the precariously balanced position of strangers. They have been expelled from one African state and resettled in another, only to find themselves facing a new mandate for repatriation; such has been the fate of the Goans who resettled in Malawi after their expulsion from Uganda.[31] Strangers in most African societies appear to face an uncertain future, a future as precarious as that of the fragile national governments which act as their hosts.

The conflict between hosts and strangers will continue to play a crucial part in all future relations between African nations, as well as in their relations with the wider political and economic world of which they are now a part. They have rejected a "pluralistic model" for their developing societies because, as Skinner claims in the Conclusion, they view pluralistic society as "basically undemocratic, since it implies that certain ethnic groups maintain control at the expense of others," for whom there would appear to be little room for maneuver. But in shaping their national policies to develop an ideal democratic society, new African nations have shown a lack of tolerance and willingness to absorb "visible" strangers, thus opening the way for elusive, "invisible" strangers—the shadowy multinational corporations—to gain control over their vital scarce resources. The struggle now being waged by African leaders with the new strangers has historical roots in the pre-colonial communities of strangers, whose contemporary analogues now exist within the boundaries of the new African nation-states.

31. *The Sunday Times* (London), May 23, 1976.

Part I
Simmel and the Stranger in Africa

1

Simmel at a Distance: On the History and Systematics of the Sociology of the Stranger

Donald N. Levine

In sociology, as in other disciplines (if not more so), certain concepts bear a special freight for being linked so closely with major figures in the history of the field. One can scarcely talk of charisma, for example, without thinking of Max Weber; or of anomie, without being mindful of Emile Durkheim; or of cultural lag, without recalling W. F. Ogburn. In the case of the sociological concept of the stranger, the relevant association is of course to Georg Simmel.

I say "of course," but there are ironies in this case. Out of a total corpus equivalent to fourteen thick volumes of philosophy and sociology, most of them untranslated to this day, Simmel is perhaps most widely known among anglophone social scientists for his six-page excursus on the stranger. What is less well known is that this "classic essay" originally appeared as a note, a mere digression, in a long chapter entitled "Space and the Spatial Ordering of Society."[1] Yet while the short excursus has been translated more often than any other of Simmel's writings, the bulk of the chapter from which it is drawn—a pioneering analysis of the ways in which the properties of physical space provide both conditions for and symbolic representations of different types of social interaction—has never been translated into English nor has it yet, to my knowledge, been alluded to in the recent upsurge of scientific work in the field called proxemics, the study of human spatial relations.

There is another, more notable irony regarding the position of Simmel's essay on the stranger in the literature of sociology. It is likely that the excursus, as a stimulus both to studies of the role of the stranger and to work on the related concept of social distance, has been cited in more social scientific research than any of Simmel's writings—and this in

This chapter is a revised version of an essay by the same title published in *Sociological Focus*, 10, no. 1 (January 1977).

1. *Soziologie* (Leipzig: Duncker and Humblot, 1908), Chapter Nine.

nearly every methodological genre, from ethnographic reportage, cross-cultural comparison, and historical reconstruction to laboratory experiment, survey research, and mathematical model-building. The abundance of materials in this literature would give the impression of a rigorous and cumulative tradition of inquiry, an impression conveyed by Alex Inkeles when he wrote some years ago that there exists "a special and well-developed sociology of the stranger."[2]

Careful inspection of that literature reveals a very different picture indeed. Far from the superbly critical treatment of Simmel's propositions which one finds in Lewis A. Coser's codification of Simmel's work on conflict, Lawrence E. Hazelrigg's analysis of Simmel's propositions on secret societies, Theodore M. Mills' conversion of Simmel's ideas into hypotheses about small groups, or Robert K. Merton's selective incorporation of Simmel's conceptions about group properties in general, one finds in the literature which draws on the excursus, both in that on social distance and that on the stranger proper, a sprawling and confused assortment of statements—an illustration, perhaps, of the special advantage which latecomers, in science as in technological modernization, have over earlybirds, since the exemplary scholars to whom I have just referred did their work on Simmel a good quarter-century after the traditions of research on the stranger and social distance were established.

Even so, it is more than an antiquarian impulse that stands to be rewarded by a review of that literature today. For if we are now to profit from the model of the latecomers and transform the sociology of the stranger from a random collection of very uneven forays into a substantial body of codified knowledge, we can learn a good deal from the many writings which have taken Simmel's formulations as a key point of reference, even though they were headed in so many different directions.

Let me begin by referring to the work of Robert E. Park, a man who did so much to make Simmel's work known in American sociology in the 1920s and who produced the first English translation of *Der Fremde*.[3] In his seminal essay of 1928 "Human Migration and the Marginal Man," Park cited Simmel's definition of the stranger and proceeded to delineate a concept of the marginal man as its equivalent—an equivalence illustrated by his remark that "the emancipated Jew was, and is, historically and typically the marginal man. . . . He is, par excellence, the 'stranger,' whom Simmel, himself a Jew, has described with such profound insight and understanding."[4]

Commenting on this adaptation of Simmel's concept, Alvin Boskoff has recently observed: "Park borrowed the concept of the stranger and

2. *What is Sociology?* (Englewood Cliffs, N.J.: Prentice-Hall, 1964), p. 12.

3. The next few pages are drawn from "Simmel's Influence on American Sociology: I," by D. N. Levine, E. B. Carter, and E. M. Gorman, published in the *American Journal of Sociology*, vol. 81, no. 4 (1976), pp. 813–845.

4. *American Journal of Sociology*, vol. 33, no. 8 (1928), p. 892.

applied it to the phenomena of migration and culture contact in complex society. Briefly, Park suggested that various kinds of deviant behavior (crime, delinquency, illegitimacy) reflected the experience of persons who, by migrating, had given up old values but had not adequately acquired the norms and skills of their new setting."[5]

It should be clear, however, that in the borrowing Park altered the shape of the concept: his "marginal man" represents a configuration notably different from Simmel's "stranger." Thinking of the experience of ethnic minorities in zones of culture contact in American cities, Park conceived the marginal man as a racial or cultural hybrid—"one who lives in two worlds, in both of which he is more or less of a stranger"—one who aspires to but is excluded from full membership in a new group. Simmel's stranger, by contrast, does not aspire to be assimilated; he is a potential wanderer, one who has not quite got over the freedom of coming and going. Where Park's excluded marginal man was depicted as suffering from spiritual instability, intensified self-consciousness, restlessness, and malaise, Simmel's stranger, occupying a determinate position in relation to the group, was depicted as a successful trader, a judge, and a trusted confidant.

In his extended study *The Marginal Man*, Park's student Everett Stonequist indicated his awareness that Park's "marginal man" was not identical with Simmel's "stranger." He observed, first, that marginality need not be produced by migration, but could also come about through internal changes like education and marriage. More explicitly, he stated:

> The stranger, [Simmel] writes, first appears as a trader, one who is not fixed in space, yet settles for a time in the community—a "potential wanderer." He unites in his person the qualities of "nearness and remoteness, concern and indifference." . . . This conception of the stranger pictures him as one who is not intimately and personally concerned with the social life about him. His relative detachment frees him from the self-consciousness, the concern for status, and the divided loyalties of the marginal man.[6]

Stonequist went on to note that the distinctive properties of the stranger identified by Simmel get lost once an individual moves into the position of being a marginal person.

In spite of Stonequist's clarity about this distinction, there has persisted in the literature a tendency to confuse the marginal man concept with Simmel's "stranger."[7] Thus more than a decade later Everett Hughes uncritically repeated Park's view that Simmel's passages on the stranger

5. *Theory in American Sociology* (New York: Thomas Y. Crowell, 1969), pp. 282–283.

6. E. Stonequist, *The Marginal Man* (New York: Scribner's, 1937), pp. 177ff.

7. One exception to this tendency is Ernest Mowrer's *Disorganization: Personal and Social* (Philadelphia: Lippincott, 1942), whose chapter "The Nonconformist and the Rebel" faithfully reproduces Stonequist's distinction between strangers and marginal men.

referred to the same phenomenon as the marginal man.[8] And Boskoff, with comparable carelessness, glossed Simmel's stranger as "vulnerable to internal uncertainties."[9] Seeking to "re-examine the ubiquitous concept of 'marginal man,'" Peter Rose did so by asking "how the 'stranger' in the midst of alien territory adapts to community life." After interviewing former urban Jews in several small towns in upstate New York, Rose concluded that their position could more aptly be described as one of duality rather than marginality, for they felt "we have the best of both." Rose considered his findings to provide evidence against the applicability of the concept of marginality, and to refute the view of "Stonequist [sic], Park, and others [who] have characterized the Jew as a disturbed marginal man, an eternal stranger [here Rose footnotes Simmel!] unable to reconcile the traditions of his people with the counterforces of the majority world."[10] In making this point, Rose, like Hughes and Boskoff, was misreading Simmel through the distorting lens formed by Park. What he actually found was that the Jews in question were not adequately characterized by Park's concept of marginality, but that they might indeed be characterized in terms of Simmel's concept of the stranger.

If Stonequist's distinction between marginality and strangerhood was made only to be lost, it was inadvertently recovered by Paul C. P. Siu. In his investigation of Chinese laundrymen in Chicago, originally carried out as a study of "marginality," Siu was dismayed to find that "none of the Chinese laundrymen I studied could be considered a marginal man." In this case, however, Siu did not use those findings to invalidate Simmel's conception of the stranger. Rather, he returned to Simmel to raise the question whether the marginal man might not more aptly be viewed as one of a possible larger number of variant types of stranger. Siu then proposed a new type, the sojourner—who, in contrast to the bicultural complex of the marginal man, clings to the culture of his own ethnic group—and added a few notes on still another type of stranger, the settler.[11] The way was thus opened for a more differentiated view of phenomena previously lumped together under the diffuse categories of strangerhood or marginality.

Another related step, albeit in a different direction, had been taken around the time of Stonequist's study. Margaret Mary Wood's *The Stranger: A Study in Social Relationships* drew freely on Simmel, but adopted a definition of the stranger that was clearly differentiated from Simmel's:

8. E. Hughes, "Social Change and Status Protest: an Essay on the Marginal Man," *Phylon*, vol. 10, no. 1 (1949), pp. 58–65.

9. A. Boskoff, *Theory in American Sociology*, p. 282.

10. "Strangers in Their Midst: Small-town Jews and Their Neighbors," in *The Study of Society*, edited by P. I. Rose (New York: Random House, 1967), pp. 463–479.

11. "The Sojourner," *American Journal of Sociology*, vol. 58, no. 1 (1952), pp. 34–44.

We shall describe the stranger as one who has come into face-to-face contact with the group for the first time. This concept is broader than that of Simmel, who defines the stranger as "the man who comes today and stays tomorrow, the potential wanderer, who although he has gone no further, has not quite got over the freedom of coming and going." For us the stranger may be, as with Simmel, a potential wanderer, but he may also be a wanderer who comes today and goes tomorrow, or he may come today and remain with us permanently.[12]

In other words, Wood's topic was not the sojourner but the newly arrived outsider, and her concern was with those internal adjustments by which different types of groups adapt to his arrival in their midst. Her work might well have laid the goundwork for an extensive sociology of the stranger, in which Simmel's formulations would properly have been understood as referring to a special type; but as S. Dale McLemore stresses in a spirited review of some of the voluminous literature related to Simmel's essay, subsequent sociologists of the stranger tended to cite Simmel as the primary point of reference for the topic and, even when citing Wood, tended to miss the distinction between Wood's newly arrived outsider and Simmel's stranger.[13] Thus Julian Greifer, in the course of reconstructing the evolution of ancient Jewish attitudes toward the stranger, defines the stranger as one who "has come into face to face contact with the group for the first time," and in the next sentence refers to this stranger "as described by Georg Simmel."[14] Oscar Grusky similarly confuses the new arrival with Simmel's stranger by using the latter concept in describing the position of a newcomer in a line of administrative succession.[15]

In this context it is instructive to examine an experimental study which claims to draw inspiration from Simmel, "The Stranger in Laboratory Culture" by Dennison Nash and Alvin W. Wolfe. In a series of experiments in which a Rorschach card stimulus was presented to small groups of subjects over a number of "epochs," Nash and Wolfe sought to create a role which "would seem to approximate in the laboratory Simmel's description of the stranger." The hypothesis they tested, however, sprang from the ideas of Park, Stonequist, and others concerning the peculiar creativity of the marginal man. What they found was that the

12. Wood, *The Stranger: a Study in Social Relationships* (New York: Columbia University Press, 1934), pp. 43–44.
13. S. Dale McLemore, "Simmel's 'Stranger': A Critique of the Concept," *Pacific Sociological Review*, vol. 13, no. 2 (1970), pp. 86–94.
14. J. Greifer, "Attitudes to the Stranger: A Study of the Attitudes of Primitive Society and Early Hebrew Culture," *American Sociological Review*, vol. 10, no. 6 (1945), p. 739.
15. O. Grusky, "Administrative Succession in Formal Organizations," *Social Forces*, vol. 39, no. 2 (1960), pp. 105–115.

"strangers" proved to be less innovative than other participants in the experiment.[16]

In spite of the experimental rigor with which this study was carried out, its value is limited by the double conceptual confusion on which it rests. It seeks to verify Simmel's formulations about the stranger by using hypotheses devised, not by Simmel, but by others concerned with a different social type, the marginal man; and to do so by constructing an experimental role modeled, not on Simmel's "stranger," but on the still different type of the newly arrived person. Nash and Wolfe were led by their unexpected findings to draw a distinction between persons socialized in a marginal situation and persons introduced into such a situation briefly as adults. The distinction seems useful, and broadly parallels the distinctions noted above between the marginal man and the newly arrived—neither of which, it should be clear, replicates Simmel's own concept of the stranger.

In a study which remains more faithful to Simmel's formulations, Robert Zajonc has in effect recovered the distinction between the "stranger" and the newly arrived. Linking Simmel's ideas about the stranger's relative independence from local customs with frustration-aggression theory, Zajonc hypothesized that insofar as strangers are expected to conform to host culture norms and find this expectation disturbing due to conflicts with values brought from their home culture, they will tend to express aggression against those norms; and that such criticism is facilitated by their unique position as stranger in the host society, and further reduces the need to conform by devaluing the norms in question. "This relationship," Zajonc notes, "hinges upon the unique role of the stranger, and it *consequently cannot be expected to hold for the newly arrived*."[17] His second hypothesis, then, is that "attitudinal aggression as a result of frustration in conformity will be greater for strangers with long residence [Simmel's 'stranger'] than for those with short residence [the 'newly arrived']"—a hypothesis that is supported by his findings.

If the materials just reviewed reflect a tale of distinctions lost and distinctions regained, other studies which remain fairly faithful to Simmel's own conception of the stranger suggest a story of distinctions still struggling to be born. One such distinction concerns whether generalizations about strangers are to refer to a category of persons or to members of a collectivity. The former usage appears, for example, in several papers which examine the effects of social detachment on moral and cognitive orientations. Lewis A. Coser, noting that "what Georg Simmel

16. D. Nash and A. W. Wolfe, "The Stranger in Laboratory Culture," *American Sociological Review*, vol. 22, no. (1957), pp. 400–405.

17. "Aggressive Attitudes of the 'Stranger' as a Function of Conformity Pressures," *Human Relations*, vol. 5, no. 2 (1952), pp. 205–216.

said about the stranger applies with peculiar force to the eunuch: 'He is not radically committed to the unique ingredients and peculiar tendencies of the group,'" has argued that the detachment of the eunuch-stranger from all group involvements makes him an ideal instrument for carrying out a ruler's subjective desires; and then extended the point to cover uncastrated but politically impotent aliens, such as the court Jews of Baroque Germany and Christian renegades who served Ottoman sultans.[18] A kindred theme is examined in papers by Arlene Kaplan Daniels and Dennison Nash which consider the ways in which the stranger's lack of social affiliations affect the degree of objectivity which social scientists can have in field research.[19]

In other writings whose authors are no less concerned to associate their work with Simmel's essay, strangers are referred to chiefly as members of ethnic communities. In *Immigrants and Associations*, for example, Lloyd A. Fallers has assembled a collection of papers on Chinese, Lebanese, and Ibo immigrant communities. Generalizing from these papers, Fallers observes that stranger communities exhibit a typical pattern: "a socially segregated and hostilely-regarded community of kinship units, knit together and defended by associational ties."[20] Similarly, Edna Bonacich has set forth "A Theory of Middleman Minorities" to account for the development and persistence of communities of this sort.[21] Elliott P. Skinner assesses Simmel's portrayal of strangers as mobile and "opportunistic" by examining the situation of alien ethnic communities in three West African societies.[22] The idea that free-floating individual strangers and those organized in ethnic communities might have quite different properties is a possibility which cannot be explored so long as the same concept is used to refer indiscriminately to both sets of phenomena.

Other distinctions of considerable analytic importance are submerged beneath the ambiguous concept of "distance" which Simmel used with such memorable effect in his excursus. The stranger relationship, Simmel tells us, involves a distinctive blend of closeness and remoteness: the stranger's position *within* a given spatial circle is fundamentally affected by the fact that he brings qualities into it that are derived from the *outside*.

18. L. A. Coser, "The Political Functions of Eunuchism," *American Sociological Review*, vol. 29, no. 6 (1964), pp. 880–885.

19. A. K. Daniels, "The Low-caste Stranger in Social Research," in *Ethics, Politics, and Social Research*, edited by G. Sjoberg (Cambridge, Mass.: Schenkman, 1967), pp. 267–296; D. Nash, "The Ethnologist as Stranger," *Southwestern Journal of Anthropology*, vol. 19, no. 1 (1963), pp. 149–167.

20. *Immigrants and Associations* (The Hague: Mouton, 1967), pp. 12ff.

21. "A Theory of Middleman Minorities," *American Sociological Review*, vol. 38, no. 5 (1973), pp. 583–594.

22. "Strangers in West African Societies," *Africa*, vol. 33, no. 4 (1963), pp. 307–320.

Generations of readers have been haunted by the imagery of distance contained in this and related passages. Some have been lured by the promise implicit in the metaphor of social distance—that social relations could somehow be represented in mathematical terms analogous to those used to represent physical space—into constructing instruments for the measurement of social distance. Although certain sociologists have become aware of the highly ambiguous character of the metaphor of social distance—one could cite, for example, the four distinct social distance scales of Westie, the four quite different social distance scales of Kadushin, and the two still different social distance scales of Laumann— none has sought to specify and relate the particular dimensions of social distance represented in the position of the stranger.[23]

A step in that direction, however, was taken by McFarland and Brown in their paper on "Social Distance as a Metric." They write that Simmel's stranger was

> described as having elements of both nearness and distance. The nearness comes from features held in common with the observer, and the distance comes from the observer's awareness that the features held in common are common to all men or at least to large groups of men. Simmel's use of the concept does not lend itself either to quantification or to a clear analogy with physical distance since in his usage two people can simultaneously be "near" and "distant." His concept of social distance actually seems to be a mixture of two different concepts: features held in common, and the degree of specificity or generality of these common features.[24]

This interpretation does serious injustice to Simmel's excursus in two respects. For one thing, it attends to only one of the meanings of distance actually used in Simmel's essay. As Simmel himself observed in a different context, there are "very manifold meanings encompassed by the symbol of 'distance.'"[25] In the stranger essay, Simmel employs his formula concerning the mixture of nearness and remoteness in at least *three* quite different senses. He says, first, that "the appearance of this mobility within a bounded group occasions that synthesis of nearness and remoteness which constitutes the formal positions of the stranger."[26] In this pas-

23. C. Kadushin, "Social Distance Between Client and Professional," *American Journal of Sociology*, vol. 67, no. (1962), pp. 517–531; F. Westie, "A Technique for the Measurement of Race Attitudes," *American Sociological Review*, vol. 18, no. 1 (1953), pp. 73–78; and E. O. Laumann, *Prestige and Association in an Urban Community* (Indianapolis: Bobbs-Merrill, 1966).

24. McFarland and Brown, "Social Distance as a Metric: A Systematic Introduction to Smallest Space Analysis," in *Bonds of Pluralism*, edited by E. O. Laumann (New York: Wiley, 1973), p. 215.

25. *Soziologie*, p. 321. See also *Conflict and the Web of Group Affiliations*, translated by K. H. Wolff and R. Bendix (Glencoe, Ill.: Free Press, 1955), p. 105.

26. *Georg Simmel On Individuality and Social Forms*, edited and with an Introduction by D. N. Levine (Chicago: University of Chicago Press, 1971), p. 145.

sage, Simmel is referring to distance in the sense of *interactional proximity:* the stranger is near in that he interacts with numerous members of the group, he is remote in that he does so incidentally and not by virtue of well-established expectations based on ties of kinship, community, or occupation.

In another passage, discussing the quality of objectivity inherent in the position of the stranger, Simmel goes on to equate the distinction between remoteness and nearness with "indifference and involvement." In this context, distance is used to refer to the degree of *emotional attachment* between actors. It is only toward the end of the essay that he comes to the usage which McFarland and Brown single out, distance in the sense of the degree of *generality of features held in common.*

In rejecting Simmel's usage as metrically unviable, since it conceived of people as being simultaneously near and far in the same relationship, McFarland and Brown do further injustice to the scientific fruitfulness of the Simmelian formulation. On the contrary, I would argue that Simmel's paradoxical formulation not only makes great social psychological sense but is indeed the key to opening up a proper sociology of the stranger.

If people can be close to or remote from one another in many ways (and the task of mapping all those ways remains on the agenda of social psychology), it is the simultaneous pressure of characteristics of closeness and remoteness along any of those dimensions—the very dissonance embodied in that dualism—that makes the position of strangers socially problematic in all times and places. When those who would be close, in any sense of the term, are actually close, and those who should be distant are distant, everyone is "in his place." When those who should be distant are close, however, the inevitable result is a degree of tension and anxiety which necessitates some special kind of response.

Two psychological mechanisms would appear to underlie this universal need, separation anxiety and group narcissism. The common observation that "the child's dread is brought into existence by the approach of a 'stranger'" can be grounded in a primal experience: the infant's dread of losing its mother aroused by the appearance of a strange person in her place.[27] In that paradigmatic situation, one who should be distant appears to be taking the place of one who should be close, and the result is immediate apprehension.

Compounding this primal anxiety is the response represented by Freud's formulation concerning the narcissism of small differences: "In the undisguised antipathies and aversions which people feel towards strangers with whom they have to do we may recognize the expression of self-love—of narcissism. This self-love works for the self-assertion of the individual, and behaves as though the occurrence of any divergence from

27. Freud, *Group Psychology and the Analysis of the Ego,* translated by J. Strachey (New York: Liveright, 1949), p. 86.

his own particular lines of development involved a criticism of them and a demand for their alteration."[28]

To translate all this into the terms of a more general group psychology: group members derive security from relating in familiar ways to fellow group members and from maintaining their distance from nonmembers through established insulating mechanisms. In situations where an outsider comes into the social space normally occupied by group members only, one can presume an initial response of anxiety and at least latent antagonism. A systematic sociology of the stranger might therefore organize itself around the types of response to this frequent social dilemma.

Logically prior to the question of the host's response, however, is the question of how the stranger himself seeks to relate to the host group. One thing to be learned from our brief review of the literature is that the stranger concept has been used to refer to a number of distinct social phenomena, phenomena which may have quite different properties. Some of these differences reflect the variety of modes of acceptance which strangers try to elicit from host groups.

Wood's discussion affords a point of departure for formulating these distinctions. In her words, "for us the stranger may be, as with Simmel, a potential wanderer, but he may also be a wanderer who comes today and goes tomorrow, or he may come today and remain with us permanently."[29] If, however, a properly sociological interest in the stranger concept is to understand it as referring to a distinctive type of relationship—as Wood herself, like Simmel, maintains—then perhaps the critical variable here is not the length of time spent in the host community, but the type of relationship which the stranger aspires to establish with the host group. In other words, the stranger may wish merely to *visit* the host community, remaining an outsider throughout his visit; or he may desire *residence* in the host community without becoming assimilated into it—to be in the group but not of it; or he may aspire to gain *membership* as a fully integrated participant in the host community.

Whatever his aspirations, the appearance of an outsider is likely to arouse feelings of anxiety and at least latent antagonism. More accurately, perhaps, it could be said to arouse pronounced ambivalence: positive feelings related to the proximity, anxiety and hostile feelings related to the fact that one who should be distant is close by. The host's response will therefore be described as compulsive, reflecting the reality of a persisting ambivalence underlying all stranger relationships and the related fact that these relationships are invested with a particularly high degree of affect. It will be compulsively friendly if positive feelings predominate, compulsively antagonistic if negative ones are dominant.

28. *Ibid.*, pp. 55ff.
29. Wood, *The Stranger*, p. 43.

Taking this dichotomy into account enables us to incorporate Stonequist's distinction between marginal men and strangers readily and, indeed, to classify each of the three types of stranger orientations just distinguished according to whether it is reciprocated in a primarily positive or negative form. The following typology of stranger relationships may then be generated by cross-classifying the two variables in question.[30] Each of these types, finally, should be further distinguished according to whether it is being taken to refer to strangers as *individuals* or as *collectivities*.

A Typology of Stranger Relationships

Host's Response to Stranger	Stranger's Interest in Host Community		
	Visit	*Residence*	*Membership*
Compulsive Friendliness	Guest	Sojourner	Newcomer
Compulsive Antagonism	Intruder	Inner Enemy	Marginal Man

This typology provides the basis for developing an analytic paradigm, one organized here with respect to three basic questions which appear to define the main areas of interest in this field:

1. What are the characteristic properties of each of these types of stranger relationship?

2. What factors are associated with the process by which persons enter into one or another of these types of relations?

3. What factors account for the changes which move persons from one of these types of relation into another?

The accompanying outline, "Paradigm for the Sociology of the Stranger," is designed to provide a means for organizing existing empirical materials and for articulating a set of specific questions for future research. I shall conclude with a few comments on various parts of the paradigm.

I. A more comprehensive typology of stranger status would include variant and specialized forms within each generic type. This would facilitate the incorporation of material that might not appear at first glance to belong to the subject. Consideration of the stranger as visitor, for example, should include whatever may exist on the sociology of tourism. The Sojourner category would encompass most of what has been discussed as

30. The resulting characterization of the Marginal Man is congruent with that of R. K. Merton, who, cross-classifying two somewhat different variables, depicts the Marginal Man as one who aspires to a group but is defined as ineligible for membership by the group. See his *Social Theory and Social Structure*, 2nd ed. (Glencoe, Ill.: Free Press, 1957), p. 290.

Paradigm for the Sociology of the Stranger

I. Characteristics of Each Type of Stranger
   (Guest, Intruder, Sojourner, Inner Enemy, Newcomer, Marginal Man)
   A. Individual strangers
      1. Personal characteristics (detachment, insecurity, etc.)
      2. Typical relations with host (used as confidants, king's men, etc.)
   B. Stranger collectivities
      1. Internal characteristics (high levels of participation in voluntary associations, etc.)
      2. Typical relations with hosts (residentially segregated, used as scapegoats, etc.)

II. Factors Affecting Assumption of Each Type of Stranger Status
   A. Factors affecting aspirations of stranger
      1. Reasons for leaving home (alienation, boredom, calling, disaster, economic hardship, political oppression, etc.)
      2. Conditions of entrance into host group (amount of prestige, movable resources, special skills, etc.)
   B. Factors affecting response of host
      1. Extent of stranger-host similarity (ethnicity, language, race, region, religion, value orientations, etc.)
      2. Existence of special cultural categories and rituals for dealing with strangers
      3. Criteria for group or societal membership (classificatory kinship, religion, citizenship, professional certification, etc.)
      4. Conditions of local community (age, size, homogeneity, degree of isolation, etc.)

III. Factors Affecting Shifts in Stranger Status
   A. Factors affecting orientations of strangers
      1. Changing conditions at home
      2. Changes in stranger's control of resources in host community
   B. Factors affecting response of host
      1. Changes in criteria of group membership (from tribal affiliation to national citizenship, etc.)
      2. Changes in local community conditions (increasing unemployment, political unrest, etc.)

"middle-man minorities." The analysis of the Newcomer would include materials on problems of succession in large organizations as well as studies on the assimilation of immigrants. The Marginal Man would include such problematic positions as that of the Homecomer, as described by Alfred Schutz, and the kindred phenomenon of the *estranged* native, discussed in recent papers by Edward A. Tiryakian and Elliott P. Skinner.[31]

I.A. The precise nature of Simmel's contribution in *Der Fremde* can now be specified. It dealt almost exclusively with the question of the characteristics of the status of the *individual Sojourner*. For the most part these concerned his relations with the host group: his freedom from its conventional constraints, the fluidity of his relations with host group members, and the ease with which he establishes a relationship of confidant with them. Wood did, in fact, make the point that the characteristics enumerated by Simmel should *not* be presumed to exist in all stranger relationships, but only in those in which the stranger does not seek to become a regular group member. Nor would they obtain when the host group expresses a compulsively antagonistic attitude toward the stranger, though Simmel's account does call attention to the host's underlying ambivalence toward Sojourners.

I.B. Much of the literature on strangers is concerned with the characteristics of Sojourner communities. Thus, Fallers speaks of the tendency of Sojourners to form a great number of interlinked voluntary associations. Wood describes the tendency of old-timers within Sojourner communities to be anxious about those newly arrived from their homeland, because the latter may not appreciate the precarious circumstances under which the Sojourners live and by some untoward act may trigger an antagonistic reaction from the host group. Howard Becker writes that such communities tend to form counter-ideologies which depict themselves as superior or chosen in defense against the low regard in which they are held by the host communities.[32]

II.A.1. I know of no studies concerning the range of motivations involved in becoming a stranger, though Robert Michels long ago enumerated some points which bear on the question.[33] It seems likely, however, that the type of status acquired by strangers will be significantly affected by whether the stranger views the host community as an asylum from political or religious persecution or natural disaster, as a market for special skills and services, as a reference group attractive because of special

31. A. Schutz, "The Homecomer," *American Journal of Sociology*, vol. 50, no. 5 (1945), pp. 369–376. E. A. Tiryakian, "Perspectives on the Stranger," in *The Rediscovery of Ethnicity*, edited by S. TeSelle (New York: Harper and Row, 1973). E. P. Skinner, "Theoretical Perspectives on the Stranger," paper presented to Conference on Strangers in Africa, Smithsonian Conference Center, Belmont Maryland, October 1974.

32. *Man in Reciprocity* (New York: Praeger, 1956).

33. "Materialien zu einer Sociologie des Fremden," *Jahrbuch für Sociologie*, I (1925).

moral or other cultural features, as a group of infidels to be converted, or as a source of stimulating adventures.

II.B.2. Some cultures may know very well how to deal with Guests, but lack any institutionalized procedures for accommodating Sojourners. Some may be able to integrate legitimate immigrants as Newcomers, but can only define short-term visitors as Intruders. There is a huge and fascinating range of variability here, all the way from the custom of those Northern Australian tribesmen who reportedly speared any stranger from an unknown tribe unless he came accredited as a sacred messenger, to that of the ancient Jews, who were told to leave the gleanings of their harvests for the poor and the strangers, and were admonished, "if a stranger sojourn with thee in your land, ye shall not vex him; but the stranger that dwelleth with you shall be unto you as one born among you, and thou shalt love him as thyself; for ye were strangers in the land of Egypt."[34] This is an ethic toward Guests, if not Sojourners, which was likewise highly developed in Arabian culture and represented among the Amhara of northern Ethiopia by the concept ye-egziabher ingida, a "guest of God."

II.B.3. The potential interest of this topic may be illustrated by considering the quite disparate ways in which different ethnic groups within Ethiopia relate to strangers. In this respect, as in so many others, the traditional patterns of the Amhara and the Galla (Oromo) stand in sharp contrast. Although the Amhara, guided by their concept of the "guest of God," are customarily inclined to receive legitimate visitors with extremely considerate hospitality, they find it difficult to integrate Newcomers, and often even Sojourners, into their local communities—a process which Galla communities in many parts of the country are reported to do almost effortlessly. I would attribute this difference in good part to the different criteria for local group membership in the two traditions. In a traditional Amhara community full-fledged status is related to the possession of rist—rights to the use of land inherited through an ambilineal descent system—and no outsider, lacking genealogical affiliations through which he might establish some legitimate claim to rist, can expect to acquire that status. Galla traditions, by contrast, derive from a style of life that historically (and among the Borana today) may be described as serially sedentary. Local camps were formed and reformed periodically on a voluntary basis; neighbors were chosen with respect to qualities of cooperativeness and personal friendship.[35]

II.B.4. Wood has dealt with the topic of the preceding section in the part of her book on "The Stranger and the Social Order." The part of her

34. Leviticus 19: 9–10, 33–34.

35. For a more extensive treatment of the structural contrasts between Amhara and Oromo societies, see D. N. Levine, Greater Ethiopia: The Evolution of a Multiethnic Society (Chicago: University of Chicago Press, 1974), Chapters Eight through Ten.

book with perhaps the most enduring value, however, is the section entitled "The Stranger and the Community Pattern." There she provides a wealth of propositions on the differential effects on the reception of strangers produced by such factors as whether the host communities consist of natives or foreigners; whether they are frontier settlements or retarded districts; whether they are homogeneous in culture or highly diverse; whether they are rural, small towns, or large cities.

III. The topical salience of the sociology of the stranger is of course related to the dramatic shifts in the position of strangers experienced in so many of the new states of Africa and Asia following independence. In many instances, Guests have been redefined as Intruders; Newcomers of long standing have been turned into Marginal Men; and most dramatically, Sojourners have been transformed into Inner Enemies, and subjected to harassment, expulsion, and even assassination. There is a great need for studies which can illuminate the dynamics of these fateful changes, studies which will consolidate and extend the pioneering analyses of this topic by Skinner and Bonacich in the papers cited above.

In conclusion, I wish to note that the sociology of strangerhood articulated by this paradigm is limited by its adherence to one essential feature of Simmel's conception: the depiction of strangerhood as a figure-ground phenomenon, in which the stranger status is always defined *in relation to a host*. Other kinds of phenomena, however, have been linked with this concept, namely, those in which *both* parties to a relationship are labeled strangers. In this usage, strangerhood is defined simply as a function of the degree of unfamiliarity existing between the parties. In Lyn Lofland's elaboration of this notion, individuals are strangers to one another simply when they lack personal, biographical information about one another. Following this definition, Lofland and others have produced some interesting insights by analyzing the modern urban milieu as a "world of strangers."[36] Applying a similar model at the collective level, relations between ethnic groups have been conceived in terms of attitudes and transactions between stranger communities, and analyzed with respect to the degrees of stereotyping, prejudice, and receptivity that obtains in their relationships.[37]

Important though such topics are, there is a danger that in characterizing the content of strangerhood so broadly, what has always been most fascinating about this subject may become obscured. The continuing relevance of Simmel's essay is its focus on what happens when people bring *into a group* qualities not inherent in it. "The stranger," writes Edward Tiryakian, "brings us into contact with the limits of ourselves . . .

36. L. Lofland, *A World of Strangers* (New York: Basic Books, 1973). See also V. Packard, *A Nation of Strangers* (New York: McKay, 1972).

37. See R. M. Williams, Jr., *Strangers Next Door: Ethnic Relations in American Communities* (Englewood Cliffs, N.J.: Prentice-Hall, 1964).

DONALD N. LEVINE

he makes us aware of ourselves by indicating the boundaries of selfhood."[38] The experience of and responses to this mixture of closeness and remoteness, of threat and excitement, is a distinctive social formation which continues to demand attention wherever there are firmly bounded groups and others who step across their boundaries.

38. Tiryakian, "Theoretical Perspectives on the Stranger," p. 57.

2

Open Systems and Closed Boundaries: The Ritual Process of Stranger Relations in New African States

William A. Shack

This essay is exploratory, not substantive. It assumes some understanding of ritual, and of the attendant symbolic and structural processes as outlined by Victor Turner in *The Ritual Process.*[1] I begin with a brief overview of Georg Simmel's concept of "the stranger" set within the broader sociological framework of ritual incorporation of outsiders by in-groups. I then move to consider Victor Turner's use of "communitas" and "structure" as analytical concepts for viewing old and new African states as "open" or "closed" social systems with respect to the structural position of strangers.[2] Finally, I set the discussion against the background of the effects of the withdrawal of European colonial rule, and the emergence of new African states, on the subsequent relations between African strangers and their host societies.

Simmel, the Stranger, and the Threshold Covenant

Georg Simmel's brief essay "The Stranger" contains several complementary sets of ideas that stimulate analysis of the phenomenon of the social status position of strangers in contemporary African societies.[3] For Simmel was not concerned, as he put it, with "the wanderer who comes today and goes tomorrow," but rather with the stranger "who comes today and stays tomorrow."[4] The stranger who came one day and remained

---

1. I am indebted to Professor Victor Turner for his constructive criticisms of an earlier version of this essay. It was further revised after presentation before members of the Seminar in Social Anthropology at the London School of Economics, on November 22, 1974, to whom I am grateful for their remarks and comments.

2. Here and elsewhere in this essay, I use the term "state" to mean "nation-state"—that is, polities larger than village communities, with types of government that range from kingdoms to chiefdoms; or "political communities" in the sense that Schapera has used the term, in *Government and Politics in Tribal Societies* (London: C. A. Watts, 1956), p. 8.

3. Several English translations have been printed of Simmel's article "Der Fremde." See, for example, K. H. Wolff, translator and editor, *The Sociology of Georg Simmel* (Glencoe: The Free Press, 1950), pp. 402–408; D. Levine, ed., *Georg Simmel on Individuality and Social Forms* (Chicago: University of Chicago Press, 1971), pp. 143–149.

4. Levine, *Georg Simmel*, p. 143.

the next symbolized a synthesis of the boundaries of both spatial relations and social relations. Remoteness and nearness, indifference and involvement were, as Simmel reasoned, explicit characteristics of the activities of the stranger—activities which were primarily, though not exclusively, economic in nature. Historical circumstances, however, more
often than not cast strangers in the occupational category of entrepre-
neur—for instance, the trader as middleman. Not surprisingly, then, the
stereotype of the stranger acting the role of the landless, mobile merchant, the economic go-between, attracted the greatest attention in
sociological writings on the stranger in various societies, including those
of Africa. Other instances have been noted of strangers having occupied
dominant political positions when objectivity was needed in mediating
disputes and arranging settlements between groups in stratified host societies.[5] In the role of mediator, Simmel's "stranger" is strikingly similar to
Elizabeth Colson's "alien diviner" among the Plateau Tonga of Zambia.
In both instances, the perceived impartiality of the outsider (stranger) is
more readily acceptable to the insiders (hosts), who for expediency and
other reasons are willing to subordinate themselves to the stranger's
arbitration.[6]

The ritual process of stranger-host relations, as expressed in economic and political activities in African societies, is a subject which I shall
take up later. It is sufficient to note here that ritual and even ceremonial
processes, of the sort which work to create a union wherein the stranger
whose relationship to the host group involves both being outside it and
confronting it, were only implied in Simmel's formulations.[7] In part, this
might be explained in terms of differences in demographic and social
scale. European societies of the type that provided the empirical basis for
Simmel's analyses of the variability of social forms, then and now, have
greater complexity and multiplicity of roles than do so-called African
"tribal" societies. In the vast majority of African societies, and virtually
all simple societies with meagre subsistence economies, kinship norms
inform the nature of political structure. Not only that, rights of citizenship are almost invariably based upon land ownership, which itself has a
kinship referrent. In such societies, ritual is seen to define more clearly
the character of social relations and often brings resolution to conflict.[8]

Arnold van Gennep drew attention to this special character of ritual

5. *Ibid.*, p. 145; see also Wolff, *The Sociology of Georg Simmel*, pp. 216ff.

6. E. Colson, "The Alien Diviner and Local Politics Among the Tonga of Zambia," in M.
Swartz, V. Turner, and A. Tuden, eds., *Political Anthropology* (Chicago: Aldine, 1966),
pp. 221–228.

7. Levine, *Georg Simmel*, p. 144.

8. This thesis has been sufficiently well advanced in the writings of the so-called Manchester School of Social Anthropology to warrant no additional comment. It began with
the interesting essay by J. Clyde Mitchell, *The Kalela Dance*, Rhodes Livingston Paper No.
27 (Manchester: Manchester University Press, 1956).

in small-scale societies.[9] His well-known thesis, which need not be summarized here, has been more recently reassessed by Max Gluckman, who asserts that "rituals of the kind investigated by van Gennep are 'incompatible' with the structure of modern urban life."[10] The overwhelming majority of examples of rituals and ceremonials that van Gennep characterized as *rites de passage* involved changes in the status relations of individuals and groups in "tribal" societies. Spatial relations of the type that concerned Simmel in the transition from one social status to another were de-emphasized but not overlooked by van Gennep, who preferred the phrase "territorial passage"; the same is true of his "rites of incorporation" of strangers. Leaving aside descriptive examples of "liminal" rites, or what H. C. Trumbull chose to call "the threshold covenant," executed prior to incorporation of strangers into the host society,[11] it is significant to note that both van Gennep and Simmel were treading upon similar sociological ground with respect to the interplay between social and spatial relations. When van Gennep wrote that "the passage from one position to another is identified with a territorial passage," and further on that "the spatial separation of distinct social groups is an aspect of social organization," his statements sound familiar to readers of Simmel.[12] That is, in the case of strangers, remoteness and closeness in social and spatial terms are, at one and the same time, characteristic of the stranger's relationship with the larger society. The stranger is symbolically in it, but not necessarily of it.

No doubt the analogy between social and spatial relations presented thus far can be pushed further than I have attempted here. The correspondence between these two sets of relations should become clear in the following sections, as I try to move the stranger figuratively beyond the threshold covenant.

Liminality, Communitas, and the New African States

Africa is replete with examples of individuals and groups who formed settled communities of occupational specialists in societies other than their own.[13] A great deal of movement from one society to the next, we are told, took place in the distant past, long before this type of voluntary

9. A. van Gennep, *Les rites de passage* (1909), translated by M. Vizedom and G. Caffee as *The Rites of Passage* (London: Routledge and Kegan Paul, 1960).

10. M. Gluckman, ed., *Essays on the Ritual of Social Relations* (Manchester: Manchester University Press, 1962), p. 37.

11. H. C. Trumbull, *The Threshold Covenant* (New York: Scribner's Sons, 1896).

12. A. van Gennep, *The Rites of Passage* (translated by Vizedom and Caffee), p. 192. Commenting on this point, Professor Julian Pitt-Rivers reminded me that van Gennep and Simmel were intellectual contemporaries. Although the evidence is lacking, it is not inconceivable that each was aware of, and was stimulated by, the other's theoretical formulations. Therefore, the conceptual similarities might be more than coincidence.

13. The chapters in this volume by Challenor, Kuper, Leighton, and Sudarkasa are particularly illustrative of this settlement pattern.

flow of human traffic became a permanent part of the historical record. It is not inconceivable that in the formative stages of communities of African strangers, the subjects were, to use Turner's phrase, "liminal entities," or better still, "liminaries."[14] The myriad examples which Trumbull and Hamilton-Grierson recorded of host societies performing the rite of the threshold covenant, symbolically incorporating strangers into their midst, provide some clue as to the extent to which ritual served to articulate social and spatial relations.[15] Trying to reconstruct ceremonials once performed to legitimate the incorporation of strangers into host societies is a fruitless task. However, enough is known of the structural position of strangers as a social category in contemporary African societies to assist in roughly sketching the contours of the ritual process before European rule was imposed on traditional African polities, during the period of colonial administration and in the post-independence era which witnessed the emergence of new African states.

African strangers, in the pre-colonial era, were neither here nor there. They moved with relative ease from one political entity to the next, often engaged in occupations disdained by the wider society. Trade, certain craft specialties, bards, jesters, minstrels, ritual practitioners of medicine, and so forth, were some of these disdained occupations which liminaries performed, and still perform today among the central Ethiopians and Boran Oromo.[16] So also, the extensive trading networks that many indigenous African states developed served to link together hostile societies through the exchange of goods and services by wandering strangers. They came one day and were gone the next. Some remained, however. Of these, very few, as individuals or groups, experienced the ritual passage from lower to higher status. Nor did strangers enjoy total rights of citizenship in the political, legal, and economic systems of the state, for these rights usually derived from ownership of land. Strangers who came and stayed were, it would appear, unrestricted in their movements between the "sacred" boundaries of one state and those

14. V. Turner, *The Ritual Process* (Chicago: Aldine, 1969), p. 95. In what follows I use "communitas" in the sense that Turner speaks of "normative communitas" as distinguished from "existential communitas," which is homogeneous and honest, and "ideological communitas" (*ibid.*, p. 132). I accept Turner's advice, made in a personal communication, that "liminal entities" could be more eloquently expressed by the term "liminaries," a suggestion put to him by Professor John Middleton.

15. Trumbull, *The Threshold Covenant;* P. J. Hamilton-Grierson, "Strangers," *Encyclopaedia of Religion and Ethics,* edited by J. Hastings, vol. 11 (Edinburgh: T. & T. Clark, 1921), pp. 883–896.

16. For a brief description of the many landless, low-status occupational groups in central Ethiopia engaged in tasks of this type, see W. Shack, *The Central Ethiopians,* Ethnographic Survey of Northeastern Africa, Part IV (London: International African Institute, 1974). The Boran Oromo (Galla) of southern Ethiopia are reported to employ as ritual surrogate parents members of low-status occupational groups. See A. Legesse, *Gada: Three Approaches to the Study of an African Society* (New York: The Free Press, 1973), p. 54.

of the next. Whatever their occupational role, the position of strangers was ambiguous. Ambiguousness was a consequence of strangers being "betwixt and between the positions assigned and arrayed by law, custom, and convention and ceremonial," all attributes of the normative structure of the wider society.[17] The weakness and passivity characteristic of the ritual status of liminal personae sooner or later became transformed into secular power in the state of "communitas." The ritual process of symbolically converting such marginal personae from the state of liminality to the state of communitas took place both before and during the earlier period of colonial rule.

Colonial rule altered social and spatial boundaries, both symbolically and in reality. Sacredness attributed to spatial boundaries demarcating distinct political entities became, as it were, "secularized." Secularization of political boundaries facilitated European administration of ethnically and culturally diverse social groups. One effect of the imposing of external authority over indigenous African societies was the creation of social systems which were more "open" than those that had existed in the pre-colonial era. Strangers who once were regarded by their hosts as "dangerous, inauspicious, or polluting" were symbolically transformed to what is best called "pseudo-communitas," a status position which served to maintain the newly imposed social structure.[18] It was a state of pseudo-communitas because it lacked the authenticity associated with normative communitas. Incorporation of previously itinerant strangers as "citizens," usually second-class citizens at that, was brought about coercively, by administrative fiat. In other words, colonial rule created "open" social systems principally bounded by the expediency of political and economic administrative functions and duties. Generally speaking, the alien system of authority ignored traditional inferior-superior status positions which differentiated strangers and hosts— except where recognition of indigenous political and religious offices was useful to the foreign administration. Social distinctions by and between Africans were still very real, although overt expression of such distinctions through hostile acts never received official sanction.

Strangers and their previous hosts were viewed by European administrators in the same social terms of reference. But more often than not, strangers enjoyed distinctive economic advantages over indigenous members of the host society, who often considered themselves to be relatively deprived of economic and political power—a point I shall return to later. Mystical fear of the "power of the weak," however, which was once wielded by individuals and groups of strangers, and was typical of liminaries in the state of communitas, declined into insignificance. This

17. Turner, *The Ritual Process.*

18. *Ibid.*, p. 109; Professor Turner suggested the term "pseudo-communitas" in a personal communication.

was because pseudo-communitas offered no ritual threat to African social life under the new, alien "normative structure" imposed by external authorities; nor did ritual symbolically call into question the moral values upon which the alien social system rested. Such a dialectic can operate only when there exist true normative structure and true communitas.

The withdrawal of European administration and the attainment of African self-government brought in its wake the breakdown of pseudo-communitas and loss of the advantageous roles strangers had occupied in it. Strangers became "reliminalized." Political and economic competition for scarce resources between former hosts and reliminalized strangers led to an exaggeration of communitas, which in turn provoked an exaggeration of the new nation-state and local-level structures. "Exaggeration of structure," as Victor Turner has argued, "may well lead to pathological manifestations of communitas outside or against 'the law.'"[19] Turner goes on to say that "exaggeration of communitas . . . may be speedily followed by despotism, over-bureaucratization, or other modes of structural rigidification."[20] I suggest that it was precisely these ritual and symbolic processes, the dialectic between re-established communitas and structure (reliminalized strangers and former host societies), which were set in motion in the post-independence era in Africa. The widespread expulsion of strangers, especially African strangers, from newly created independent African states is an aspect of that ritual process which I shall attempt to take one step further in the next section.

The Ritual Process of Stranger Relations

Now the ritual processes that are expressive of different symbolic states of stranger-host relations, and occur under different historical circumstances, represent only one side of the problem. Why strangers have been expelled from some African societies and not others cannot be explained satisfactorily by ritual and symbol. Ritual and symbol are not explanatory of social processes; they are expressive of them. Social rank, status, attitudes, and behavior are all significant attributes of stranger-host social interaction. The sociological task is to seek an understanding of these attributes in order to furnish a set of explanations complementary to those furnished by an analysis focused on ritual and symbol. A case in point can be excerpted from the social history of stranger-host relations in Ethiopia, with special emphasis on Europeans as liminal personae.

The earliest record of any sizable contingent of Europeans in the ancient Christian state of Abyssinia was the small army of mercenaries who

19. *Ibid.*, p. 129.
20. *Ibid.*

landed at Massawa, on the Red Sea coast, in 1541.[21] Commandeered by Christopher da Gama, these four hundred matchlockmen had been requested by the Christian kingdom to help stem the tide of the Muslim invasion that was threatening its existence. After decisively defeating the Muslim armies, the Portuguese embarked from Abyssinia, unheralded by their hosts. However, the Portuguese military presence had pierced the floodgates, allowing a small but steady stream of European and non-Ethiopian strangers to flow into Abyssinia. The trickle of liminal personae continued in varying rates of flow from the sixteenth century right up to the present. Roman Catholic and Protestant missionaries;[22] skilled artisans, envoys, and counselors in the temporary employ of successive rulers; physicians, technicians, and teachers in service to governments in more recent times;[23] merchants, traders, shopkeepers, and the like—all were typical of the liminal stranger who comes today and goes tomorrow. So few European strangers experienced ritual and symbolic change in status through the transition from liminality to communitas that a case for them can hardly be made.

Ancient Abyssinia and modern Ethiopia are representative of societies with "closed" boundaries, at the threshold of which have stood strangers, of one sort or another, in the state of liminality. As such, they never came to hold "the power of the weak," as strangers do in the state of communitas, enjoying privileges of higher rank and status than did indigenous groups of Ethiopians, even lowly peasants and landless serfs. Whenever European strangers came dangerously close to posing a threat to the closed morality and routine behavior upon which Ethiopian social life depended, they were expelled forthwith.

In other cases, strangers were imprisoned in the confines of the royal court, or denied permission to leave the country. Indeed, Ethiopians from the time of Fremnatos, in the fourth century, have always shown

21. Leaving aside, of course, that it was a "religious stranger," Fremnatos, who introduced the Christianity of the Roman Empire to the royal court of King Ezana (about 330 A.D.). Various adventurers, itinerant traders, and the like had visited the court of Abyssinian kings long before the famous Portuguese embassy led by Father Francisco Alvarez to the court of Emperor Lebna Dengel (Prester John) in 1550. See, for example, C. F. Beckingham and G. W. B. Huntingford, *The Prester John of the Indies*, Hakluyt Society, Series II. Vol. CXIV (Cambridge: Cambridge University Press, 1961), 2 vols. On the activities of some "religious strangers" in East Africa in the nineteenth century, see Southall, Chapter Eleven.

22. An excellent account of the role of foreign missionaries in the politics of Ethiopia is presented by D. Crummey, *Priests and Politicians: Protestant and Catholic Missions in Orthodox Ethiopia, 1830–68* (Oxford: The Clarendon Press, 1973). See also my review article "Religious Strangers in the Kingdom of Ethiopia," *Journal of Modern African Studies*, vol. 13, no. 2 (1975), pp. 361–366.

23. For a review of Afro-Americans as liminal personae in Ethiopia, see W. Shack, "Ethiopia and Afro-Americans: Some Historical Notes, 1920–1970," *Phylon*, vol. 35, no. 2 (1974), pp. 142–155.

greater readiness to receive visitors from the outside world than to allow them to depart. Sir James Bruce, who explored northern Ethiopia in search of the source of the Nile, was as much a prisoner as a free man during his lengthy stay in the country. Father Alvarez, after having enjoyed six years (1520–1526) of relative freedom of movement, had difficulty obtaining permission from Lebna Dengel to leave Ethiopia. All these instances represent rigidification of the state of liminality.[24]

Ethiopians were never dispossessed of the attributes of power and wealth, whether symbolized in political office, honorific titles, land, cattle, or access to sacred accoutrements or ceremonial rites peculiar to major and minor religious groups. Tolerance and indifference, and the absence of overt forms of hostility, for the most part characterize the attitudes of Ethiopians toward strangers, whatever the strangers' racial or ethnic origins or religious leanings.[25] Historical fact reinforced the centuries-old conviction of the Ethiopians that they have never been deprived of power, even to a relative extent, by immigrant groups, either in the distant past or under contemporary conditions.

It might well be argued that the historical circumstances of stranger-host relations in Ethiopia present too extreme a situation from which to advance sociological generalizations that would broaden our understanding of strangers in other African societies and elsewhere. I believe not. Instead, the juxtaposition of Ethiopia alongside African states from which strangers who once experienced the state of communitas have been expelled, or incorporated, has a functional purpose also. It extends the baseline for comparison with societies having both similar and different historical features, and either greater or lesser complexity of social, economic, and political organizations. By making such comparisons we can learn a great deal more about the social-structural and cultural capacities of particular African societies to make use of ritual and symbol in regulating the social position and spatial movement of strangers.

Let me recapitulate briefly the essential points of the argument set forth thus far. Strangers, in the Simmelian sense, were marginal as well as integral elements of African social and political systems long before the beginning of colonial rule. In many African states, especially in West Africa, strangers as liminaries often engaged in occupations disdained by the indigenous host societies in which they settled, temporarily or per-

24. From the reign of Fasilidas (1632–1665) to that of Iyasus (1682–1706), Ethiopian kings continued their firm policy of prohibiting entry by Europeans. If admitted, their activities were severely curtailed.

25. However, it is of interest to note that historically, "religious strangers" have always been perceived as posing the most serious threat to the Ethiopian polity, numerous missionaries having lost their lives attempting to spread a foreign gospel. The most obvious explanation for the fierce reaction of Ethiopian rulers toward religious strangers is that new religious ideologies, rituals, and symbols had the capacity to undermine the politico-religious structure of the monarchy.

manently. Colonial administration transformed the character of what were in essence ritually "closed" boundaries demarcating distinct indigenous African political entities. This alien authority, in turn, created "open" systems which facilitated the spatial passage of strangers between one polity and another. Threshold rites of incorporation, which had been social and ritual requisites for the initiation of stranger-host interaction, faded. Status differentiation, formerly expressed symbolically in social and spatial relations between strangers and hosts, became less clearly marked. Under European administration, Africans were viewed as forming a social structure of undifferentiated social categories. Political independence and the emergence of new African states brought about a rebirth of the "closed" system. Taking the colonial legacy of multiethnic and culturally heterogeneous social systems within their political boundaries, the new states defined more rigorously than ever before the social, structural, and status positions of one African group as against another. Normative structures were re-established in which previously privileged strangers found no place for accommodation. Thus in several new African states, strangers who were formerly "accepted," despite rank and status discrepancies, have been expelled, or mandated for repatriation to their homelands.

In most societies around the world, strangers and other immigrant groups seldom receive entitlement to rank and status congruent with that of the wider society, at least not at first. Social discrepancies engender different attitudes, sometimes tolerant and liberal, at other times intolerant and conservative.[26] These attitudes may not always correlate with the same social discrepancies, or if so not always to the same degree; but a difference of some sort or another will be made between those who are and who are not "in equilibrium."

Status consistency is more likely to obtain among strangers, immigrants, migrants, and the like, who from the viewpoint of the host society represent an undifferentiated social category. Status consistency is *less* likely to obtain among the many people of different status and rank who constitute the host society, and who are more intensively engaged in competition for limited goods whatever their exchange value or symbolic worth. Status and wealth are not inevitably linked to political influence, power, and authority. In some cultures, historical circumstances have rendered those with high rank and access to wealth essentially powerless, or at least they believe themselves to be so. Conversely, in the same cultures, historical circumstances have provided ground for the weak to gain power. And when the "power of the weak" becomes possessed by strangers, then persons or groups of higher status who believe themselves to be dispossessed of the attributes of power and wealth are likely to feel deprived.[27] In the words of W. G. Runciman, "those who in general view their position in such a way as to feel a sense of relative deprivation will be more likely to express hostility to out-groups and specifically to immigrants [or strangers]."[28]

I have attempted to point out that historical circumstances of European colonial fiat created in many dependent African territories "open" social systems in which strangers were deliminalized and became components of plural societies. In these cases there was an enforced pseudo-communitas in which strangers came to symbolize the "power of the weak." As I have already said, strangers were accorded economic, occupational, and educational privileges that were denied to indigenous members of the wider society; and examples of strangers being accorded favored treatment are not wanting.[29] Simmel noted the same phenomenon for some medieval societies.[30] In some former colonialized African territories, the subordination of higher-status groups to strangers, who were thrust into the role of quasi-political and administrative functionaries or entrepreneurs, was commonplace. Colonial authority provided few safeguards for in-groups to preserve their identity against structurally inferior, "marginal," out-groups of strangers. If social conditions engendered hostile in-group attitudes toward strangers—and it is reasonable to assume that such attitudes arose in many societies—few outlets existed for the overt expression of hostile sentiments. However, in the "closed" or bounded societies of the new African states, reliminalized strangers threatened the "closed morality" and the routine behavior upon which post-independence social life depended. The various modes of structural rigidification instituted by new African states, including the expulsion of strangers, symbolize efforts to renew idealized social norms.

I have deliberately overstated the case for communitas and structure in order to sharpen the focus on ritual and symbolic processes as explanatory models for understanding the past and present position of strangers in African societies. If the models of communitas and structure, and the interaction between "open" and "closed" social and moral systems which Turner calls the "dialectic of the developmental cycle,"[31] are applicable to African societies generally, then the question of why strangers have

27. *Ibid.*, p. 183.
28. *Ibid.* The most striking example of this attitude in modern historical times is, of course, the hostility expressed toward Jews in European societies. European Gypsies experienced a similar fate, and in late nineteenth-century England, Anglo-Saxon attitudes had hardened and were expressed in open hostility toward Gypsy strangers. Professor Elizabeth Colson brought to my attention an excellent account of Anglo-Saxon attitudes toward strangers in the Victorian study by Mrs. Gaskell, *My Lady Ludow and Other Tales* (London: Sampson Low, Son & Co., 1861); see the chapter entitled "An Accursed Race."
29. See, for example, the chapters in this volume by Challenor and Leighton.
30. Wolff, *The Sociology of Georg Simmel*, pp. 216–217.
31. Turner, *The Ritual Process*, p. 97.

been expelled from some new states and local communities in Africa but not from others has been answered, at least implicitly.

The dialectic of the developmental cycle has been articulated with greater intensity in the new states in West Africa than in the southern, central, and eastern regions of the continent. It is also the case that in the pre-colonial era, West African states had developed more complex political and economic structures than those in other regions of the continent, including the interlacustrine kingdoms of East Africa. The petty Bantu kingdoms in southern Africa, for example, represent a mid-nineteenth-century stage of political development, a transformation from segmentary states to state formation. The mass expulsion of Nigerians from Ghana, and of Asians from Uganda, suggests an exaggeration of communitas which, in turn, provoked an exaggeration of structure.[32] Africans and non-African strangers in states outside West Africa have, in the main, been treated with relative tolerance—as for instance, the Lebanese in Sierra Leone.[33] I suggest that in such cases strangers have remained liminaries, and have not yet become intensively engaged in serious economic and political competition with the indigenes—which indicates an absence of the exaggeration of structure in the post-independence era.

Strangers are not considered strange because of distinguishable features of race, color, language, dress, custom, habits, modes of livelihood, and so forth, or because of the demographic scale of the society which by convention defines the boundaries of their social and spatial relations. Rather, strangers are considered strange because they are cast in the role of "interpreters," a term Monica Wilson has used to refer to individuals and groups who stand at the frontiers of conflicting social systems.[34] It may be true, as Victor Turner has suggested, that without the dialectic between communitas and structure, no society can function adequately.[35] If so, then interpreters, or strangers, have a more important role in this dialectical process than has been recognized heretofore: they serve to translate material and organizational needs into systems which enable them to be adequately met.

32. See the chapters by Kuper and Sudarkasa in this volume.
33. See the chapter by Leighton.
34. M. Wilson, "The Interpreters," Third Dugmore Memorial Lecture (Grahamstown, South Africa, 1972).
35. Turner, *The Ritual Process*, p. 129.

Part II

Historical Processes and Strangers' Roles

3

Strangers in Africa: Reflections on Nyakyusa, Nguni, and Sotho Evidence

Monica Wilson

Movement of people in Africa is nothing new. The physical variations in populations are evidence of the merging of different streams: archaeological evidence points to the arrival of strangers of differing physique with new techniques; and there is a rich and diverse oral tradition of journeys and arrivals. Within historical times Nguni-speakers from Zululand spread northward 1600 miles as the crow flies, nearly to Lake Victoria, and southward 600 miles to the Fish river in the eastern Cape, with a handful going on to the Tsitsikamma. Sotho-speakers spread 700 miles from near the Drakensberg to the upper reaches of the Zambezi. These were not movements of armed warriors alone but migrations by large parties including women and children, who drove cattle and planted grain when they halted for a season; they covered the distance within one generation.

The recurrence of the same salutation (*isiduko* or *isibongo*) among the Nguni and the same avoidance (*siboko*) among the Sotho in distant chiefdoms is certain evidence of the dispersal of one lineage through many political units.[1]

The chiefdoms of southern Africa made provision for strangers. This can be traced in written records beginning early in the sixteenth century. At least from the nineteenth century, and probably long before, every chiefdom included two categories of people: the kinsmen of the chief, more or less distant, and unrelated people. Schapera found that the nuclear stock formed only one fifth of the Ngwato population; J. D. and E. J. Krige found that it formed one tenth among the Lobedu.[2] Among the Xhosa the nuclear stock was larger: J. H. Soga, the grandson of a Xhosa councillor, identified twenty-five Xhosa clans claiming descent from Xhosa himself, five of them of doubtful origin, and sixteen clans of refugees received, so the nuclear stock probably formed more than half

---

1. I. Schapera, *The Ethnic Composition of Tswana Tribes* (London: London School of Economics, 1952), p. v.

2. *Ibid.*; E. J. and J. D. Krige, *The Realm of a Rain Queen* (London: Oxford University Press, 1943), p. 85.

51

the population.[3] In Pondoland in 1932, clans claiming kinship with the royal line formed much more than half the total population of the two Mpondo chiefdoms.[4] In both Nguni and Sotho chiefdoms, rank turned on closeness of relationship to the chief, and all those of the founding stock claimed higher status than strangers.

The status of unrelated people varied: they might be either earlier inhabitants or refugees coming in. If the earlier inhabitants were hunters and gatherers, and the incoming people were cattlemen, the early inhabitants might become clients of the cattle-owners, with the cattle-owners establishing themselves as chiefs. How closely clients were bound to patrons depended upon space and opportunity for self-support in hunting: they might become near serfs, or they might live almost independently, exchanging goods and services only when convenient. The relationship can be traced during the last century between Tswana and Sarwa, and in historical documents from the seventeenth century between Khoikhoi and San in the western Cape. It existed also between Xhosa, Thembu, Mpondo, and San until the nineteenth century.[5] Schapera and others have described how Sarwa lacked civil rights in Tswana chiefdoms in the early twentieth century; they could not bring cases to court or join a regiment, and intermarriage with Sarwa was strongly disapproved.[6]

The status of strangers coming in depended on whether they were individuals or members of a large group with a leader of their own. Survivors of shipwrecks on the southeast African coast left records dating from the sixteenth century, which make clear that a number of them, differing in race and status, were absorbed into Xhosa, Thembu, Mpondo, and Natal Nguni chiefdoms (not yet identified as Zulu). Those absorbed only became known to the outside world if they were met by survivors from a later wreck, so their numbers were no doubt larger than reported.

In 1554 six individuals, survivors from previous wrecks, were mentioned as meeting the survivors of the ship *Sao Bento* in Natal. Of the six one was a young Bengali; one, named Gaspar, was a Moor by birth; two were slaves, one was a Portuguese, and one was a man from Malabar. Only Gaspar chose to travel with the 1554 party "to return to a Christian country." The party from the *Sao Bento* left behind two Portuguese and thirty slaves.[7] In 1622 survivors of yet another wreck, the *Sao Joao*

3. J. H. Soga, *The Ama-Xosa; Life and Customs* (Lovedale: Lovedale Press, 1931), pp. 17-20.

4. M. Hunter, *Reaction to Conquest* (London: Oxford University Press, 1936), pp. 58, 398-399.

5. M. Wilson and L. Thompson, eds., *The Oxford History of South Africa*, 2 vols. (Oxford: The Clarendon Press, 1969 and 1971), I, pp. 63-64.

6. I. Schapera, *Handbook of Tswana Law and Custom* (London: Oxford University Press, 1938).

7. G. M. Theal, *Records of South Eastern Africa*, 9 vols. (London: Government of the Cape Colony, 1898), I, pp. 235-238.

Bahtista, met in Natal a Portuguese, Diogo, who was old and had children and chose to remain, and a "black of Malabar," left behind in 1593, who now had two wives and twenty children. Asked why he did not return "as a Christian" with the 1622 party, the man of Malabar replied that it was impossible to bring his two wives and twenty children: he had married one of the king's sisters, and had cattle from which he lived. Another survivor from a previous wreck was "a kaffir speaking Portuguese." He, too, refused to come because "he made rain." This 1622 party also left many of its members behind.[8]

In 1635 survivors from the wreck of the *Nossa Senhora de Belem* met a man of mixed descent who had been left behind as a child forty years earlier on the Transkei coast west of the Mthatha. He had become very rich, married three wives, and begotten many children. His Portuguese was "confused" but he was helpful in persuading the local people to trade in cattle. There was no question of his leaving.[9]

The shipwreck which excited most interest at the Cape was that of an East Indiaman, the *Grovenor*, in 1782, on the Pondoland coast, east of the Mzimvubu. Six survivors (five sailors and a boy) reached the eastern outposts of the Cape Colony, and two expeditions were sent to look for others of the 136 survivors. The first expedition found twelve: three English sailors, seven Lascars, and two black women. The second expedition found a village of mixed descent, survivors not of the *Grovenor* but of previous wrecks, living on the Mgazana river on the Pondoland coast "subject to Hamboonas" (Mpondo). Jacob van Reenen, journalist of the second expedition, reported finding "a village of *bastaard* Christians" in which "the people were descended from whites, some too from slaves of mixed colour, and the natives of the East Indies. There were three old women, who said they were sisters, and had when children been shipwrecked on this coast, but could not say of what nation they were being too young to know at the time the accident happened. We offered to take them and their children back with us on our return; at which they seemed very much pleased." But when the time came to leave, they chose rather to "remain with their children and grandchildren" until they had reaped their crops, "after which, with their whole race, to the amount of four hundred, they would be happy to depart from their present settlement."[10]

In 1828 the missionary William Shaw visited a minor chief, Mdepa, "an infirm old man" living on the same coast some distance further west. His mother, who had died "some twenty years before," had been one of the three women seen by van Reenen. She had married an Mpondo chief, Sango, or Xwabiso, and Mdepa's sister (whom Shaw also visited) was

8. Theal, *Records*, VIII, pp. 103–107.
9. *Ibid.*, 217–218.
10. G. Carter and J. van Reenen, *The Wreck of the Grovenor* (Cape Town: van Riebeeck Society, 1927), pp. 160, 170.

married to another minor chief, Mjikwa, living a little way inland.
According to their story their mother was Besi. She had been wrecked
with her father, Badi, and another white man, Tomi, both of whom had
married African women. Nothing was discovered about the two other
women survivors mentioned by van Reenen.[11] Henry Francis Fynn, who
also visited Mdepa after his mother's death, reported that she had been
regarded as "remarkably handsome." He also met the son of the black-
smith from the *Grovenor*, who had survived and married, and the son of
a cooper, also of European extraction.[12]

In the 1920s J. H. Soga visited a clan known as the abeLungu
(whites), who were living on the coast west of the Mthatha among the
Bomvana, and collected their genealogies. According to their stories,
three men and a little girl, Gquma (roar of waves) had been wrecked. She
grew up and married Xwebisa, a minor chief, as his senior wife, and bore
him three sons, the youngest being Mdepa, and a daughter Bessie, who
married Mjikwa. One of the wrecked men was taken off by a ship which
approached the shore, and the two men who remained were the progeni-
tors of the abeLungu.[13] The details given by Soga differed somewhat
from those given by Shaw and Fynn, but in outline the stories are consistent.[14]

Another clan on the same coast, mentioned first by Soga, was the
amaMholo, who also claimed to be descendants of survivors from a
wreck. By 1931 their customs approximated to those of their neighbors,
but they had a tradition that before slaughtering an animal they cut its
throat (as Muslims do); and in appearance, the one member of this clan
whom I knew (a woman) looked like an Arab, with long hair and sharply
cut features.[15]

It is certain, therefore, that from the sixteenth century onward individual survivors from shipwrecks were absorbed into Nguni society irre-
spective of race. Again and again, those who had been absorbed in this
way refused to leave with a later party. In two known cases the descendants of foreign men formed separate clans living on the coast. The jour-
nals of survivors make it clear that many of those who got ashore after a
wreck died while traveling to Moçambique or the Cape—from hunger,
exposure, exhaustion from walking and swimming rivers, or sickness.

11. Wm. Shaw, *The Story of My Mission in South-Eastern Africa* (London: Hamilton,
Adams and Co., 1860), pp. 492–499.

12. H. F. Fynn, *The Diary of Henry Francis Fynn*, edited by J. Stuart and D. McK.
Malcolm (Pietermaritzburg: Shuter and Shooter, 1950), pp. 112–113.

13. J. H. Soga, *The South-Eastern Bantu* (Johannesburg: Witwatersrand University
Press, 1930), pp. 330–332, 376–387.

14. Shaw was told that Besi was the girl wrecked, Soga that Besi was the daughter; Fynn
was told that the mother of Mdepa was Dawa; and the name of the wrecked woman's husband is variously given as Xwabiso, Xwebisa, and Sango.

15. Soga, *The South-Eastern Bantu*, pp. 489–490; Hunter, *Reaction to Conquest*, pp.
6–7.

Repeatedly, members of the larger parties stole food, or were involved in fights, some admittedly started by themselves. Individuals were more readily assimilated than large parties, and food was sometimes provided for a child when refused to adults. Relationships between the people of the country and different parties of survivors varied greatly: the party which fared best (1593) was disciplined in behavior, never stealing food or killing people, and it had a member—a slave from Moçambique—who could communicate with Nguni speakers.[16] Large parties were regarded as a threat, and cattle were driven to kraals at their approach. Shaw was told that the "jealousy and fear of Faku's father [the Mpondo chief] was excited by the large number of survivors—136—from the *Grovenor.*"[17] The 322 survivors from the 1554 wreck must have been seen as a serious threat.

Besides survivors from shipwrecks, there were individual refugees from the Cape of all races: slaves, convicts, seamen, and soldiers who took refuge with Xhosa, Sotho, or Khoikhoi and were incorporated by them. One of these, named Trout, who was met in 1782 and 1790 on the Pondoland coast, had been a slave of van Reenen the elder at the Cape, and had committed murder, according to van Reenen the younger. He had married and settled in Pondoland. Fynn met another runaway slave and heard of a European who had died but left a son in Pondoland.[18]

During the wars of 1820–1837, which spread from Zululand to the highveld, and north and south along the coast from the Save river to the Mthatha, thousands of African people were displaced and scattered; some were absorbed as individual refugees into other chiefdoms; others were accepted as groups under their own leaders and allocated land; still others established conquest states such as those of the Ngoni under Soshangane, Mzilikazi, Zwangendaba, and of the Kololo on the Zambezi.[19]

Attitudes toward strangers varied with time and place. Very generally, in Southern Africa men were scarcer than land, and because the power of a group depended upon its fighting strength, strangers were welcome; they added to the dignity and power of a chief. For this reason, a chief commonly used medicines to attract men; he welcomed strangers provided they acknowledged his authority by formally presenting a gift; and he protected the traveler. Among the Xhosa, at least from the seventeenth century, every man was "a shield of the chief" and therefore under his protection: to injure a man was to injure the chief who represented the state. Dutch survivors from the wreck of the *Stavenisse* in 1686 remarked that a man might travel safely in what is now the Transkei and

16. Theal, *Records*, I, pp. 224ff.
17. Shaw, *Mission in South-Eastern Africa*, p. 499.
18. Carter and van Reenen, *Wreck of the Grovenor*, pp. 161–164; Fynn, *Diary*, pp. 113–114.
19. Wilson and Thompson, *Oxford History of South Africa*, I, pp. 98–102, 391–405.

Natal: "One may travel 200 or 300 *mylen* through the country, without any cause of fear from men, provided you go naked, and without any iron or copper, for these things give inducement to the murder of those who have them. Neither need one be in any apprehension about meat and drink, as they have in every village or kraal a house of entertainment for travellers, where these are not only lodged, but fed also; care must only be taken, towards night fall, when one cannot go any further, to put up there, and not to go on before morning."[20]

From 1600 onward, there are references to trade in metals, furs, and ivory, and to travelers encountered: thus Alberti reported men who were almost certainly Zulu west of the Fish in 1807, and John Brownlee met Tswana from northwest of the present Kuruman at Hintza's great place north of the Kei.[21] Hintza was the senior Xhosa chief ruling from before 1809 to 1835, and he is described as receiving Zizi, Bhele, and Hlubi refugees from Natal "very *kindly*," and ordering his people to feed them.[22]

But security for movement and trade did not extend everywhere. Survivors of the *Stavenisse* reported in 1688 that they were told by Xhosa that if they tried to travel westward they "must pass tribes, armed with bows and arrows, who would obstruct their passage and murder them," and van der Stel, commenting on reports received, wrote to the Dutch East India Company in 1689: "Those Makriggas live by plunder, chiefly residing in the mountains; they are very populous, and in constant war, attacking all travellers and robbing them of every thing; but that these people lie between, the Hottentots could travel safely from the Cape to Rio de la Goa, or even the Tropic of Capricorn."[23]

There is evidence from the early seventeenth century of a regular trade route between the Zambezi and Lake Malawi, crossing the Lake.[24] Though sometimes obstructed, it appears to have been used over a long period. But in the isolated valleys in the Corridor between Lakes Malawi and Tanganyika, a trader bringing iron or salt in the late nineteenth century (and probably for long before that) did not risk traveling through strange chiefdoms: goods were passed on by local residents from one village to the next, for a stranger without kinsmen was liable to be killed and his goods seized. Cases are recorded of strangers being killed by a chief himself, even though the stranger had friends in the chiefdom, because the chief wanted the man's cattle or wife.

In this same Corridor area, however, one people after another tell of how their chiefs came as strangers and were welcomed as benefactors.

20. D. Moodie, *The Record, 1838–1842* (Cape Town and Amsterdam: Balkema, 1960), I, p. 431.

21. L. Alberti, *Des Cafres* (Amsterdam: Maaskamp, 1811), p. 9. G. Thompson, *Travels and Adventures in Southern Africa* (London: Colburn, 1827), p. 461.

22. T. B. Soga, *Intlalo ka-Xosa* (Lovedale: Lovedale Press, n.d.), pp. 10–12.

23. Moodie, *The Record*, I, pp. 427, 432.

24. John Gray, "A Journey by Land from Tete to Kilwa in 1616," *Tanganyika Notes and Records*, vol. 25 (1948).

Before they came, authority did not extend beyond one village. They were welcomed because they brought "lordship" symbolized by fire; because they brought iron weapons and tools; cattle; and new crops; and sometimes, it is said, they also brought trade contacts, which meant that cloth could be exchanged for ivory. The chiefs established ritual links which extended far beyond their political power, and priests traveling to celebrate a ritual would beat their sacred drum and passed through many chiefdoms safely, even though they carried valuable gifts of iron hoes and salt.[25]

The manner in which strangers were welcomed as chiefs because they had authority to maintain order and were thought to control rain and fertility has been splendidly described by Aidan Southall for the Alur people, on the border between Uganda, Zaire, and the Sudan. He has described groups who had no chiefs carrying off the son of a chief from elsewhere and establishing him among themselves to stop fighting.[26] Order in society is, after all, one of the things men seek, and the outsider sometimes has the prestige which an insider lacks to maintain order. In Africa, this prestige was commonly associated with the power of fertility—a power of growth thought to inhere in the chief's own body—and control over rain, as well as force of personality and self-confidence. All these things were fostered in a chief through medicines: leopard's whiskers, lion claws, crocodile hide, python flesh—the most fearful things men could imagine—and the heir to a chiefdom was commonly given such a mixture as he grew up, and later during his reign. Among the Nyakyusa an explicit association was made between majesty and the fearfulness of beasts of prey.[27] This also happened in Europe of course, as coats of arms show—an English stamp in use in 1974 shows Robert the Bruce with lion rampant. Authority was something valued and cherished, more or less consciously.

In 1959, Tutsi pastoralists were still being welcomed as immigrants by cultivators living in what was then the Belgian Congo, west of Lake Tanganyika and a little way south of Bukavu. They were welcomed because they provided the cultivators with milk, and with manure for their fields. They had not yet established themselves as chiefs, as in neighboring Burundi, but potentially they were overlords, and a Belgian agricultural officer expressed astonishment that they should be welcomed, in view of the tension in Burundi and Rwanda between Tutsi and Hutu.[28]

In the nineteenth century, various Europeans established themselves

25. Monica Wilson, *Good Company* (London: Oxford University Press, 1951); *Communal Rituals of the Nyakyusa* (London: Oxford University Press, 1959); *Peoples of the Nyasa-Tanganyika Corridor* (Cape Town: University of Cape Town, 1958).

26. A. W. Southall, *Alur Society* (Cambridge: W. Heffer & Sons, 1963) pp. 12-18, 92-96, 181-186.

27. Wilson, *Communal Rituals*, p. 58.

28. Verbal communication in Bukavu from a Belgian Agricultural Officer, May 1959.

as chiefs with followings; they hunted for ivory, traded, and participated in frontier politics. Medicines and weapons were sought from them. Among these men were Dunn in Zululand, deBuys on the eastern Cape frontier and then in the northern Transvaal, and Fynn on the border of Natal and the Transkei. Each of them married a number of wives and left many descendants who formed a recognized people concerned with land rights and securing a status in the South African caste society more favorable than that of blacks.

John Dunn was of Scots descent, thought to have been born in Port Elizabeth in 1833. He was a conspicuously brave fighter, who supported the Zulu claimant against Cetshwayo in 1856, and formed his own independent chiefdom. After Cetshwayo's installation as king in 1872, Dunn supported him, negotiating on his behalf with the Natal government and growing wealthy by gun-running—or so it was alleged. He was also the "supervisor" of Tsonga people from Moçambique who passed through Zululand to work in Natal. But in the colonial war against Cetshwayo, Dunn fought along with the British, and was rewarded with a grant of land in Mangete district. He married 48 wives according to Zulu custom, as well as one wife of mixed descent, and was reputed to have over 100 legitimate children. Some of his descendants were absorbed into the white community, and a few into the black, but the great majority (245 in 1945) continued to live at Mangete and Emoyeni in Zululand; they attended a "Coloured" school (for those of mixed descent) instead of a Zulu school, and were acutely color-conscious, distinguishing between light and dark Dunns and separating themselves from the Zulu. They farmed more or less efficiently, and worked as carpenters and blacksmiths, and many moved to jobs in industry. A prolonged battle over title to their lands continued until 1976.[29]

Nearly a century before Dunn, there was living on the eastern Cape frontier a farmer named Coenraad de Buys, an enormous man who spoke fluent Xhosa and became notorious for seducing the wives of leading Xhosa men. He even ingratiated himself with the widowed mother of the Xhosa chief, Ngqika, much to the anger of the Xhosa councillors— though according to custom, a widow might herself choose her lover. He became an outlaw in the Cape, fled north, and with his followers established Mara in the northern Transvaal, where he traded in ivory and salt. His descendants became a distinct community at Mara.[30]

Henry Francis Fynn, who arrived in Natal in 1824, became an ivory hunter, trader, and political negotiator. He lived close to the people and also left a group of descendants by African wives.[31]

29. Research Team, University of Natal, The Dunn Reserve (Pietermaritzburg: University of Natal Press, 1953).

30. J. S. Marais, Maynier and the First Boer Republic (Cape Town: Maskew Miller, 1944), pp. 29-32, 47, 72, 78-79, 99-103, 115, 123-124, 127. Wilson and Thompson, Oxford History of South Africa, II, p. 55.

31. Fynn, Diary, and personal fieldwork.

The lineages of stranger chiefs who arrived with cattle have increased fast in numbers. They did so because in a patrilineal and polygynous society with cattle-marriage, the men of a rich lineage marry many wives and beget many children; the men of a poor lineage marry late and each can afford no more than one wife. So dominant lineages have spread: the *abanyafyale* (chiefs) called "the sons of Lwembe" among the Nyakyusa, the Luo among the Alur, the Dlamini among the Nguni, the Kwena among the Sotho, and in colonial times the descendants of John Dunn, Coenraad de Buys, and Henry Francis Fynn.

Cattle-owners may have spread rapidly for another reason also: they could provide milk for children. I found some evidence to suggest that families of laborers on dairy farms in South Africa increased faster than families of laborers on sheep or cereal farms. And stranger groups bringing new crops or techniques of cultivation may also have increased faster than the indigenous population; thus the population increase of the Nguni in the eighteenth century may have been associated with the introduction of maize on the southern African coast.

In some areas, the strangers coming in merged with the indigenous community. This happened with survivors from shipwrecks along the southern African coast, and with individuals who escaped from the Cape and sought refuge with Xhosa or Tswana chiefs or Khoikhoi groups.[32] The Nyakyusa chiefs—the *abanyafyale*—merged with the people among whom they spread: chiefs married commoner women as well as daughters of other chiefs; and children of junior sons, whoever their mothers, became commoners. The status of a woman was reflected among the Nyakyusa in the number of cattle given at her marriage, or in the fine imposed for her seduction; the status of a man was indicated by the number of cattle demanded in fine if his wife committed adultery, and the difference between chiefs and commoners in this regard was defined. In Nguni chiefdoms there were similar rules distinguishing chiefs and commoners, and the number of cattle expected for a chief's own daughter was greater than for a distantly related girl of the royal clan, for although she might be Dlamini or Nyawuza or Tshezi, she was no princess.

In Rwanda, Burundi, and Ankole, the Tutsi or Hima remained a separate caste, not intermarrying to any extent with indigenous Hutu or Iru, and strongly disapproving such intermarriage. Among the Ngwato, a Tswana could not contract a legal marriage with a Sarwa; in South Africa in 1949 it became illegal for white to marry black or Coloured or Indian; and in East Africa generally, white and Indian have not intermarried with each other or with black.

An anthropologist must ask the reason for the differences. The Nyakyusa chiefs claimed that they "differed in their bodies" from the cultivators among whom they spread, as well as from the pygmie people who had once occupied the forests of Rungwe; and the diversity of

32. Wilson and Thompson, *Oxford History of South Africa*, I, p. 234.

physical types in the valley supports this claim. There is good reason to suppose that the Nyakyusa were an offshoot of the incoming people who spread round the Lakes, but one which merged rather than staying separate, as did the Tutsi of Rwanda and Burundi, and the Hima of Ankole. A generation ago the missionary anthropologist John Roscoe raised the question why some of the incoming peoples in the lacustrine area had merged with the indigenous inhabitants while others had stayed separate; he thought it depended upon relative numbers of population and sex balance.[33] If the numbers of indigenous inhabitants, or of incomers, is very small they are likely to be absorbed; if both groups are large a caste system is more likely to develop. If the incoming group consists solely or mainly of men (or women) they will inevitably intermarry with the earlier population and fuse with it. Roscoe was correct in thinking that demographic factors are of major importance. Studies in anti-Semitism and of immigrants in Europe support this, but demography is not the sole factor.

In Africa, six other factors demonstrably affect absorption or separation: these are visibility, relative skills, living space, employment, language, and values. Where strangers are visibly different from indigenous inhabitants, fusion between them is less likely than where they are physically indistinguishable. Tutsi and Hutu in Rwanda and Burundi, Tswana and Sarwa in Botswana, and Xhosa and San in the Cape Province all differed in stature, features, and complexion. So did Caucasian (white), African (negro), and Indian in South and East Africa. Between these different physical stocks intermarriage has at some periods been disapproved, or illegal, or both: despite some mingling, there has been continuing separation. Nyakyusa chiefs, indigenous cultivators, and pygmie hunters also differed in physical type, but fusion between them has been complete. In the Rungwe district, the pygmie physical type was rare by 1934 and thought ugly: once, in a whisper, a man with an unmistakably pygmie physique was pointed out to me as I passed the field in which he was hoeing; it would have been impolite to let him hear the comment. According to genealogies recorded a hundred years ago, there has been intermarriage between San and Xhosa, Thembu, and Mpondomise. The son of a San woman was even chosen as a Thembu chief (one of the Thembu praises is still "the tiny man"), and Xhosa chiefs repeatedly married Khoikhoi women in the eighteenth century, the Khoikhoi being of the same physical type as the San, but cattle-owners. In the same way, when the Dutch first settled at the Cape, marriage between white and Khoikhoi was accepted, and on the frontiers marriage between white and black African (negro), as well as white with those of mixed descent, was common until this century.[34] It did not become illegal until 1949.

33. J. Roscoe, *Immigrants and their Influence in the Lake Region of Central Africa.* Frazer Lecture, Cambridge: Cambridge University Press, 1927.
34. Wilson and Thompson, *Oxford History of South Africa,* I, pp. 104–106, 245–246.

Physical difference is not, therefore, the sole reason for strangers remaining separate; it does not always operate, and groups who were physically different have merged many times. South Africa has an admittedly mixed population of 2,306,000, which is 9.3 percent of the total, and the de facto mingling is certainly much larger. One of the myths that repeatedly emerges in South Africa and elsewhere is the myth of a clean break, of an earlier total separation, which does not accord with archaeological, historical, and linguistic evidence. The mingling of Xhosa with San, or Tswana with Sarwa, is no more readily admitted than the mingling of white with black or Khoikhoi is admitted at the Cape. Moreover, San and Khoikhoi have now been shown to be physically of the same stock and culturally very close, not the separate groups that modern myths have made them.[35] What is not clear is *when* these myths emerged, and whether or not they are a reflection of the white preoccupation with race.

Differences in skills may be complementary, and may create antagonism and disdain only when people with different means of subsistence come into competition for scarce resources. The skills of the Nyakyusa as cattlemen and cultivators merged with those of earlier cultivators, and a people living solely by hunting disappeared from the Rungwe valley. Skillful hunters remained important in defending stock and crops, especially against wild pig, but a hunt was organized by a chief like a military expedition; its success depended upon cooperation beyond one village, and upon organization rather than individual skill. Competition between groups differing in physical type and skills never emerged.

In most of South Africa, and in Botswana, the hunters and gatherers could hold their own against the cattle-owners until land and game became scarce. Their client relationship was a relatively equal one so long as it could be terminated at will; but once the client could no longer hunt for himself (because hunting grounds were shrinking and game had been shot out) he became a dependent. Then the physical difference, coinciding with the difference in skills, increased disdain. This connection can be traced in the relationship of Sarwa or San with Tswana, Sotho, Xhosa, Thembu, Mpondo, white, and mixed people in South Africa. So long as population was sparse, hunters and cattle-owners lived amicably, exchanging certain products and sometimes intermarrying; when population increased in relation to available grazing and hunting land, bitter war developed. The fighting is depicted in the cave paintings of the hunters along the foothills of the Drakensberg and in the Queenstown district, where they clashed with Xhosa and Thembu and later with white colonists.[36]

35. *Ibid.*, I, pp. 104–106. In Ankole a myth of total earlier separation was reported in 1974, but it does not appear in previous accounts. Y. Elam, "Relationships between Hima and Iru . . . ," *African Studies*, no. 33 (1974), pp. 159–172.

36. E. Rosenthal and A. J. H. Goodwin, *Cave Artists of South Africa* (Cape Town: Balkema, 1953), pp. 56–58.

Competition for living space is *one*, but only one, of the basic conflicts. I do not agree with Robert Ardrey that it is the most fundamental, though it is certainly true that conflict between groups often increases when pressure on land increases. How the competing groups are defined varies. Sometimes, as among the Nyakyusa since 1950, it appears as competition between generations, or between men and women, for scarce land. Among the Xhosa of the Ciskei, there is now increasing conflict between long-established landholders and immigrants coming in from white-owned farms and country towns, even though the landholders and immigrants are all Xhosa-speakers and culturally and physically alike. Tension rises as the number of immigrants increases, though the cleavage between landholders and "landless-wanderers" is nothing new.[37]

In an industrialized society unemployment exacerbates tensions, and as Africa industrializes conflicts between groups appear as competition for jobs, sometimes for the better-paid jobs, sometimes for any sort of employment. The color-bar legislation in South Africa, reserving certain occupations to whites, was passed during a period of recession and unemployment. In 1974 among laborers in the gold mines, there were repeated clashes between Sotho and Xhosa speakers who were competing for jobs. The Xhosa resented promotion of Sotho workers from Lesotho to foremen's jobs—"boss boy" jobs as they are called. There is no physical divergence between the groups in conflict, but there is a difference in language and custom.

Where integration has occurred between earlier inhabitants and strangers coming in, their accounts of history and the myths they tell, and celebrate in ritual, are more or less consistent. Both chiefs and commoners among the Nyakyusa told the same stories and participated in enacting the same ritual, the "coming out," which celebrated the arrival of chiefs, depicting them as benefactors who had brought such good things as lordship, cattle, and iron, but which *also* asserted the chiefs' dependence upon commoners, and demonstrated cooperation between them in kindling fire, the symbol of authority and civilization. Where, on the other hand, a caste system has been established, accounts of history given by members of the different castes differ. Vansina has reported this for Rwanda, and it is conspicuous for South Africa.

The myth told by whites in South Africa, and still repeated by political leaders there, is that the whites at first occupied an *empty* land: Bantu-speakers were only crossing the Limpopo as van Riebeeck landed in the Cape! This is still widely believed by whites. Blacks have long been sceptical. As one of my friends, an elderly clergyman, put it: "We knew it was not true, but we lacked evidence." In fact, the earliest written records, dating from the end of the fifteenth century, show that southern

37. M. Wilson, S. Kaplan, T. Maki, E. M. Walton, *Social Structure*, Keiskammahoek Rural Survey, III (Pietermaritzburg: Shuter and Shooter, 1952), p. 5.

Africa was occupied, sparsely in some areas and densely in others, by negroes speaking Bantu languages, and by yellow-skinned people living as hunters and herders. Archaeological evidence, now piling up fast, shows that an iron-age people, with skeletons of negroid type, existed from the fifth century A.D. in the Transvaal. Reville Mason is now digging up such an iron-age village at Broederstroom near Johannesburg.[38] F. R. Schweitzer and others have shown that sheep were kept on the coast near Cape Town "2,000 or more years ago," and skeletal remains suggest that the herders were ancestors of the Khoikhoi, the yellow-skinned herders whom van Riebeeck found there.[39] Robin Derricourt has shown that there were cattle-keepers, probably Khoikhoi, on the Keiskamma river fifty miles from the southern coast in the eleventh century A.D.[40] The tools of hunting peoples may go back nearly a million years; there is argument over which ape-men did or did not make tools, but no archaeologist doubts that they were made in South Africa 500,000 years ago.

It seems necessary for every group to have a history which justifies its existence and social position, something that Malinowski called their "social charter." The typical settler myth takes one of three forms: we came first, we occupied an empty land; or the earlier inhabitants died out, and almost none are left; or we brought civilization—we brought fire to people who ate their food raw, we taught people to cook, therefore we are the chiefs. This third form, the civilization myth, is told not only by the Nyakyusa but by various Sotho-speaking peoples, and has many layers of meaning: fire stands for "lordship," authority, and chieftainship. It stands also for cooked food, as distinct from the raw flesh eaten by witches and animals.[41]

Sometimes, though less often, the settler myth is matched by an autochthones myth asserting that: "We, the original inhabitants, had everything good and necessary; we borrowed nothing. Our language is pure, and our culture was perfect until it was destroyed." I was amused to hear of horses being fitted into just such a myth in Lesotho, horses being claimed as ancient, despite solid evidence that horses were first imported into Southern Africa by van Riebeeck in 1655.

In July 1974, I participated in celebrations at the opening of a cultural center commemorating the arrival of British settlers in South Africa

38. R. J. Mason, "First Early Iron Age Settlement in South Africa: Broederstroom 24/73, Brits District, Transvaal," *South African Journal of Science*, no. 69 (1973), pp. 324–326.

39. F. R. Schweitzer, "Archaeological Evidence for Sheep at the Cape," and Hertha de Villiers, "Human Skeletal Remains from Cape St. Francis, Cape Province," *South African Archaeological Bulletin*, vol. 29, nos. 115 and 116 (1974), pp. 75–82, 89–91.

40. R. M. Derricourt, "Archaeological Survey of the Transkei and Ciskei," Interim Report for 1972, *Fort Hare Papers*, no. 5 (1973), pp. 453–455.

41. Wilson, *Communal Rituals*, pp. 1, 3, 7, 10–11, 14–15, 51–54, 56, 83, 103–105, 111–112.

a hundred and fifty years ago. What was being celebrated were British contributions to South Africa in language and literature, economy, law and government, religion, education, and so forth. To the participants, self-respect turned on trying to define honestly the contribution made by English-speakers, for the crude "We brought civilization" myth does not impress scholars even of my generation, still less does it impress students. An individual's realization of his own identity depends upon his belonging to a group with an identity that can be respected, and the groping after this is obvious. But an African friend was surprised at the speeches, for he had expected self-glorification. His comment was: "The English are very good at finding fault with themselves."

Where there is a caste system, with a marked disparity in the size of caste, a minority that increases in wealth or power is often attacked, regardless of whether it is the dominant or a subordinate caste. Rwanda and Burundi are examples of this, the first driving out the dominant Tutsi, and the second apparently trying to wipe out that section of the subordinate Hutu which had gained power through education. Germany driving out Jews or Uganda driving out Indians are other too-familiar examples of the expulsion of identifiable minorities that have excited envy. For a hundred and fifty years in South Africa blacks have dreamed of driving whites back into the sea whence they came. Whites, for their part, keep talking about excluding blacks from most of South Africa, the parts referred to as "white areas," and families are still being evicted from these areas in 1978. I believe that throughout history, dominant groups have repeatedly succeeded in expelling, or wiping out, or absorbing subordinate minorities. In a preliterate society, it is often hard to know which process has occurred.

The security for a minority lies in absorption through cultural assimilation and intermarriage. Examples of this are numerous in African and European history. I have already mentioned the Nyakyusa chiefs who integrated with commoners. Among the Nguni people generally, the earlier hunting people were absorbed, and that process of absorption is proceeding now in Botswana. At the Cape, the French-speaking Huguenots were absorbed by the ruling Dutch.

Even where merging is asserted as a value, the process is not always straightforward. Nathan Glazer and Daniel Moynihan have shown how in New York City ethnic cleavages still exist, with differences in religion and in race proving the most persistent.[42] Even the "melting pot" does not quite jell: people remember their roots and feel back after them. Erik Erikson has shown how a successful American felt guilty for having left his orthodox Jewish father in Eastern Europe, and had to recall his roots to achieve individual integration.[43] I kept thinking of the Xhosa accounts

42. N. Glazer and D. P. Moynihan, *Beyond the Melting Pot* (Cambridge: M.I.T. Press, 1963), pp. 290–314.

43. E. H. Erikson, *Insight and Responsibility* (London: Faber and Faber, 1964), pp. 87–88.

of those who *tshipa* (abscond to town) when I read Erikson. It seems that individuals must realize themselves in terms of their own remembered roots, and not attempt to bury the past (because it never stays buried), and perhaps the same applies to groups.

In Africa, as elsewhere, cleavages are deepest when the lines of economic class, race, language, education, and religion coincide, when people who differ in skills and language are visibly different, and worship different gods. In a caste society, such as Rwanda before 1960, or South Africa today, law and convention buttress the coincidence of cleavages. In South Africa, for nearly two hundred years, there has been a struggle over religion: do churches conform or not conform to a caste system? The struggle over that issue continues: Manas Buthelezi has described the church as a "monument to race" in South Africa; he is right when one looks at half the evidence; and not right when one looks at the continuing struggle against that heresy. Everywhere historical cleavages are exploited by political parties and leaders for their own aggrandizement, and this maintains and deepens the divisions. Even within one caste, or in societies without castes, the principle of "divide and rule" is exercised by those in power, and those out of power may seek to gain it by exploiting class, religious, ethnic, racial, language cleavages. I watch with fear as politicians in the Ciskei exploit a cleavage, one hundred and fifty years old, between the Xhosa and the Bhele, Zizi, and Hlubi refugees from Natal. The people are alike in race, language, economic class, education, and religion, and intermarriage has gone on for over a hundred years; the divergence had almost disappeared, but it is in the interest of certain politicians to revive it now (1978), and differences in mythologies are recalled. One party argues that Bhele, Zizi, and Hlubi refugees were welcomed by the Xhosa, the other that they were treated as slaves, and accusations are made that the refugees always sided with the whites in the frontier wars.[44]

Such examples are common, but it is important for the anthropologist to note, alongside them, cleavages which have been overcome. In African oral tradition and physical anthropology there are hints of cleavages that have disappeared, and I have cited examples of absorption. We know more about antagonisms that once existed, and the historical process by which they disappeared, in literate societies. The Huguenots, as mentioned earlier, were quickly absorbed both in South Africa and in England, though they came and settled in relatively large groups and spoke a foreign language. Northern Scotland remained a tribal society until the eighteenth century, and violent antagonisms existed between highland clans, as well as between highlanders and the lowlanders whom they raided for cattle. I come from a Scottish family, and a much respected

44. On the conflicting accounts of how the Xhosa treated refugees from Natal, see T. B. Soga, *Intlalo ka-Xosa;* and R. T. Kawa, *I-Bali lama Mfengu* (Lovedale: Lovedale Press, 1929). On sides taken in the frontier wars, see Wilson and Thompson, *Oxford History of South Africa,* I, pp. 244, 349, 252.

umkhozi (in-law), when a political prisoner in a Southern African jail, took pleasure in reminding me that for nearly two hundred years after 1603, a meeting of more than four MacGregors (my mother's people) constituted an illegal gathering in Scotland.[45] I had forgotten the fact— if ever I knew it—for it is not relevant to contemporary life, even in Scotland. Scottish nationalism remains a political force insofar as it is linked to diverging economic interests, but tribal (clan) loyalties are of negligible political importance.

I think of these things when the cleavages in Africa or Ireland appear overwhelming. Conflict in societies persists, but the lines of cleavage are not constant: sooner or later, he who was once a stranger becomes a brother.

45. W. C. Dickenson, *Scotland from the Earliest Times to 1603* (Edinburgh: Nelson and Sons, 1961), p. 377.

4

Strangers as Colonial Intermediaries: The Dahomeyans in Francophone Africa

Herschelle Sullivan Challenor

The expulsion of non-European resident strangers constitutes an increasingly serious after-effect of the dismantling of colonial empires in Africa and Asia. Not since the balkanization of the Ottoman Empire after World War I have there been so many large-scale, politically forced movements of minorities. On the Indian subcontinent, Indian functionaries were forced to leave Burma and Ceylon; in Southeast Asia, Chinese were expelled from Indonesia and Malaysia, and in North Africa, Algerian civil servants had to withdraw from Morocco.[1] Dahomeyans were expelled from the Ivory Coast in 1958, from the Congo (Brazzaville) in 1962, and from Niger in 1964.[2] Ghanaians were sent out of Sierra Leone and Guinea; Nigerians were driven from the Cameroon in 1967[3] and from Zaire in 1971; over a million West Africans were ousted from Ghana in 1969; "Asians" were forced out of Kenya, and Malawi, and were expelled en masse from Uganda in 1972; and "down islanders" have left the Virgin Islands under duress. Despite the different occupational composition of these strangers, they can attribute their presence in large numbers in a host country to the circumstances surrounding colonial rule.

The central hypotheses of this chapter are as follows. The status of a stranger class of bureaucrats and clerks, introduced and protected by a European colonial administration, depends upon the perpetuation of colonial rule. It follows that any host country which feels politically or economically threatened by a stranger group will expel that group when it gains the power or authority to do so. Five different occupational

1. Howard Wriggins, *Ceylon: Dilemmas of a New Nation* (Princeton: Princeton University Press, 1960), pp. 212–228. Victor Purcell, *The Chinese in Southeast Asia*, 2nd ed. (London: Oxford University Press, 1965). On the Algerian departure from Morocco, see I. William Zartman, *International Relations in the New Africa* (Englewood Cliffs: Prentice-Hall, 1966), p. 103.

2. Herschelle S. Challenor, "French Speaking West Africa's Dahomeyan Strangers in Colonization and Decolonization." Ph.D. dissertation, Columbia University, 1970.

3. Willard Johnson, *The Cameroon Federation: Political Integration in a Fragmentary Society* (Princeton: Princeton University Press, 1970), p. 367.

groups of strangers can be identified in colonial societies, and the assault upon them tends to be sequentially ordered by their occupational function. And finally, one can identify a five-stage process to explain the colonial stranger's transition from a position of privilege to the privation of status and personal safety.

Strangers in colonial societies belong to five principal groups: (1) intermediaries—civil service bureaucrats and clerks in the private sector; (2) pariah entrepreneurs—money-lenders and large wholesale and retail merchants, especially in the export-import sector; (3) small independent businessmen—market traders, craftsmen, and small shopkeepers; (4) wage-earning laborers—workers in agricultural, mining, service, or public works sectors, often on term contracts; and (5) entrenched Europeans—businessmen, colonial administrators, teachers, and technical advisers to host governments.

Generally, the intermediaries are the first to go. Assaults upon the second and fourth groups—pariah entrepreneurs and wage-earning laborers—accompany periods of nationalistic fervor and increased unemployment. Violent confrontations with the fifth group—entrenched Europeans—are likely to occur only in the context of cataclysmic revolutionary changes, domestic or international; but partial sanctions against Europeans, such as nationalization, will follow the emergence of revolutionary ideologies.

Reaction against intermediaries occurs for these basic reasons: they are envied because the position they hold is accorded high status; they have previously exercised real or imagined political influence; and they are viewed as vestigial symbols of colonial rule. Also, it is often easier for the government to exert pressure against civil service bureaucrats and clerks. Indigenization of the civil service is usually justified as being in the national interest; and a clerk class, a parasitic group, is easier to replace than a class of pariah entrepreneurs, which needs capital, stocks, a distribution network, and external contacts which can only be built up over time. Finally, intermediaries are seen as providing support for political leaders.

The use of stranger intermediaries who are also political "subjects" as instruments of power is a relatively recent phenomenon in the history of empires. With rare exceptions, ancient empires tended not to incorporate provincial subjects into the imperial service; such positions were usually reserved for citizens of the conquering state. It was not until Western European nations began to colonize or exercise control in Africa, Asia, and the Middle East that wide-scale use of westernized "subject" intermediaries began.[4]

4. In the Roman Empire, from the period of the Republic (from 500 to 27 B.C.) through the late Empire (from 285 A.D. to 475 A.D.), when the imperial bureaucracy was most highly developed, the civil service was structured along class lines and accessible only to full citizens (William C. Beyer, "The Civil Service of the Ancient World," *Public Adminis-*

The evolution of the colonial intermediary, from recruitment to re-patriation, can best be explained by a five-stage model which assumes three principal actors: supply-country nationals, host-country nationals, and European third powers.

Stage one: Contact. This stage is marked by European identification of a group in a non-Western society which exhibits greater receptivity to westernization or already possesses certain attributes of Western society, such as adherence to the Christian religion.

Stage two: Marginalization. In this process, as described by Donald Horowitz, a local "horizontal" ethnic structure, defined as a system of parallel ethnic structures each with its own criteria of stratification, is transformed. In the first step of the transformation, the parallel structures are changed into a pattern of "vertical" ethnic differentiation according to ethnicity or race, with the European colonizers at the top.[5] Later, as partial access and greater privilege are accorded to a westernized or

tration Review, vol. 19, no. 4 (1959), p. 247). While the magistracies were reserved for patricians, stratification within the service became more pronounced under the late Empire. Divided into three distinct divisions, the upper division was reserved for the senatorial class; the intermediate division was recruited from the equestrian class and the lower division from the "humbler" citizens, freed men and slaves (ibid., p. 248).

Although in principle the civil service was more open in the Byzantine Empire, access to important posts was in fact restricted to the upper classes. Eunuchs often gained short-term power and influence, but they were not accorded prestige, and of course there was no concern about the transferability of their status to their progeny (W. Ensslin, "The Emperor and the Imperial Administration," in N. H. Baynes and H. St. L. B. Moss, eds., Byzantium: An Introduction to East Roman Civilization [London: Oxford University Press, 1948], pp. 268-358).

In the Spanish-American Empire, all but the most menial jobs were reserved for the European Spanish. Recruitment of Creoles, American-born Spanish, was either proscribed or restricted. This policy was attenuated for local administrative posts beginning in the seventeenth century, when more posts were sold or became hereditary. There were notable permutations in these general policies in all of the empires, which gave some flexibility to the caste-like system. Thus slaves under the Roman Empire often occupied important positions in the administration of finances and in tax collection; they remained servants of Rome, however, and acquired little prestige (S. N. Eisenstadt, The Political Systems of Empires: The Rise and Fall of the Historical Bureaucratic Societies [New York: The Free Press, 1969], p. 81). Under the Suleiman regime in the Ottoman Empire, Christian children were taken from the provinces to the court, where they were schooled and, depending upon their abilities, recruited into the corps of the Janissaries (ibid., pp. 76-78); many of them gained wealth and some influence, but they were prohibited by law from passing on their positions to their children (A. Hourani, Minorities in the Arab World [London: Oxford University Press, 1947]). In the Spanish-American Empire, at least as early as 1773, wealthy mulattoes or blacks could purchase a royal dispensation from blackness called gracias al sacar (grateful deliverance), which entitled them to enter the civil service, the Church, or the guild organizations (A. Lyber, The Government of the Ottoman Empire in the Time of Suleiman the Magnificent [Cambridge: Harvard University Press, 1913]). However, all of these exceptions reinforced rather than reversed the traditional vertical ethnic stratification system existing between the imperial citizens and the indigenous people in the provinces.

5. Donald Horowitz, "Three Dimensions of Ethnic Politics," World Politics (1971), pp. 232-244.

other non-European "subject" group, the vertical stratification becomes diagonal: the new marginal group having adopted Christianity, or having been socialized in European schools, is recruited into the colonial service or into the offices of European companies. Such upwardly mobile groups tend to emulate Western culture, and in the eyes of host populations, they become para-Europeans. Hence in Africa such terms as Toubab, and Yovo, normally reserved for Europeans, are also used against the marginals. This aspect of the process, whereby one's race or ethnicity comes to be perceived by the host population more as a function of one's racial or ethnic affinities, measured in terms of behavior and loyalties, than by simple ascription, is apparently ignored by Horowitz.

Stage three: Coalescence and Nationalism. This stage finds the marginals frustrated by the ceiling on their upward mobility and by the persistence of racial antagonism shown toward them by unreconstructed colonizers. They form a fragile coalition with host intellectual and political elites to exert pressure against the colonial administration, seeking reform and eventual independence.

Stage four: Self-Determination and Indigenization. This stage is characterized by the erosion of European authority and the disintegration of the fragile alliance between the host and the stranger marginals. Self-government provides the authority that permits the host-country nationals to give expression to their disdain for strangers. Popular xenophobic acts against non-European strangers, and government-instituted sanctions against them, bring an end to their privileged status. The strangers either return home, migrate to another country, or try to ride out the storm and accept new constraints imposed by the host government.

Stage five: Expulsion and Repatriation. When its expelled nationals suddenly return, the supplier country faces economic and political problems. Trying to absorb the civil servants overloads its administrative bureaucracy and creates a strain on national resources; incorporating them into the private sector is possible only in a relatively well-developed country. The initial sympathy of other supplier-country nationals for their returned compatriots sours as the prodigal sons become competitors for scarce jobs. The repatriates tend to settle in the urban areas, thereby swelling the level of the unemployed and creating a pool of dissatisfied persons receptive to political unrest.

The Dahomeyans in Francophone Africa

The problem of the Dahomeyan colonial intermediaries merits study not only because it involves strangers who are clerks and bureaucrats as opposed to pariah entrepreneurs, but also because their expulsion had implications for the entire political and administrative structure of the former colonial federation of French West Africa, as well as for Dahomey.[6]

Dahomeyans figured prominently as colonial intermediaries in French West Africa because of factors directly related to the slave trade. As one of the important slaving centers during the late eighteenth and the nineteenth centuries, Dahomey attracted both Europeans and Africans to its ports of trade, Ouidah and Porto Novo. Portuguese, French, and Dutch company representatives were joined by Fanti seamen, local officials of the Fon and Goun kingdoms, and most importantly, by mulattoes and manumitted or expelled slaves from Brazil, especially after 1845.[7] The Catholicized "brésiliens" encouraged the establishment of mission schools. Their descendants, along with mulatto offspring of European-African unions and the African ruling elite, formed the nucleus of Dahomey's educated elite. By the time the French established the West African Federation (AOF) in 1904 and the first federal school in 1907, Dahomey had produced a cadre of students who excelled in the entrance examinations required to enter the federation's major educational institutions.[8]

Despite the additional privileges that French citizenship had conferred on those Senegalese born in the four original communes, Dahomeyans were disproportionately represented in all of the elite schools supported by the AOF: the schools of medicine and midwifery at Dakar; the William Ponty normal school at Dakar; the girl's normal school at Rufisque, Senegal; the school for veterinary medicine at Bamako, Mali; and the later restricted Pinet Laprade school for business and vocational training, also in Senegal. Dahomeyan pre-eminence was particularly notable in the girls' schools; for instance, 15 members of the 1929 graduating class of 22 midwives were Dahomeyan.

Most of the Dahomeyans attending federal schools in the prewar period, particularly the mulattoes and the brésiliens, came from the coastal elite families. Names recurring on school enrollment lists include offspring from such important families as the d'Almeidas, de Souzas, Talons, Oliveiras, Lawsons, Quenams, Paraisos, Johnsons, Martins, Da Piedades, Comlavis, and Dossou-Yovos. Eased out of their dominant role in the commercial sector after the French conquest, this bourgeoisie, like the Senegalese elite of Gorée and St. Louis before it, turned to the French colonial service as a source of income and continued prestige.[9]

6. Challenor, "Dahomeyan Strangers."

7. Robert Cornevin, Histoire du Dahomey (Paris: Editions Berger-Levrault, 1962), pp. 255–266.

8. Pierre Verger, "Les Afro-Américains," Mémoires de l'IFAN, No. 27 (Dakar: Imprimerie Nationale, 1953), pp. 18, 191–192, 205, 218.

9. Challenor, "Dahomeyan Strangers," pp. 70ff.

French Colonial Service

The French colonial service embraced a wide range of employment, and until 1950 was divided into two parallel three-tiered groups. At the top were the Metropolitan and General Cadres, who were directly responsible to the French Government in Paris and could serve anywhere in the colonial empire—in Asia, Africa, the Caribbean, or in France itself, The Metropole. The middle level, the Joint Superior and the Joint Secondary Cadres, were directly responsible to the federal government of French West Africa at Dakar; they could serve only in the seven states of the federation and Togo. Finally, the governor of each territory recruited the Local Cadres. In addition, there were subordinate categories of "auxiliaries" and contract laborers. The vertical difference between cadres depended not only upon the locus of recruitment and control, but also upon educational prerequisites and fringe benefits. The horizontal differences—Metropolitan, Superior, and Local on the one hand, and General, Secondary, and Local on the other—initially reflected de facto if not de jure caste distinctions between *citoyens* and *indigènes*.[10] The greater fringe benefits available to Europeans constituted a source of conflict between Africans and French Metropolitans as early as 1910 and were only partially resolved by the Lamine Gueye Law of 1950.[11]

Recruitment of Africans for the middle cadres of the civil service occurred either when they successfully completed a course of study in one of the federal schools or when they passed a competitive examination. Only Africans with diplomas from the upper elementary schools were eligible for the Local Cadres. In theory, the Local Cadres could serve only in their country of origin. In fact, however, Governors from disadvantaged colonies such as Niger and Mauretania often recruited Local Cadre functionaries from the neighboring states of Dahomey and Senegal.

Generally, the federal government assigned graduates of the federal schools to posts in their own territories. The principal exceptions were that the top medical school graduates were often attached to the hospital in Dakar. Once a state's most glaring civil service manpower needs were satisfied, its surplus cadres were posted outside their own territories. Given Dahomey's small size and disproportionately high number of cadres, as early as 1912 the AOF federal government began to assign Dahomeyans to other countries, particularly to Senegal, the Ivory Coast, and Niger. In that year, two "brésiliens," Felix Martin and Julien de Souza, were assigned teaching posts in the Ivory Coast.

10. Louis Rolland and Pierre Lampué, *Droit d'outre mer*, 3rd ed. (Paris: Dolloz, 1959), p. 354.
11. Law No. 50-572 of June 30, 1950, *Journal officiel* of AOF, 1950, p. 1231.

Private Enterprise

The private sector also recruited Dahomeyans to work in other territories. Inter-territorial recruitment was facilitated by the existence of three giant corporations which owned or controlled most of the European export-import houses and commercial firms in French Africa: CFAO (Compagnie Française de l'Afrique Occidentale, founded by Marseille-based commercial interests); Chargeurs Réunis (the shipping line that held the monopoly for postal and administrative shipping between France and its African colonies); SCOA (Société Commerciale de l'Ouest Africain, established by Swiss merchants in 1907), and Unilever (the British-Dutch company whose African companies included John Holt, Walkden and Company, and the United Africa Company). From their branch offices in Cotonou, Porto Novo, and Ouidah, these companies recruited Dahomeyans to work in companies located in other parts of the AOF, Togo, and French Equatorial Africa.[12]

Once Dahomeyans began to occupy positions in firms located in other territories, the recruitment process became more informal. A Dahomeyan would notify relatives or friends when a vacancy appeared or when a recruitment examination was scheduled. Having earned a reputation for intelligence, industry, and frugality, Dahomeyans in many cases were preferred to local people.

One could argue that the presence of a coastal elite in Dahomey and its relative wealth until World War I worked to its own disadvantage in the long run, in view of French colonial policies. Those who sought the greater status and financial reward that accompanied admission to the upper civil service levels were subject to recruitment elsewhere in the federation, and so many of the best-trained Dahomeyans were siphoned off to other areas. Even so, there were enough trained Dahomeyans left to deprive the colony of a large resident French community of clerks and entrepreneurs. Despite the obvious disadvantage of having too many Europeans in a colony, their presence does create residual benefits which tend to have a spill-over effect: jobs multiply in the service sector, urban improvements occur, a large consumer sector appears, and a local lobby of Europeans can press the mother country for additional economic advantages.

France expected its colonies to pay for themselves—that is, to assume financial responsibility for local administrative and development costs. In view of the lack of basic infrastructure, the French government decided that it would be cheaper to transport labor than to ship products. As a result, the early years of colonial effort were devoted to developing other coastal colonies, which unlike Dahomey and Senegal had

12. Jean Suret-Canale, *Afrique noire occidentale et centrale* (Paris: Editions Sociale, 1958), pp. 214–229.

not yet built up an important external trade. One observer noted wryly that "Dahomeyan palm oil production developed before the arrival of the French and has hardly developed since they came." In contrast, the Ivory Coast, the colony considered the poorest and most backward at the time of European penetration, emerged as the wealthiest country in the AOF after 1951 because of the spiraling growth set into motion by French inputs in the 1920s and 1930s.[13]

Anti-Dahomeyanism in the Ivory Coast

African strangers have played a major role in the development of the Ivory Coast. Initially, stranger Africans, especially those from the Gold Coast, controlled the timber market in the Ivory Coast. As a result, until the end of World War I, two-thirds of Ivoirian timber was exported to Great Britain. By 1926 the colonial government, in collaboration with French companies, passed export tax measures that had the effect of squeezing Gold Coasters and Ivoirians out of the timber market. Earlier efforts in 1902 and 1915 to exclude Gold Coast peoples from the fish trade had failed. Realizing that Ivoirian subsistence fishermen could not supply the colony's needs, the French government passed decrees that reestablished the fishing rights of outsiders in April 1919. This action by the colonial government established a significant precedent: the rights of Ivoirians were subordinated to those of African strangers in the interest of economic development. However, many Gold Coasters left the Ivory Coast when the government revoked their right to export dried and smoked fish. By 1938 many Awonlon people from Togo settled in the Port Bouet areas, and reopened the fishing trade abandoned by the Gold Coasters.

Starting in the 1930s, Europeans opened coffee and cocoa plantations, and imported primarily Voltans and Malians as agricultural laborers. The expansion of these plantations created a serious labor shortage by 1941. As a result, the French colonial government, favoring European planters, prohibited Ivoirian farmers from recruiting foreign labor. This form of discrimination not only created anti-European attitudes among Ivoirians, but may also have heightened resentment of the stranger communities whose presence was sanctioned by the colonial government.

As early as 1928 and again in 1938, Ivoirians vented their hostility against the Dahomeyans, who were often accused of treating their indigenous hosts with condescension. By 1928 there was a strong reaction among local people to an editorial that appeared in *La Voix du Dahomey*:

> Grand Bassam, Ivory Coast—It seems that in this part of the AOF federation, people aren't very gentle with the blacks. It is true that most of the natives are very backward and are naturally treated like bushmen. They are beaten by the whites there, who it seems

13. George Hardy, *Histoire sociale de la colonisation française* (Paris: Larose, 1947).

behave like veritable torturers towards the black brothers—Our
compatriots who are stationed in the Ivory coast and are among the
most civilized blacks there, have been unjustifiably mistreated by
certain European officials there. They [Dahomeyans] are prevented
from opening the local natives' eyes and stopping them from bow-
ing and scraping to the whites.[14]

Though, on the face of it, this article would seem to imply racial
solidarity between the Dahomeyans and the Ivoirians, the Ivoirians
viewed it as condescending. The emerging Ivoirian elite continued to re-
sent Dahomeyans and in 1937, after at least two other minor incidents,
the Ivoirians gave political focus to their formerly diffuse concern. They
established an Association for the Defense of the Interests of the Natives
of the Ivory Coast, to represent their interests to the colonial administration, citing the predominance of Dahomeyans and Togolese in the
private commercial houses, and suggesting repatriation as a possible
sanction against the strangers. Apart from transferring one or two of the
most offensive Dahomeyan civil servants, the colonial government
responded only by admonishing the Dahomeyans to behave more
responsibly.

The early anti-Dahomeyan incidents demonstrated the impotence of
subject groups in host countries to remove the stranger groups. The
French response to the Ivoirians' articulation of their interests was to
encourage gradual change. The government appealed to the private sector to replace Dahomeyans and Togolese with Ivoirians, but this was
viewed as a warning, and not a directive. The French Governor of the
Ivory Coast optimistically predicted in 1938 that "progressively our subjects, whose cultural evolution has been slower than that of the
Dahomeyans and the Togolese, will soon occupy the jobs given to the
latter."[15] But twenty years later, more, not fewer, Dahomeyans and
Togolese held jobs in the modern sector of the Ivory Coast's economy.

Postwar liberalization and reform by the French colonial administration intensified local resentment of Dahomeyans in the Ivory Coast
and Niger. In this process, four factors were particularly important: the
elaboration of an economic development program, the Lamine Gueye
Law, the right of political associations, and the Basic Law of 1956.[16]

The economic development program contributed to the expansion
of French private enterprise in urban areas such as Abidjan and to the
proliferation of public works programs, thereby attracting more extra-
territorial labor; furthermore, the expansion of the school system put

14. *La Voix du Dahomey*, March 13, 1928. See Dossier of AOF, "Renseignements et
environs divers en Côte d'Ivoire," 1928, No. 59125.17, Archives of Dakar.

15. Gouvernement-Général de L'Afrique Française Occidentale, *Rapport politique 1938*
(Dakar: Imprimerie Nationale, 1938), pp. 283–285.

16. Thomas Hodgkin and Ruth S. Morgenthau, "French-speaking Africa in Transition,"
International Conciliation, No. 528 (1960), p. 396.

into training the hundreds of Ivoirians and Nigeriens who by 1958 began to compete for jobs held by strangers.

The Loi Lamine Gueye of 1950 markedly reduced the differences in salary between French and Africans in the civil service, thereby increasing the cost of maintaining African stranger functionaries, and making these positions more attractive to host populations. Perhaps it should be stressed here that the application of this law was more important for Niger, where 51 percent of the Dahomeyans worked in the public sector and 28 percent in the private sector, and 21 percent were self-employed. In the Ivory Coast, Dahomeyan wage-earners were more evenly divided between the public and private sectors: 37 percent were in the public sector and 38 percent in the private sector, and 21 percent were self-employed. Thus strangers became not only more numerous but more expensive as well. At no point did African expatriate functionaries cost more than French civil servants, but host-country African complaints against the European presence could not be made with impunity.[17]

As a result of the opportunity to participate in political parties and electoral politics, local African leaders and the public at large began to develop a parochial nationalism. Furthermore, when the AOF developed two rival factions in 1950, Dahomeyan leaders had sided with the one called the Overseas Independents, a loose alliance led by Léopold Senghor, which placed them in opposition to the African Democratic Rally Party (RDA), which was led by Félix Houphouet-Boigny, and included the state of Niger.[18] Reacting to territorially based nationalism, which was in conflict with French colonial federation, the Ivory Coast led the move to split up the West African federation in 1956; by so doing it avoided any obligation to subsidize the powerful states in the AOF and hastened the time when African local governments would exercise the authority to dispose of African stranger groups.

The Basic Law of 1956, by making the federal government an agency of coordination only, and politicizing the once purely administrative Territorial Councils, neutralized the power of the AOF and opened the way for its disintegration into eight self-governing territories.[19] Among the expanded powers granted to the territories under this new law was local control over the majority of their civil servants. The reorganization of the colonial service bisected the pyramidal structure of the service: the State (French) Civil Service became one part, and the Territorial Civil Service the other. France maintained financial responsibility for the services dealing with foreign relations, defense, the courts, interstate commerce, economics, finance, and higher education. All other divisions of

17. Lamine Gueye, *Itinéraire africain* (Paris: Presence Africaine, 1966), p. 94.

18. Ruth S. Morgenthau, *Political Parties in French-Speaking West Africa* (London: Oxford University Press, 1964), p. 167.

19. Law No. 56–619 of June 23, 1956. This law is often referred to as the Loi Gaston Deferre. The institutions went into effect in April 1957.

the civil service came under the Territorial Service. In order to minimize its financial responsibilities, France regarded all subordinate functionaries in the State Service as members of the Territorial Service who had been seconded to the State Service. By this device, lower-level functionaries retained the salaries and benefits of the Territorial Service. Efforts by Léopold Senghor to create an intermediate category of federal inter-territorial civil servants was rejected by the French National Assembly. Each territory was empowered to determine the salaries, fringe benefits, and other regulations pertaining to the Territorial Service, and to hire and fire civil servants working in its territory—a provision which jeopardized the status of stranger functionaries.[20]

France's acceptance of financial responsibility for all the State Cadres, many of whom were formerly paid by the Territorial budgets, might be thought to have reduced local personnel expenditures. However, the cost of setting up eighty-nine ministries, coupled with French measures to recoup their newly added personnel expenditures, offset any saving that the territories might have made.

For our purposes the most important provision of the civil service reform gave local authorities statutory control over functionaries in the Territorial Service. This policy made possible arbitrary contraventions of the formerly uniform regulations. Although territories were prevented by law from lowering the salary and rank of civil servants, local political considerations could now affect promotions and post assignments. The colonial government's power over transfers and post assignments had formerly been one of its most effective means of controlling "agitators." Niger capitalized on its new authority and tried to restrict stranger recruitment into the Local Cadres by requiring knowledge of at least one Nigerien language. The purpose of the ruling was "to decrease the local budget by reserving administrative jobs to indigenous Nigeriens."[21]

The Basic Law reforms were intended to placate local African leaders. However, substituting administrative decentralization for effective local control merely galvanized early pressure for greater African decision-making power into a movement for autonomy and complete independence. Besides creating a situation conducive to raising tensions among stranger civil servants, local leaders, and local potential civil servants, the Basic Law proved in another respect disadvantageous to the position of Dahomeyans in the Ivory Coast and Niger.[22] Disagreement over the law led to great debates in the AOF and the development of opposing blocs over the issues of decentralization versus federation, and independence versus self-government within a larger French community. This debate lasted from 1957 to 1960, and not only revealed past rivalries

20. Challenor, "Dahomeyan Strangers," pp. 113ff.

21. Ibid., pp. 123–124.

22. Samir Amin, Le Développement du capitalism en Côte d'Ivoire (Paris: Les Editions du Minuit, 1967), p. 44.

but also conditioned post-independence relations among the states of French West Africa.

The Ivory Coast's postwar boom, a result of the coffee subsidies and the completion of Abidjan's deep water port in 1950, attracted more European and African strangers into the territory. In fact, the country's European population increased almost sevenfold between 1936 and 1955. For the first time many European women joined the labor force, taking over many lower-level positions that might otherwise have been available for Africans. As many as 34 percent of the European wage-earners in the Ivory Coast held unskilled jobs in 1950. The decrease in the number of jobs open to Africans was complicated by the growing number of Ivoirian "school-leavers" and dropouts who demanded local employment. For instance, 85 percent of all pupils graduating from elementary schools entered the labor market; furthermore, most of them disdained agricultural work and sought white collar employment in the urban areas. The few Africans who did obtain positions in the top civil service cadres were primarily strangers; as indicated in Table 1, 300 out of 500 Africans at the highest occupational levels in the Ivory Coast were expatriates.[23] At least eight of the fewer than twenty Africans in the top administrative and technical positions in the civil service were Dahomeyans. Even the lowest labor category, which included agricultural workers and domestics, was dominated by outsiders. Most were Voltans, who by 1958 contributed 90 percent of all wage-earning migrant labor in the country. The Dahomeyans either held white collar jobs or owned their own farms, transport companies, or shops. It has been reported that Dahomeyans represented 80 percent of the personnel in some of Abidjan's commercial businesses. In addition, many Dahomeyans who belonged to the civil service were attached to those divisions which offered the greatest upward mobility to Africans: teaching and public health. To make matters worse, these two branches of the service, though relatively small, had the greatest contact with the masses of the population, and were thus highly visible.[24]

Dahomeyans attracted increasing resentment for their condescension toward local peoples. It was not unusual for a Dahomeyan to comment that he had come to the Ivory Coast to "civilize" the Ivoirians. As practicing Catholics, many Dahomeyans believed themselves to be more "Western" than local Africans, who adhered to Islam or traditional African religions. Moreover, although Dahomeyans did not live in separate quarters but were scattered throughout the African settlements of Abidjan, Port Bouet, and Grand Bassam, they socialized primarily among themselves, and formed particularistic voluntary associations.

23. *Annuaire statistique*, AOF, 1951–1954, p. 49.

24. Challenor, "Dahomeyan Strangers," p. 129. See Jean Rouch, "Second Generation Migrants in Ivory Coast," in *Social Change in Modern Africa*, Aidan Southall, ed. (London: Oxford University Press, 1961), p. 301.

Table 1
Number of European and African Workers by Occupation in 1950
(excluding highest-level metropolitan cadres)

Occupations	Europeans				Africans				
	Managers	Employees	Laborers	Total	Managers	Employees	Laborers	Menial Laborers	Total
PUBLIC SECTOR									
General Admin.	90	85	14	99		490	670	9,039	10,199
Technical Services		57	158	305	36	469	1,185	5,392	7,082
Total	90	142	172	404	36	959	1,855	14,431	17,281
PRIVATE SECTOR									
Agriculture	69	92	43	204	17	432	437	17,485	18,371
Forestry	33	45	70	148	22	381	405	7,345	8,153
Mining	25	13	42	80	1	100	270	6,438	6,809
Industry	80	21	163	264		419	2,579	3,938	6,936
Construction	30	11	129	170	6	109	2,834	4,872	7,821
Transportation	27	117	40	184	3	543	958	7,543	9,047
Commerce	213	446	161	820	96	3,156	1,536	6,974	11,762
Professionals	2	4		10		53	58	47	158
Banks, Insurance	25	98	4	123		185	2	8	195
Domestics									2,500
Total	504	847	652	2,003	145	5,378	9,079	54,650	71,752
Grand Total	594	989	824	2,407	181	6,337	10,934	69,081	89,033

SOURCE: Ministère de la France Outre Mer, Annuaire Statistique de l'Afrique Occidentale Française, édition 1951, p. 455.

The union of Dahomeyans and Togolese that existed in 1958 gave way to associations that regrouped Dahomeyans from particular areas. For example, the *originaires* of Ouidah formed an association called the Gléhouéens, and Dahomeyans from Abomey established their own organization. These groups performed vital socialization and support functions for newcomers and older resident strangers, but they defined primary relationships as excluding Ivoirians.[25]

It was only in the political arena that there was some interaction between Dahomeyans and Ivoirians. Houphouet-Boigny, the Ivoirian leader, involved them in the political institutions of the territory, such as the Assembly and the RDA Party bureaucracy. In fact, approximately 20 percent of the membership of these two institutions were strangers. Albert Paraiso, a Dahomeyan from Porto Novo, was one of Houphouet's closest political associates and a long-time member of the RDA executive bureau. However, most Ivoirians ignored these links as their preoccupation with the Dahomeyan stranger problem increased and they believed themselves capable of supplanting the Dahomeyans. Less than a month after the 1958 referendum granting internal self-government, an anomic group led by Béte dissidents in the Ivory Coast rioted against the resident Dahomeyans and forced 10,000 to return to their homeland. This group of Ivoirians had felt economic discrimination because of the Dahomeyan domination of white collar jobs. Houphouet-Boigny was constrained to accept this fait accompli because his political position was in jeopardy.[26]

Anti-Dahomeyanism in Niger

The Dahomeyans in the Sahelian Republic of Niger had the same difficulties with the indigenous population as they did with the Ivoirians. Nigeriens had criticized the dominant status of the Dahomeyans as early as the 1950s.[27] As late as 1957 African strangers outnumbered Nigeriens at all four major levels of employment except menial work. Not one of the top positions open to Africans was held by a Nigerien. Tensions between Nigeriens and Dahomeyans increased during the decolonization process and for the same reasons as in the Ivory Coast. The situation was exacerbated when Dahomeyans became involved in the political struggle that took place in Niger from 1958 to 1960. Certainly the "no" votes cast by most local Dahomeyans in the September 1958 referendum on independence, or continued association with France, did not endear them to the Nigerien government.

Matters came to a head in June 1960, just before the independence of both Dahomey and Niger, when a serious clash broke out between

25. Challenor, "Dahomeyan Strangers," pp. 129–130.

26. *Le Monde*, September 28–29, 1958. See "Les Epulsés dahoméens de Côte d'Ivoire," *Echos d'Afrique noire* (Dakar), March 3, 1959.

27. Challenor, "Dahomeyan Strangers," p. 163.

Dahomeyans and Nigeriens on Lété, a small island in the Niger River that forms a boundary between the two countries. When the island is not submerged by the Niger River during five months of each year, the land is cultivated by Dahomey agriculturalists from Gourouberi Village, and it is also used for grazing cattle by Nigerien Fulani. As tempers rose, President-designate Hubert Maga of Dahomey and his Nigerien counterpart, Hamani Diori, agreed to postpone indefinitely any final resolution of the territorial dispute in order not to create further antagonism between their peoples. They did authorize a bipartite committee to investigate both the incident and the question of ownership of the Isle of Lété.[28]

No sooner had this dispute been quieted when, in 1961, a fight broke out between Nigeriens and Dahomeyans in Niamey. Some Dahomeyan civil servants were expelled "in the interest of national security," but it seems that only the friendship between Presidents Maga of Dahomey and Diori of Niger prevented harsh action against the resident Dahomeyans.

The removal of Hubert Maga during Dahomey's October 1963 revolution excited enmity in Niger and the Ivory Coast and caused the re-emergence of political tension between Dahomeyan strangers and their hosts. Maga and Diori had been warm personal friends since their school days together at the Victor Ballot school in Porto Novo and the William Ponty school in Dakar (1930–1936). Maga was also a close political associate of both Hamani Diori and Félix Houphouet-Boigny, and in 1959 under Maga's leadership Dahomey had joined the Ivory Coast, Niger, and Upper Volta in the Council of the Entente.

Significantly, in November 1963, less than one month after President Maga was overthrown, the Isle of Lété again became a hot political issue, and the Niger government announced the expulsion of all Dahomeyans working in the department of the interior and the police. Subsequently all Dahomeyans were included in the repatriation order. Hostility toward Dahomeyans was aggravated by allegations of Dahomeyan support of the Sawabaists, a banned Nigerien opposition party led by Djibo Bakary.[29] This hostility increased in October 1964, when the Sawabaists launched what proved to be an abortive invasion into Niger. Some of the invaders had crossed through Dahomeyan territory, and Nigeriens also believed that the Sawabaists, who were based in Ghana, had received support from Dahomey and the People's Republic of China. Tensions between Niger and Dahomey did not ease until January 1965, and the dispute was not resolved until September 1966.

The process of tension reduction between Dahomey and Niger provides an interesting case study of the peaceful settlement of inter-state conflicts in Africa. That study cannot be undertaken here, but it is important to note that so long as the expulsion of Dahomeyans involved

28. *Ibid.*, p. 165.
29. Pierre Bearnes, *Le Moniteur africain*, December 12, 1963.

only the francophone African states, France remained neutral. However, when Ghana and the People's Republic of China were alleged to be third parties involved in the dispute, France felt that her influence in the area was threatened, and she intervened. France was not prepared to permit Ghanaian and Chinese support of external subversion to threaten the existing power relationships in the region. Houphouet–Boigny, Diori's closest ally, was so concerned about the Ghanaian threat that he switched from quiet diplomacy to a diplomatic offensive designed to isolate Ghana on the African continent. Finally, it is instructive to note that during the period when Dahomeyans were being expelled from both the Ivory Coast and Niger, the French took no official notice of their plight. It appears that as far as France was concerned, the Dahomeyan intermediaries, who were created as a result of French colonial rule, were expendable. France did offer sympathy and some financial assistance to Dahomey after the events of 1958, but she did not actively help her former servants and did not participate in the political resolution of the dispute. When France did intervene in 1964 and 1965, it was to subordinate the conflict of Dahomey and Niger to the larger problem of Chinese and Ghanaian threats to her dominance in francophone Africa.[30]

Reintegration

Faced with the sudden return of thousands of repatriated strangers, a supplier country like Dahomey has essentially only three main options: to absorb them into Dahomey, to search for new external job markets in African countries other than the Ivory Coast and Niger, or to seek labor guarantees for them in the old markets of Ivory Coast and Niger. Dahomey's problems seem to suggest that the political and economic costs of absorbing a clerk class are higher than those of absorbing a class of pariah entrepreneurs. Survey data collected in Dahomey show that the self-employed—the traders, artisans, and farmers—experienced very little loss of occupational status as a result of their return. They stayed with the jobs they had held before in the host country, though with reduced incomes. In contrast, middle-level bureaucrats and clerks in the private sector suffered greatly. They were an educated quasi-elite corps who had become redundant labor in their homeland, where educational expansion has outstripped economic development. Moreover, migrating to another state was no longer an attractive option; most other newly independent states, fearing the wrath of their citizens if local employment is jeopardized by strangers, now insist, in any multilateral agreement signed with other states, upon the right to expel "non-nationals."

The return of thousands of Dahomeyans had other far-reaching implications for Dahomey. Educated Dahomeyans found it hard to rec-

---

30. Challenor, "Dahomeyan Strangers," pp. 189–191. See *Chronologie politique africaine*, vol. 5, No. 6 (1964), p. 26.

oncile their allegiance to Dahomey with loyalty to France and the federation, particularly since Dahomey has a dismal record of political and economic achievements. Dahomeyan strangers were repatriated physically, but psychologically they were incapable of becoming "repatriots." Given the slightest opportunity, these repatriates leave Dahomey for other countries. The only hope that Dahomey has for truly integrating the expatriates into its society may be to develop its economy rapidly—so that expatriates can achieve in their own country the status and wealth they enjoyed in other African states during the colonial period. Only this could create the conditions for building a successful national state, and with it the "symbolic capacity" needed to coalesce the country and cut off its chronic brain drain. In the case of Dahomey, it is the lack of economic development that induces political instability. The tragedy of Dahomey is that, through no fault of its own, it possesses the manpower for a Gulliverian administrative bureaucracy in a Lilliputian state.

Ironically, it was the French rather than the Ivoirians or Nigeriens who benefited most from the Dahomeyan expulsions. French nationals from the empire had been returning to France's public and private sector since 1954. However, many of those who left Indochina and Algeria were posted to sub-Saharan Africa and Madagascar. As these countries became independent, these French expatriates were seconded to them as technicians, and many of these personnel replaced the Dahomeyans who were expelled from such countries as the Ivory Coast and Niger. Today, both Niger and the Ivory Coast have more French citizens working in the public sector than they had during colonial rule. France has been able to soften the effects of decolonization on its own economy, and has gained time in which to absorb its expatriates gradually. This is why France sees a genuine need to maintain its political and economic influence in francophone Africa, and is prepared to respond energetically to any threat to its position.

The countries of French-speaking Africa have been able to expel the Dahomeyan strangers who were imposed upon them by colonial administration. The Ivory Coast and Niger were able to remove Dahomeyans with impunity because these strangers had no political leverage. However, these states have had only marginal success in eliminating other colonial legacies. President Ahomodegbe's attempt to "decolonialize" Dahomey's civil service was one reason for his demise. Guinea's and Mali's attempts to decolonialize their monetary systems pushed them into a position of economic isolation within Africa, and even the world at large. At great cost to its national prestige and political stability, Mali capitulated and returned to the franc zone. Only time will tell when these nations will expel French expatriates and thereby enter the final stage of decolonization.

5

The Political Economy
of a Stranger Population:
The Lebanese of Sierra Leone

Neil O. Leighton

This chapter examines several of the political problems which have arisen from the presence of an alien middleman minority, the Lebanese, in a new nation, Sierra Leone. We begin with a brief review of the colonial legacy.

The arrival of the Lebanese in the 1890s was a period of considerable economic activity in Sierra Leone, as in Africa generally. The extension of imperialism by European powers had reached Africa following the Berlin Conference of 1885, and the rush to stake out territorial claims on the continent was in full swing during the 1890s. Colonial governments sought to open up the hinterland of Africa and exploit its agricultural and mineral resources. Private investment in mining and in large commercial trading enterprises increased greatly during this decade, as colonial governments created territorial-based institutions. These included not only communications and transport, but expansion of the civil service to administer the territories, and schools to supply personnel for the lower ranks of the new bureaucracy as well as the private firms.

The period of the 1890s witnessed the growth of closer ties between the colonial government and private commercial interests. As government sought to provide business with law, stability, and wage labor, as well as such essential services as railways, roads, and port facilities, private investors in Europe became increasingly willing to invest in the colonies. This investment was on a small scale in 1850, during the premodernization period, but by the 1890s it was substantial.[1] The demand for tropical produce during this period increased at the same pace as world trade as a whole.

It was into this rapidly changing economic and social environment that the foreign middleman came. Colonies were becoming big business

1. W. Arthur Lewis, ed., *Tropical Development, 1880-1913* (Evanston: Northwestern University Press, 1970), pp. 13-14. Between 1883 and 1913 the volume of tropical trade increased three times.

and in a period of laissez faire economics they were held to be justified, at least by the British, less for prestige reasons than for their ability to stimulate and expand trade abroad and manufacturing at home. As big capital came to dominate the reorganization and expansion of the colonies, the middleman also changed from itinerate peddler to full working partner in the new expansion.

The role of agent for private firms is of course analogous to that of the "comprador." Traditionally this concept, derived from the activities of merchants in the coastal cities of China, applied to indigenous peoples. But in Africa and perhaps elsewhere, strangers historically have filled these roles: mulatto and European-assimilated "gourmettes" in eighteenth-century Senegambia; a new mulatto and African merchant elite in seventeenth-century Angola; Asians in twentieth-century East Africa; and ex-slaves or re-captives in nineteenth-century Sierra Leone and Western Nigeria.[2]

As a link in the chain of distribution and collection of imported goods and agricultural produce, the Lebanese received the protection of the dominant sector of colonial society—government and the larger expatriate firms. The price for this protection was a close identification, in the minds of the indigenous population, with colonial rule.

The Arrival of the Lebanese Strangers

The demise of the Creole trader left the European firms in an unchallenged position in retail trade, particularly during the Protectorate. Their superiority was short-lived. During the 1890s the first Lebanese arrived in Freetown. Why the Lebanese decided to immigrate to Africa is still debated, but it is known that most of the emigrants in the period from 1860 to 1910 left to find a new life in the United States or South America. When the gates were closed to them in the United States prior to the First World War, many Lebanese began to look elsewhere. Since the route of emigration was from Beirut to Marseilles, the first few, because of ignorance or deceit on the part of shipowners, landed in Dakar as early as the 1860s. The Lebanese thus began to move down the coast, the first arriving in Freetown in 1893.[3]

By 1901 there were 41 Lebanese residents in Freetown, all Maronite Christians who had been driven from Lebanon by poor economic conditions and Turkish persecution of their religious sect. The first Shiite Mus-

2. Paul A. Baran, *The Political Economy of Growth* (New York: Monthly Review Press, 1957), pp. 194–195. Baran argues that the emergence of this group of merchants, which derive their profits from the operation of foreign business, slows down and may even prevent the transformation of a "developing country" from merchant capitalism to industrial capitalism.

3. Marwan I. H. Hanna, "Lebanese Emigrants in West Africa" (Ph.D. dissertation, St. Antony's College, Oxford University, 1959), pp. 46–49. See also Jean Gabriel Desbordes, "L'Immigration Libano-Syrienne en Afrique Occidentale Française" (Ph.D. dissertation, Université de Poitiers, Imprimerie Moderne, Renault et Cie, 1938), pp. 40–41.

Table 1
Lebanese Population of Sierra Leone, 1891–1963

Year	Colony	Protectorate	Total
1891	0	0	0
1901	41	0	41
1911	175	91	266
1913	212	?	212
1921	177 (riots of 1919)	386	563
1931	413	153	1,766[a]
1948	873 (post-war immigration)	1,201	2,074
1957	? (diamond boom)	?	2,612
1963	813	2,408	3,221

[a]There were 1200 in 1939.
SOURCES: R. R. Kuczynski, *Demographic Survey of the British Colonial Empire*, Vol. I (London: Oxford University Press, 1948), pp. 3, 191, 192, 196.

Great Britain: Colonial Office, *An Economic Survey of the Colonial Territories*, 1951, Vol. III (London: H.M.S.O., 1952), p. 77.

Marwan Hanna, "The Lebanese in West Africa," *West Africa*, No. 2142 (May 3, 1958), p. 415.

1963 Population Census of Sierra Leone, Vol. I, "Number of Inhabitants" (Freetown: Central Statistics Office, 1965).

lims arrived in 1903 from the south of Lebanon, again due to an impoverishment of agriculture and population pressure on the land.[4] As can be seen in Table 1, the Lebanese were not slow in arriving and moving up-country into the Protectorate.

What accounted for this rapid dispersion of the Lebanese petty trader into the Protectorate was large-scale intervention by the colonial government in the economy of Sierra Leone. As early as 1872 Dr. Edward Blyden, the famous Sierra Leonean scholar-adventurer, called for a railroad to reach into the interior to facilitate trade. By 1894 surveys were completed and actual construction began in 1895. By 1903 the rail line was completed to Bo Town, 136 miles from Freetown. By August of 1905 the line reached Baiima, 220 miles from Freetown. Three years later the line reached its present terminus eight miles further at Pendembu, thus completing the first railway in British West Africa.[5] As with other early railways, trade was only a partial reason for the line, the main reason being to provide an administrative instrument for opening the country, and for quelling possible rebellion by speeding the movement of troops. In any event, wealth did begin to flow from the interior. The European demand for lubricants, margarine, and explosives, all of

4. Hanna, *Lebanese Emigrants*, pp. 75–79.
5. T. N. Goddard, *The Handbook of Sierra Leone* (London: Grant Richards, 1925), p. 170.

which relied on palm produce, caused an immediate rise in exports. By 1904 the export figures surpassed those of 1897 (the intervening years had witnessed a worldwide depression), and by 1909 exports had doubled, trebling in 1912 to a figure of £1.4 million. Customs receipts, which had yielded £102,969 in 1900, rose to £301,140 in 1912.[6] As each intermediate stage of the railway was finished, Lebanese traders moved up the line.

The Lebanese were important in the establishment and spread of the territorial market. The market was to prove an institution which fostered considerable social change, particularly in the creation of a new stratification order. Where the European or Creole was unwilling to go, the trader penetrated the bush, showing a keen interest in the African as a potential consumer, taking the time to learn the customs of his customers as well as their needs. The compatriots who remained in Freetown began to supply the upcountry trader with newer and more varied trade items in exchange for agricultural produce, particularly palm kernels and kola nuts. Kola nuts were retained by the Freetown merchants and sold locally and along the West African Coast. In time, those Lebanese traders who had gone upcountry began to build small stores on land leased from the Paramount Chiefs whose chiefdoms lay along the railway, and the traders could stop making time-consuming trips back to Freetown for supplies.[7]

The economy of the Protectorate of Sierra Leone at the turn of the century was still largely characterized by subsistence production. In order to establish a territorial market it was necessary for someone to go into these more remote areas and induce African farmers and sylvan crop collectors to produce a surplus. The reliance on this method of establishing a market system was dictated in part by the fact that land in the Protectorate was inalienable—it was communally held and could not be bought and sold. The expansion of British colonial rule retained this land tenure pattern under the new legal system.[8] This, of course, was one factor among many which was to assure the Lebanese the status of "strangers." This rule, however, applied to Creoles and Europeans as well; only through marriage could they achieve a claim to ownership of land, although long leaseholds of small parcels for commercial establishments was secured.

Unable to buy land and engage in commercial agriculture, the Lebanese were forced to attempt to expand commerce by creating new consumer tastes and providing a more efficient means of bringing the

6. S. A. J. Pratt, "The Development of the Sierra Leone Railway," vol. 1 (Freetown, June 1966, mimeo.), p. 51.

7. Harry Ransome, "The Growth of Moyamba," *The Bulletin* (Freetown: The Journal of the Sierra Leone Geographical Association, No. 9, May 1965), pp. 54–55.

8. Allen McPhee, *The Economic Revolution in British West Africa* (London: Routledge, 1926), pp. 35, 190, 191.

market to the farmer. With their profits from street trading they reinvested in shops in Freetown, and on occasion pooled their resources with those of kinsmen to buy goods in wholesale lots from European import firms. As a result they were able to increase exports of palm kernels and kola nuts. Kola nuts, which had totaled £60,516 in 1902 and was still largely in the hands of the Creole traders, rose to £276,530 in 1912 and was almost exclusively in the hands of the Lebanese.[9] By the early 1920s they were also buying store frontage in Freetown (Freetown and its environs did have freehold land tenure) from the very Creoles they were driving out of business.

As early as 1905 the Creoles were beginning to feel the pinch of increased competition, and they sought to remedy the situation through political influence. A few Creoles were appointed members of the Legislative Council and they sought to exclude their trade rivals by legislative action, a tactic they would follow even beyond independence. The antipathy toward the Lebanese on the part of the Creoles was well in evidence when a Mr. Davy, a Creole member, stated his case regarding the exemption from license fees of hawkers who traveled by land. The recording secretary wrote:

> Further, [Mr. Davy] was of the opinion that this system of hawking encouraged a class of people which this Colony would be better without. He referred to the Syrians who were the worst type of traders on the West Coast: they were nothing less than parasites who came here in large numbers impoverishing the Colony, were filthy in their habits, lived in unsanitary conditions, paid practically no rates or taxes and very little rent, lived cheaply and thereby were enabled to compete unfairly with others, did absolutely nothing for the Colony, brought no industry in their wake, in fact had only come to take every farthing they could away from the place. The Government should do all it could to discourage and limit their operations and as far as practicable, prevent their coming to the Colony altogether.[10]

The Creoles were to lead the opposition to the Lebanese almost alone until after the Second World War, when they were joined first by the Europeans and finally by the Protectorate elite. It is interesting to note that the Europeans, who created the stranger-middleman, eventually sided with the indigenous elite's aspirations for greater autonomy; the Lebanese had become such serious rivals that they became determined to drive them out of competition even if it meant granting political independence—a condition which they felt they could control.

9. Christopher Fyfe, *A History of Sierra Leone* (London: Oxford University Press, 1962), pp. 613–614.

10. CO 270/41 Colony of Sierra Leone, *Legislative Council Debates* (September 21, 1905), pp. 519–526.

While expanding trade in the Protectorate, the Lebanese did far more than introduce new wares and stimulate agricultural production. To begin with, they dealt directly with the African farmer, in his own locale, and in cash. Although modern currency was first introduced in the Eastern Province by the British Army as early as the Hut Tax War of 1898, it was Lebanese and European agents who accelerated its general use. As cash dealings grew common, the Lebanese trader began to bind the African producer to him by means of small cash advances. During the 1920s the Lebanese became entrenched in the two-way trade which was financed by the big firms and in some individual cases the banks. The Europeans considered the Lebanese good credit risks, inclined to repay promptly because their business and hence their family reputations depended on it. The traders in turn extended credit to the farmers in the form of cash loans or trade goods, which the farmers would repay at harvest time when they brought their crops to the traders to sell.

As the Lebanese began to bind the African producers to them through control over their buying and selling habits, they also tied them indirectly to the advanced sector of the new territorial market system. This "binding" is what Fred Riggs has called the "debt cycle."[11] The traders perpetuated the debt cycle by undervaluing the crops presented to them by the farmers. Thus a farmer's debt, though reduced temporarily by the sale of his crop, was soon increased because he needed more than food and supplies; he needed additional cash to meet social obligations. The farmers had few alternative sources of credit, because the European firms, with their large overhead and accounting procedures, were in no position to risk lending to small producers. The same was true of the banks, who considered the producer a poor credit risk because he had little or no collateral to pledge.[12] The Lebanese traders therefore became the principal source of agricultural credit in rural Sierra Leone.

The Lebanese expanded their operations rapidly in the first half of the twentieth century. The two World Wars brought troops and support facilities to Freetown, and the stimulus these gave to agricultural production and export trade enabled many Lebanese to enlarge the scope of their operations. Many used their accumulated profits to purchase war surplus materials, some of which were used by the traders directly, while the rest were sold at a handsome profit.

As early as 1925, the first public transportation system in Freetown was founded by a Lebanese; it was so successful that the colonial government bought him out in 1928. The census of Sierra Leone for 1931 lists

11. Fred W. Riggs, *Administration in Developing Countries* (Boston: Houghton Mifflin, 1964), p. 115.

12. Vernon Dorjahn, "African Traders in Central Sierra Leone," in Paul Bohannan and George Dalton, eds., *Markets in Africa* (Evanston: Northwestern University Press, 1963), p. 76.

814 miles of all-weather roads, and refers to the fact that all motor transport in the Protectorate was in the hands of the Lebanese. Following the
Second World War, some traders were in a position to begin importing
on their own. Since British and French goods were controlled by the large
European trading firms (also British and French), the Lebanese turned to
Japan, Italy, and Germany. By the 1960s Lebanese firms were the sole
importers for Japanese passenger and commercial vehicles, and they held
the franchise for Mercedes Benz, Fiat, certain makes of textiles, and other
trade items.

During the 1960s Lebanese control over the produce trade was also
completed. The Sierra Leone Produce Marketing Board, a price stabiliza-
tion fund and export operation solely owned by the government and set
up in 1949, had originally appointed seventeen buying agents. In 1954,
five of these buying agents were Lebanese, four were African, one was an
Indian, and seven were Europeans. By 1961 there were twenty-six agents
of the Board, and half of them were Lebanese. By 1966 the European
firms had abdicated the produce buying field, leaving a handful of small
African agents and the large Lebanese agents clearly in command of pur-
chasing produce for the Marketing Board.[13]

The Lebanese traders had clearly established themselves as middlemen. They bought in bulk from the European firms, on credit or with
bank financing; they broke bulk and became a vital link in the chain of
distribution by retailing directly to the African farmer-producer; they extended agricultural credit; they collected and transported produce and
even warehoused it. Then they sold crops to the European firms and later
to the Produce Marketing Board for export overseas.

The Diamond Trade

After the Second World War the Lebanese entered a sector of the
economy which was to enable them to substantially influence the political development of Sierra Leone. This event was their entry into the diamond trade. During a geological survey undertaken in all of Sierra Leone
in 1930, alluvial diamonds were discovered in the Gboboro stream of the
Kono District. Actual mining of the precious stones began in 1932 under
a lease arrangement between the colonial government and a British concern, Sierra Leone Selection Trust (SLST). By 1964 this company exported £7.4 million worth of raw diamonds, employed close to 4,000
people, and produced 5.8 percent of the world's diamonds.[14] What
makes diamonds so important to Sierra Leone is that the yield of gem

13. Sierra Leone Produce Marketing Board, *Annual Reports* (Freetown: Government
Printer, 1967).
14. Ralph G. Saylor, *The Economic System of Sierra Leone* (Durham: Duke University
Press, 1967), p. 132.

stones to industrials is very high, so that the valuation per carat of diamonds exported is correspondingly high. Thus in 1963, while mining (iron ore, rutile, bauxite, and diamonds) accounted for 83.7 percent of the total exports of Sierra Leone, diamonds alone accounted for 75.9 percent of all mineral exports and 65 percent of total exports.[15]

Expansion of the diamond industry after World War II brought about increased awareness on the part of the general population concerning the wealth to be gained in diamond mining—and smuggling. The illicit trade in diamonds by Africans, and by Lebanese who acted primarily as buyers and financiers, grew to gigantic proportions in the early 1950s. The monopolistic position of SLST ceased to exist with this rise in illicit digging (primarily on the company's leaseholds) and smuggling. Between 1954 and 1959 an estimated £10 to £15 million in revenue was lost to the firm.[16]

What were the reasons for this increase in illegal mining, and what was the role of the Lebanese trader? This role, both real and as it was perceived by Sierra Leonean decision-makers, was to have a profound influence on the policies which were directed toward the alien middleman group in the years following independence. The economic roles of some Lebanese in the chaotic situation which prevailed up until 1959 were essentially those of diamond dealers, produce buyers, retailers, and perhaps part-time smugglers. Very few Lebanese had been involved in diamond smuggling during the 1940s, but by the 1950s, following an increase in the number of immigrants, their number engaged in smuggling also rose. Nevertheless, the risks were high because the Lebanese were relatively few in number, quite visible and equally vulnerable.

In 1956 the government enacted the Alluvial Diamond Mining scheme and abolished the monopoly position of SLST, allowing Africans to mine diamonds on small leaseholds. The Alluvial Diamond Mining scheme had provisions for dealers and was for the most part supported by the trading community, because if one had a dealer's license possession of diamonds was no longer grounds for arrest. Two months after the scheme went into effect, 32 Lebanese and 51 Africans had been granted licenses. By January of 1958 smuggling had increased, and the Minister of Mines, Lands, and Labor sought an amendment to the scheme whereby a £3,000 deposit was required of foreign dealers. The purpose was twofold: to increase the number of Africans in diamond dealing, and to decrease the possibility of "non-natives" contravening the diamond regulations, which was made grounds for forfeiture of their deposit. By the end of 1958 there were 209 dealer's licenses granted, and just over 30 percent of them were to Africans. Of the remaining 146 which were to "non-

15. *Ibid.*, p. 143.
16. Sierra Leone, *Report of the Mines Department* (Freetown: Government Printer, 1962), pp. 4–5.

natives," 101 were to Lebanese.[17] The new regulations failed and the smuggling continued.

The reasons for the continued smuggling were easy to discover. When the fixed price for diamonds paid by the Diamond Corporation of Sierra Leone (a private company) failed to keep pace with the prices offered on the black market operating in nearby Monrovia, Liberia, the dealers often managed to sell their stones to illicit dealers who had contacts in that city. Some dealers went themselves, frequently by road to the border and then by private aircraft to Monrovia.

The Lebanese dealer was in an ideal position vis-à-vis his African competitors, not only within illicit operations but in the legal buying and selling of diamonds as well. The Lebanese dealer could finance his buying operations from the profits of his other commercial activities, such as produce, transport, and retailing. This explains why in the early years of the diamond boom, the 1950s, there were relatively few specialists in diamond dealing among the traders; few were so highly skilled in the appraisal of stones that they could afford to neglect their other operations. Besides, one bad purchase of considerable size could and frequently did wipe them out; the stories of dealers buying pieces of mineral water bottles or quartz and mistaking them for diamonds are legend. By the 1960s, however, a number of Lebanese diamond dealers had become quite expert at judging stones, and the best dozen or more of them were judged by the European buyers of the Government Diamond Office (GDO) to be as skilled as themselves.

The middleman operation is as important to the diamond trade as it is to the produce industry. The middleman's function is one of advancing money to African miners to buy mining equipment, rice, and other staples. This is a form of credit in return for which the miner is expected to bring his stones first to his benefactor for appraisal. One diamond dealer may have several hundred miners bringing their stones to him under this type of arrangement. The diamond dealer will also advance cash of up to several hundred pounds to itinerant dealers who purchase stones for him from small unstaked miners and illicit diggers. A large dealer may even stake illicit diggers, who then bring the stones directly to him. In almost all cases, it is the dealers who act as the channel for both legal and illicit stones, which go either to the GDO or the black market, depending on the price.

The essential difference between the diamond trade and the produce trade is that the Lebanese diamond dealer does not operate on credit obtained from the GDO or large firms and banks. A dealer must have substantial capital of his own to get started, which mitigates against Africans dealing for large amounts of large individual diamonds. The mechanism

17. H. L. Van der Laan, *The Sierra Leone Diamonds* (London: Oxford University Press, 1965), pp. 16–17.

whereby the dealer ties the "producer" to him in a debt cycle, however, is basically the same. Because of the nature of the product, and the availability of a ready market (other dealers) or the possibility of smuggling, the itinerant miner-dealer is in a more flexible position vis-à-vis the middleman. Nevertheless it is estimated that an astute Lebanese dealer can earn a steady 25 percent profit on his capital investment, and he may turn that investment over many times in a single month. Most of the top dealers were successful businessmen in other trade areas or were staked by relatives who were. Most of the top dealers have since given up their other enterprises or turned them over to family members to operate, preferring to keep their assets in more liquid form (diamonds and cash) should their hasty departure from the country be required.

Political Development

The colonial government, the prime mover in the early stages of economic growth, attempted to create territorial as opposed to communal institutions. Once opportunities were provided, large business with the necessary capital moved in to exploit the most lucrative aspects of trade, mining, and later tertiary industries. The Lebanese, with little capital and low levels of technology at their disposal, were able to ensconce themselves as intermediaries. They succeeded in changing consumer tastes, creating a dependency on the part of the African producer-consumer for cash, and in some cases they provided the incentive for the adoption of new technology, especially in diamond mining. Finally, the middleman succeeded in tying the producer-consumer to the market economy through this two-way trade and the vehicle of the debt cycle. The middleman was therefore significant in stimulating participation by Sierra Leoneans in the new territorial economy. This participation was by no means characterized by equity, since the African was and still is primarily found in the menial tasks—in agricultural production and in the lower-paying white collar occupations. In short, their access to wealth and income is greatly restricted.

The key role played by the Lebanese middleman extends beyond economic considerations. As mentioned above, in the process of penetrating the rural subsistence economy it was necessary for the traders to have both credit facilities and trading partners; and these were invariably the European firms. Indirectly this meant that the colonial administration was instrumental in guaranteeing the minority group some modicum of stability and order, by providing personal security and enforcing contracts. The Lebanese always had access to the courts, whether the District Commissioner's or the Appellate Court, and most traders felt that British justice was harsh but fair. These conditions obtained largely because of the close ties which existed between European business and the colonial government. Just as the European firms used the Lebanese as formal and informal agents of their enterprise, the colonial regime relied heavily on the firms in their economic development plans. Very early on, therefore, the Lebanese came to identify their interests closely with those of the European firms and colonial society generally. The trading minority, although for the most part excluded on the purely social level by the colonial and expatriate elite (and thus unable to shed the mantle of the "stranger"), identified with this ruling class in terms of political support, educational ambitions, business ethics, and other social attitudes.

In the rural areas of Sierra Leone a similar process took place; the Lebanese there worked closely with the most conservative element of society, the Paramount Chiefs. It was from the chiefs that the traders leased land, contributed to coronations, marriages, and funerals, provided gifts for wives of chiefs, and sometimes even settled their local trade disputes with Africans in the Chiefdom Courts rather than taking them to the District Commissioner.[18] Just as their urban counterparts supported the colonial administration, the Lebanese traders never attempted to undermine tribal authority, preferring instead to work through the existing machinery. This meant that even in rural areas the Lebanese were allied closely with the colonial regime, which accorded the Paramount Chiefs a position within the colonial administrative hierarchy. Even in the Protectorate it was impossible for the Lebanese to escape the status of "stranger," because membership in chiefdom society was primarily defined by birth. It also meant that both urbanized workers and the younger educated Africans in the Protectorate perceived the Lebanese as being closely tied to the colonial regime. This identification, along with their position as strangers in a racially categorized society administered by the colonial power, was to cost them dearly following independence.

Because of their central economic role and racial distinctiveness, the Lebanese were often thought to be present in Sierra Leone in vast numbers, when in fact they never exceeded 3,000 (see Table 1). They were viewed as representatives of the dominant or capital-intensive sector of the economy, as opposed to the subsistence or labor-intensive sector. When conditions in the subsistence sector turned against the producer— as when the technologically deficient sector swelled in population and outstripped capital accumulation, or when government economic policies failed—the highly visible Lebanese minority became extremely vulnerable. It was frequently blamed for deteriorating conditions, whether in food supply and prices or in agricultural commodity prices. The Lebanese have historically been the scapegoat for the failure of elite policies, both under colonial rule and in post-independence Sierra Leone.[19]

18. File P/9/4 Commissioner, Southeastern Province, *Chief's Courts* (September 25, 1941), p. 33.
19. An early example of this took place during the world influenza epidemic of 1919. The colonial government stepped aside for a period of time and allowed the mob in Freetown, led by disaffected Creoles, to wreak "vengeance" on the "Syrians" as the

The Stranger Question and Political Vulnerability

The first group to exhibit a sense of nationalism and the exclu-
sionary policies which it entails were the Creoles. An indigenous elite
within the colony (Freetown and environs), this group was very much
influenced by the rise of anti-colonial nationalist movements after World
War I. They were an unusual group in that they had a mercantile origin
and they had acquired during the nineteenth century some of the characteristics of an independent bourgeoisie. This began to change rapidly
around the turn of the century. Social ostracism on the part of the European ruling elite, plus the education and subsequent professionalization
of the offspring of the old Creole merchant group, changed their occupational base. As more Africans—and in the case of Sierra Leone particularly, more Creoles—went into government service, they came to look
on the government as the primary source of employment. Only the colonial government was capable of providing enough jobs of the sort for
which the colony elite had been trained. Most of the higher-level jobs,
however, were in the hands of British expatriates, which constituted a
barrier to the aspirations of the new elite group. As early as 1920 this
new group discovered that the barrier "could be overcome only with the
demise of the colonial regime."[20]

Although the rhetoric of the early Creole-led movement was nationalist in scope, it was limited by the fact that it perceived the colonial
problem as one affecting only the emerging middle class. During the
interwar period there were many popular forces at work, producing
labor strikes, the anti-Lebanese riots, tax disturbances in the Protectorate, trade boycotts, and so on. Yet the middle-class base of the
colony's new elite caused it to narrow its focus and to acquire, as one
author has remarked, "a false consciousness," a belief in its own efficacy
which ignored the limits set by the political context in which they found
themselves.[21] The truth of the matter was that the colonial government
possessed the power to shape the limits of political change. By forcing a
division between the Colony and Protectorate elites, it was able to maintain this power until independence. This power was also employed to
keep the Lebanese middlemen, who were under continual attack from the
Colony elite, from being defined out of the emerging society.

At the same time that the offspring of the old Creole merchant elite

---

Lebanese were officially called then. The government had failed to meet the resulting crisis
through lack of adequate distribution of rice, stockpiled in government warehouses. Great
Britain, Colonial Office, "Anti-Syrian Riots of 1919," CO 267/582-7 (London, 1920-1922).
For the post-independence period, see Sierra Leone, Restriction of Retail Trade Act No. 30
of 1965 and subsequent legislation.

20. Martin Kilson, "The National Congress of British West Africa, 1918-1935," in
Robert I. Rotberg and Ali A. Mazrui, eds., *Protest and Power in Black Africa* (New York:
Oxford University Press, 1970), p. 575.

21. *Ibid.*, p. 581.

were actively agitating against the colonial administration—for increased political participation as well as for restrictions on or expulsion of the Lebanese—a new elite group was forming in the Protectorate.

The Protectorate elite consisted of the young, educated kinsmen of the Protectorate aristocracy. They were for the most part conservative, and supportive of the institution of chieftaincy. Their relationships with the Lebanese traders were highly particularistic. Many members of the Protectorate elite had grown up in towns where there were traders, had known their families, had gone to school with Lebanese, and in some cases had even worked in their shops. But in the period preceding independence, despite the vast political differences which separated the Creoles and the Protectorate elite—differences stemming from their rival claims to control of the machinery of the state—common interests began to surface. Both groups were articulate, educated, and politically frustrated. The Creoles felt fenced in by the colonial administration and the Lebanese; the Protectorate elite felt limited in their effectiveness by the administration, and to a lesser extent by their own kinsmen, the hereditary rulers of the Protectorate.

Sierra Leone achieved independence under the political leadership of Dr. Milton Margai, a member of the Protectorate elite (an M.D.), bound by ties of kinship to the aristocracy and pledged to strong support for the institution of hereditary rule.[22] After founding the Sierra Leone People's Party (SLPP) in 1951, Dr. Margai sought to maintain a careful balance between the aristocracy and their educated progeny. When the SLPP attained political power under majority rule ten years later, the Party was in the hands of the Protectorate elite. It was their interests which became paramount, though dependent to some extent on support from the aristocracy.

In the last few years before independence (roughly 1955 to 1961), the younger Creoles and the more independent of the Protectorate elite came to realize their common interest in controlling the machinery of the state. The communalism of both Creoles and Protectorate elite began to give way to a more national outlook on matters of social advancement, political participation, and economic freedom. It was their ideas on economic freedom which brought this emerging middle class into conflict with the Lebanese minority.

The Politics of the Powerless

When the British government decided to begin an orderly transfer of power to indigenous hands in Sierra Leone, the Lebanese were faced with the prospect of having to deal with African political organizations. There had been no need (and little opportunity) for the Lebanese to seek power

22. *Protectorate Assembly*, Proceedings of the Eleventh Meeting, 1955 (Freetown: Government Printing Department, 1955), pp. 13–14.

or even to try to influence decision-making so long as they could conduct business with the approval of those who held power—which meant the colonial administration at the top and the Protectorate aristocracy at the local level. But when the dominant power in this relationship, the British colonial administration, withdrew its protective mantle, the Lebanese found themselves increasingly the objects of a struggle for power because of their control over a portion of the new nation's wealth. The Lebanese community was therefore forced to rely increasingly upon what Riggs has termed "intrusive access."[23]

The Lebanese realized that there was little to be gained from supporting the various Creole-led political movements because of the antagonism between the Colony and Protectorate elites; once majority rule was established, the Creoles as a restricted elite were doomed as a political force. Not surprisingly, some members of the Lebanese community began to respond to the Protectorate elite's need for funds to support their nascent political movement. The Lebanese perception of their own vulnerability vis-à-vis other indigenous groups in the coming power struggle played no small part in their decision to support the group with which they had existed in a complementary economic relationship.[24]

Dr. Milton Margai, the leader of the SLPP, had worked as a government medical officer throughout the Protectorate. He was well known to the Paramount Chiefs and also to the Lebanese community, which thought him to be kind, honest, and competent. The SLPP, because of its widespread connections with the Protectorate aristocracy, was in a good position to solicit funds from the Lebanese community.[25]

Lebanese support for the SLPP, though immediately forthcoming, was covert because the response of the colonial government was unpredictable—even though it was known to be sympathetic to the SLPP because of its strong ties to the most conservative element of the Colony's social structure. The Lebanese, through a large merchant in the major Protectorate town of Bo, provided Land Rovers, sound equipment, and contributions to the new political party. Such support, which continued after independence, was rewarded with contracts to import rice for the Sierra Leone government, as well as 35 cars for the Independence Day

23. Riggs, Administration in Developing Countries, pp. 274–275. Riggs argues that this relationship results not only from the middlemen confronting a set of official codes inimical to their interests, but also from the fact that the bureaucracy is recruited from communities which are hostile and insensitive to the needs of the foreign middlemen. The middlemen then encourage inefficiency by making the implementation of policy unworkable because of bribery and corruption.

24. For a similar situation in the Central African Federation at the time of its collapse (1963), see Floyd and Lillian O. Dotson, The Indian Minority of Zambia, Rhodesia, and Malawi (New Haven: Yale University Press, 1968), p. 321.

25. Martin Kilson, Political Change in a West African State (Cambridge: Harvard University Press, 1966), pp. 110–111.

celebrations, a justice of the peace appointment, and licenses, leaseholds, and other emoluments from time to time.[26]

What appeared to be an astute political move on the part of some of the wealthier members of the Lebanese community began to run aground after 1961. As independence became imminent, the Lebanese, faced with increased demands by the Creoles for the Africanization of commerce, had aligned themselves with the Protectorate elite. What they had not counted on was the extent to which these demands would eventually appeal even to the Protectorate elite.

As late as 1959, the "Africanization of commerce" remained almost totally a concern of the urban (Creole) middle class. But as Sierra Leone approached independence, the Protectorate elite was faced with a dilemma concerning commerce in general and the Lebanese trader in particular. Most of this elite's constituents, the rural populace, depended upon the trader for agricultural credit, for the purchase of their cash crops, and for the distribution of retail trade including staples. If complete Africanization were to take place as recommended by the Colony elite, serious dislocations in the economy might result, particularly in the absence of African businessmen or experienced government agencies. Secondarily, there was the very real and continued need for Lebanese and other expatriate financial support for the conduct of political activities. This need continued until after independence, when the SLPP was able to gain access to public revenues and other government facilities. There were also private financial relationships between Lebanese businessmen and Sierra Leonean politicians and traditional rulers—such as jointly owned companies and loan arrangements—which would be jeopardized if a policy of Africanization were vigorously pursued. On the other hand, certain groups within Protectorate society, and many politicians as well, had reason to favor increased Africanization. To maintain the party and insure continued electoral support, it was necessary to reward some of the better educated and trained followers with economic positions. In some cases this meant providing better opportunities for investment in land in Freetown, transportation contracts, shares in the rice trade, and positions in retail trade.

The need to accommodate these competing demands occupied a great deal of the time and energies of the Protectorate elite in the years following independence. The resolution of the dilemma in favor of both the Colony and the Protectorate elites' interests amounted to the merger of the two groups into a new national middle class. It also served to

26. Government of Sierra Leone, *The Report of the Commission Appointed to Enquire into and Report on the Matters Contained in the Director of Audit's Report on the Account of Sierra Leone for the Year 1960-61 and the Government Statement thereon.* (Cole Commission) Mr. Justice C. O. E. Cole, Chairman (Freetown: Government Printer, 1963), pp. 128-129.

further define the Lebanese as a *national* stranger group, and hence to push them steadily out of the new stratification order which emerged after the transfer of colonial power to the new middle class in April of 1961.

Independence and Nationalism

The decision to nationalize or "de-alienize" is often deemed as essential to emergent nationalism as political autonomy. Only in rare cases, however, is a clean sweep of aliens attempted. The usual reasons for this are significant control of the economy by foreign groups and the need to earn foreign exchange, maintain the availability of rural credit, collect import revenues, and preserve distribution functions. These reasons for caution, however, are countered by an equally strong set of motives. As the new power-holders are confronted by demands from various indigenous groups for greater participation in the economy, they respond by assigning increasingly higher priority to some policy of "de-alienization." The corresponding priority placed on enlargement of the economic sector may remain static or in some cases be reduced.

In Sierra Leone, the result of these increased demands, which appeared to come from various middle-class groups as well as urbanized workers, was a series of restrictive laws directly affecting the Lebanese community. These laws placed quotas on the hiring of expatriates, on types and quantities of goods to be handled by them, on immigration, citizenship, and hence political participation, and on ownership and leasehold of land. The linchpin of a nationalization or Africanization policy is the definition of citizenship. For the first time the new middle class viewed the Lebanese as potential rivals for political power. The case was exaggerated, of course, because the Lebanese group within their community was too small to constitute an independent political threat. Nevertheless, it was felt that the wealth of this minority group, if left unchecked, could seriously hinder the emergent middle class's own efforts to gain control of the state and access to wealth. The middle class believed that Lebanese politicians, wise in the ways of Sierra Leone society, might be able to buy their way into office. The SLPP promptly set about formalizing the "stranger" position of the Lebanese community politically and legally in the Constitution of the new state. They even went so far as to insert a grandfather clause into the document.[27]

It soon became obvious that formalizing the Lebanese community's stranger status involved much more than exclusion from the political and economic life of the country. In almost every case where restrictive legislation was introduced, the opposition to the Lebanese trading community

27. The grandfather clause stated that to become a citizen a person had to have been either a British subject or British Protected Person (many Lebanese were one or the other), and also that his paternal grandparent *must* have been born in Sierra Leone. No Lebanese could meet this last requirement, because Lebanese immigration had begun only in the 1890s. See Sierra Leone, *Constitution* (sections 1–10), Public Notice No. 78 of 1961.

was parliamentary. Each restrictive legislative act was a concession to the various interests of an emerging bourgeoisie, which was increasingly synonymous with the political and administrative elite. That this elite was using the machinery of the state to advance its own business interests is borne out by the figures below. Almost all of these interests were acquired after the passage of restrictive legislation, between 1962 and 1967. A Commission of Inquiry set up following the military coup d'etat of March 1967 revealed that 29 former ministers and deputy ministers held substantial interests in the following restricted areas of trade and commerce:

Transport	18
Stock in Manufacturing Company	9
Bakeries	1
Cement Block Manufacturing	3
Mineral Water	1
Construction	2
Market Gardens, Livestock	9
Rice Purchasing and Importing	6
Other Restricted Trade	17

Of these same 29 persons whose assets were investigated, 23 had acquired houses and land in the Western Area (Freetown and environs). Most of these properties were acquired after independence, with the greatest number occurring after 1964 when Sir Albert Margai became Prime Minister. Of the 23 ministerial officials who acquired properties, only 4 were Creoles—that is, indigenous inhabitants of the freehold areas.[28] These figures do not account for holdings in business or land by ordinary M.P.'s or senior civil servants. Some of these persons were later tried and convicted by the military government after March 1967.

The Anatomy of Corruption

After the attainment of independence and the passage of restrictive legislation against the Lebanese immigrant community, corruption became more than ever a means of survival in business. The newly independent government had acquired control over a patronage system which had formerly been exercised by foreigners located in London and only secondarily in Freetown. The demands placed on the new officeholders by constituents and kinship relations were often so great that they could be met only from public coffers or from private commercial operations. Dipping into public funds was risky because they were subject to audit, but using private money was often condoned, given that both European and Lebanese firms had been invulnerable to indigenous political pressure during colonial rule.

28. Government of Sierra Leone, National Reformation Council, *Report of the Forster Commission of Inquiry on Assets of Ex-Ministers and Ex-Deputy Ministers* (Freetown: Government Printer, 1967).

In the new state there were various degrees of vulnerability within the foreign business community, and the independent but wealthy Lebanese merchants became a prime target. In this situation the "stranger" is forced to become a buyer in a seller's market. Precluded from seeking posts of authority (power) or honorary positions (status) by reason of their existence outside of the constitutionally defined political system, the strangers are forced to "purchase" influence. The trading minority in Sierra Leone, besides lacking constitutional legitimacy, was not large enough or sufficiently well organized to purchase continued access to wealth by influencing the policy-making process. Efforts in this direction would have been doomed anyway because the policies on Africanization and economic growth were being formulated by the same people—the parliamentarians and the new national middle class. This left the stranger community with no alternative but to purchase influence at the enforcement stage of policy implementation. Corruption in this context can therefore be viewed as a "transaction," an alternative to coercion as a means of gaining influence.[29]

Before the military coup of 1967 corruption had reached epic proportions. As early as 1963 the Lebanese community had protested that politicians and civil servants had secured large amounts of money from them. A political rally in the diamond fields had raised £25,000 from diamond dealers, and sums only slightly smaller than this changed hands almost weekly. "Purchases" of influence affected the Immigration Quota Committee, which had been overruled several times by Prime Minister Margai because he wished to allow *more* "strangers" to enter the country.[30] Virtually every government agency which dealt with commerce had been "bought"—from the Produce Marketing Board, the Rice Board, and the Provincial and District Administration all the way to the office of the Prime Minister. After the coup in 1967, a military commission of inquiry ordered former Prime Minister Margai to repay the government £385,517, a large portion of which had come directly or indirectly from the Lebanese trading minority.

Conclusion

It may be correct to say that the wealth of the Lebanese trading minority served to unify disparate elite groups into a new middle class. But that wealth also served, in the face of growing opposition in the postwar period, to reinforce their stranger status. As they achieved greater wealth, the Lebanese were able to send for relatives and wives from Lebanon. This reversed the earlier trend toward assimilation and reinforced group cohesion; the elite groups began to notice that the trading

29. James C. Scott, "The Analysis of Corruption in Developing Nations," *Comparative Studies in Society and History*, vol. 2, no. 3 (1969), pp. 321–322.

30. Theo Azu, "Fireworks from Kai-Samba," *Daily Mail* (Freetown, July 21, 1967), pp. 1, 9.

minority was greatly increasing its numbers while socially isolating itself. The greater availability of regular transportation and communications with the mother country also served to strengthen communal identification on the part of the Lebanese community, both Muslim and Christian. Their political and social awareness of the Middle East, Lebanese politics, and their own situation vis-à-vis the new elite groups grew as their educational level increased. The new Sierra Leonean nationalism began to clash with their own, and the Lebanese increasingly came to view Sierra Leone as a temporary residence. They liquified their assets into sterling, precious metals, or diamonds, and proceeded in the years just prior to and following independence to engage in capital flight. As the accusations against them soon became fact, the Lebanese found themselves in the typical stranger position—they became more marginal. The ensuing state of "pariah-hood" during the 1960s increased their visibility, and corruption became their defense against increased vulnerability. Although they were given a temporary reprieve by the military coup of March 1967, when much of the restrictive legislation was rolled back, their long-term prospects in Sierra Leone remain bleak.

The Lebanese strangers were instrumental in creating a rural class of farmers who produced an increasing surplus for a cash-oriented economy. They were a source of credit for farmers, truck owners, drivers, and itinerant indigenous traders. They also aided directly in the creation and perpetuation of one sector of the working class, the diamond miners. Last but not least, they directly provided the means by which an emerging middle class came to rely less on traditional sources of wealth and prestige, and thus became less dependent upon the population for its income. As this new middle class became less dependent on the rest of the society, it also became less responsive to mass demands for an equitable redistribution and allocation of societal wealth.

Having played a role in the creation of a new stratification order, the Lebanese find that they have been defined out by the very bourgeoisie they had supported. The Lebanese will continue to be used as a source of revenue for the more powerful groups within the new middle class, as they struggle to gain control of the state. But once agreement is reached by these competing forces, the Lebanese will be of no further use to them. Barring an unlikely social revolution, they will be driven out and replaced by indigenous members of that same middle class.

6

Strangers, Nationals, and Multinationals in Contemporary Africa

Ruth Schachter Morgenthau

New political rulers in Africa insisted on choosing new economic partners. The colonizers did, and so, more recently, the leaders of the independent African states have done so. Commerce was too important to be outside African nationalist control, particularly since their economies remained dependent on markets controlled by foreigners living overseas.

Colonial rule had protected African markets for European manufacturers. They began to set up factories in Africa only after independence threatened the colonially established markets. In overseas commerce, similarly, colonial rule had made it possible for the big European trading companies to eliminate most Africans from the ranks of management and even to crowd them out of the wholesale and some of the retail trade; in West Africa, for example, to take over an estimated two-thirds to three-quarters of the overseas trade. They relegated Africans to subordinate positions and reduced African traders to minor retail trade, even though there had been a flourishing African trading tradition.

Indigenization

Indigenous African trading companies were the precursors of multinational enterprises in Africa.[1] Some African traders have had the potential of becoming direct investors, as traders did in many industrializing countries, but until recently only a few Africans invested their money productively outside of real estate, good living, and charity. Few had opportunities to put their experience at the disposal of the African governments. Displaced by foreigners, for a time they became victims in the crisis of loyalty that followed the end of colonial rule.

For many African traders, this was unexpected. Where nationalist parties developed, African traders had often contributed resources. They wanted the opportunity to take part in wholesale as well as retail trade,

1. For a working definition of multinational enterprises, see Raymond Vernon, *Sovereignty at Bay* (New York: Basic Books, 1971), Chapter One.

to obtain import and export licenses, to start manufacturing. In the nationalist era, many African traders, talking the language of socialism, usually meant that Africans should be in control of their own economic institutions, whether private or public. Yet with the coming of independence, even where they had been active in the nationalist movement, as in Ghana, the Ivory Coast, Guinea, and Mali, the African traders lost ground. They were shouldered aside by others. Most African founding fathers were trained as administrative assistants to the colonizers. Fearing local rivalry, for a while some new African governments made peace with foreign businessmen and preferred dealing through them.

African trading families were often internationally minded, and few stopped their transactions at the borders of the new states. Since many were not born in the country where they lived, they were treated as strangers. In the first decade of independence there was an almost autarchic African nationalism: some new governments, especially the smaller ones, viewed multi-African connections as politically suspect. Strangers like the Hausa in Ghana, the Dioula in the Ivory Coast, and the Dahomeyans in many parts of West Africa were sometimes expelled and often harassed. Yet some had the contacts to create their own international enterprises, linking commerce and eventually manufacturing in several African countries. Some Africans did this in diamonds, in foreign currency, and in cattle and kola nuts, linking Angola, Zaire, and the West African states.

In West Africa, these items were often in "unofficial" African trade, a pattern that persisted in spite of partition by the different colonial powers, and the disparate tax, tariff, and currency barriers between French- and English- and Portuguese-speaking colonial territories. There were no effective payment arrangements among the monetary zones. It could take a year, for instance, to pay legally for cattle coming into Upper Volta from Ghana. Moreover, in 1975 Ghana had an overvalued currency. Merchants found it worthwhile to import at the official rate of exchange, and export at the parallel market rate of the depreciated *cedi*; but for political reasons the government of Ghana did not want to devalue. Thus it is not surprising that clandestine trade, including transit trade, thrived in Dahomey and Togo or Gambia. Official statistics recorded that almost all West African states received no more than 5 percent of their imports from neighbors. Unofficially, however, Nigeria absorbed at least 75 percent of Niger's exports and provided at least 20 percent of her imports. Legal imports from Nigeria were subject to a 30 to 50 percent tariff in the franc zone states.[2] Officially, therefore, importing European goods was often cheaper.

The official economic structures sometimes made smugglers out of

2. Robert Smith, "West African Economic Cooperation—Problems and Prospects," *Foreign Service Journal* (Washington, D.C.), April 1974.

traders who wanted to survive. The same was true of government officials who had to find spare parts or badly needed foodstuffs, particularly in outlying regions. Some might call it illegal for Guinean officials to drive English cars which they had clearly managed to get in from Sierra Leone, but practical reality required they have cars, and a car eased across a border was the only one available. Similarly, on the Mali-Mauretanian border the legal system might require maintenance of tight customs control, for a currency change was involved. But in practice the post was usually deserted, and people moved unhindered across the border, exchanging cattle for vegetables and other products.

Such necessities help explain a gradual turn toward the Africanization of commerce. Within a decade after independence, most new African governments moved to Africanize in the private as well as the public sector. This did not eliminate the stranger issue from public consideration, but it changed the prospects of some African entrepreneurs. While stranger African traders were hard-pressed by new national regulations, many "citizen" political leaders moved to reward their best supporters with special advantages in the economy. Experience often counted less than loyalty.

Outside of white minority-ruled areas, Africanization had already begun in some states shortly before independence—the collecting of export cash crops through official marketing boards (*caisses*) and cooperatives. In addition, the Nigerian Enterprises Promotion Decree, enacted in February 1972, took effect in April of 1974 and required that all small enterprises be Nigerian-owned, and that medium-sized enterprises have 40 percent Nigerian participation. In Zaire, "authenticity" became official policy and Zairization led to a replacement by Zaire nationals of the Greek, Pakistani, Portuguese, and other foreign traders. As early as 1962 Ghana took over the Leventis trading enterprises and set up the Ghana National Trading Corporation. In 1968-1970, it became compulsory that only Ghanaian nationals take part in retail trade and small businesses. In Kenya, Europeans found it prudent to take African partners, and many European landholders sold out to Africans. In Senegal, a number of well-trained African civil servants have left their secure government positions for the uncertainties of private business.

Though commerce and medium-sized business is by no means wholly Africanized, the process has begun. Many African governments favor giving bank credits, import licenses, and other supports to their nationals, while pressing the foreign establishments to move out of the import-export trade and small businesses and shift to investment. A few new African governments also tried to take over the retail trade of imports and displaced all middlemen, whether of overseas expatriate, alien African, or local African origins. In Guinea, Mali under the Union Soudanaise, and Tanzania, wholesale and retail transactions in imported consumer goods became state monopolies. Many enterprising traders migrated to neighboring states while some took posts in the government trading monopolies.

These policies, political in motivation, have not been adopted everywhere. There are few signs of them in white-ruled Africa, or in the black-ruled states immediately surrounding South Africa. It is hard, for example, to find an African business employing as many as ten people in Malawi or Swaziland.[3] Many of the Africanization policies have been implemented with uneven energy and somewhat inconsistent policies, even under successive regimes in the same state. The government of Ghana's President Nkrumah, for example, was reluctant to create a class that might compete with the government for control over economic policy. Even in post-Nkrumah Ghana, in which Ghanaians are operating practically all businesses with an annual turnover of under half a million dollars, most Ghanaian businessmen find it prudent to take a cautious position in relation to government, because they worry what new regulations may require of them next. Moreover, the governments carrying out Africanization policies have realized that those policies alone cannot give them control over the forces governing their economies, nor assure them an expanding economy in which the size of everyone's share will grow.

The experience with Africanization measures has made many African governments painfully aware of economic constraints and limitations. The measures did not increase production, and in some states they temporarily decreased it. Many African entrepreneurs, like many African workers, lived on slim margins and could take only limited risks; they had little credit, skill, organization, and technology. Indigenization measures did not improve the prospects of strangers. They did not alter the relationship of the national economy to the international market, and barely touched the domains of overseas-based multinational enterprises. The problem of growth, of interaction between African and global economic structures, remained. Within the global structure, many African leaders might characterize themselves as strangers.

Technology

Both the nationalism that speeded the departure of European foreigners from Africa and the reaction against African strangers from within communicated popular resentment against the rich. Many Africans felt poor, and nationalism seemed to promise equality. The anti-stranger reaction that followed independence carried with it bitter disappointment at post-colonial reality. To understand that reality, it will be helpful to look at technology. Technology, of course, never caused a stranger problem. Whether they come by camel, wheel, or

3. See Bruce Dinwiddy's *Promoting African Enterprise* (London: Croom Helm and the Overseas Development Institute, 1974), and *West Africa* (London), May 27, 1974.

wing, travelers are still tourists with money who intend to go home or newcomers who may want to settle. The effects of technology depend on the uses people make of it. Nevertheless, technology does affect the terms on which integration or rejection of outsiders takes place. It can quicken communication, the spread of language, the transmission of institutional and social patterns that make people feel they belong together. It can bring prophets of a universal religion predicting the unity of Africa, or all mankind. It can allow them to overcome previously insurmountable barriers. It can make the Niger river navigable. It is very important in deciding the outcome of wars.

The transfer of new technology and its products has long impelled people in Africa to take the risk of leaving home. Jack Goody for West Africa and de Gregori for the whole continent have pointed out that until the time of Christ, iron-working on an advanced level for its time characterized the sub-Saharan savannah agriculture from the upper Niger to Abyssinia.[4] From there, the Bantu, probably originating in the Lake Tchad area, spread iron technology through the tropical rainforest, and with it many food crops originating from Asia. By the time the Portuguese came to southern Africa, Bantu-speaking peoples were farming there. This Bantu movement involved a spectacular spread of technology, and included conquering, replacing, or incorporating various hunters, gatherers, and cattle-raising nomads, long before the Europeans improved their navigation techniques and came to the shores of Africa. Not everything strangers brought was acceptable to Africans. Wheels are represented in the rock drawings of the caves and stones of the Sahara, and those who traveled across it knew that the wheel was in use in the Mediterranean world.[5] Yet the wheel did not become widely used in tropical Africa until the Europeans reintroduced it by sea. This had social consequences. Through iron technology, agriculture allowed the development of greater social distinctions than were possible in the societies using stone tools, even though the social distinctions in precolonial Africa remained slight in comparison with many Asian and European societies.

That situation changed when the Europeans used technological superiority to colonize, and then used colonial rule to keep control of their technological superiority. Their new techniques remained in enclaves, in cities, where there were roads, in the fertile rain forests, where cash crops grew in coexistence with traditional agriculture, hunting, fishing, and cattle-raising. The new African nations were characterized by far greater social inequalities than had existed before the colonial era.

4. Jack Goody, *Technology, Tradition and the State in Africa* (London: Oxford University Press, 1971). See also the elaborate, longer study by T. R. de Gregori, *Technology and the Economic Development of the Tropical African Frontier* (Cleveland: Case Western Reserve, 1969).

5. L. A. Thompson and S. Ferguson, eds. *Africa in Classical Antiquity* (Ibadan, 1969).

Where the Europeans introduced palm oil, coffee, cocoa, rubber, peanuts, cotton, and sisal, they helped produce a surplus that spread some new wealth among those Africans that grew the new crops. These African farmers and a few traders apart, the rest of the African rich were the post-colonial rulers and their immediate allies. Few produced anything, but they held power. Unlike the peasants and farmers and workers, they often lived extremely well. Many new military and civilian rulers hastened to acquire large tracts of land, to become a kind of landed aristocracy.

In contrast, African wage-earners, though perhaps better off than rural peasants, held low-skill and low-wage jobs introduced in the colonial era. Often stranger Africans from across the borders of poorer countries were recruited to hold these jobs. Low wages still blight the lives of Africans in the industries of South Africa, and the stereotype of the low-wage laborer persists among foreign business managers setting up operations in Africa. Africa is on the whole labor scarce, needing a high-skill, high-wage labor policy.

The technological superiority which allowed the Europeans to conquer left a legacy of sharp social inequality in the new African states. The new leaders needed weapons, cars, trucks, and telephones from outside Africa. Yet they had little control over the dynamics of growth, and thus over what could be produced locally or used to satisfy popular expectations for a better life. The privileged group of Africans who inherited the chairs of the Europeans needed the benefits of long distance trade, and on the whole they valued the foreign connections that made it possible. Their attitude has not necessarily been shared by the rest of the population, who have sought their own real prosperity. In the long run, that prosperity depends on the productivity of the artisans, the productive wage-earners, and those who work the land.

Multinational Entry

The end of colonial exclusivity and the world shortage in raw materials attracted multinational enterprises to Africa. They found entry easy. The new African states lifted colonial barriers to entry, and little resistance came from African entrepreneurs. What have been some of the effects of this, on the availability and distribution of resources; on the patterns and paths to development; on the struggles for power in the new states; on the evolving pattern of connections between African social groups, including strangers; and on the African state system?

Multinational enterprises sit astride a mountain of wealth, technology, and techniques of organization developed over hundreds of years. They control valuable markets. Their spokesmen are trained not to release acquired advantage. Their structures allow them to control from parent headquarters abroad even indigenous African employees in

top positions. The customary processes of acculturation and incorporation which have assured the integration of many layers of strangers into
African society in the past cannot now be counted on to draw multinational enterprises closer to defined national objectives.

If it is understood that strangers are vulnerable and do not have a
place to return to; but that foreigners are secure, have a place to return
to, and deal through the national elites, then it could be said that multi-
nationals can change their managerial employees—even strangers or
nationals—into foreigners. This is not unique to Africa. In France, the
French government has considered IBM a threat even when the management in France is composed of French nationals.

Multinational enterprises, though often efficient stimulants to economic growth, can contribute to social stagnation. The development of
mining and subsoil extraction, for example, poses great problems of distribution and often increases the gap between the few rich and the rest,
far more than development through small-farm agriculture would. Except in oil and copper, new mines often meant only a little more real
wealth to the nationals of the new African states. The mines remained
prosperous enclaves. Few Africans worked for the mines, even where
there were ore-processing plants. Long lead time, much capital and
machinery, and little labor characterized most multinational activity.
Enterprises prospered but the people did not. Even in the better-organized
new African mining states, the most affluent level broadened only a
little. The syndrome of growth without development has accompanied
multinational entry into many new states.[6] The new money rarely
reached the people; it stayed rather in the enterprise, in the capital city,
and with a top few government leaders.

Multinationals can make the difference between the survival and the
disintegration of an African political elite. Where would the political
leaders of Mauretania be without copper and iron, Liberia without rubber and iron, Guinea without bauxite and iron, Zambia without copper,
Nigeria without oil? The rewards that multinational enterprises can offer
their African allies are considerable. They are as attractive, for example,
to Sékou Touré of Guinea as guns and cannons were to Samory Touré
almost a century ago.

Multinationals sometimes furnish the leaders with enough resources
that they can afford to pay little attention to other problems. And where
multinationals enter agriculture, it is often to drain the produce out of
Africa; production for home consumption suffers.

While a few African governments have seriously sought to equalize
distribution—through mechanizing agriculture, encouraging African

6. See my essay "Multinational Enterprises in Africa," in "Multinational Enterprises and
Economic Development." Institute of Policy Studies Papers, Yale University, 1974. Mimeographed.

enterprise, improving infrastructure and social services, and developing an internal market—many governments have not yet tried. In several states, most wealth has stayed largely in the hands of the allies of the rulers in power. Especially when agriculture was in trouble, multinationals generated revenues and sometimes made it possible for governments, even with slim popular support, to stay in power. Most African armies are small, funds are scarce, and great advantages can be drawn from access to technology—radio, telephone, telegraph, and other means of communication.

Oil and copper and some other minerals appear to contribute enough resources to allow some countries to grow, to begin genuine development, and to make a redistribution of wealth which is not simply a superimposition of new wealth upon old. Algeria, Zambia, Angola, Zaire, and Nigeria have these resources. Yet only the political institutions of the country can evolve policies that diffuse the wealth, promote reinvestment, and generate opportunities for the bulk of the population. Multinationals have quite different objectives. If new African countries had better distribution of income, more diverse and larger sources of revenue, a wider net of national institutions than the army and the civil service, more technically skilled people, stronger and more diverse institutions connecting leaders and the rest of the population, more avenues of social mobility—then the entry of multinational enterprises and the consequent tightening of links to the world market would not so exacerbate the extremes of power, health, and wealth.

Multinationals figure prominently in the calculations not only of those in power, but also of those outside, who try to find levers for dislodging or altering what are often autocratic but inefficient regimes. Opposition groups must do their work in the city, through the police and the army (which have access to modern weapons and communication), or they must go to the grassroots and mud paths. And unless an opposition group has funds, it can rarely fight its way into the city from the hinterland. The uncertainty in national integration, the lack of control over the hinterland by the capital cities, also weakens the opponents of a government. No wonder opposition leaders view the revenues from multinational enterprises as keys to power, more accessible and easier to manipulate than agricultural revenues, the prize and support of any government. In the post-OPEC (Oil Producing Export Countries) era, few spokesmen of autarchy or isolationism can be found even in African opposition or guerrilla groups. Their object is simply to take over the political kingdom—with outside help, if necessary. Such calculations affected the timing of the 1974 coup d'état in Niger, for example.

In many international industries, it is hard for Africans to find a foothold without accommodating multinational enterprises. Even the leaders of socialist states find this to be true. African leaders seek access to markets and productive technologies, which govern availability of credit. They control many such techniques and seek to perpetuate the control. They can change Saharan rock into valuable uranium, or the Niger delta into oil—valueless things into resources. At the same time they rapidly transfer to Africa inflation, recession, and world market highs and lows. With a few significant exceptions, multinational entry into new African states has resulted in continued or increased dependence on overseas markets, less local or regional self-sufficiency, a draining of African resources from the countryside, and a reinforcement of economic and social differences. Only if African leaders use political pressure to force changes are any changes likely to occur.

It is possible to speculate about the effects of multinational entry upon the processes of state formation in Africa, and upon the organization of post-colonial African societies. It is clear that a struggle for more African control is taking place between the leaders of new African states and the stranger managers of multinational enterprises.

In the midst of political disturbances, nationalist leaders sometimes blew up the industrial installations they had worked hard for in times of peace. But even guerrillas have been careful with capital installations. The Algerian and Angolan nationalists wanted the oil wells, and did not destroy them.

Faced with old-style contracts and colonial-style behavior, African political leaders have at times acted in ways that seemed irrational or illegal to managers of foreign enterprises. But they were rational to Africans, who had little at stake. An example is the well-publicized decision by President Eyadema of Togo to nationalize the French-owned Togolese Benin Mining Company (CTMB), which processed phosphate, after a company pilot shook him up in a crash landing. The President of Togo accused the mining company of wanting to kill him, and refused an offer by the company of compensation for damages.[7] He had other reasons: he knew that profits in the phosphate market were not being transferred to benefit Togo, and he wanted closer links with Nigeria.[8]

Many African leaders have denounced prior contracts unilaterally, to force their renegotiation. Many African leaders have found ways to control and shape foreigners indirectly, by playing on multinational rivalries, seeking sweeteners in multinational packages either from the enterprises themselves or from the government of the parent country. They have explored the mixed blessings of suppliers' credits and other export incentives offered by the industrialized countries, and have considered a variety of loans that might facilitate direct African participation in projects located in their own countries. Companies are under

7. *West Africa*, February 18, 1974.
8. *Economist Intelligence Quarterly, Quarterly Economic Review, Ivory Coast, Togo, Dahomey, Niger, Upper Volta*, No. 2, 1974; and Philippe Decraene "Togo: Eviction des prives du secteur minier," *Révue Française d'Etudes Politiques Africaines*, no. 98 (1974), pp. 15–16.

increasing pressure to accord producing countries a larger part of the profits, a voice in pricing, and participation in management and ownership. This does not affect every African country, every company, every industry. But it has spilled over beyond oil, beyond bauxite and copper, and is kept in motion by changing market conditions and increasing competition among rival multinational groups.

The capacity of multinational enterprises to fish in troubled waters in Africa is limited only by the political systems they find there. Partly because most African societies were at a relatively early stage of economic and social change at the time of multinational entry, surprising connections were sometimes forged. Since many African nations are new and not closely integrated, with few national structures, the balance among local groups is rarely stable. Therefore, the advent of strong outsiders, such as multinationals, can and has led to competition for support among local interest groups, undercutting the already weak national political balance. This is not unique or new to African politics.

Though limited, the capacity of African political leaders to mediate between their own interests and the interests of foreign multinational enterprises is growing. At first, successfully reaching into the United States or European internal political processes seemed possible only for the white-ruled states of Africa. The Smith government of Rhodesia skillfully manipulated its control over a significant supply of chrome and its connection with Union Carbide, as well as the susceptibility of the southern lobby in the U.S. Congress to arguments of white racial superiority, to speed Congressional passage of the Byrd amendment. In contrast, the government of Zambia was able to obtain only a partial boycott of trade with Rhodesia after its Unilateral Declaration of Independence. On rare occasions, African political leaders have even manipulated separatists in a developed country. For example, President Hamani Diori of Niger was able to get economic aid from the Canadian government in Toronto; in exchange, he agreed to oppose General de Gaulle's support of the French-speaking separatist movements of Quebec, and negotiated Canadian membership in the association of French-speaking peoples through the federal government.

The hope of wealth through a favorable multinational connection affects how many national governments behave toward their neighbors. For example, the Mobutu government of Zaire intervened in the internal quarrels of its Angolan neighbors, partly because their common frontier divides relatives, and partly because of Cabinda oil. The border wars in the Saharan region are affected by expectations of sub-soil resources.

There are many examples of regional or ethnic separatism in Africa being heightened by multinational enterprises. The hope of wealth affects how political rivals within nations behave toward each other. Leaders coming from regions which have the resources that multinationals seek—oil or copper, for example—have frequently expressed separatist ambitions; as class, regional, and ethnic issues became superimposed. For example, in Zambia's copper belt, the politics of many miners deviated from the rest of the country.[9] In Zaire's copper belt, the Union Minière in Katanga became a chief support of Moise Tshombe's separatist movement. A policy of encouraging rivalry between U.S.-based multinationals and Belgian monopolies helped make it possible for General Mobutu to contain Katanga separatism.[10] The revenues from the oil companies in Nigeria were disputed by the combatants in the Nigerian civil war. Though it was certainly not the only reason, given the availability of oil money it made economic sense to set up a Biafran state. Ibo leaders frightened at becoming strangers within Nigeria sought to build a separate nation of their own. Thus, links between local and international interests are not necessarily mediated through national governments. When structures of the scale and power of multinational enterprises are involved, we speak less of strangers and more of transnational relations. By affecting the political balance within and between African states, multinational enterprises play a part in state formation of Africa.

Changing State Relations

The coming of multinational enterprises to Africa has caused political relations to shift both within and between African states. Accompanying the energy crisis of the 1970s have been shifts in most raw material industries. Many parts of Africa have become very attractive to multinational enterprises; many are now in a race for concessions and connections. The largest hydroelectric potential in the world exists on the African continent, and multinational enterprises can develop that potential. Inga in Zaire and Cabora Bassa in Mozambique are only two of the important energy projects. When completed, the Inga project alone promises to yield more hydroelectric output than all of Western Europe. The Cabora Bassa dam in Mozambique is important to the South African economy, and its possible loss would be a blow. Needless to say, such large projects involve the movement of thousands of people across national borders, people who become strangers in their new homes.

Increasingly, Africa is producing oil—in Algeria, Libya, Nigeria, Gabon, Zaire, and Angola, for example. Much exploration is taking place, along the coast, in the Saharan area and elsewhere. Nigeria was seventh among world oil producers in 1973, when it exported about 2.2 million barrels a day; and oil politics have involved some African states in complex OPEC maneuvers.

9. See Richard Sklar, *Corporate Power in an African State* (Berkeley: University of California Press, 1975).

10. See David Rochefort, "American Policy Toward the Congo Since 1960," Brandeis University Honors Thesis in Politics, April 1975.

Oil brought Nigeria's government more resources in 1973 than were available to the South African government, and at the same time the value of Nigerian exports surpassed the value of South Africa's exports. Gold values, like oil, tripled in 1973, which saved the South African government from ruin because of its total dependence on imported oil. Yet South Africa's economic strength has declined since the new high oil prices went into effect in the early 1970s.[11]

Oil is not the only resource leading to new wealth in Africa. Changes are also taking place in copper, the principal export of Zambia and Zaire; in bauxite, which Ghana exports and of which Guinea has some of the world's largest known reserves; in uranium, found not only in South Africa but also in Gabon and Niger; and in nickel, of which Burundi has large reserves. African iron, if found near water power, has become more attractive economically than it was before the new militant OPEC oil price policy. There are many other examples of structural changes in the economy, which naturally affect African rulers.

These shifts have had several consequences. The relative weight and power of South Africa in continental affairs has declined. The coup in Portugal and the advent of black-ruled governments in Mozambique and Angola have further reduced the South African radius of power and influence. The rich African states, previously dependent upon or accustomed to trading with Europe, can now afford to shop around the world. Many African markets, previously small, can broaden in the future.

Within Africa, the disparity in wealth between rich and poor countries is growing. The rich African states are increasingly able to exercise power in the world and are becoming centers for regional regrouping within Africa; they are also attracting strangers looking for work. Meanwhile the drought afflicted millions with poverty and misery and sickness. The high oil prices made uneconomic many new industries in African oil-importing states. Conditions are no longer, however, quite the same as those which provoked the organizers of the Bandung conferences in the 1950s and the UNCTAD meetings of the 1960s to speak of the widening gap between developed and underdeveloped countries, and between white and black. In Africa, the extremes are great, but rich is no longer white and poor is no longer black.

How are strangers affected by these changes? The rich African states are becoming centers of power and could become centers of growth, and growth at a sufficient rate to allow for the harmonizing of communal conflicts. These economies are likely to need more workers than are available. Algeria, Nigeria, Gabon, Zambia, and Zaire, for example, are already attracting more strangers looking for work. Multinational enterprises can generate wealth which affects the capacity of leaders to act.

11. See my "The Developing States of Africa," *Annals of the American Academy of Political and Social Science*, (1977), pp. 80–95.

Much depends on what policies the leaders in the rich states choose to follow.

They have the opportunity of shaking off dependence upon long-distance trade and developing self-sustaining growth. With such growth some of the gaps between the leaders and the rest could be bridged. Oil, copper, and cheap energy are scarce enough in the world market that the nations producing them are in a very strong bargaining position. The leaders will have more than enough to share. Dynamic growth in these countries could allow the African strangers to take root comfortably, to grow and produce descendants and institutions that are in time regarded as native.

The establishment of new borders created problems of nationality in the new states, just as the colonial rule had done a few generations ago. It is too early to know whether the newly created West African Economic Community will make citizenship, and belonging, open to many who are now considered strangers, by making borders fewer and less rigid. If barriers were reduced, and economic cooperation became the official goal, a new economic pattern might well emerge.

Some of the rich states are already looking beyond their borders and following policies which could lead to a reduction of economic barriers between the African states. It is to the interest of manufacturers in Nigeria, for example, to be able to count on a larger market in all of West Africa. If a dynamic of self-sustaining growth spreads outward from the rich enclaves in Africa, the stranger issue might fade in significance, and the peaceful absorption of strangers might again be possible.

The Importance of Politics

There is, however, an important condition. African political authorities must follow integrating policies that give some weight to performance rather than origins, to merit consideration. Otherwise growth can only reinforce estrangement, and produce differential incorporation of groups in a hierarchy defined by ethnic or racial externals. South Africa is the most extreme example; there, growth has armed the whites and financed the repression of blacks. Until the change in oil prices, multinational enterprises had their largest African investment in South Africa and reinforced the apartheid system—which is perhaps the ultimate instrument of estrangement, since it made strangers of Africans on their own soil.

Growth does not necessarily favor integration. This means that the political process is of great importance in setting the terms on which strangers are to be treated. On the other hand, economic stagnation, declining living standards, reduced political consensus, and reduced tolerance of strangers have often come together. Migration and misery are the lot of millions in the poor parts of Africa. Crossing of international borders does not appear to be reduced by a lack of hospitality to strangers. Often expelled strangers do come back. If the need is great enough, people move even among hosts who are not hospitable. Genuine growth could absorb the energy of all layers of the population around a common sense of identity, but only if other institutions and policies encourage this.

If integrating policies are followed, and growth is maintained, then institutions can take root which are capable of involving different groups around a common sense of identity. In precolonial days, such integrating institutions were the religious structures, both Muslim and animist; the army, the schools, and the bureaucracy; and the artisan, professional, and ethnic organizations. Through these, communities took in strangers and allowed them land, property, status, and perhaps wives.

Multinational enterprises have a significant effect on African class structure, state formation, and relations among African states; they can influence the allocation of resources within African states and the choice of development policies. Multinational enterprises bring in strangers who carry some of the strongest ties that bind Africa to the world economy. But an elimination of multinational enterprises as we know them would not eliminate existing ties to the world economy. Moreover, though the multinationals affect growth, and can provide some African strangers with jobs, they cannot automatically solve the stranger problem. Meanwhile, it is hardly realistic to expect political policies to stop human movement and contact. A solution can only be found by reinforcing integrating structures and gradual assimilating of strangers.

For there are deep cleavages in African society, which surfaced as the European colonizers left. There were cleavages between chiefs and commoners, young and old, and even men and women within many African ethnic groups. Marabouts and animist sages struggled for support. These social and cultural cleavages have often been clearly connected with a conflict over resources. Conflicts became more acute, for example, between shepherds and farmers. As rainfall declined, overuse of new well-digging technology allowed shepherds on the desert fringe to breed too many cattle, who foraged for food and denuded the fragile environment of existing vegetation. The result was a growth of the desert, and a Malthusian solution to the overproduction of cattle.

Another cleavage has resulted from the loss of the delicate balance between town and countryside, between land, peasants, and food. Since the 1960s many African countries have produced less food and imported more while their cities grew in size but not in productivity. The increase in civil servants, soldiers, and police made the problem worse.

Because of the rapid influx to the cities by people deserting the countryside, most African cities expect to double their population every ten years, which is three times the national growth rate. In response, many urban-based governments have sought devices to reduce population pressure. Fewer and fewer farmers have been expected to nourish more and more eaters, but industrialization is still in its infancy. These cleavages have made it difficult for the authorities at the administrative center of a country to keep a hold on people living on the periphery. Frequently, African governors or regional authorities have tremendous autonomy—and few facilities from the center. Thus in Mali there were even internal customs barriers, across which people and goods were not permitted to move—an example of the emergence of strangers within national borders. Such tragic results come from the deformation of market mechanisms. These encouraged peasants to grow crops for export, only to find themselves without food. People wandered far from home to live as strangers, willing to accept exploitative wages for fear of total destitution. In such conditions even brothers can become strangers.

Conclusions

Strangeness is a matter of degree, perceived in ways that differ with circumstances. Strangeness is a process which involves changing institutions, resources, numbers, and technologies. Strangeness involves a power relationship, which varies according to rulers and to the institutions of the geographic unit—whether village, town, city, region, nation, or even world. Strangeness involves the very dynamics of change itself. Where many become viewed as strangers, there is a loss of equilibrium between power, production, and distribution which can be acute enough to undercut any assimilating institutions that might exist. Harassment of the weakest strangers shows that there is a crisis, but it is not necessarily its cause; the weak strangers may be scapegoats, who suffer in place of richer and more powerful objects of resentment.

These ideas have been discussed in the context of an abbreviated account of African political and economic development. Strangers may come from rural areas, leaving inadequate subsistence economies. In contrast, multinational enterprises bring in strangers who are firmly attached to the international economy. The recent attempts of African leaders to manage the multinationals and turn the usual contact more in their favor—through OPEC, CIPEC (Community of International Petroleum Exporting Countries), and the organization of producer groups in wood, coffee, cocoa, bananas, and other major African exports—have a bearing on the conditions of change, and hence on the processes and the power relationships involved in the perception of degrees of strangeness.

Meanwhile, even though there is everywhere a stranger problem, it is hardly realistic to expect a full stop in human movement, or an end to the clash over resources, power, institutions, and ideas. The formation of nations involves far more than changes in borders, and in who rules, who belongs, and who does not. The withdrawing colonizer assaulted African values and customs and institutions, in varying depths according to the nature of the colonial relationship. The resulting reaction has varied according to the depth of impact. This explains the drive toward authenticity, négritude, and African personality, expressed in the use of African names and styles of dress and the use of African languages.

It would be wrong to explain the stranger problem only in terms of political power or economics. Reactions to outsiders express decisions about what kind of society, what kind of civilization, what kind of group identity future Africans will have. Fernand Braudel pointed out that the Spanish reaction against the Muslims, and the expulsion of the Jews and others from Catholic Spain in the fifteenth and sixteenth centuries, were part of a Spanish reassertion of cultural identity. It was a process of decolonization, sometimes violent. Institutions, languages, education, even architecture and art forms were being decided upon then.[12] Will future observers, with the benefit of more hindsight, be able to make some comparisons with contemporary intolerance of strangers in some parts of Africa?

12. Fernand Braudel, *The Mediterranean* (New York: Harper and Row, 1973 edition), vol. 2, pp. 790–797.

Part III

Special Studies: Ghana

7

Host Reactions: Aliens in Ghana

Margaret Peil

This chapter will examine the role of strangers in Ghana, especially African aliens, within the framework of Donald Levine's typology (see Chapter One). It seeks to explain two things: first, the interaction between the stranger's intended level of participation in the host community and the host community's response, whether friendly or antagonistic, as this has been experienced mainly by southern Ghanaians; and second, the factors involved in that community's decreased tolerance of alien strangers over the past twenty years. Many of the points to be made will apply to other countries which have had similar problems with African and non-African strangers. Ghana serves as a useful case study because of its notable tolerance of strangers in the past and its equally notable expulsion of over 100,000 aliens in late 1969 and early 1970. The first part of the chapter focuses on the motivations of migrants—citizens and aliens alike—and their position in the local society. The second part deals with the expulsion of aliens, examining the factors leading up to it and its repercussions in the local and stranger communities.

Migrants and Hosts

Sojourners

Ghanaians tend to see integration into their society as dependent upon the wishes of the outsider: no one need remain a "stranger" unless he chooses to do so. Historically, Akan society assimilated slaves and other strangers by marriage and subsequent adoption into the kinship group; but these were mostly people who had no choice about leaving. The great majority of today's migrants to the towns and cocoa farms are free to leave. Most do not seek to be completely integrated because they have no intention of staying permanently; they would rather maintain hometown ties than become full members of a new community. This applies as much to Ghanaian citizens as to aliens. Busia's comment on Sekondi-Takoradi in 1950 could still be applied to most large towns: "very few of the large population manifest civil loyalty or responsibility for the town in which they make their living. They may own property

123

here, marry and have children, but they are always considered, and they consider themselves, 'strangers.'"[1]

The situation has changed somewhat; recent migrants have extended their stay in town and found that participation in local elections enhances their power with local authorities; but in general they have only moved from the status of "guest" to that of "sojourner." In a recent survey in Tema and Ashaiman (a new port and industrial town and its suburb), 820 respondents were asked, "Do you think it is better for older people to live in town with their children or should they go back home when they retire?" Only 10 percent of those in Tema and 7 percent of those in Ashaiman thought migrants should settle permanently. Because these towns were minor villages twenty years ago, and the indigenous inhabitants therefore form only a minute proportion of the present population of over 100,000, the fierce struggle for power between migrants and hosts which occurred in many Nigerian towns (notably Lagos, Ibadan, and Warri) has not taken place here. Rather, the opposite problem exists—finding local leadership willing to take an interest in pressing the government for the services the town needs. Sojourners generally are not concerned about these things.

Other Ghanaian towns have a larger core of indigenes—the Ga in Accra and the Akan in Kumasi are good examples. In both cases, migrant members of the local ethnic group regard the city as their home and are assimilated into the local kinship group upon arrival; they may not even go through a "newcomer" phase. Other migrants tend to be sojourners who leave local politics to the local people, though various stranger communities have established links to the local power structure for self-protection. But many migrants, especially southerners, belong to no stranger community and establish their position as individuals within eclectic networks; ethnic "ghetto" communities of the type described by Mayer are unusual.[2]

Segregated housing and employment are the exception in Ghana. The *zongos* (areas set aside for stranger residence) still exist, but their population today is usually a mixture of aliens and northern Ghanaians of long residence who are traders or laborers.[3] The majority of migrants live elsewhere, sharing houses with the local population. The opportunity to assimilate is present, and most people accommodate to local customs, but the migrant who actually changes identification so that his

1. K. A. Busia, *A Social Survey of Sekondi-Takoradi* (London: Crown Agents, 1950), p. 73.

2. P. Mayer, *Townsmen or Tribesmen* (Cape Town: Oxford University Press, 1961).

3. See C. Dinan, "Socialization in an Accra Suburb: the Zongo and Its Distinct Sub-culture," in C. Oppong, ed., *Legon Family Research Papers No. 3: Changing Family Studies* (Legon: Institute of African Studies, University of Ghana, 1975), and E. Schildkrout, "Strangers and Local Government in Kumasi," *Journal of Modern African Studies*, vol. 8, no. 2 (1970), pp. 251-269.

new residence becomes "home" is rare indeed. He may speak the local language (this is less frequently the case in Accra, where the Ga are a minority and most migrants have enough education to communicate in English, than in smaller cities where a local language has more utility); he may have many friends from various groups including the hosts, and be indistinguishable in dress or behavior from others in the neighborhood; but there is almost always a reserve, an attitudinal and emotional distance which makes it clear that he remains at least partly a stranger. He shares many common features with residents, interacts frequently with them and has economic and social ties with them, but his deepest emotional attachments are reserved largely for his home town and his kinsmen. The widespread practice of sending money home, a strongly valued behavior even among migrants who find it difficult, is a material measure of the migrant's true allegiance.

The same lack of integration applies even more strongly to rural migrants from Upper Volta or northern Ghana. They have usually come for the cocoa harvest, and are guests for the season. Some have remained as farm caretakers or year-round laborers, but the food farms allotted them by their employers are for temporary tenure only, and almost all return after a few years to their own farms at home. It is, of course, harder to be assimilated into a small-scale farming community than into an urban neighborhood, so rural migrants tend to remain more fully strangers than urban migrants. This position is strengthened by their intention (and the local expectation) of a shorter residence.

Two Communities

Sojourners are most likely to be seen as such where their culture or their position in society differs most clearly from that of the local people. At the most general level, Ghanaian society is divided into two communities, northern and southern. Although Nkrumah placed considerable emphasis on being Ghanaian, the southerners' advantages in education and economic development, along with their greater access to political power, have magnified the cultural and environmental differences between north and south so that northerners who migrate to the south are as much outsiders as the aliens, and they generally share a low prestige in southern society. Prestige in Ghana is closely related to economic position, which is generally correlated with education. While there are some wealthy farmers and traders who are greatly admired within their local community, the most prestigious positions in the society as a whole are held by well-educated professionals, senior civil servants, and members of the government, almost all of whom belong to the southern community. Insofar as southerners look down on northerners (who may in turn look down on southerners), the role of stranger is reinforced whenever the migrant is out of his home territory; the gap is seen to be greater and assimilation is less acceptable to both host and migrant.

In the past, northern migrants have been largely guests, staying in the south for only a short time and interacting much less with the local people than southern migrants do. Northern migrants to the southern cities now tend to stay long enough to be classified as sojourners, but their interaction is still largely within the northern community. Most can readily be identified as strangers and few attempt to overcome this identification. Southerners in the north also tend to be guests. Because most of them are government personnel on transfer, they usually intend a short stay and fill roles which local residents see as usually filled by outsiders. The education and life style of southerners in the north give them a more prestigious position than that of northerners in the south, and their governmental employment makes it difficult to consider them truly "outsiders"—though few of them interact more than is necessary with the host community and most leave as soon as work in the south can be arranged. It is, for example, very difficult to attract or keep southern teachers in northern secondary schools. As the number of northerners qualified for these positions increases, southerners may come to be considered intruders—as has happened in northern Nigeria.

Immigrants belong to the northern or the southern community according to their religion, education, and cultural orientation. Aliens from along the coast (coming mainly from Togo and southern Nigeria, but including the Kru of Liberia and people from the southern Ivory Coast, Dahomey, Cameroun, and Sierra Leone) generally fit into the southern community if they are educated or Christian. Although only a minority of northern Ghanaians are Muslim, the northern community in the south is largely Muslim in ethos, and in the past its members have had little or no state education. It has been led by Hausa immigrants from northern Nigeria, whose long-term residents might be considered hosts in the southern *zongos*. For instance, they have acted as *maigida*, housing and servicing visiting traders.[4] The use of Hausa as a lingua franca by the northern community gives the Hausa a status not available to other foreigners. The Hausa built up their prestige by obtaining leadership roles over other strangers housed in the *zongos* and becoming their representatives to the local and colonial governments.[5] As the *zongo* communities grew and various groups chose their own headmen and through them established patronage links to local authorities, Hausa prestige has been limited to religious and linguistic dominance. Hausa pre-eminence in the northern community has been challenged by northern Ghanaians, notably in the longstanding dispute over who should be *imam* of the

4. P. Hill, "Landlords and Brokers: a West African Trading System," *Cahiers d'études africaines*, vol. 6, no. 23 (1966).

5. E. Schildkrout, "Strangers and Local Government in Kumasi."

Kumasi Central Mosque.[6] This nationalist dispute has coincided with the general development of less favorable attitudes toward aliens, to be described below.

The Hausa have also achieved considerable importance in northern towns. Though here they are more clearly outsiders, some are far closer to full membership than they could be in the majority community in the south. Immigrants from Upper Volta, Niger, and Mali also join the northern community in both areas, though these have usually stayed in Ghana for shorter periods and remain sojourners if they get beyond the guest stage. Migration as a result of wars and trading in the precolonial period, and the dry climate suitable for cereals and herds, give the northern savannah and Sahelian peoples many common forms. Islam provides a further tie in a strange place, so that migrants may practise it while they are strangers and drop it when they return home. The northern community, as found in southern towns, has been character-ized by Rouch as a "supertribe," though this level of unity was less evi-dent by the late 1960s.[7]

Coastal Ghanaians share myths of migration from the east, and a common environment has increased cultural similarities with other coastal peoples. A large measure of acceptance and integration seems to be characteristic of educated southern aliens (the few in clerical jobs or in the universities); these mix freely with Ghanaians of equal education. Further down the scale, coastal peoples are also less "strange" than illiter-ate northern Ghanaians. Thus, each community feels closer to some aliens than to others, even among groups with whom they share no ethnic heritage.

Some evidence of these community ties can be presented in data on shared housing in Tema and Ashaiman. Censuses were taken of all the residents of 572 randomly selected houses. In Tema, where houses are sublet from employers and limited space is available to the self-employed, there were three obvious divisions: coastal peoples, northern peoples, and Nigerians (excluding the few Ibo, who usually shared with coastal Ghanaians). The divisions in Ashaiman were not so clear, since people are free to live anywhere in the town and houses tend to be larger and more heterogeneous than in Tema. Nevertheless, it was possible to distinguish a tendency for coastal and northern peoples to live separately, with most of the Nigerians sharing housing with southern Ghanaians. The Songhai in Ashaiman were an interesting exception to this norm; in 1968 and in 1970, Songhai shared more often with southerners than with northerners. No explanation is yet available for this. It should also be

6. E. Schildkrout, *Islam and Politics in Kumasi: an Analysis of Disputes over the Kumasi Central Mosque*, Anthropological Papers of the American Museum of Natural History (New York), vol. 52, part 2, 1974.

7. J. Rouch, *Migration in the Gold Coast* (Accra, 1954); and E. Schildkrout, "Strangers and Local Government in Kumasi."

noted that in 1968, during the Nigerian civil war, the Ibo and Yoruba in Ashaiman were as closely associated with each other as with members of any other group.

While there are many factors aiding the assimilation of immigrants into either the northern or the southern community, their lack of education and their religion often set them somewhat apart, even from northerners. Aliens generally are less educated than the average Ghanaian of the same age, and they are more likely to be Muslim. Aliens born in Ghana are only somewhat less likely to attend school than citizens (this can be explained by their greater adherence to values of the northern than the southern community), but few of the foreign-origin population who were born abroad have any education.[8] This is because the countries from which they come are less developed educationally than Ghana, so that those who do obtain schooling tend to find sufficient employment opportunities without leaving their country. This lack of education hinders their integration into Ghanaian society in several ways.

First, most of them migrate to southern or central Ghana, where a majority of the children now attend school. Those who lack education are relegated to the bottom level of the society, and are considered fit only for the lowest jobs. Second, they have not learned English, and thus find it difficult to communicate with officials except through intermediaries. Misunderstandings inevitably occur, and the alien can be blamed for things which he does not understand. Third, participation in the school system would provide socialization into Ghanaian society for young immigrants, enabling them to "pass" if they desire to do so later, as well as to qualify for the same occupational roles as Ghanaians if they wish to move away from immigrant monopoly areas. Schildkrout reports that Muslim strangers resist sending their children to school, not only because they fear Christian influence (this reason has been often given in northern Nigeria), but also because they think the Kumasi school system will make their children "become Ashanti."[9] If the strangers should decide that their future can only be secured through integration, the schools might be seen as performing a useful function. So far, however, they have preferred to remain sojourners.

Religion is also an important differentiating factor between Ghanaians and immigrants. According to the 1960 census, 42 percent of the Ghanaian population were Christian, 12 percent were Muslim, 38 percent followed a traditional religion, and 7 percent had no religion at all. The proportion of Muslims is somewhat higher and there are more followers of traditional religions among northern Ghanaians than among southerners, but in no Ghanaian group are more than a quarter of the

8. N. O. Addo, "Assimilation and Absorption of African Immigrants in Ghana," *Ghana Journal of Sociology*, vol. 3 (1967), pp. 17–32.

9. E. Schildkrout, "Strangers and Local Government in Kumasi," p. 267.

adults Muslims. By comparison, 61 percent of the Yoruba and over 90 percent of the Hausa, Fulani, Kokokoli, Mande, and Songhai are Muslim. This clearly sets them apart from local people, since Muslim habits of prayer, marital customs, scholarship, and so on tend to integrate Muslims into their own community, and to separate them from non-believers. Because few Muslims in Ghana have been educationally qualified for good jobs and because so many are aliens, their prestige among the general population is low. Many of the Yoruba Christians are also isolated because they belong to the Baptist church, which has few Ghanaian adherents.

The cosmopolitan acceptance of outsiders in Ghanaian society over a long period has meant generally favorable attitudes toward guests and sojourners, with the occasional assimilation of those who wanted to stay permanently. The hosts have been willing to take strangers on their own terms, and the maintenance of stranger status has been due to the reluctance of migrants to commit themselves more fully to the host society, largely because the dual role was more profitable to them. Most migration is for economic reasons, and the migrant who cannot cover his costs (which is almost inevitable in old age) is considered better off at home. Lack of segregation in housing and jobs, and the presence of ethnically open northern and southern communities in which they could find a place, ensured a generally easy entrance of strangers into the host society. The next section deals with the change in public opinion whereby relations between hosts and aliens became antagonistic, so that sojourners and guests who were redefined as aliens were expelled from the country. The incompleteness of this expulsion is a measure of the integration achieved by many immigrants and the unwillingness of many in the host society to make this redefinition, at least in regard to individuals they know personally.

From Sojourners to Aliens

The word "alien" was not in common use in Ghana until the promulgation of the Compliance Order in November 1969, which gave all non-citizens two weeks in which to obtain residence and work permits or leave the country. Before this time, foreign Africans had been referred to as Wangara, Mossi, Lagosians (though only a small proportion of the Yoruba actually came from Lagos), Ewe (who could come from either side of the international border), and so on. Europeans (including Americans), Asians, and Lebanese (including Syrians) were collectively called expatriates; these will be excluded from further discussion, leaving the word "alien" as a collective noun applying to African residents of Ghana who are not citizens. In present Ghanaian usage, the word "alien" has a pejorative connotation suitable for stereotyping and scapegoating. It is applied to people one does not know or like; a friend is seldom perceived as an outsider to the society. Thus, the "inner enemy" is an alien, but one's workmate or co-tenant, a sojourner like oneself, is an Ibo or a Malian.

Although there were occasional incidents, especially when immigrants became politically active (in a sense stepping out of their sojourner role and trying to act as members), the attitude of the Ghanaian host community toward immigrants has been generally benevolent or at least tolerant. Expelled Nigerians often speak of the friendliness of the Ghanaian people, and their regret at having to leave is not based solely on economic loss. Caldwell reports that half of the immigrants from Togo and Nigeria in his sample thought they were liked by Ghanaians; fewer than expected thought that their success in getting jobs was envied by the local people.[10] Very few of the respondents interviewed in Ashaiman six months after the expulsions were sharply critical of aliens or engaged in ethnic stereotyping. About half claimed to have known aliens well (they had formerly constituted about a fifth of the town's population), and a majority of those who had had alien co-tenants said they were easy to get along with.

Factors of Change

The change of attitude has been far greater at the community or societal level, where relationships are categoric, than at the personal level, with its stress on particularism. The chief factors in the change appear to be economic and, to a lesser extent, political. While the country was prospering and there was work for all, additions to the work force were welcomed. Caldwell's 1963 survey of economically superior areas in four cities found a fairly even division between those favoring an increase in the proportion of immigrants and those who thought there were already too many for the economic opportunities available.[11] Foreigners often moved into the least desirable occupations and expended considerable energy supporting themselves during formal unemployment, whereas local people found it easier to get support from kinsmen or return home to the farm until conditions improved. This meant that aliens interested in wage employment tried harder to find jobs and were more committed to keeping them than the local people. The job stability of alien factory workers compares favorably with that of local workers, even though they were usually in laboring jobs which generally have the highest turnover.[12] The aliens' hard work did nothing to raise their pres-

10. J. C. Caldwell, "Migration and Urbanization," in W. Birmingham et al., eds., A Study of Contemporary Ghana: Some Aspects of Social Structure (London: George Allen and Unwin Ltd., 1967), p. 110.

11. Ibid. p. 119.

12. M. Peil, The Ghanaian Factory Worker (Cambridge: Cambridge University Press, 1972), p. 101.

tige in Ghanaian eyes, but the success it sometimes brought was accorded a rather grudging admiration.

Three-fourths of the male respondents interviewed in Ashaiman in 1970 had worked with aliens at some time. Half of these found no difference between foreign and Ghanaian workers, and the rest were divided evenly between those who thought aliens worked harder and those who favored local workers. Caldwell's evidence indicates that Nigerians and Togolese are convinced that they work harder than Ghanaians.[13] Given the easygoing nature of southern Ghanaians, this may be a valid comparison within the coastal community. However, the aliens had an additional motivation for hard work, because they were far from home and had only limited local sources of aid.

But as the economy stagnated, school leavers (who completed primary and middle schooling) could not find employment, and as the cocoa price fell local people began to feel that the competition from outsiders was unfair and should be restricted if not stopped. As cocoa farming became less profitable and the average age of the farmers increased, enthusiasm for opening up new lands declined and less labor was needed in cocoa areas; more of this labor than formerly could be supplied by local school leavers and migrant northern Ghanaians. At the same time, Ghanaian businessmen felt that their greatest competition came not from the multinational corporations, but from the small trading and manufacturing firms of Lebanese, Indians, and Nigerians, and they sought to change the balance in favor of themselves. The Ghana Business (Promotion) Act of 1970 made it impossible for most of these small-scale entrepreneurs to operate; Nigeria took similar action in 1974. Thus, the late 1960s were a time when the contribution of aliens to the Ghanaian economy was questioned as it had never been before.

Changes on the political front affected the position of aliens over a longer period. These have been discussed at length by Skinner, Schildkrout, and Peil, and need only be summarized here.[14] Aliens in Ghana had generally kept on the right side of both colonial and local officials (if the latter had any real power), but they got into trouble at independence because citizenship suddenly became an important issue. They had considered themselves members of a recognized (northern or southern) community, but they now found themselves defined as outsiders (a potential if not actual inner enemy) and sometimes deported for taking too great an interest in local affairs—their assimilation in this field was unwelcome. In response to the new situation, they began to segregate themselves

13. Caldwell, "Migration and Urbanization," p. 120.

14. E. P. Skinner, "Strangers in West African Societies," *Africa*, vol. 23, no. 4 (1963), pp. 307–320; Schildkrout, "Strangers and Local Government in Kumasi"; M. Peil, "The Expulsion of West Afican Aliens," *Journal of Modern African Studies*, vol. 9, no. 2 (1971), pp. 205–229.

somewhat more than formerly, trying to abstain from participation in activities which could be construed as political. However, as members of a highly politicized society where casual arguments could take on political implications, this was not always easy to do. The Convention Peoples Party government appointed and deposed headmen of various groups and made other regulations to which the strangers were supposed to conform. (The Compliance Order merely enforced a registration requirement of the Aliens Act of 1963.) Politics in the alien community sometimes went underground, but it continued.

The military coup of 1966 brought some relief; various groups regained the right to select their own headmen and were given more freedom to develop patronage relationships with local authorities without being accused of political activity. But there was inevitably conflict between those who had supported and those who had opposed Nkrumah, which demonstrated to the Ghanaian public that aliens could not live in the country and remain politically neutral. The return of politics under the Busia government posed many of the same problems as the previous civilian government, but the stagnation of the economy produced an additional handicap; the government needed a scapegoat for its troubles. The honeymoon following the election was short; corruption reappeared and dissatisfaction began to spread. The government hoped that it could silence its critics by blaming all the country's ills on its alien residents—they were said to be responsible for crime, inflation, the lack of jobs, the shortage of social services, and so on.

The Results of Expulsion

Unfortunately, extensive or long-term studies of the effects of the Compliance Order are not yet available. It is generally agreed that well over 100,000 people left the country within a short period, in conditions which it would be hard to describe as humane. Some I met in Nigeria over a year later were still unemployed. But many aliens returned after a short time or did not leave at all, passing as Ghanaian or hiding until the furor died down. It is a measure of the position of the two communities in Ghana that aliens could successfully pass as southerners but that some northern Ghanaians were forced to prove that they were not aliens—which was not always easy, because only Europeans had identity papers. A few of those who were deported were second- or third-generation Ghanaian residents who no longer knew where their "homes" were; some of these returned clandestinely to Ghana and tried not to get caught again.

Generally, the greatest pressure to leave was exerted on traders, mostly Nigerians, who were found in most markets and hawked their wares in villages throughout the country. Alien male traders often had sections of the market to themselves (because they traded in different commodities than the women who dominated the markets), or they wandered from place to place, and so they did not get to know traders outside their own group. Being men in what is a women's occupation in Ghana also helped them maintain separation. Their wives also traded, making closer contacts with local women than the male traders did. They were often competing more directly with local women, but they got to know them through sharing the same sources of supply and sitting all day in the markets together. It is notable that the uprising in Kumasi market in 1953 was against Gao men controlling the yam market.[15] Alien women traders continued to work peacefully with their Ghanaian colleagues for over fifteen more years.

Ghanaians objected at least as much to the alien traders' isolation as to their economic success (though the success was often seen by villagers as being achieved at their expense). The Yoruba, who were the most heavily engaged in trading, usually maintained subgroup endogamy, as they do in Nigeria. This was facilitated by the division of Ghana into spheres of influence, so that immigrants from certain towns and villages in Nigeria were concentrated in certain Ghanaian towns.[16] There were also many Hausa traders, and they had a near monopoly on butchering in the urban markets of the south. (In 1960, 59 percent of the country's butchers were aliens, mostly Nigerians.) They are freer to marry interethnically than the Yoruba, since religion rather than ethnicity is their criterion of endogamy. But their prestigious social position within the northern community set them somewhat apart and increased the envy of the northern Ghanaian butchers, who were largely excluded from southern markets.

Comments by Ashaiman respondents reflect the type of personality which leads to success in trading (Simmel's prototypical stranger): "Immediately they get a few cedis they go into retail trade—and they prosper too." "They are impatient with buyers, arrogant and difficult to come to terms with." In a society where trading is a social as well as an economic activity, and where credit is a recognition of personal bonds between buyer and seller, these traders are seen as not conforming to societal norms and stubbornly maintaining their social distance. This separation is reinforced by distinctive dress and by not making friends with local people: "They are unfriendly and do not help friends when they are in financial difficulty." "They are thrifty and clannish." "They don't seem to trust Ghanaians and confide in them." Since Ghanaians are generally very friendly, this unwillingness to mix socially emphasizes the role of stranger more strongly than differences of language, religion, or culture.

15. Skinner, "Strangers in West African Societies," p. 312.
16. M. Hundsalz, "Die Wanderung Der Yoruba Nach Ghana und Ihre Ruckkehr Nach Nigeria," *Erdkunde* (Bonn), Band 26 (1972), pp. 218-230.

At the other extreme, it was more difficult to redefine as "inner ene-mies" those peoples whose lands straddle Ghana's international bound-aries. They often move from place to place for farming or schooling without much regard for formal boundaries. Some hold dual citizenship, and most have regarded themselves as belonging primarily to a people (Ewe, Busanga, Lobi) rather than to a country. Only in situations of po-litical conflict between the hetero-national group and neighboring ethnic groups does the question of being outsiders arise. For example, Lobi have been moving back and forth across the border between the Ivory Coast and Ghana for three generations. In recent years, the local Gonja hosts have become aware that more and more of the farmland they have neglected has been appropriated by Lobi cash crop farmers, and that the increase in Lobi residents in Bole (the local market town) is threatening to turn the Gonja into a minority of voters. They have tried taking legal action, claiming that Lobi are Ivoriens, not Ghanaians; but this is very difficult to prove where births are not officially registered and the cri-terion of citizenship is belonging to "any tribe or region comprising Ghana."[17]

The Ewe people of the Ghana-Togo border area have not faced the same difficulty as the Lobi because there has been no other ethnic group to contest land ownership. There is considerable movement across the border to visit kinsmen and for schooling, farming, and trading (legal and illegal), even when the border is officially closed. With few jobs available at home, the Togolese Ewe have profited from dual nationality and considered themselves as much a part of the Ghanaian community as the local migrants. Many of the thousands who left following the Com-pliance Order soon returned, but they are now far more aware of their position as strangers. Nationality took on a new meaning, with respon-dents carefully specifying that they were Togolese rather than merely saying they were Ewe. Others, who felt less secure, claimed to be Ghanaian Ewe or even identified themselves with the neighboring Adangbe to avoid being asked which branch of the Ewe they belonged to.

Those who were in wage employment usually found it easier to stay on than the majority who were self-employed or farm laborers.[18] Large-scale employers often obtained the necessary papers for their alien employees. However, some of the employees later chose to leave the country voluntarily. As one of them put it, "It is better to go now, when arrangements can be made, than to be suddenly thrown out without warning at some future date."

Although most aliens had in the past planned to retire to their homes, quite a few never got around to leaving. Aliens were relatively

17. *Ghanaian Times*, December 4, 1969.
18. Farm laborers sometimes work for wages and sometimes for a share of the crop.

well-represented among the elderly population in several towns, serving as leaders of their groups and helping new migrants get started. Quite a few aliens in their fifties or sixties who had been working for a long time in Ghana remained because they were sufficiently integrated into the community so that they were under no pressure to leave. They had changed in self- and host-community identification from sojourner to member, insofar as this is possible without blood ties. Some were farm workers or caretakers; others were farming on their own or were former wage-workers or traders who chose to retire in Ghana. Finnegan reports that none of the Voltaics in the village he studied who had spent "thirty years" in Ghana had gone home; the recent immigrants (under fifteen years) had been expelled, though not all of them had returned to their village.[19]

Men of the next generation (in their thirties and forties) have been shown that they cannot depend on a stable situation and had better make serious plans for an eventual return home. Although the present military government has again made it easier for aliens to enter Ghana, there is no guarantee that a future civilian government will not reverse this policy. From being relatively integrated sojourners, they have moved toward the guest end of the continuum.

Respondents in Ashaiman were asked two questions about the change they had observed over the eight months since the Compliance Order: "Do you think things in Ghana are just the same, now that many aliens have left?" and "Do you think Ashaiman is just the same, now that so many aliens have left?" More persons were able to comment on local than on national changes. Over half (56 percent) had noted no particular change for the country and 30 percent saw no change in Ashaiman. Some of these said that many aliens were still resident and things wouldn't change until they also left. About a fifth (22 percent) mentioned that Ghanaians could participate more freely in trade, or that there were now more job openings for local people. Ten percent and 17 percent respectively thought that the markets in Ashaiman and in the country as a whole had been affected; 13 percent felt that crime had decreased nationally, but 49 percent had perceived a local decline.

There were three theories about how the departure of aliens would affect the job situation: it might help (since jobs vacated by aliens could be filled by Ghanaians), hinder (since many small alien businesses hired Ghanaian workers), or make no difference (since employers could arrange for alien workers to get work permits and therefore they wouldn't leave). While it seems likely that the first theory was right over the long term, if not right away, there is very little evidence one way or the other. There were immediate gaps in what had formerly been alien

19. G. A. Finnegan, "Mossi Social Fields." Paper presented at fifteenth annual meeting of the African Studies Association, Toronto, Canada, 1972.

monopolies (such as collecting used bottles), which were filled fairly quickly (in this case, by Ghanaian women). Smuggling proved to be much less exclusively an alien preserve than the government had publicly assumed. Generally, few aliens held white collar jobs, and the better paying the employment the more likely the alien was to remain in the country. Thus, it seems unlikely that many "good" jobs were vacated. Nevertheless, opportunities for those willing to accept employment of any kind did improve, at least temporarily. This is most easily demonstrated from the data by Addo on employment of farm laborers.[20]

Before the Compliance Order, nearly half the employees on cocoa farms were foreigners. Although the Order was amended early in 1970 to exempt farm workers, the proportion of aliens on Brong/Ahafo cocoa farms had dropped in 8–11 months to 26 percent, and about a third of the Ghanaian employees had been hired during that period. About half of the new Ghanaian employees were northerners and a quarter were from the locality. This indicates that the really large-scale beneficiaries of the exodus were young men willing to work on cocoa farms, especially illiterates from the north, who took over from the Voltaics. These two groups contributed 34 percent and 14 percent respectively of the workers in Addo's sample; in 1960, 43 percent of farm workers in Ghana were from Upper Volta.

The Ghanaian recruits are still largely illiterate; there is as yet little evidence of interest in this work on the part of school leavers. Those who must take it up temporarily usually escape by the time they are twenty. The pay is not notably low considering subsistence costs, but the work is hard and there are no opportunities for advancement. Insofar as middle school leavers become farmers, they more often do so by inheriting a farm after a period of urban employment. Aliens' children have in the past shown the same tendency as rural Ghanaian youths to migrate to town if they get schooling.[21] Newly recruited aliens and local farm workers in Addo's 1970 sample both averaged 34 years of age, an indication that this job no longer appeals to young men and that the alien exodus from the farms had little effect on the unemployment rate for young men, which is certainly far more serious than that for men in their thirties.

Four-fifths of the alien married employees on cocoa farms had their wives and children with them, an indication that they planned a longer stay than was characteristic in the past. Aliens were more likely than Ghanaian employees to live in the farm hamlet, whereas Ghanaian employees more often lived in the village and even in the compound of their employer. If this is general throughout the cocoa area, it would also

20. N. O. Addo, *Migration and Economic Change in Ghana*, Vol. I. (Legon: Demographic Unit, Department of Sociology, University of Ghana, 1971).
21. Addo, "Assimilation and Absorption."

mean that aliens have been fairly isolated socially, with limited opportunities for socializing with Ghanaians other than their employer and his family, or with other aliens (the farmers in Addo's study employed an average of less than three workers each).

The new opportunities in the towns have probably allowed Ghanaians more scope for self-employment, especially in trade, but created few vacancies in wage employment. Newspaper publicity about reallocating vacated stalls in urban markets made people more aware of this result nationally than they might have been locally. However, in 1970 there were local men trading from kiosks and tables in Ashaiman where in the past male traders had been aliens. One Ga who had purchased a kiosk business was pleased with his success, but felt somewhat guilty about it. In a sense, aliens had established the possibility of men trading, and their departure provided an opportunity for Ghanaian men to take it up. (Southern men, especially Kwahu and Asante, had operated small stores in the past, but petty trading was left to women and aliens.)

It is difficult to assess the effect of the Compliance Order on the availability and price of goods, and relatively few people connected the two. Immediately after the exodus there was a shortage of transport in Ghana, since the best way to get a substantial sum of money out of the country was to buy a lorry, fill it with immigrants going home and drive it across the border. This shortage seems to have been rectified over the following six months, since by summer there were no more public complaints than usual about the shortage of vehicles. Comments on changes in the availability and price of goods were often complaints about inflation. Newcomers to trade could not immediately reproduce the aliens' supply lines (which were not always legal), so some items disappeared from the markets. The prices of other items soared because of profiteering by Ghanaians determined to make the most of new opportunities. Some petty traders complained that their sales were lower because so many of their customers had left and too many Ghanaian women had thought it a good time to go into business.

Much of the government's propaganda effort at the time of the Compliance Order concerned alien involvement in crime, prostitution, and smuggling. It was claimed that almost all the nation's criminals, in and out of prison, were foreigners. Statistics disprove this. The alien community was at least as law-abiding as the local people, but the government obviously thought that their best ideological line of attack lay in implying that these outsiders, who maintain their distance from us, are preying on us. The extensive propaganda effort was successful in the sense that many people came to accept the truth of the allegations. Thirteen percent of the respondents said that the alien departures had lowered the Ghanaian crime rate (for which the newspapers, in spite of considerable interest in the matter, could provide no evidence), and half of them thought that Ashaiman was a safer place than it had been.

There is some truth in this last assessment, but it would be difficult to prove that the departure of aliens was solely responsible. When first studied in 1968, Ashaiman was well known as a hideout for thieves of varying origin operating in the Tema area; most people stayed at home in the evening to protect their belongings. Although there were many complaints about thieves at that time, nothing was said about their nationality, and there was evidence that the police post was inefficient. In the next two years, serious efforts were made to round up thieves in the area and the police service was improved considerably. Thus many thieves probably moved to safer quarters and others, especially aliens, were in hiding and relatively inactive. The result was a more peaceful community.

Nevertheless, it was surprising to find that respondents who claimed to have known aliens well most often said that there was now less crime in Ashaiman. There was no difference in this tendency between those who were generally favorable to aliens and those who disliked them, and the relationship was consistent over several questions involving different types of contact. The only explanation which can be given is that the alien element in Ashaiman was much less law-abiding than the foreign community as a whole, and that some of the aliens these respondents knew had been thieves or con men. The normality of such behavior in a community like Ashaiman can be seen from Hart's discussion of various ways of supporting oneself in Nima, a low-income area in Accra.[22] Citizens in similar economic circumstances are as involved in such activities as aliens, but it aids national self-esteem to believe that only "strangers" participate. (Hart was mainly studying the Frafra, who form a large proportion of the northern community in Accra.) If one considers northerners as well as aliens to be "strangers," the stereotype fits even better.

There were many more aliens than northern Ghanaians in Ashaiman, giving it something of the appearance of a foreign enclave (especially to officials who had no idea of the real proportion of aliens to local population). One respondent hoped that the aliens' departure would give Ashaiman a new image and thus strengthen the drive to get improved amenities for the town. As he put it, "The town's development would now be a concern of the government, since they know it's her nationals in it." From his point of view, the citizen sojourners had become members, and should no longer be treated as strangers. In response to strong pressure from local residents, the development of Ashaiman was taken seriously by the government in 1970, though this had

22. K. Hart, "Informal Income Opportunities and Urban Employment in Ghana," *Journal of Modern African Studies*, vol. 11, no. 1 (1973), pp. 61–89.

little to do with the proportion of aliens in residence because no statistics were available to the authorities.

Like other comments mentioned earlier, this one demonstrates a tendency to use aliens as a convenient explanation for anything wrong in the society, a tendency encouraged by the Busia government and difficult to resist by those who had no opportunity to get to know aliens well. It is to the credit of Ghanaians with alien workmates or co-tenants that they were usually unwilling to make blanket statements when they had something unfavorable to say, but were willing to suggest that their experience might have been exceptional. Ghanaians generally have more tolerance of strangers than citizens of many other countries, perhaps because so many Ghanaians are or have been strangers themselves.

Conclusion

The Ghanaian host community, north and south, urban and rural, has usually been friendly in its acceptance of strangers. These have mostly come as guests or sojourners, with the proportion of the latter increasing in recent years. The emphasis on blood ties to the ancestors has made full incorporation in the host community difficult, but there have always been mechanisms for the assimilation of strangers who chose to become members. Migrants have usually preferred the role of stranger—living in the community but not of it.

The large number of strangers who can be accommodated by a secure host community may be seen as potential or actual inner enemies by a less secure community. The insecurity may be political (to maintain our independence we must be able to make our own decisions), economic (if jobs are short, local youths should be given first chance), or social (the maintenance of our local language and culture and the quality of life in our cities depends on decreasing the influence of outsiders). Persons or groups who are categorized as strangers because they keep themselves apart lay themselves open to the suspicions of their hosts. It is not at all surprising that the transition to independence should produce this insecurity and subsequent action against those who are in any sense strangers, or that the strongest reaction should be against those who hold themselves apart from the new national entity.

The shift from a friendly to an antagonistic attitude is also stimulated by checks in the development process, and by the combined inflation and stagnation which plagues nations throughout the world. (Is it Britain's economic position rather than the number of Commonwealth immigrants which makes the National Front so popular?) Immigrants are generally at the bottom of the social and economic structure, so in good times they fill roles the hosts do not want; in bad times, these roles assume a new significance.

But attacks on aliens can rebound by threatening the security of minority groups who have migrated in search of greater opportunity.

They, too, are strangers, and attachment to nation is less important for most citizens than attachment to one's locality. Thus, government backing for discrimination against aliens may diminish a people's feeling of national unity. In the aftermath of the Compliance Order, Ghanaian citizens became more aware of national identity than they had been in the past, but their awareness of ethnic differences also increased.

The results of the expulsion of alien strangers from Ghana appear to have been more ideological than economic. The method used did not redound to the government's credit or increase public confidence in it, and any economic effect was inevitably confounded by the world commodity markets, which are far more important to Ghana's economic health than the contribution or withdrawal of a hundred thousand aliens.

8

From Stranger to Alien: The Socio-Political History of the Nigerian Yoruba in Ghana 1900-1970

Niara Sudarkasa

On November 19, 1969, the Ghanaian Ministry of Information, on behalf of the Ministry of Interior, issued this statement:

> It has come to the notice of the Government that several aliens, both Africans and non-Africans in Ghana, do not possess the requisite residence permits in conformity with the laws of Ghana.
>
> There are others, too, who are engaging in business of all kinds contrary to the term of their visiting permits.
>
> The Government has accordingly directed that all aliens in the first category, that is those without residence permits, should leave Ghana within fourteen days, that is not later than December 2, 1969.
>
> Those in the second category should obey strictly the term of their entry permits, and if these have expired they should leave Ghana forthwith.
>
> The Ministry of Interior has been directed to comb the country thoroughly for defaulting aliens, and aliens arrested for contravening these orders will be dealt with according to the law.[1]

The initial research on which this paper is based was carried out in Ghana by the writer (then Gloria A. Marshall) between June 1968 and June 1969, and in December 1969 and January 1970, with the financial aid of the Center for Research on Economic Development of the University of Michigan and a Faculty Research Grant by the University of Michigan's Rackham School of Graduate Studies. Supplementary research was conducted in Nigeria and Ghana in collaboration with Rasaba Delmer Sudarkasa from September 1973 to September 1974. The Joint Committee on African Studies of the Social Science Research Council and the Middle East and Africa Field Research Fellowship Program of the Ford Foundation provided partial funding for this research. Acknowledgement must also be given to the Nigerian Institute of Social and Economic Research, with which I was affiliated as a Research Associate in 1973-1974.

1. Quoted in *The Pioneer* (newspaper), Kumasi, November 19, 1969.

141

With the issuance of what an editorial in *The Pioneer* of November 20 termed this "simple announcement," the government of Prime Minister Dr. K. A. Busia, leader of the recently elected Progress Party, triggered a chain of events that culminated in the expulsion from Ghana of hundreds of thousands of "aliens," almost all of whom were Africans.

According to newspaper reports, commentaries, letters to the editor, and editorials, the Ghanaian populace was of the opinion that the expulsion of the non-Ghanaians was long overdue. It does not seem an overstatement to say that the expulsion of the *African* "aliens," toward whom virtually all the unleashed aggression was directed, was heralded as a panacea for the amelioration of the economic plight of the "ordinary Ghanaian citizen." Foremost among the accomplishments envisioned by the expulsion of the "alien" Africans was the demise of "foreign dominance of [Ghanaian] commercial activity," and a resultant opening up of employment opportunities for hitherto unemployed or underemployed Ghanaians.[2] The anti-alien sentiment in the country was at such a pitch that ships and market stalls were looted, many people were physically assaulted, and lives were threatened.[3]

By all accounts, the prime targets among the foreigners thought to "dominate" retail market trade in Ghana were the Nigerians, in particular the southern Nigerians, of whom the Yoruba were the most numerous,[4] the most widely dispersed throughout Ghana, and the most easily identified because of their mode of dress and, in many cases, because of their facial "tribal marks." Moreover, they were easy targets in many cities and towns because of their tendency toward concentration in specific residential areas and in specific areas within the major daily markets.

The clamor for the expulsion of Nigerian traders, coupled with the fact that most of them did not possess the required permits, led to the exodus of thousands of southern Nigerians from Ghana in late Novem-

2. J. Oppong-Agyare, "Test Case of Credibility," *The Pioneer*, November 28, 1969.

3. See, for example, "Police Save Aliens from Molestation," *The Pioneer*, November 24, 1969; and "Don't Molest Aliens, Gov't Warns," *Daily Graphic* (Accra), November 25, 1969. For additional data on the ouster of Africans from Ghana, see M. Piel, "The Expulsion of West African Aliens," *Journal of Modern African Studies*, vol. 9, no. 2 (1971), pp. 205–229; and "Ghana's Other Africans," *West Africa* (December 20, 1969), p. 1.

4. In Ghana, the term "Nigerian" usually referred to a person of Yoruba origin. Hausas and Ibos, who made up the other two large Nigerian stranger populations, were usually referred to by their ethnic group designations. Although figures are not available on the size of the various Nigerian populations in Ghana in 1969, the population figures from the 1960 Census are: Yoruba, 100,560; Hausa, 61,730; Ibo (Igbo), 14,050; other southern Nigerians, 24,350. (Figures are not available for Northern Nigerian groups other than the Hausa.) Although all these groups are predominantly of Nigerian origin, approximately 39 percent of the Yoruba and 53 percent of the Hausa populations were born in Ghana. (Statistics taken from *Special Report "E": Tribes in Ghana*, by B. Gil, A. F. Aryee, and D. K. Ghansah, 1960 Population Census of Ghana, Census Office, Accra, 1964, Tables 1, 5, and 8).

ber and in December of 1969.[5] The Hausa of Northern Nigeria were less harassed, apparently because they were thought to hold fewer strategic positions in the commercial sector of the Ghanaian economy, and also because they were not easily distinguishable from (and, reportedly, successfully "passed for") Northern Ghanaians.

This essay deals with the socio-political history of the largest Nigerian ethnic group in Ghana at the time of the Compliance Order—namely the Yoruba, who migrated to Ghana from various parts of Nigeria. I begin by tracing the changing relationship of the Yoruba community in Kumasi to the Ashanti host population and to other strangers in the Kumasi Zongo, in which the Yoruba first settled.[6] I then examine some of the political developments that paved the way for the expulsion of the Yoruba and other African "aliens" from Ghana, and conclude with a discussion of the implications of the Yoruba sojourn in Ghana for the study of stranger-host relations in contemporary West Africa.

The Yoruba as a
Stranger Community in Ghana

To the layman, and to scholars unfamiliar with the technical usages which sociologists, beginning with Georg Simmel, have attached to the concept of "stranger," the application of this label to *African* populations living on the African continent might require some explanation. From the perspective of the second half of the twentieth century, the label of "stranger" might seem much more appropriately applied to the foreigners from outside the African continent, whose intrusions onto that continent culminated in the establishment of colonial rule. The term "stranger" might also seem appropriate to those non-Africans whose entry into the continent was facilitated by the fact of colonial rule. In any case, because the technical concept of the "stranger" has been used by some scholars in reference to these non-African populations, it should be explained why the same concept has also been used to describe *African* populations who live and work in areas that are not considered to be their "indigenous homelands."

The concept of the "stranger" is ultimately derived from two basic facts of human social existence: the fact of group differences, and the fact of individual and group mobility. In Africa, as in other parts of the

5. Estimates of the actual number of Nigerian deportees ranged from about 100,000 to 500,000. It seems a conservative estimate to say that at least 200,000 persons of Nigerian origin left Ghana within a few months after the Government's aliens Compliance Order. For a fuller discussion of the impact of this Order on the Nigerian population in Ghana, see N. Sudarkasa, "Commercial Migration in West Africa, with Special Reference to the Yoruba in Ghana," *African Urban Notes*, Series B, No. 1, (1974–1975), especially pp. 95–98.

6. For an overview of the economic activities of the Yoruba in Ghana between 1900 and 1970, see N. Sudarkasa, "The Economic Status of the Yoruba in Ghana Before 1970," *Nigerian Journal of Economic and Social Studies*, vol. 17, no. 1 (1975).

world, past and present, various cultural and linguistic factors and social interactional codes have combined to delineate different groups. The groups so delineated were of the scale of entities we term "societies," or they were subdivisions of these societies. The fact of population mobility in precolonial as well as present-day Africa has meant that various peoples have come into sustained or sporadic contact with persons or groups who were "outsiders"—that is, members of different societies or different communities.

It was Elliott P. Skinner who first applied Simmel's concept of the "stranger" to one such set of "outsiders"—the African populations which have "moved out of their homelands and . . . established relatively long-term residence in the territories of other groups."[7] Without accepting the applicability of all of Simmel's formulations to the West African context, Skinner did show that the West African "strangers," like Simmel's prototype, were "mobile" and "opportunistic in that [they] profited from the relationship with [their] hosts, especially in trade and finance."[8]

Skinner's discussion of the politics of the relationship between the host societies and the communities of outsiders in their midst showed the relevance to the West African context of another of Simmel's postulates concerning stranger-host relations—namely, that of "distance." In the words of Donald Levine (Chapter One), this refers to "a distinctive blend of closeness and remoteness: the stranger's position *within* a given spatial circle is fundamentally affected by the fact that he brings qualities into it that are derived from the *outside*."

According to Levine, Simmel used the concept of distance—that is, simultaneous closeness and remoteness—in reference to three different aspects of the stranger-host relationship: (1) the nearness and distance which characterize interaction between the stranger and the host; (2) the simultaneous "involvement" and "indifference" which characterize the stranger's emotional attachment to the host; and (3) the similarity and difference manifest in the social and cultural attributes of the stranger and the host. Although Skinner himself did not use the distance concept, his work showed that at least some of the problems which characterize the relationship of West African strangers to their hosts arose because the strangers were close at hand and at the same time attempting to maintain a detachment from the host community.

If Skinner's work demonstrated the utility of using the stranger concept to analyze certain situations of ethnic group interaction in Africa, it also raised the question whether it is appropriate to use this concept in analyzing the relationship between the Europeans who settled in Africa and the African populations they met there. Skinner himself has solved

7. E. P. Skinner, "Strangers in West African Societies," *Africa*, vol. 33, no. 4 (1963), pp. 307–320.
8. *Ibid.*, p. 307.

this problem by developing the concept of the estranger. He points out that because of their political power, Europeans in Africa and elsewhere in the colonial world had the

> facility of *estranging* autochthonous peoples and transforming them into aliens, and of turning foreigners into "people of the soil".
> . . . The Europeans who went to South Africa called themselves Afrikaners [while they] exterminated, absorbed, or herded many of the indigenous populations into reserves and transformed them into *natives*. . . . The conquerors insisted the conquered territory was "their country" . . . Europeans called Kenya "white man's country," and those in Matabeleland and Shonaland renamed it Rhodesia.
>
> Because they assumed complete military, economic, social, cultural, and psychological control over the indigenous populations, the conquering aliens or foreigners should never be considered "strangers." They could be considered "*estrangers*." They had the ability to determine who the natives were and could treat the indigenous people as "aliens" if they so desired.[9]

The concept of the stranger as defined by Simmel and refined by Levine, and that of the *estranger* as developed by Skinner, provide a very useful framework within which to analyze the changing relationship of the Yoruba in Ghana to the local African populations, to other stranger groups, and to the European *estrangers*, whose presence was a key factor in determining the relationship between the African hosts and strangers.

Before 1900, the only major Yoruba settlement in what would become Ghana was located in Salaga, a Gonja town which, like all other precolonial international (inter-ethnic) and inter-regional trading centers in West Africa, had an area (called the Zongo) on the outskirts of the town set aside for the residence of its stranger population. As was normally the case in precolonial West African cities, virtually all the strangers in Salaga were either circulatory migrants or settled migrants (whom Levine would term "sojourners") who were involved in commerce. Indeed, the only other types of strangers who appear to have lived for any length of time outside their home communities in precolonial West Africa were foreign wives, enslaved captives (both of whom usually became absorbed into the host society), and foreign ruling groups who moved into an area to "conquer" it or otherwise establish political hegemony over it. (These foreign rulers, too, often became assimilated into the indigenous population of the area.)[10]

9. E. P. Skinner, "Theoretical Perspectives on the Stranger," 1974, pp. 8–9.

10. It is important to note that even when these "conquerors" did not assimilate, or become assimilated into, the indigenous population, they did not play the role of *estrangers* as did the Europeans. The indigenous populations were not converted into aliens in their own land.

The political rights of strangers in Salaga, like those of strangers in other precolonial towns in West Africa, derived from the rulers of the town. The various stranger communities in Salaga had their own chiefs and community leaders who were responsible for maintaining order among their respective populations, and through whom official communication with the authorities in Salaga was maintained. The strangers were allowed to oversee their own internal affairs, and only when there was real or threatened conflict with the local populations did the strangers call upon the Chief of Salaga to intervene.[11]

These commercial migrants were allowed to reside in the area because of the importance of their role as intermediaries who facilitated the movement of goods between different societies and communities.[12] Through their trade activities, the strangers contributed to the economic prosperity of the town and surrounding area. They provided revenue (in the form of taxes and gifts) for the chiefs and constituted an important consumer population for goods produced in and around Salaga.

The establishment of British colonial rule in West Africa at the turn of the twentieth century led to profound changes in the socio-political status of the stranger communities which were attached to various cities in Ghana and elsewhere in the region. Foremost among these changes, as Skinner has pointed out, was the fact that

> the relationship between the stranger and traditional African political leaders changed. The new strangers entered these foreign areas under the aegis of the Europeans, even when they were not directly brought by them. The result [being] that, unlike the earlier strangers, they had only secondary relationships with the local African political authorities (who were now also controlled by the Europeans) and were relatively free to deal with them as they saw fit.[13]

Except for the fact that the Yoruba community in Ghana could never afford to deal with the traditional authorities "as they saw fit," the above statement is an apt and succinct introduction to the socio-political history of the Yoruba in Ghana after 1900.

The Yorubas who migrated to various parts of Ghana in 1900 and for almost six decades thereafter came as "British subjects." The first Ọba

---

11. Marian Johnson, *Salaga Papers: Vol. I*, Institute of African Studies, University of Ghana, 1966. For a discussion of precolonial trade in Salaga, see Kwame Arhin, "Strangers and Hosts: A Study in the Political Organization and History of Atebubu Town," *Transactions of the Historical Society of Ghana*, Vol. 12 (1971), pp. 63–82; and Ivor Wilks, "Asante Policy Towards the Hausa Trade in the Nineteenth Century" in *The Development of Indigenous Trade and Markets in West Africa*, C. Meillassoux, ed. (Oxford University Press, 1971), pp. 124–141.

12. Sudarkasa, "Commercial Migration in West Africa"; E. P. Skinner, "West African Economic Systems" in *Economic Transition in Africa*, M. J. Herskovits and M. Harwits, eds., (Evanston: Northwestern University Press, 1964).

13. Skinner, "Strangers in West African Societies", p. 309.

(king) of the Yoruba community in Kumasi would recall, in a petition sent to the British government in 1930, after he had been "de-stooled" and "banished" to Accra (through the connivance of the British administration in Kumasi and the head of the Kumasi Zongo):

> I entered Kumasi with the victorious British Punitive Force in 1900, and for thirty years Kumasi has been my home, the present site on which my house stands having been granted me by Chief Commissioner Fuller himself. . . . All through my thirty years stay in Kumasi, I have been a conscientious, faithful, and loyal subject of His Majesty, our Gracious King Emperor, having never once failed to obey, comply with, or fulfill any orders or demands made upon me by his lawful representatives.[14]

The history of the Yoruba community in Kumasi provides an excellent example of how the fact of being "British subjects" served to foment ill-will and strife between the local host population and the strangers, as well as between the different strangers groups themselves.

The Struggle for Political Control in the Kumasi Zongo, 1900–1932

The first Yoruba community in Kumasi, which was predominantly Muslim, was centered in the Zongo, as was the case in Accra, Sekondi, Tamale, and most other Ghanaian towns. The other ethnic groups in the Kumasi Zongo in the early 1900s may be listed along with their homelands as follows: Dagomba, Mamprusi, and Frafra (mainly from Northern Ghana); Mossi and Grunshi (mainly from Upper Volta); Kotokoli (mainly from Togo); Hausa (mainly from Northern Nigeria); Wangara (also known as Djoula, mainly from Upper Volta, Ivory Coast, and Mali); Zabrama (mainly from Mali); and Fulani (mainly from Upper Volta, Niger, and Northern Nigeria).[15]

There had been a stranger quarter in Kumasi before the establishment of British rule, but the first British Chief Commissioner for the Ashanti Region moved the Zongo to the site at which it developed from the early 1900s to the present day.[16] By the early 1900s, each of the ethnic

14. Ghana National Archives (GNA), Ashanti Regional Branch (Kumasi), File No. D-12, *Kumasi Zongo Affairs*, p. 117, April 5, 1930.

15. In listing the "home countries" of these groups, the oft-repeated fact that colonial boundaries in Africa cut across ethnic group ("tribal") boundaries, and the less frequently mentioned fact that many West African peoples had a precolonial history of dispersal over wide areas, must be borne in mind.

16. For a political history of the Kumasi Zongo, see E. Schildkrout, "Government and Chiefs in Kumasi Zongo," in *West African Chiefs*, M. Crowder and O. Ikime, eds. (Ile-Ife, Nigeria: University of Ife Press, 1970). The data in the present discussion of the Kumasi Zongo were obtained mainly from the Ghana National Archives file, *Kumasi Zongo Affairs*, and from three Yoruba community local historians: Alhaji Raji Bakari, Alufa

groups in the Zongo had a chief (called the Headman by the British) who was officially recognized by the colonial government, and the Hausa chief was accorded the official title of Serikin Zongo (Chief of the Zongo).

Between 1900 and 1919, each stranger community in the Zongo was virtually responsible for the running of its own affairs, much as had been the case in the Zongo in Salaga and other West African market-towns in the precolonial period. Thus, even though the British had officially established a system of Native Tribunals and Magistrates' Courts, most of the disputes which arose in the Zongo were handled by the chiefs and elders of the various stranger groups. Disputes not satisfactorily resolved by the traditional authorities were referred to the Magistrate's Court rather than to the Native Courts presided over by the Ashanti chiefs. Reportedly, such instances of referral from the Zongo to the Magistrate's Court were rare. However, the relative autonomy of each of the various stranger groups in the Zongo, and their relative insulation from control by the colonial government, ceased after the appointment of Mallam Salao Katsina as Serikin Zongo in 1919.

The period of Mallam Salao's reign as Serikin (1919–1932) was a turbulent one for the Zongo, and very instructive as to the extent of British intervention in the relations between stranger groups in Kumasi. Events during the period also reveal the relative lack of power of the traditional Ashanti chiefs (the Omanhene) in dealing with affairs in the Zongo. This was especially true for the period before 1924, during which time Prempeh I the Asantehene—the title given the Ashanti King—was in forced exile in Sierra Leone and in the Seychelles Islands off the coast of East Africa. But even after the British allowed the Asantehene to return to Kumasi, reducing him to the rank of Kumasihene, they did not permit the Ashanti chiefs to exercise any control over or to intervene significantly in Zongo affairs. In his official position as Kumasihene, the Asantehene could and did make recommendations to the colonial administrators concerning matters in the Zongo, but these usually went unheeded. The Serikin Zongo was not in any way accountable to the Asantehene for his actions, a situation that would have been unthinkable in the precolonial context.

Early in his reign as Serikin Zongo, Mallam Salao made himself very popular with the various important colonial administrators in Kumasi (the Kumasi District Commissioner, the Commissioner for the Eastern Province of Ashanti, and the Chief Commissioner for Ashanti Region) by keeping them informed on happenings in the Zongo, and by conscripting Zongo residents to work long hours, without pay, on projects

Lardan, and Chief Aliu Alao, Oba of the Yoruba Community. Alhaji Raji was born in Ibadan in 1905 and brought to Kumasi by his parents in 1909; Alufa Lardan, whose father was from Ilorin, was born in Kumasi in 1906; Oba Alao was born in Ilorin in the late nineteenth century, and had migrated to Kumasi in the early 1900s.

such as cleaning the Zongo and cutting weeds in various parts of the town. However, his methods of enforcing compliance with his work orders (notably by commanding the public flogging of those who disobeyed) made him distinctly unpopular with residents of the Zongo. In 1927 the colonial government rewarded the Serikin Zongo for his cooperativeness by establishing a Zongo tribunal under his jurisdiction.[17]

One important rationale for the establishment of the Zongo tribunal stemmed from the fact that after the return of the Asantehene, the Ashanti chiefs were seeking to reclaim at least some of their traditional authority over Kumasi, and one of the means of doing so would have been to bring the residents of the Zongo under the authority of the system of Native Courts, over which the Ashanti chiefs themselves presided. (Of course, by law, major civil and criminal cases had to be handled by the Magistrates' Courts, the lowest of which was presided over by the District Commissioner.) The establishment of the Zongo tribunal gave the Serikin authority to handle all minor civil and criminal cases involving Muslim strangers resident in the Zongo, with the right of appeal being directly to the Magistrate's Court rather than to the Asantehene's court. Thus, the colonial government effectively insulated the largest stranger community in Kumasi from any possible vestige of control by the Asantehene.[18]

The establishment of the court in the Zongo exacerbated the existing tensions in the community. Mallam Salao (and apparently the District Commissioner as well) interpreted it to mean that he was being given absolute authority over his "subjects" in the Zongo. As might be expected, this interpretation annoyed and offended a number of Zongo "sub-chiefs" (the chiefs of the various constituent communities), who considered this a usurpation of their powers. Once the Zongo tribunal was in operation, all minor civil and criminal disputes had to be referred in the first instance to the Serikin Zongo. No chief dared to be caught holding a court "on his own." Even though certain "sub-chiefs" (specifically the Mossi, Kotokoli, Frafra, Fulani, Grunshi, Yoruba, Wangara, and Dagomba chiefs) were supposed to sit with Mallam Salao in judgment of all cases, the Serikin apparently expected them to serve mainly to add their assent to his decisions.

The Serikin's attempt to undermine the chiefs was also signaled by his dictate that all ceremonies, such as weddings, naming ceremonies, and funerals, had to be presided over by him or his appointed deputy.

17. The Zongo tribunal was established under an amendment to the Native Jurisdiction Ordinance, passed in 1924. (See Schildkrout, "Government and Chiefs," pp. 377–379.)

18. At first there seems to have been some question as to whether the Serikin's tribunal would have jurisdiction over all strangers (including non-Muslims) in Kumasi. However, the District Commissioner, in interpreting the law, recommended that it be understood that "all Akan-speaking people in the Zongo shall have their cases tried direct by the Kumasihene." (*Kumasi Zongo Affairs*, D–12, January 19, 1928.)

This symbolized to the peoples of the Zongo that none of their chiefs had the authority to carry out even those routine functions normally associated with their office. It also meant that Mallam Salao could collect any gifts or fees exchanged on these occasions. Among the Serikin's other dictates was that he should receive a portion of the property of all strangers who died in the Zongo, and all the property of anyone who died in the Zongo without a family.

Mallam Salao's excesses were particularly offensive to the Yoruba community, which saw them as affronts to the dignity of their chief, Qba Sule.[19] They considered him to be the senior-most chief in the Zongo, inasmuch as he had officiated at the ceremonies at which both Mallam Salao and his predecessor were installed as Serikin Zongo.[20] In 1927 and 1928, the Yoruba community leaders led a move to curb Mallam Salao's powers. They sent a number of petitions to the colonial government asking permission to take cases directly to the Magistrate's Court. This was desirable, they said, because Mallam Salao applied Hausa law in the adjudication of Yoruba disputes, and consequently caused them to incur the expense of appealing the decisions in the Magistrate's Court. Since the colonial government had set up Mallam Salao's court to serve its own ends, it was predictable that the Chief Commissioner (acting on the advice of the District Commissioner) refused to grant the Yoruba request. In 1929 the Yoruba community petitioned the government for a tribunal of its own. Needless to say, this request was also turned down.

The Asantehene's lack of power to intervene effectively in the disputes surrounding the Zongo tribunal is indicated by informants' recollections as well as by written colonial records. From as early as 1927, the Yoruba chief, supported by the Mossi, Grunshi, and Kotokoli chiefs, had sent emissaries to the Asantehene to keep him abreast of the developments that followed the establishment of the Zongo tribunal. Of course, the Asantehene was also kept informed by means of his own intelligence-gathering network, which operated all over the city. In a meeting held in June 1928 with the District Commissioner, to discuss

19. It is interesting to note that the Yoruba chief and his followers claimed for him the title of Qba, the highest of the Yoruba offices, rather than that of Bale, which is traditionally the title given to the rulers of small dependent Yoruba towns. The term Qba might have been chosen for the Yoruba chief in Kumasi in order to indicate rulership over groups from different towns, each one of which might have had a leader who was equivalent, in this foreign context, to a Bale.

20. This point was made in a petition which Qba Sule sent to the colonial government after he had been exiled to Accra. The petition states: "Your Petitioner materially assisted Sir F. C. Fuller in the election and installation of the Chiefs of the Hausa Community particularly Chiefs Mallam Alidu and Mallam Asumanu the former of whom was deposed and the latter died about twelve years ago (ca. 1965) and also in the election and installation of the present Mallam Salao all of which took place during the administration of Sir F. C. Fuller [Chief Commissioner of Ashanti]." (*Kumasi Zongo Affairs*, D–12/77, December 20, 1929.)

Zongo affairs, the Asantehene "put forward the following suggestion: That the various Zongo Headmen be given jurisdiction under the Native Jurisdiction Ordinance up to £12.0.0 in civil cases with appeal to the Serikin Zongo."[21] The District Commissioner dismissed the Asantehene's proposal with the following report to the Commissioner for the Eastern Province of Ashanti Region:

> 2. The Kumasihene, when asked for reason to support his proposal was unable to convince me of the necessity for the proposed change.
> 3. In my opinion, such action would be ill-advised as the Serikin is perfectly capable of ruling the Zongo with the assistance of the various Headmen who sit with him in the Tribunal.
> 4. The chief mover in this scheme is the Lagos Headman who is an old enemy of the Serikin Zongo.
> 5. The Serikin Zongo would strongly oppose any such alteration; as it would greatly weaken his authority.[22]

After the Yoruba community petitions and other efforts received a firm and final rebuff from the colonial authorities, Qba Sule stopped attending Mallam Salao's court. Mallam Salao immediately cut off the Yoruba chief's monthly allowance of £3.00, which was the amount allocated by the Serikin as each "sub-chief"'s stipend for attendance at court. There followed a number of letters in which the Serikin first requested and then demanded the Yoruba chief's attendance at his court. After Qba Sule refused (on the grounds that he had been threatened by Salao and was therefore afraid to attend the Tribunal), Mallam Salao, with the connivance of the District Commissioner, engineered a trial of Qba Sule in his court in October 1929; upon finding him guilty of disobeying a constituted authority, the Qba was "de-stooled from his Headmanship" and deported from Kumasi.[23] Chief Sule went to Accra, where he took up residence with Chief Braimah, the head of the Yoruba community in that city.

After many petitions, written between 1929 and 1931 by members of the Yoruba communities in Kumasi and in Accra and by Chief Sule himself, the colonial government agreed to permit the chief to return to Kumasi, with the stipulation that upon his return he should enter into a bond to keep the peace for one year. Chief Sule returned to Kumasi on April 27, 1931, and two days later he posted a bond in the amount of

21. *Kumasi Zongo Affairs*, D–12/16, June 13, 1928.

22. *Ibid.*

23. The process resulting in the "destoolment" of Chief Sule was probably set in motion shortly after August 30, 1929, when the District Commissioner wrote to the Commissioner for the Eastern Province of Ashanti, complaining that the Yoruba and Mossi chiefs had for years "been a thorn in the side of the Serikin," and concluding "I would strongly recommend the deposition and removal of both the Lagos [Yoruba] and Moshi Headmen." (*Kumasi Zongo Affairs*, D–12/68A, August 30, 1929.)

£100 and "two sureties" as a guarantee that he would keep the peace with the Serikin Zongo for one year.

With Chief Sule back in their midst, the Yoruba community in Kumasi began to campaign to have the colonial administration recognize him as their official head. According to information given me by Yorubas who had been in Kumasi during this period, the government did not recognize Chief Sule as the Yoruba chief up to the time of his death in 1936.[24]

After the banishment of Chief Sule from Kumasi in 1929, relations between the Serikin Zongo and most strangers in the Zongo steadily deteriorated. The Mossi, Grunshi, Mamprusi, and Kotokoli chiefs sent a number of petitions through the Asantehene to the British administrators, detailing charges of abuse of power by Mallam Salao. In 1932, about a year after Sule's return to Kumasi, tensions in the Zongo exploded. After several incidents, one of which involved the imprisonment of a young Hausa man who failed to obey the Serikin's order to cut grass and weeds in the town, the young men of the Zongo, with the encouragement of the Mossi, Grunshi, Mamprusi, and Kotokoli chiefs, instigated a series of full-scale riots that were quelled only after the police and the army had been called out in full force.

In the wake of the Zongo riots, the national colonial government in Accra initiated an investigation that further documented abuses of power by Mallam Salao. Although Salao's supporters among the colonial officials in Kumasi tried to justify his actions, the investigations resulted in Salao's forced resignation and his forced but supposedly voluntary return to Katsina, Nigeria, which was reported to be his hometown.[25]

After Mallam Salao's swift and secret exit from Kumasi, the colonial government jailed a number of instigators of the riot and deported the Mossi, Grunshi, and Kotokoli chiefs. (The first two were described as "French subjects" who had abused their privilege of residing in a "British territory.") The Zongo tribunal was discontinued, under the announced pretense that it had been an "experiment" in the first place. Minor civil and criminal cases from the Zongo would in the future be heard in the Asantehene's court. Although a new Hausa chief was elected, he was not officially appointed to the office of Serikin Zongo.

The Yoruba Town Union

During the late 1920s and 1930s when the Yoruba in Kumasi were fighting to maintain control over their community centered in the Zongo, thousands of new migrants from Ogbomosho and more

24. I do not doubt these reports, but the government had at least taken note of the Yoruba community's re-election of Qba Sule as their chief (*Kumasi Zongo Affairs*, D-12/264, April 3, 1933).

25. Schildkrout, "Government and Chiefs," states that Mallam Salao was actually born in Yendi, Ghana, "of a Hausa father and a Dagomba mother" (p. 376).

southerly Yoruba towns greatly increased the size of the Yoruba population in Kumasi. Many of the new migrants settled outside the Zongo, thereby increasing the Yoruba dispersal from the Zongo, which had begun in 1923, when the Sabon Zongo (New Zongo) was founded. By the end of the 1930s Yoruba communities existed not only in the Zongo and Sabon Zongo but also in the areas that came to be known as Aboabo Number 1 and Aboabo Number 2.

The founding of Aboabo Number 1 in 1937 coincided with the period when Oba Aliu Alao was chosen as the head of the Yorubas in Kumasi to succeed Oba Sule, who had died in 1936. The Yoruba Oba continued to reside in the Zongo, but a large percentage of the Yoruba population became increasingly insulated from its politics. This was due not only to their dispersal (first to Aboabo, then to Ashanti New Town and Akwatia Line, and in later years to Lagos Town at Oforikurom),[26] but also to the increasing number of Christians among the migrants. By and large, the Zongo and its affairs continued to concern only Muslims in Kumasi.

As the Yoruba population became larger, more dispersed, and more diversified (in terms of the different Yoruba towns that were represented in the Kumasi population), the mechanism of the Oba-in-Council was not sufficient by itself to maintain community cohesion and community control. Between the 1940s and 1960s, the Yoruba developed a network of associations known as Parapos (Unions), which were designed to promote solidarity and maintain order within the Yoruba community, and to facilitate the articulation of that community with the colonial government, the Ashanti host community, and the other ethnic communities with which the Yorubas had contact in Kumasi.

Each Parapo was comprised of males and females from the same town (as was the case, for example, with the Ogbomosho Parapo). In one instance—that of the Ekiti-Ijesha Parapo—the association embraced Yorubas from closely related but different subgroups. These Town Unions or Descendants' Unions (which are the two English phrases used to designate the Parapos), actually had their origins in the early twentieth century, when Yorubas from each of the various towns represented in Ghana began to meet to render assistance to one another and to discuss hometown affairs. However, it was in the 1940s and later that most of these associations took on the formal organizational characteristics which they had when I studied them in Kumasi in 1968–1969.

By the decade of the 1960s, in each major Ghanaian town (and in the small towns where sizable Yoruba populations existed), there were Parapos which catered to the welfare of their townsmen. Moreover, in at least two cases (that of the Ogbomoshos and the Egbas) there were formally organized national Parapos which comprised branches of the Parapos

26. These were the major centers of Yoruba concentration in Kumasi between 1937 and 1969, but small groups of Yorubas lived in Suame, in Ahinja, and elsewhere in Kumasi.

from different Ghanaian towns. The annual meetings of these national Parapọs were attended by delegates from towns and villages all over Ghana. Even where there was no formal Ghana-wide organization, Parapọs in one Ghanaian town maintained communication with their counterparts in other towns, and the Ghanaian town with the oldest Parapọ (which was usually also the place with the largest number of descendants of the Yoruba town in question) served as headquarters for all the rest. For example, Koforidua served as the headquarters for the Ọffa Descendants Union which had branches in various Ghanaian towns.

A primary aim of the Parapọs was to settle all internal dissensions without going through the Ghanaian courts, and by so doing, to "protect the community's good name." The Parapọs adjudicated disputes over financial matters and handled all types of serious domestic quarrels, especially those involving the breach of marital contracts. Many instances were recounted to me of different Parapọs having granted divorces and determined the appropriate terms of settlement in the particular cases. The parties concerned had been married under Yoruba customary law, and the Parapọs decided on the amount of the bridewealth to be returned to the husband, and on the manner in which jointly acquired properties would be divided. When there was some question as to whether the husband should be allowed custody of the children (as is normally the case among the Yoruba, who are predominantly patrilineal), the Parapọ decided the matter. If a Parapọ could not effect a satisfactory resolution to a dispute, the parties concerned were usually ordered to go to their hometown in Nigeria to settle the matter. The most elaborate Parapọ court system reported to me was that organized by the Ọffa Descendants Union, which had four branches of the court, located in Koforidua, Kumasi, Nsawam, and Accra. Ọffa descendants from all over Ghana brought cases to be settled in these four courts.

Members who insisted on bypassing their Parapọ by taking "internal" matters to a Ghanaian court would have substantial fines levied against them by the Parapọ. The ultimate sanction used by the Parapọs against recalcitrant members was forced repatriation to Nigeria. This they accomplished with the aid of relatives or friends of the person (including, where necessary, those in Nigeria as well as those in Ghana), who together with the Parapọ officials put pressure on the person to leave Ghana. The decisions of the Parapọ councils (comprised of the officers and most highly respected elders) were usually adhered to because normally a Yoruba would not want to incur the consequences of alienating the Parapọ elders and, more especially, of alienating his family and friends.

In addition to settling disputes among members, the Parapọs always tried to effect out-of-court settlements of any disputes that might arise between their members and outsiders. On various occasions different Parapọ in Kumasi had sent delegations to the police station to plead for the release into their custody of a member who had been arrested for a minor offense, such as 'fighting in the market. It appears that before Ghana became independent, Yoruba leaders often succeeded in obtaining the release of such persons. After 1957, however, the local police and courts increasingly sought to assert their authority over all residents in Kumasi, and it was harder to free a violator of the law without the case going through the "normal channels." Nonetheless, even after independence it seems that where offenses were minor, the Parapọ leaders were usually able to arrange for acceptable redress without the case having to go to court.

The judicial functions of the Parapọs served not only the social and political interests of the Yoruba communities but their economic interests as well. By keeping "internal" matters out of the courts, the Parapọs saved their members lawyers' fees as well as court costs and fines. This was considered very important by all the Parapọ leaders whom I interviewed in 1968–1969. Here, they said, was a way of saving money as well as of insuring that disputes were settled "in the Yoruba way."

In addition to their judiciary functions, nearly all of the twenty-five Parapọs in Kumasi in 1968–1969 maintained facilities for accommodating migrants who had no friends or relatives in the city to provide them with lodgings. The chairman of a smaller Parapọ usually assumed responsibility for lodging newcomers who needed this assistance. Some Parapọs rented rooms that were used solely for this purpose. A few of the large Parapọs in Kumasi owned particular houses which were rented to provide an income for the association; in these, there was at least one room reserved for "guests" of the Parapọ. The newcomer was always allowed at least two weeks' free lodging before he would be asked to pay rent. A lodger who found it difficult to find a job could spend months in the Parapọ's room without paying rent.

The Parapọs also helped to defray the major expenses incurred by their members in connection with birth, marriage, illness, death, or any unforeseen circumstance (such as the need to make an unplanned trip back to the hometown). Usually, the association's charter or constitution stipulated the amounts to be given for naming ceremonies for newborn babies, for funerals, and so on. Members of the Parapọs contributed money to their townsmen who traveled back to their hometowns to marry, as well as to those who married in Ghana. Not only did the Parapọs make contributions toward funeral expenses, they normally bore all the funeral expenses for members who died destitute or without relatives in Ghana. A number of Parapọs reported having paid for the repatriation to Nigeria of widows and children. Some of them had also repatriated old people who had no relatives or means of support in

Ghana. At times, they rendered financial assistance, in the form of loans, to members whose businesses had faltered, or to indigent newcomers who lacked the necessary capital to begin their trade.

Although the official membership in each Parapo in Kumasi consisted of those males and females who paid the stipulated monthly or weekly dues, in fact the Parapos served non-members as well as members. In emergencies, for example, a townsman who was not a dues-paying member could receive help from the Parapo. The reverse was also true: when a Parapo launched a general financial appeal, regardless of the status of their official relationship to the Parapo, descendants (and many spouses of descendants) of the town contributed to the campaign. This indicates that regardless of the size of the official membership of a given Parapo, it represented all the people from the hometown.

The larger Parapos in Kumasi had constituent branches, and the largest Parapo (that of Ogbomosho) had many sub-branches as well. The term "egbe," which is the general Yoruba word for "association," was normally used to refer to the smaller subdivisions of the Parapos, but some of the Parapos themselves used the term "egbe" in their official titles. For example, the Ilorin Parapo was named "Egbe Omo Ibile Ilorin" (literally meaning: Association of Descendants of Ilorin). Historically, the term "egbe" is an older usage that was replaced by the term "parapo" as it became important to distinguish the smaller associations, of which there are hundreds wherever Yorubas reside in large numbers, from the larger Town Unions. Whereas the egbes usually restricted membership by age, sex, or religion, the Town Unions were open to all people who traced their origin (or in the case of females, whose husbands traced their origin) to the town in question.[27] The smaller egbes that were branches or sub-branches of the Parapos in Kumasi in 1968–1969 were usually convivial or religious organizations that met more frequently and with less formality than the Parapos.

One of the reasons for the Parapos' success as mechanisms for maintaining the cohesiveness of each Yoruba subgroup was that this cohesiveness was rooted in the domestic organization of the Yorubas. Most men chose their wives (or at least their first wife) from among their own townswomen. Those Yorubas who did not marry persons from their hometown usually married Yorubas from other towns. The instances I encountered of marriage outside the Yoruba ethnic group were extremely few. An indication of the Yoruba's "own-group bias" as regards the choice of spouses is provided by the data from the life histories I collected in Kumasi. Of the 177 married or previously married persons interviewed,

27. Yoruba women could belong to their own Parapos and still be active in their husbands' Parapos. This was generally consistent with the Yoruba tradition of concurrent participation by married women in the affairs of their natal and their affinal lineages (see N. Sudarkasa, *Where Women Work* [Ann Arbor: University of Michigan Museum of Anthropology, 1973], Chapters Five and Six.

68.4 percent (121 persons) were married or had been married, polygy-
nously as well as monogamously, only to spouses from their hometown.
Moreover, 173 of the 177 persons, or 97.8 percent of the sample, were
married or had been married only to Yoruba spouses, and in two of the
remaining four cases, at least one of the spouses was Yoruba. In other
words, in only two cases (1.1 percent of the sample) had the respondents
(both males) never been married to Yoruba. One of these two males was
a divorcé, who had been married to a Gā female; the other was married
monogamously to a Hausa female. (The man with the Hausa wife hastened to tell me, when I asked to which ethnic group his wife belonged,
that she had lived with Yorubas for so long that she "had become a
Yoruba.")

From 1959 to 1969, the Parapos in Kumasi collectively formed the
core of the official governing body of the Yoruba Community.[28] Prior to
1959, the official Yoruba Community leadership in Kumasi had been
structured along the lines of a traditional Yoruba town, with the Oba
and his council of advisors (who were recognized elders in the community) constituting the official governing body. Although there was not a
full roster of titled chiefs, as would be found in a Yoruba town, some
members of the Kumasi Yoruba Oba's council were given traditional
titles. In 1959 the official governing body of the Yoruba Community
became the Executive Committee, consisting of four representatives of
each of the twenty-five Parapos plus the elected officers of the
community. Although the Oba remained the head of the Yoruba Community, the Chairman, who was elected by the Executive Committee,
was the official who presided over the meetings of that body.

One of the main responsibilities of the Yoruba Community's Executive Committee was the adjudication of disputes between members of
different Yoruba subgroups. The Executive Committee also deliberated
upon and decided the overall policy or position the Yoruba Community
as a whole would take on any local (Ghanaian) governmental issues that
came up. Where there was an official Nigerian government policy on any
issue, the Yoruba Community's Executive Committee took responsibility
for seeing that this policy was adhered to by the community. In 1968–
1969, one of the major concerns of the Executive Committee (and of the
various Parapos) was the effect which the National Liberation Council's
policies on aliens in business would have on the Yoruba Community in
Ghana. Even though it was not evident that the Compliance Order
would be immediately forthcoming, the community leaders were concerned over the increasingly negative attitudes toward non-Ghanaians

28. According to Mr. A. H. Alao, Secretary to the Nigerian Community in Kumasi, the
following Parapos were officially represented in the Yoruba Community Council: Aiyetoro
(from Osun Division, Nigeria); Ajashepo; Ede; Egba; Ejigbo; Editi-Ijesha; Eko (Lagos);
Erin; Ibadan; Iduoshun; Ijabe; Ijebu; Ilero; Ilorin; Inisha; Iseyin; Iwo; Offa; Ogbomosho;
Ojoku, Okeho; Oshogbo; Oyan; Oyo; and Shaki.

that were circulating in the press, in the market, and elsewhere. In fact, before I was allowed to undertake my research, the Yoruba Community's Executive Committee had to be assured (ultimately by means of a letter from the Nigerian High Commission) that I was not conducting an investigation designed to supply the Ghanaian authorities with information that would jeopardize the position of Yorubas in Ghana.

The Yoruba Community in Kumasi was formally affiliated with the Kumasi District Nigerian Community, which was an executive body inaugurated in Ghana in 1960 some months prior to Nigeria's independence. It consisted of two representatives of each of the fourteen Nigerian ethnic ("tribal") groups in Kumasi District, plus seven officers elected from among the constituent groups. The Kumasi District Nigerian Community, in turn, was one of fifteen similarly constituted organizations that made up the Ashanti Regional Nigerian Community. (In all of Ghana, there were twenty-seven Nigerian Community organizations, some of which embraced districts, others of which represented entire regions.)

According to the constitution of the Kumasi District Nigerian Community, that body was "the head of all the Tribunal Unions" (such as the Yoruba Community and the Hausa Community) and, as such, was empowered to settle disputes between the different member Unions. Although the Kumasi District Nigerian Community was subordinated to the Ashanti Regional Community, both these groups maintained direct communication links with the Nigerian High Commission in Accra. The High Commission used the various Nigerian Community organizations throughout Ghana as vehicles for communicating official Nigerian government policy on various issues that affected Nigeria-Ghana relations, and as channels through which it promoted the general welfare of Nigerians in Ghana.[29] The various Nigerian Communities, in turn, were channels through which inquiries, requests, and complaints could be passed up to the High Commission. In some cases, local communities would report extreme cases of misbehavior to the High Commission, with the recommendation that the persons concerned be repatriated to Nigeria.

It will be noted in Figure 1 that in addition to the relationships already described, the Yoruba Community is represented as still maintaining a formal link with the Kumasi Zongo. By 1968–1969, this linkage was considerably less significant than it had been in the first three decades of this century. There are a number of reasons for this. First of all, with the growth and dispersal of the Yoruba population, the Zongo ceased to be the center of activities within the overall Yoruba Community. Second,

29. In 1968–1969, while the Nigerian civil war was being fought, most of the Ibos in Ghana considered themselves members of the "Biafran Community" and sought to remain independent of the various Nigerian Community organizations. In fact, when the aliens Compliance Order was issued, many of the "Biafrans" sought to remain in Ghana as "refugees."

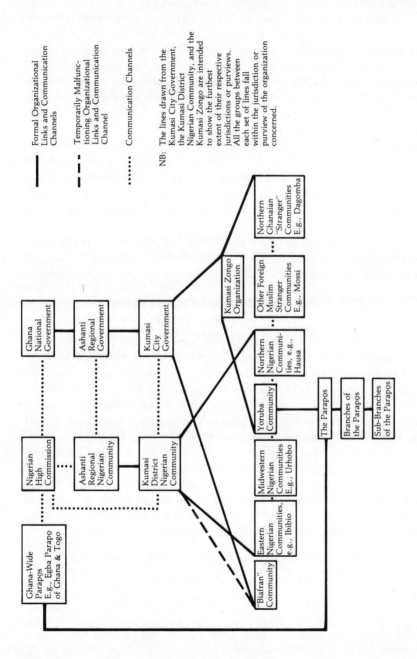

Figure 1. Organization of the Yoruba Community in Kumasi in 1968–1969 and Its Links to Other Formally Organized Bodies in Ghana

with changes in the structure of local government in Kumasi, the Zongo lost much of the official autonomy it had enjoyed during the period between 1900 and 1932. It became just another ward within the Kumasi municipal government (later Kumasi city), with the result that the Kumasi city governmental apparatus, rather than the Zongo per se, became the local authority to which the Yorubas and other strangers living in the Zongo deferred. Third, the changing local government structure meant that Yorubas were directly represented in city government through the various wards in which they resided; the center of their municipal influence thus became Aboabo, where they were most numerous, rather than the Zongo, where they were outnumbered by Hausas and other (predominantly Muslim) stranger groups.[30]

Despite these changes, the Yorubas maintained a link with the Zongo for two reasons: (1) the Ọba still resided there and was considered one of the Zongo chiefs, who were at least titularly and ceremonially under the leadership of the (unofficial) Serikin Zongo; and (2) the Yoruba Muslim community, comprising about two-thirds of the Yorubas in Kumasi, continued to be involved with and affected by many issues that developed within the wider Kumasi Muslim community which was centered in the Zongo.

Nationalist Politics and Changes in the
Status of Stranger Groups

It was through the linkage of the Yoruba Muslim community in Kumasi with the wider Muslim community (both of which had a recognized leadership) that some of the Yoruba leaders became involved with national politics in Ghana in the 1950s. During the 1940s and 1950s, when Ghana's pre-independence nationalist political activity was most intense, most of the Yoruba community's organizational efforts were focused on the Parapọ and other ethnically homogeneous associations, and this had the effect of insulating the majority of Yorubas from more broadly based political organizations in Ghana. Nevertheless, between 1949, when Kwame Nkrumah's Convention Peoples Party (CPP) was founded, and 1957, when Ghana gained its independence, a number of Yoruba leaders were active in the Muslim Association Party (MAP), which had its origin in the Muslim community in Kumasi.[31]

30. Although the Yorubas were not the largest stranger group in the Kumasi Zongo, they were the largest stranger group in Kumasi as a whole, outnumbering any other single ethnic group of foreign origin. In fact, the Yoruba population in Kumasi was larger than that of any single "stranger" group of Northern Ghanaian origin. According to the 1960 Ghana Census (*Special Report "E"*, Table S-1, pp. C-3 to C-9), the following stranger groups in Kumasi had populations of 2,000 or more: Yoruba, 9,530; Hausa, 8,010; Mossi, 5,150; Busanga (mainly of Ghanaian origin), 4,270; Dagomba (of Ghanaian origin), 3,830; Wangara, 2,100; and Songhai or Gao, 2,010.

31. For a general discussion of the impact of nationalist politics on the Kumasi Zongo political leadership, see Schildkrout, "Government and Chiefs," pp. 384–388.

From its inception around 1950, the MAP was opposed to the CPP. This opposition has been described as an instance of the opposition of traditional chiefs to emergent nationalist political forces.[32] However, some of the Yorubas who had been leaders in the MAP told me that the initial basis for the opposition to the CPP was its failure to support government sponsorship and establishment of Islamic schools in Ghana.

Alhaji Raji Bakari, a Yoruba Muslim and MAP leader who had been prominent in the Islamic movement before it formally launched the MAP, reported that as early as 1948 Muslim leaders in Kumasi had sent a delegation to Accra to meet with leaders of the United Gold Coast Convention (UGCC) to discuss the possibility of establishing government-supported Islamic schools in Kumasi and elsewhere in Ghana. After the CPP separated itself from the UGCC in 1949, the CPP leadership opposed efforts to obtain public financing for such schools. As a result, the Muslim leaders withdrew their support of Nkrumah and the CPP.

In 1950 and 1951, the Muslim leadership in Kumasi organized and rallied support for the MAP. Halidu Suame, an Ashanti Muslim convert, became the Party's first President, and Alhaji Alufa Lardan, a Yoruba, became its Chairman. Halidu Suame and the other MAP leaders subsequently moved to consolidate the Party's position among the Kumasi Muslims by handing over the presidency to Ahmadu Baba, the Hausa chief who was then the unofficial Serikin Zongo. In the local government elections of 1954, the MAP put up candidates in six wards, including Aboabo, where most of the Yorubas lived. Four of the six candidates were elected, including the Yoruba candidate for Aboabo, Akani Smith (son of the Chairman of the Egba Parapo in Kumasi).

According to Mr. Bunyamin T. Oni, a Yoruba Muslim who served as General Secretary for the MAP between 1954 and 1958 and as Assistant General Secretary in 1953, one of the main reasons why the Yoruba opposed the CPP and supported the MAP was the CPP's harsh treatment of Yoruba market women in 1952 and 1953. He reported that some Yoruba women had been beaten and others stripped of their clothing in the Kumasi Central Market by "CPP party thugs" who were seeking to obtain the active support of all the market traders.

In any case, shortly after the 1954 local elections, the MAP declared its alliance with the National Liberation Movement (NLM), whose leaders it had actually supported even before the NLM was officially launched. (Alufa Lardan had accompanied Dr. Busia on his campaign tours and had traveled separately all over the Ashanti Region and in the North, campaigning for support of the Ashantis and the MAP.) The MAP-NLM alliance further incensed the CPP, and in 1957 the newly elected government of Ghana deported Alufa Lardan and Ahmadu Baba to Nigeria. Both leaders were sent to Kano, which was Ahmadu Baba's hometown. Alufa Lardan was a "son" of Ilorin; he had been born in

32. Skinner, "Strangers in West African Societies," pp. 312–313.

Kumasi in 1906, but his father had had extensive trade connections with Hausas in Kano.

In 1957, the MAP and NLM joined to form the United Party (UP) under the leadership of Dr. Busia. According to Mr. Oni, the majority of the active supporters of the UP in Kumasi were Nigerians. In the same year that the UP was formed, the CPP government passed a law barring non-Ghanaians from holding seats on local councils, thereby disqualifying Bunyamin Oni from representing Aboabo on the Kumasi council. In 1958, Mr. Oni, who had been warned that the CPP was making plans for his imprisonment, fled from Kumasi to Lagos.

In 1957, the CPP had moved to gain control of the Kumasi Muslim population by installing one of its Hausa supporters, Chief Mutawakilu, as the Serikin Zongo. Subsequently, the government "banished" twelve Muslim "troublemakers" from Kumasi to Accra. Among those "exiled" was Alhaji Raji Bakari, a leading Yoruba spokesman in the Muslim community and a strong supporter of the UP. Despite these moves, Muslim opposition to the CPP continued into the 1960s.

The various strangers whom the CPP expelled from Ghana in the late 1950s were deported on the grounds that they were non-Ghanaians (even though some of them were born in Ghana) whose activities were not in the national interest. The deportations, and the laws under which they were effected, signaled the beginning of the legal transition in the status of "populations of foreign origin" in Ghana from that of "strangers" to that of "aliens."[33] By the promulgation of the Nationality Act and the various Deportation Acts, the newly elected CPP government accomplished two ends. First, it asserted a right which all contemporary nation-states claim, namely the right to define citizenship and to specify the rights, privileges, and duties of non-citizens as well as those of citizens; and second, it divested the *traditional polities* within the nation-state of Ghana of their ancient prerogative of defining the terms upon which "strangers" would be permitted to reside in their midst. This latter point is of particular significance for interpreting the socio-political changes in the status of the Yorubas (and other strangers) in Kumasi, for one of the aims of the Nkrumah regime was to make it clear to these strangers that they now had to accommodate themselves to the Government of Ghana, and not to the Ashanti political leaders.

Throughout the colonial period the Yorubas in Kumasi had sought to accommodate their organizations and activities to two realities: the fact that the British were the authority over the Gold Coast; and the fact that the Ashantis were the host community with which they, as strangers, had to maintain good relations. As "British subjects," the Yorubas were compelled to obey the laws made by the colonial administration.

33. See the Ghana Nationality and Citizenship Act, 1957 (Act 1); the Deportation Act, 1957 (Act 14); the Immigration Act, 1957 (Act 15); the Deportation (Amendment) Act, 1958 (Act 49); and the Deportation (Amendment) Act, 1959 (Act 65).

Inasmuch as these laws often ran contrary to the traditional protocols by which strangers related to their hosts, the very colonial structure under which the Yorubas existed made it difficult to maintain good relations with the Ashanti community. Nevertheless they tried to do so.

I have already pointed out, for example, that even in the period between 1919 and 1932, when the Yorubas lived in the Zongo under an authority which was made independent of the Ashanti chiefs by the colonial administration, the Yoruba leaders still channeled most of their communications to the colonial government through the Asantehene. No doubt this was an indication of their hope that the head of their host community could find the means of asserting his traditional authority over strangers in his domain. It was also an indication of the Yorubas' desire to show their respect for Ashanti authorities, even though these authorities were being ignored by the Serikin Zongo.

The attempt on the part of the Yorubas to maintain good relations with the Ashantis is also indicated by the functions assumed by the Yoruba community organizations. In the early years of the settlement in Kumasi, the Yoruba Oba and Council viewed themselves as being primarily responsible for maintaining order within the community, and thereby minimizing the possibility of conflict with the Ashanti hosts. As had been customary in precolonial West Africa, the Yorubas sought to regulate their affairs according to their own customs and usages. After the mid-1930s, when the expansion of the Yoruba community (in terms of absolute numbers, in terms of sub-groups represented, and in terms of spatial distribution) made it impossible for a single structure (represented by the Oba and Council) to oversee, regulate, and serve the entire Yoruba community, the Parapos, representing different Yoruba towns or sub-groups, were established to undertake these functions.

Although the Parapos can be said to have increased the insulation of the Yoruba community from its hosts, the Yorubas conceived them as an appropriate mechanism through which to *articulate* with their hosts. The activities of the Parapos in maintaining internal order, and in interposing themselves between their members and Ghanaian authorities, were viewed as legitimate functions that would contribute to good relations with the Ashanti host community. Moreover, the Parapo leaders, along with the Oba, were the Yoruba community's representatives at official and ceremonial functions to which they were invited by the Ashanti chiefs or the Kumasi city government. It was also through the Parapos that contributions were raised for various Ghanaian local or national fund-raising appeals.

Somewhat paradoxically, it was because the Ashantis and other Ghanaians came to accept many of the colonially established institutions as part of their own developing national structure that some of the traditionally derived functions of the Parapos came to be viewed as antithetical to the interests of the host community. Thus, the judicial functions of the Parapos came to be seen as a usurpation of the functions of the judicial system established by the colonialists, and ultimately maintained and supported by the Ghanaians. Whereas in precolonial West Africa each stranger group was allowed to have at least its own "court of the first instance," in the colonial Gold Coast and thereafter the local populations sought to bring the strangers under the direct jurisdiction of the system of customary courts presided over by indigenous chiefs. Of course, money was the key element in this abandonment of the traditional practice of allowing strangers to settle their internal disputes. The courts (and their law-enforcement mechanism, the police) derived much of their revenue from the cases they handled. When strangers settled their own disputes, they deprived the indigenes of a source of income.

As the colonial period moved toward a close in the Gold Coast, the Yorubas in Kumasi sought to remain in the good graces of their hosts by aligning themselves with the political structures and aspirations of the Ashanti community. Even though the MAP had had an independent basis for opposing the CPP, there is no doubt that its members, including the Yorubas, saw the political expediency of an alliance with the Ashanti-led NLM and its political successor, the UP. By aligning with the NLM, the Yorubas and other strangers in Kumasi were responding to a situation that arose in the nationalist period and was without precedent in the early colonial period: that is, one in which they had to choose between two Ghanaian "host communities" which were vying for their allegiance.

During the colonial period, there were two main power groups with which strangers had to deal. One was the monolithic national political authority—the colonial government. (If the British disagreed among themselves, as colonial documents suggest, they took care to conceal their differences from both the indigenous and the stranger populations.) The second was the indigenous host community—the ethnic group that predominated in the particular town or area in which the strangers resided. With the emergence of nationalist political control over Ghana in the late 1940s and the 1950s, strangers were no longer confronted with the dichotomy of a monolithic national interest (a colonial host community) and a single, local host-community interest to which to respond. They found themselves caught between rival indigenous Ghanaian (host) groups that were vying for power on the local as well as the national levels. The fact that these groups were multi-ethnic political parties rather than unitary ethnic groups was partially obscured in the Kumasi situation, where the NLM, and later the UP, was comprised mainly of Ashantis. The Yorubas and most other strangers in Kumasi cast their lot with the leaders of Ashanti host community—who, of course, were vying against Nkrumah in the national struggle for power.

What the CPP did after it won the initial power struggle in 1957 was to let strangers know that as *aliens* they owed allegiance to the government of the state of Ghana rather than to any region, segment, or ethnic group within that state.[34] In contrast to the concept of "stranger," the concept of "alien," which embraced all "persons of foreign origin," including those born in Africa, carried no connotation of the slightest degree of political autonomy within the nation-state. In fact, it clearly signaled that the political and legal status of these outsiders prohibited them from presuming the right to exercise any of the prerogatives of citizens, such as holding political office, which they had done as British subjects in the colonial context. That the Yorubas heard and heeded the warnings sounded by the laws regarding aliens is indicated by the fact that they took a distinctly low profile in Ghanaian national political affairs after 1960. It is also shown by the fact that they sought, through the structure of the Nigerian Community Organization which they spearheaded, to create a climate of friendship between themselves and the Ghanaian government. By this time, however, it was too late.

What is particularly ironic in the Ghanaian situation is that even after the overthrow of the Nkrumah government, which many of the African strangers had opposed, the opposition to "aliens" had become so strong and the economic situation in the country so desperate that the successive governments of Ghana found it convenient to blame many of the problems on the presence of "aliens" in their midst. The supreme irony was that Dr. Busia, for whom a number of Yorubas and other strangers had actively campaigned in the 1950s, and to whom many hundreds of thousands more had given their support, should be the head of state who put the capstone on the Ghanaian anti-alien policies by expelling most of the African "aliens" from the country.

Conclusion

The expulsion, in the 1960s and early 1970s, of resident African strangers from various African countries, on the grounds that they were aliens whose presence was inimical to the national interest, points up a major difference between contemporary African nation-states and their precolonial precursors. These contemporary states, unlike the precolonial ones, *could not accommodate groups of settled strangers (sojourners) living in semi-autonomy in their midst.*

In the precolonial situation, groups of strangers could be permitted to reside on the periphery of market towns and to manage their internal affairs because it was understood by strangers and hosts alike that the rights of citizens (indigenes) did not extend to strangers. Regardless of the

34. Although the Nkrumah government publicly proclaimed an "open door" policy toward Africans from sister countries, the Deportation Acts which it promulgated in the late 1950s formed the basis for the anti-alien legislation passed in the 1960s and 1970s. The Ghana Nationality Act of 1961 and its amendments of 1967, 1969, and 1972; the Aliens Act of 1963 and its amendment of 1968; the Ghana Enterprises Decree of 1968; and the Ghanaian Business (Promotion) Act of 1970 are representative of the laws that had their genesis in CPP legislative acts of the late 1950s.

length of their residence in the host area, the *stranger groups* could not presume the right to participate in the host country's political affairs, nor could they claim any inalienable right to the lands on which they had settled. Moreover, the strangers' economic activities did not threaten the hosts because their activities were complementary to rather than competitive with those of the local population.

The introduction of European models of statehood into West Africa during the colonial period made profound changes in the political relationship between the African host communities and the strangers in their midst. A most critical change was the fact that citizenship, and hence the right of access to power, was defined in such a way as to blur the distinction between those whom the Africans had considered insiders (citizen-hosts) and those whom they defined as outsiders (non-citizen-strangers). In the colonial situation, strangers and hosts alike were defined as subjects (second-class citizens) of a state represented locally by the resident European functionaries. Birth in a given colonial territory, and in many cases residence in that territory, were considered sufficient to confer the right of participation in key political processes, such as voting or holding political office. In the precolonial situation, a stranger would not claim the political rights of an Ashanti simply because he had been born in an Ashanti town.

Under the colonial state apparatus, stranger groups sought to maintain as much community autonomy as possible from the indigenous hosts, but at the same time they sought to exercise political power in the nationalist state which the indigenous peoples were trying to create. With independence, the host nations moved to bring under their complete political and jural control the resident stranger populations, which had in many instances played important roles in pre-independence nationalist politics. The stranger groups could no longer be tolerated living both within the state and outside it. In other words, the strangers could not be permitted to exercise the rights of citizens of the state while claiming autonomy or quasi-autonomy for their communities. They could not be accorded the prerogatives of citizens without their assuming the civil responsibilities that this entailed.

In order to alleviate some of the problems caused by the ambiguity of the stranger status, the new African states chose to define citizenship in such a way as to exclude persons who would have been defined as strangers (non-citizens) according to precolonial protocol. The government of Ghana, for example, maintained that birth in the Gold Coast did not confer citizenship in the newly independent state. It was only those persons who had been born in Ghana *after* its independence who could claim citizenship by birth.

Whereas the efforts of the new African states to define and safeguard the rights of their citizens could be appreciated, there was genuine concern that the anti-alien legislation passed in many countries would work against the efforts to achieve regional economic cooperation in different parts of the continent. No doubt, the anti-alien legislation reinforced, and in some cases created, xenophobic tendencies toward other Africans on the part of the indigenous peoples of various countries. The Economic Community of West African States (ECOWAS), inaugurated in 1975, clearly recognized the necessity of reversing this trend, and to that end, the ECOWAS treaty provides that all citizens of member states should be considered "Community citizens," and that all restraints on their movement and residence within the Community should be removed.[35] When this treaty is fully implemented, the rubrics of "stranger" and "alien" should become outmoded as concepts with which to analyze intergroup relations between West African peoples.

35. "What ECOWAS Says," *West Africa*, June 16, 1975, p. 679.

9

Kinship and Entrepreneurship among Yoruba in Northern Ghana

Jeremy S. Eades

This paper considers in detail a specific instance of a very general phenomenon, members of a stranger minority group being successfully engaged in entrepreneurial activity in the area in which they have settled. It is concerned with the success of Yoruba migrants from western Nigeria in commercial activity in northern Ghana. Two main questions will be dealt with. What advantages did the individual Yoruba trader in one city, Tamale, gain from participation in this process of chain migration, and what advantages did he derive from membership in the Yoruba community in Ghana? Answers will be sought first by examining in detail the histories of two groups of related migrants from Ogbomosho in Nigeria.

In northern Ghana, the general pattern was for clusters of migrants from the same town in Nigeria, and even from the same compounds within these towns, to build up through a process of chain migration. This was certainly true of Tamale, the largest town in the north, where this research was carried out. By 1969 the city of Tamale was a major urban center, with a number of educational and military establishments in addition to the government offices; its population was approximately 60,000, of which 3,000 were Yoruba. Nearly all the large trading firms had branches there and there was a large wage-earning population creating a demand for manufactured goods.

The town had two main markets. The older Central Market was the main stronghold of the Yoruba traders: a third of the 700 stalls owned by the Tamale Council were rented by Yoruba, and a further 200 Yoruba had built stalls for themselves on land allocated by the Council. In general, the Yoruba women in Tamale were trading on a smaller scale than the men, and only 42 of the stalls were listed in their names. Women without stalls of their own sold either from tables outside their husbands'

The research on which this paper is based was carried out in northern Ghana and western Nigeria, 1969-1971, and was financed by a Smuts Studentship from the University of Cambridge and a Hayter Studentship from the Department of Education and Science. My thanks are due to Jack Goody for his help and advice.

169

stalls, from stalls and kiosks outside their houses, or from headloads which they hawked around the town. By 1969, the great majority of the Yoruba men were selling manufactured items. These included European cloth, provisions, and *worobo:* flashlights, batteries, ballpoint pens, cutlery, wallets, razor blades, and other cheap items. While the men selling provisions did so mainly at the wholesale level (by the carton or in larger units), the women for the most part sold single items direct to the consumer. Very few of the Yoruba in Tamale dealt in local foodstuffs, and few of them had stalls in the newer Aboabo Market on the road to Daboya, where the foodstuffs trade was located.

A brief discussion of the Yoruba kinship system will be useful at this point because the core of the Yoruba community in Tamale consisted not only of migrants from a small number of Yoruba towns, but of migrants from a small number of compounds within these same towns. After this discussion, we will consider in detail two of the four groups of related migrants which formed the core of the Ogbomosho migrant community in Tamale.

Yoruba towns consist of a large number of compounds (*ile*) in which normally reside the male members of a single agnatic lineage (*idile*) together with their wives and children. These lineages are localized corporate groups which are exogamous and in which are vested rights over property, residential land and farm land. Traditionally a compound consisted of a single large rectangular structure, but with the growth in population and the process of segmentation, these large structures have been progressively demolished to make way for a number of smaller buildings, each housing a lineage segment. The head of the lineage or segment (*bale*) is the oldest male member of the group concerned, and he has the final authority in matters which affect the members as a group.[1]

Yoruba kinship terminology is basically Hawaiian, but in addition it takes into account seniority. All collateral relatives of the same generation as ego, regardless of sex, are referred to as *ẹgbọn* (senior sibling) or *aburo* (junior sibling). This reflects the emphasis on seniority within the compound, defined by order of birth for members of the core lineage, and by order of marriage for their wives.[2] To his senior relatives in the compound, ego is expected to show deference and respect and to be willing to perform services for them when necessary. He expects the same from his junior relatives. The agnatic lineage therefore represents a pool of potential helpers for the successful migrant abroad.

1. Kinship organization varies between different areas of Yorubaland. For a description of the system in the northern part of Oyo State, from which most of the migrants in northern Ghana came, see P. C. Lloyd, "The Yoruba Lineage," *Africa*, vol. 25, no. 3 (1955), pp. 235–251.

2. On the Yoruba system of seniority, see W. R. Bascom, "The Principle of Seniority in the Social Structure of the Yoruba," *American Anthropologist*, vol. 44, no. 1 (1942), pp. 37–46.

Two other features of Yoruba kinship organization are relevant to an understanding of the cases presented in the next section. The first is the emphasis on the unity of the sibling group. The relationship between full siblings (ọmọiya) is expected to be one of affection and cooperation. It is expected that the relationship between half-siblings of the same father only (ọbakan) may be marked by more tension.[3] The second feature is the cognatic component in Yoruba kinship. Marriage is virilocal, but a woman retains rights and seniority in her natal compound, and maintains close contact with it in a situation where town endogamy is the norm. Therefore matrilateral links played an important part in the recruitment of some migrants to Ghana.

Ile Isalẹ

The first member of Ile Isalẹ in Tamale was Joseph Ọla, who arrived there in the 1930s.[4] Arriving before him in Ghana, however, was another member of the lineage, Braimah, who migrated first to Kumasi in the 1920s. Initially Joseph was trading in partnership with Shittu, a sister's son from another Ogbomosho compound. Each of the two men had gathered his own capital from farming, but they cooperated in buying and selling when necessary, and initially they dealt in Yoruba cloth brought from Nigeria.

In around 1934 they were joined by Rahimi, Braimah's senior half-brother's son, and his own eldest son, Ganiyu, who up to then had also been farming at home. Braimah was in charge of the cloth-buying in Nigeria, while the others sold in Kumasi and the surrounding villages. Later on, in the slacker parts of the year, Rahimi began to go to Navrongo, Tamale, Bawku, and the other towns in the north to buy foodstuffs for the market in Kumasi. The war disrupted the flow of cloth from Nigeria, and in around 1940, the whole group moved to Tamale to join Joseph. He was by then selling waist-beads assisted by Peter, his eldest son. By this time, also helping were Mohammed, Braimah's second son, and Lawani, a half-brother of Shittu. Up to the 1950s the members of both lineages were living in the same house in the Mossi Zongo in Tamale, which they rented from a Fanti man.

Immediately after the Second World War, there was another period of expansion in the cloth trade because of a shortage of European cloth. First Rahimi and then Mohammed took over the buying and transport from Nigeria. In addition to Yoruba cloth, from time to time group members took foodstuffs to Accra and bought European manufactured goods for sale in Tamale. It was in this postwar period that the group started to

3. This is also related to Yoruba inheritance patterns; see, for example, P. C. Lloyd, *Yoruba Land Law* (Ibadan: Oxford University Press, 1962), pp. 279ff.

4. All the names of the migrants and their compounds in the following sections have been changed.

break up. In 1948 Rahimi was given $550 and some goods to start trade on his own. From then on he dealt in *worobo*, changing to fishnets in the 1950s and shoes from around 1960. He was soon followed by Mohammed, Ganiyu, and Lawani, all three of whom also started to sell *worobo* on their own.

This was a period of rapid growth for Tamale. By 1950, after the war years, goods had started to come back onto the market and real incomes were rising rapidly.[5] The result was an increased level of trade and a rapid influx of Yoruba to exploit it. The house rented by this group was soon bursting at the seams with younger relatives recruited as helpers by those already established in Tamale. Most of them were helping Mohammed, Rahimi, and Peter Ọla, by this time the most successful traders, Peter having taken over when his father died just after the war. Rahimi was being helped by Raji his half-brother and by four sons of other siblings. Shittu was being helped by Gbademasi, his second son, and later by Salami, the third son. Lawani had working for him a brother's son and the son of a friend. Mohammed was helped by two father's brother's sons and a mother's brother's son. Peter was helped by his two junior full brothers, a half brother, and the son of a friend.

The only failure was Ganiyu, the eldest son of Braimah. He had been given his own capital about the same time as Mohammed, but he had spent it all. He moved to join Ogbomosho friends in Atebubu, then went on to Damongo where he stayed for three years. Despite repeated help from his brother Mohammed, he gave up trade. He came back to Tamale and learned tailoring from an Ede friend, paying him $8 for the tuition. Six months later his father Braimah returned to Nigeria to become *bale* of the compound.

After the heady days of market expansion in the early 1950s, the going became harder.[6] Besides Ganiyu's chronic financial difficulties, Shittu and Peter were in trouble as well. Mohammed did better, but made unsuccessful attempts to diversify his activities. Trade had been going well—he was taking $1500 to Accra two or three times a month and his three assistants were helping him to increase his turnover by cycling out to the rural markets every day. After his father went home he sent money to him to help build an "upstairs" house in Ogbomosho, and he also invested in a taxi and a diesel truck for a time. Neither of these two investments paid off. As many Yoruba in Tamale discovered, the problem was supervising the drivers. He eventually sold both vehicles and started to build a house in Tamale instead.

5. See E. J. Berg, "Real Income Trends in West Africa," in M. J. Herskovits and M. Harwitz, eds., *Economic Transition in Africa* (Evanston: Northwestern University Press, 1964), pp. 199–238.
6. See D. Rimmer, "The Crisis in the Ghana Economy," *Journal of Modern African Studies*, vol. 4, no. 1 (1966), pp. 17–32.

The difficulties of Peter and Shittu were more serious. As their trade declined, their helpers drifted off into other occupations. Yesufu, Shittu's eldest son, had already fallen out with his father over education and had been working for an expatriate for some time. Gbademasi, the second son, went to Ibadan to learn tailoring. After Salami finished primary school in 1959, Shittu packed up and followed Braimah home to Ogbomosho, where he went back to farming. Salami was sent to join another relative in Jos, where he attended technical school and then helped sell motor parts in the market there. Peter soldiered on with trade, but his brothers dropped out. In 1960 one of them became a driver and the second followed his lead in 1962. The third brother became a Public Works Department laborer. Finally Peter himself gave up trade in 1966 and became a daily contribution collector.[7]

The final stage in the development of the group came with the younger members separating during the 1960s. The economic climate by this time was much more difficult. While the senior established traders still continued to make money, the junior ones found increasing difficulty in getting started. Rahimi and Mohammed were both able to build houses of their own in Tamale, and both of them had three wives by this time. However, Raji, Rahimi's half brother, spent the capital he had been given in 1961. Rahimi was at first angry, and refused to help him again. Raji learned watch repairing from an Ogbomosho friend in the market. After a while the brothers patched up their quarrel and Raji started to trade again. He was in his own stall, but he also helped Rahimi with the buying when required. Peter's remaining helper, the son of one of his friends, had similar problems. Peter arranged his marriage in 1966 and gave him $40 starting capital. This was too small to allow him to become established. By 1969 he had given up and gone off to join a brother in Nkoranza.

The other helpers of Rahimi and Mohammed had gradually dropped out as well. Three of the boys helping Rahimi left for Kumasi and later joined relatives in Zaria. Two of them left in the early 1960s and the third left in 1968 after Rahimi had arranged his marriage and given him $170. The fourth of the brother's sons fared better in Tamale. He too was given $170 in 1968, and soon had a stall in the market nearly as large as Rahimi's.

Of Mohammed's helpers, the mother's brother's son disliked trade and his master's attempts to convert him to Islam. His own father was a Christian in Ogbomosho. After completing middle school he took a secretarial course and became a clerk in a secondary school. Raufu, the

7. Daily contribution collectors saved money for anyone who required their services. They collected a fixed amount from each client each day, and recorded the contributions on a special card. As payment, they retained the first contribution from each client each month.

father's brother's son, was given capital, and Mohammed arranged his marriage in 1967. His brother Kelani was working for him in 1969, and was still unmarried.

A final chapter in the family migration history was the reappearance of Shittu, who had been farming in Ogbomosho since 1959. Rahimi and Mohammed suggested that he come back to Ghana in 1968 and he did so, bringing Salami with him. He started to trade with the help of loans from the other two, in a spare stall of Mohammed's.

The general pattern, therefore, is one in which the original migrant recruits junior, mainly agnatic relatives, who in turn become independent and recruit their own helpers. A successful trader may over time recruit a number of these, some of which fare better in the market than others. The successful ones are normally given starting capital, often at the time of their first marriage, for which the master also pays, and after this they are left to trade on their own. Those that are able to become established remain trading in Tamale, and the less successful ones go elsewhere or turn to other occupations. Over the years, the main trend among the traders in this group was to move out of selling Yoruba cloth and to take up selling European cloth and other manufactured goods purchased from expatriate and Levantine firms in Accra and Kumasi. By 1969 the process had resulted in this case in the establishment of eight separate trading enterprises by related men, all working in the same area of the market and selling either *worobo* or shoes. It should also be noted that the dozen or so wives of the men were also trading.

Ile Oke

The first member of Ile Oke to go to Ghana was Joseph Ade. He made his first journey there in 1912 and spent 10 years trading in Accra, selling *adire* cloth. He returned to Ogbomosho to marry in 1922, and after three more years in Kumasi, went on to Tamale in 1925. In 1931 he took his brother Luke with him, and in 1937 he took Isaac, a son of his father's half-brother. Isaac had completed primary school before leaving Nigeria. At first the group was selling the usual Yoruba cloth, Joseph himself buying the cloth in Nigeria, traveling back and forth on the coastal route. Luke took over the traveling in the 1930s. During the Second World War, following the disruption of trade along the coast, the cloth was transported by Isaac and others on cycles.

After the war, Joseph spent increasing periods of time in Ogbomosho, leaving the trade to the others. Until 1953, Isaac did most of the traveling, and by the 1950s he was flying over from Accra to Lagos every three months to buy some $800 to $1500 worth of cloth at a time. Most of this was bought in Okeho, where he placed orders for the types of cloth in demand and then remained in Nigeria until the weaving was completed. After 1953, Moses, Joseph's eldest son, took over the traveling until they gave up the Nigerian cloth trade completely in 1958. They had been selling it not only in Tamale but also in the nearby villages, where it had been taken by Isaac and the younger members of the group on cycles.

Luke remained in control in Ghana when his brother left for home, and in 1950 he became a licensed dealer for the CFAO (Compagnie Française de l'Afrique Occidentale). This required a large amount of capital—$1400 or more as a deposit—but it was a logical step for the wealthier traders. It meant that they did not have to travel themselves to the south to collect the goods, that they would be given preference for any goods available, and that they would receive a commission for all goods sold, which would be added to their deposits. Luke continued with this arrangement until 1955, when he transferred to the United Africa Company (UAC). In 1958 he opened a second UAC store in Bawku, putting Moses in charge. In 1962 he disposed of his agency with the company and started his own store instead. With the accumulated commission and deposit he bought his first grinding mills.

Isaac also branched out. In 1950 his marriage had been arranged by Joseph in Ogbomosho, and in 1953 he started to trade on his own. At first he sold cloth and provisions. These he bought in Kumasi and Accra once a month, though he also had passbooks for CFAO and UAC in Tamale, which he could use when the goods were available. He had brought over his junior brother John, to help him, after John had completed school in Ogbomosho in 1950. Between 1953 and 1958 the brothers were also exploiting the trade in the neighboring countries of Upper Volta and Togo, where they sold goods from Kumasi. In 1958, Isaac was badly injured in a lorry accident. After his recovery he put down a deposit of $2000 with UAC and sold cycles and provisions until the exodus from Ghana in 1969.

Thus by 1960, Luke and Isaac were both with UAC. Isaac was helped by John and Luke by Gabriel, Moses' brother. Moses ran the UAC store in Bawku for Luke and was joined there by Matthew, a senior sister's son. For a time after the end of the war, Isaac's half brother, Peter, had been helping to transport the cloth, though he gave this up later and went back to farming. Ezekiel, another son of Joseph, helped Luke with odd jobs; but he was not good at trade and up to 1969 he had received neither a wife nor capital. By that year he had drifted off to become a carpenter-laborer with the Ministry of Agriculture.

By this time, Luke had begun to turn in other directions. Besides his house in Ogbomosho which he had built with Joseph, he had started to acquire houses in Tamale; by 1969 he had at least six there. Second, he had been buying more grinding mills; he had seven of them located in the town in 1969, which he and Gabriel supervised. The persons operating them were Dagomba, including relatives of one of his wives. (He had five wives by this time, two from Ogbomosho, one from Shaki, and two Ghanaians.) After 1962 he was selling grinding mill spares and provisions. Provisions became less important after the 1966 coup; there was a drastic fall-off in sales for many Yoruba, and Luke responded by going into farming. In 1967 he started a large maize and rice farm on the Walewale road, which he expanded with the help of a government loan for which he was able to use his houses as collateral. Moses, in Bawku, withdrew from trade around the same time and bought three grinding mills, which he ran with the help of Matthew and hired local laborers; this remained his full-time occupation until 1969.

Isaac had been less fortunate. His cycle store had done well until the middle 1960s. He paid for John's marriage in 1962 and soon after that suffered two expensive setbacks. First, a load of smuggled goods belonging to him was confiscated at the border. Then John, who had become a part-time daily contribution collector, absconded with some of the money. Isaac paid off John's creditors and kept the matter out of the hands of the police. In 1967 local memory of the scandal had softened enough to allow John to return to Tamale. He got a job as a sales assistant in a Lebanese shop across the street from his brother's store. Relations between the two brothers were not good, and Isaac was criticized by many, especially John's friends, for his failure to help his brother start trading on his own. He himself had brought over a younger half-brother, Paul, to help him with the cycles. Despite these setbacks, Isaac had managed to retain an air of prosperity by building a house in Tamale— though it was said that most of the money came from his wife, one of the richest Ogbomosho women in the town. In 1968, he followed Luke's example and started a farm.

Summary and Analysis

We may now summarize the main input which these traders derived from membership of the Yoruba group. First, the Yoruba in Tamale, though trading on a small scale, were a relatively prosperous group by north Ghanaian standards. The median turnover of the male traders we interviewed was $640 per month, but 18 percent of them had turnovers of $1700 or more per month. It must be remembered that it was the wealthy traders who were most likely to recruit junior relatives to assist them. Unsuccessful traders and assistants would normally be advised or assisted by the other Yoruba to go home or to find other work in Ghana so that they would become self-supporting. In a situation where the majority of migrants were being recruited by relatives who were already established traders, capital was fairly readily available. In time, the successful migrant might recruit a number of assistants and eventually give them capital; and at least some of them might be able to establish themselves in their own right.

Second, there was the training factor. The success of the early traders was based on their access to Yoruba cloth, for which there was a heavy demand from the end of the First World War onward. Over the years, however, as their interests diversified, they were more and more likely to face competition from members of other ethnic groups. Continued Yoruba success was promoted by the training process inherent in the pattern of recruitment. During the course of his apprenticeship the junior relative would learn all aspects of market trade—bargaining techniques, pricing, sources of supply (both legal and illegal), and the areas of supply and demand.

Third, within the Yoruba community in Tamale there was a complex network of short-term credit arrangements between close friends and spouses, which enabled traders to make their buying trips to the south even though not all of their creditors were paid up. Other credit mechanisms operating within the Yoruba community included esusu, or rotating credit associations,[8] and daily contribution collectors; in addition, there was access to association funds for the members of some of the Yoruba town unions with branches in Tamale.

Fourth, the ongoing communications system within the Yoruba community in and outside the market served as a source of information on market conditions both in Tamale and farther afield. Close friends confided in each other and asked each other's advice in economic as well as other matters, and useful market information would thus often be shared. Even if a trader attempted to hide information or a successful deal in the market, other Yoruba with their eyes and ears open could often deduce information which outsiders could easily miss. Besides having access to these complex patterns of information, a new trader could benefit from reciprocal stall-minding, the passing on of customers to fellow Yoruba who were known to stock the goods required, and other services of this kind.

Fifth, as the trader built up his turnover, junior relatives from home became a source of labor he could draw upon. In Tamale, this meant that the demand for goods in the rural areas could be met. Most of the older Yoruba traders had once spent time traveling round the larger rural markets in the vicinity, either by lorry, cycle, or on foot, selling goods for senior relatives; and many still had junior relatives doing the rounds for them in 1969. Others went further afield, taking goods to customers as far away as Wa, Bolgatanga, and Bawku. Junior relatives could also be sent to buy in the south, enabling their masters to keep the Tamale stall open more of the time.

Finally, the migrant could take advantage of his ethnic group membership in his relations with the authorities. The wealthier Yoruba

8. On the esusu, see W. R. Bascom, "The Esusu: a Credit Institution of the Yoruba," Journal of the Royal Anthropological Institute, vol. 82 (1952), pp. 63–69.

traders like Luke had a wide and well-developed network of contacts with the police and the bureaucracy, and this network could be used by other Yoruba if they ran into trouble. The usual sort of trouble in the 1960s concerned trade in smuggled goods and infringements of price-control regulations.

From his membership in the minority group in Tamale, then, the individual derives training and capital. Training combined with the presence of the required psychological traits determines his routine entrepreneurial ability—by which I mean his ability to handle business on a day-to-day basis without necessarily making innovations in technique. His ability to increase his turnover, on the other hand, depends on the information at his disposal (both inside and outside the Yoruba community), the size of his available capital, the support he can gain from short-term loans, and the use of junior relatives as assistants.

We should next consider the nature of the links between the Yoruba and their Ghanaian hosts. A common view of minority trading groups emphasizes the restriction of interaction between group members and outsiders.[9] In the case of the Yoruba in Tamale, this would be an oversimplification. Many Yoruba, such as Luke, had extensive friendship networks outside the Yoruba community, which on occasion could yield important benefits for them. Though Isaac was prominent within the Yoruba community through his position on the Baptist Church committee, his primary-school education—which distinguished him from most Yoruba of his age group—drew him naturally toward educated businessmen and civil servants in Tamale who belonged to other ethnic groups. He was a member of a quasi-masonic order which drew its membership from this semi-elite stratum, and was frequently called upon to help sort out matters involving other Yoruba and the bureaucracy or the police. Though Nigerians were technically ineligible to vote in the 1969 election campaign, Isaac did so and openly supported the National Alliance of Liberals, as did Luke.[10] Luke's networks were rather different but equally extensive. As a prominent member of the Nigerian community committee and the Yoruba community in the town, he was one of the most influential Yoruba elders. Through his Dagomba wife he was allied to the Andani family, which he supported in the longstanding Yendi chiefship dispute.[11] Thus besides being prominent Yoruba leaders, these men were unusually active in local politics, which they could not have been with-

9. For a stimulating discussion of the concomitants of exclusiveness, see E. Bonacich, "A Theory of Middleman Minorities," *American Sociological Review*, vol. 38, no. 5 (1973), pp. 583–594.

10. The NAL was the main opposition party in the Ghanaian Parliament after September 1969; the seats they held included Tamale.

11. This dispute over the paramount chiefship of the Dagomba kingdom flared into violence in September 1969 with a serious shooting incident in Yendi, 60 miles east of Tamale. See M. Staniland, *The Lions of Dagbon* (Cambridge: Cambridge University Press, 1975).

out strong ties with the host group. These ties persisted beyond the alien compliance order and exodus of 1969. The last I heard was that both men had returned to Ghana.after the coup of 1972 which ousted the Busia regime.

So far we have considered the impact of Yoruba identity on the career of the individual migrant. We may now ask a reverse question: What are the implications of entrepreneurial success for the maintenance of Yoruba identity, and the links of the migrant with his place of origin? This is a complex question, because the wealthier the trader is, the more options are available to him. It is the wealthier trader who has the money to make frequent visits to Nigeria, to bring junior relatives from Nigeria to work for him, to build a house in which to retire at home, and so on. On the other hand, he is also the individual with the largest assets in Ghana, and the one who stands to lose most financially by returning home and leaving his assets in Ghana to the care of junior relatives, if he does not choose to sell them completely.

For the earliest Yoruba traders in northern Ghana, this dilemma did not arise. They came to Ghana to sell cloth, and having sold it they returned to Nigeria to buy more. Before long, however, they began to acquire assets in Ghana. By the 1930s some of the more prosperous Yoruba had begun to acquire houses in Tamale; it was not until the 1950s, however, when the trade in Yoruba cloth dwindled, that the main thrust of Yoruba housebuilding in Tamale began. Even in 1969, most Yoruba in Tamale said that the construction of a house at home was still high on their list of priorities; but the currency restrictions of the 1960s made the repatriation of funds ever more expensive, and so housebuilding in Tamale increased steadily.[12] Nevertheless, the pull of ties with home was still strong: some old Yoruba traders with assets in Ghana had retired to Nigeria to assume the position of *bale* in their compounds in the late 1960s, even before the Compliance Order, and very few Yoruba died in Tamale. However, the Yoruba in Northern Ghana were comparatively recent arrivals. Whether this pattern would have continued or whether the migrants with assets in Ghana would have become more and more reluctant to leave them there is an open question.[13]

Thus far, we have limited ourselves to spelling out some of the implications of the structure of social relations obtaining within a minority group, and between it and its place of origin, for the type of entrepreneurship in which it is engaged in the migrant situation. For a complete evaluation of Yoruba success in trade in Ghana, a number of other elements would have to be considered, notably the inputs available to other

12. It was more expensive because of the necessity of using the black market to obtain Nigerian currency. See Rimmer, "Crisis in the Ghana Economy."

13. On this, see F. Oyedipe, "Some Sociological Aspects of the Yoruba Family in Accra" (unpublished M. A. thesis, University of Ghana, Legon, 1967), p. 92.

ethnic groups in a competitive market and the way in which the Yoruba were able to avoid or overcome competition.[14] Without attempting an exhaustive evaluation, we may use the two cases presented earlier to discuss several other factors in the Yoruba success in Ghana.

To begin with, there were the financial remittances to Nigeria, made both by the migrants as individuals and through their town associations. While the remittances made through the associations have been well documented,[15] they were probably only a small fraction of the total. Most remittances consisted of money sent back to Nigeria by individuals for the support of relatives, marriage payments, and the construction of houses. It would be extremely difficult to perform a cost-benefit analysis of investments of this sort versus the alternatives available in Ghana. While multiple marriages and the construction of houses in the remoter areas of the Western State of Nigeria did withdraw capital from circulation, they still remained high on the list of priorities for the successful trader, given the goal of eventual prestigious retirement at home.

Next there is the question of the proliferation of enterprises. It is possible that whereas one-man or small-scale trading units were a rational adaptation to the trading conditions of the 1950s, such units were becoming less viable in the increasing economic gloom that followed independence.

The history of Ile Isalẹ enterprise in Tamale is typical of Yoruba commerce there, resulting in a number of traders in the same part of the market, all of them related to each other and selling similar lines of goods. The career of the Ile Oke group, by comparison, was marked by a considerable degree of innovation: Luke was the first Yoruba in Tamale to be a licensed agent for the large firms, and one of the first to see the potential of grinding mills and farming as alternatives to trade. While the Ile Isalẹ group was becoming a series of small one-man enterprises, the Ile Oke group grew in a more diverse and capital-intensive pattern. It is worth noting the point at which fission occurred in each group. Luke and Rahimi were both married around 1940, but while Rahimi was given capital and started on his own in 1948, no split took place in the other group until 1953, by which time they had opened the CFAO store. By that time the original capital of the other group was already divided between Braimah, his two sons, and Rahimi.

The two groups also responded differently to the market expansion of the 1950s. The Ile Isalẹ response was labor-intensive: large numbers of

14. It is easy to lapse into circularity in an analysis of this type and see all aspects of Yoruba migrant social structure as being functional in the market. It could be argued that in some ways, the maintenance of strong links with home was a drain on the entrepreneurial capacity of the Yoruba migrants.

15. For example, A. L. Mabogunje, *Regional Mobility and Resource Development in West Africa* (Montreal: McGill-Queen's University Press, 1972), pp. 135–137.

junior relatives who could cope with the demand in the rural areas joined the others in Ghana. The Ile Oke response was to become established with the large firms and use them as a base from which to move into other areas. Thus when the market contracted in the 1960s, the Ile Oke capital remained in the hands of two men, who could shift it into investments which they considered to have the most potential. The legacy of the recruitment of assistants in the 1950s was a number of impatient young men in the 1960s—men who were expecting marriage arrangements and trading capital from their masters in a time of reduced prosperity.

A final point to be made about this material relates to the distinction Leibenstein makes between innovative and routine entrepreneurship.[16] Most of the Yoruba traders in Tamale were not innovative entrepreneurs. They dealt in standard lines of goods, exploiting the steady demand from public-sector employees in the town, and using methods which changed little over the years. Their access to training and capital, together with their access to information, made them competent in this, but it remained essentially routine activity bringing in a steady return. Returns diminished, however, after independence and the coup. In 1969 the wealthiest Yoruba traders in Tamale were those, like Luke, who had realized this and moved into different fields.

Looking further, there may be a connection between the patterns of recruitment described, the commercial conservatism which they gave rise to, and the patterns of ethnic specialization which have developed in many markets in West Africa. With rapid change in patterns of demand, particular ethnic groups such as the Yoruba have the assets to exploit a particular economic niche very successfully once it is opened up. However, this does not guarantee their success in new niches that might open up, or in their old niche in the face of changing market conditions. In Tamale, the Yoruba have remained almost entirely dealers in manufactured goods, whereas the local Dagomba have moved successfully into the foodstuffs, cattle, and transport industries, and have become some of the wealthiest local entrepreneurs; the Yoruba, despite attempts by individuals, have on the whole been unable to compete. The result of a conservative training and recruitment process is a pattern in which particular ethnic groups become entrenched in successively developing economic niches. A few Yoruba, such as Luke, were able to break away from this pattern of ethnic specialization and establish new types of enterprise. Others continued in set ways until forced out of the market, either by the declining demand which affected most of the Yoruba traders in the 1960s, or by the political pressures of the Compliance Order in 1969.

16. H. Leibenstein, "Entrepreneurship and Development," *American Economic Review*, vol. 58 (1968), pp. 72–83.

Conclusion

This chapter has touched on two themes common in the literature on trade in West Africa. The first is the role of the "extended family," however defined, either in aiding the development of entrepreneurship or in hindering it.[17] We have seen in this case that kinship links were crucial to the Yoruba traders in Tamale, both in the recruitment and socialization of assistants and in the mobilization of capital for the aspiring Yoruba trader. In a sense, the migrant trader is in a fortunate position vis-à-vis his kin at home. He can call on the labor of junior relatives when it suits him, but he is insulated by distance from the day-to-day demands on his capital by fellow lineage members. But despite this he eventually has to face the cost of the capitalizing junior relatives; and it can be argued that this process of fission leads to a fragmentation of capital and a diminution of the group's economic effectiveness. Thus while kinship links are crucial in the establishment of trading enterprises, their other implications for trading patterns are more ambiguous.

The second theme is the factor of minority group status and the inputs which derive from it for the individual entrepreneurs. The case material suggests that the most important of these inputs were credit, information, and support in dealings with the authorities, all within the framework of trust and understanding within the minority group, with its efficient communications system. However, this is not to say that relationships of trust did not occur with outsiders. In fact, several individuals in the Yoruba community in Tamale had many close contacts with Ghanaians. These functioned in the interests of the Yoruba community in two ways: when other Yoruba required assistance, and when they allowed the individuals concerned to reestablish themselves in Ghana after the Compliance Order. The Yoruba in Tamale must not therefore be seen as a monolithic whole, with impermeable social barriers between it and outsiders. Individuals within it had a range of options open to them—options leading either to maintenance of links with home or further involvement in Ghana—and the wealthier migrants were in a position to seek the best of both.

17. On this point, see W. Penn Handwerker, "Kinship, Friendship and Business Failure among Market Sellers in Monrovia, Liberia, 1970," *Africa*, vol. 43, no. 4 (1973), pp. 288–301.

10

The Ideology of Regionalism in Ghana

Enid Schildkrout

O ne of the more unfortunate legacies of much that has been written on Africa is a reification of poorly defined ethnic categories. Whereas naive observers still think of Africa in terms of "tribes" and "nations," Africans themselves obviously employ a much wider and more subtle range of social categories in their daily lives. This becomes clear when one looks at the way strangers are defined in a number of African societies. Strangers are indeed sometimes designated on the basis of ethnicity or nationality; but a stranger may also be someone from a different kin group, an affine, or someone from another locality, clan, or cultural or linguistic group; or he may come from another country, race, or continent. These definitions obviously change in context, but some definitions of strangers are much more tenacious than others, reminding us that the distinction between stranger and host is not always equivalent to that between outsider and insider. This chapter will examine one of the more persistent dichotomies between "us" and "them" among a small group of people in Ghana and suggest some reasons for its tenacity.

In much of West Africa the most persistent category of inclusion and exclusion is neither tribe nor nation, but regional identity.[1] Definitions of strangers in regional terms are more persistent than many other social boundaries, except perhaps those such as nationality, which are reinforced through legal sanctions. It is curious that regional categories of identity have been neglected in the literature, for they are older than those of the modern nation-states and more persistent than the tribal or cultural units often recognized by colonial administrators and anthropologists. In West Africa, as in many other areas, regional categories persist, and indeed have developed as cognitive categories in the first place,

The research on which this chapter is based has been supported by the National Institute of Mental Health (grant No. MH 11859), the Wenner-Gren Foundation for Anthropological Research (grant No. 2597), and the University of Illinois at Urbana. Among the several people who assisted in the analysis of data, I would particularly like to thank Duane Orlowski, who worked on this project for a year at the University of Illinois. Marcia Darlington, Frances Fosburgh, and Sarah Meltzoff also helped with the analysis at the American Museum of Natural History. An earlier and quite different version of this paper was presented at the New York Academy of Sciences in 1974.

1. Regions here are defined as distinctive geographical areas, not as administrative units.

because they are based upon differences in resource availability and subsistence patterns. These variations structured relations between peoples of different regions even in precolonial times. Trade relationships, migration, and patterns of warfare all exploited regional variations. In Ghana, as in almost the whole of sub-Saharan West Africa, the most significant variation is that between the southern coastal and forest region on the one hand, and the northern savannah on the other.[2] There are obvious differences in mean annual temperature, rainfall patterns, and vegetation which support variations in subsistence patterns and cultural traditions.[3] These variations have deeply affected the ways in which people of the savannah and peoples of the forest have interacted and perceived each other for several centuries. In colonial and postcolonial times these regional contrasts have been exaggerated by a pattern of unequal economic development. In some cases, regional complementarity has become regional inequality, when, in a national context, one area has developed at the expense of another.

People inevitably elaborate on differences such as these in order to symbolically express their perceptions of their interaction. Stereotypes are elaborated around those social categories which are most relevant at any given time; regional categories become particularly important in situations involving the distribution of scarce resources, including labor, within a national context.

In the analysis which follows, cultural differences between peoples of different regions are *not* seen to be the underlying reason for the existence of social categories based on regional identity. However, real or mythopoeic cultural differences do provide the content of stereotypes which express the pattern of regional dichotomization. Stereotypes, then, are part of a cognitive superstructure. Although they consist of attributions of cultural traits, they are not necessarily accurate descriptions of cultural variation.[4] They are descriptions of the ways in which

2. Although there are ecological differences between the forest and the coast, communication has been much easier in this area. The distinction between forest and coast is therefore not as significant as that between the south as a regional zone, including the forest, and the northern savannah. In this light, unless otherwise specified Asantes are referred to as southerners in this paper.

3. See D. Forde, "A Cultural Map of West Africa: Successive Adaptations to Tropical Forests and Grasslands," *Transactions of the New York Academy of Sciences*, vol. 15, no. 6 (1953), pp. 206–219.

4. Ethnic categories or groups are not necessarily based on the possession of a distinctive culture. See E. Schildkrout, "Ethnicity and Generational Differences among Urban Immigrants in Ghana," in A. Cohen, ed., *Urban Ethnicity*, Association of Social Anthropologists Monograph No. 12 (London: Tavistock, 1974), pp. 187–222. The minimal definition of an ethnic unit, as defined here, is the idea of common provenance, recruitment primarily through kinship, and a notion of distinctiveness whether or not this consists of a unique inventory of cultural traits. Stereotypes are the cognitive counterpart of ethnicity, in that they consist of a selection of cultural attributes which may or may not correspond to cultural reality or to the self-concept of members of the stereotyped group.

members of a particular category are thought to be different; they are, in this sense, folk ethnographies. They consist of sets of symbols which are used to define boundaries, and they may be read as rules about permitted and restricted areas of social behavior. Through the use of cultural symbols, stereotypes describe, and sometimes proscribe, relationships between insiders and outsiders, expressing limits, potentials, and expectations of interaction.

Although stereotypes are sometimes constructed, as well as exploited, quite consciously and deliberately by demagogues, in many cases they are simply learned generalizations about the world, accepted unquestioningly until they are believed to be perceptions of reality.

The attitudes held by one group about another may be described as an ideology, if this is understood in the minimal sense of "a set of closely related beliefs or ideas, or even attitudes characteristic of a group or community."[5] Stereotypes about strangers often reflect the ambivalence of the position of the stranger which Simmel and others (see Levine, in Chapter One) have pointed out. In some cases the attitudes held about stranger groups are replete with contradictions and consist of complex concatenations of positive and negative attitudes. The attitudes which are expressed depend upon the context in which they are elicited. From the point of view of a student of social relations, the most important thing about an ideology is not its content, however, but the way in which it is used. There is no necessary correlation between these phenomena. In discussing the attitudes of southern Ghanaian children towards northern Ghanaians, and in reviewing attitudes to northerners in nineteenth-century Asante, we shall be dealing with the content of an ideology, and not necessarily at all with the behavior of the individuals whose attitudes are described.

Strangers in Asante:
Concepts and General Background

The Akan term for stranger, *ohoho*, Rattray speculated, derives from *eho*, literally "one from over there." It refers to someone from another political division, tribe, or locality who may or may not be Asante. Basically it refers to any outsider or visitor, one lacking rights of membership in the community.[6] A number of Asante proverbs illustrate the attitude of the Asante to the *ohoho*. To give only two: "a stranger does not break laws" (he is not expected to conform to the Akan legal code); and "a stranger may have big big eyes, but he does not see into what is going on among the people he is with, whereas the town's man, with little little eyes, knows all the town's affairs."[7]

5. J. Plamenatz, *Ideology* (London: Macmillan, 1970).
6. R. S. Rattray, *Ashanti Law and Constitution* (London: Oxford University Press, 1929).
7. Two versions and translations are in Rattray, *Ashanti Law*, pp. 142ff.

Besides the *ohoho*, or sojourner, there are other individuals and communities which are in some ways defined as outsiders, but which have very clear statuses and roles in, or in relation to, Asante society. From an observer's viewpoint, there is a series of more and more inclusive stranger-host dichotomies in Asante, and in various situations an individual can place himself at any point within this series. Thus many Asantes in Kumasi are strangers from the point of view of the few whose families have claims to land in the town. When the community of inclusion is defined in terms of ethnic categories such as Asante or Akan, all Asante or all Akan are strangers. In Kumasi, with a population of almost a quarter million, non-Akans constitute 40 percent of the population. If birthplace is the relevant criterion, a non-Asante born in Kumasi may not be a stranger, while an Asante may be. If the distinction is made on a national basis, the stranger category becomes congruent with that of alien. At one time or another, all of these distinctions are made and used as a basis for behavior.[8] Depending upon what rights, privileges, or resources are at stake, those with legitimate claims to access will be defined differently.

Thus the population of Kumasi and of the Ashanti Region can be broken down into a number of categories whose members may or may not be defined as strangers in different situations. According to the 1960 census, less than half of the Kumasi population identified itself as Asante and 26 percent were non-Asantes from southern Ghana.[9] At least one-third of the total consisted of northerners, including peoples from northern Ghana—Dagomba, Mamprusi, Tallensi (Frafra), Dagati, and others —and people from the savannah areas of the surrounding countries, including the Mossi, Hausa, Yoruba, Zabarama, and others.

In the region as a whole, the population also exhibits considerable heterogeneity. For the past several hundred years, the Asante population has absorbed numerous northern immigrants who are now culturally, if not socially, indistinguishable from other Asante.[10] It also contains many

8. For example, in the long dispute over the Imamate of the Kumasi central mosque, see E. Schildkrout, "Islam and Politics in Ghana: An Analysis of Disputes over the Kumasi Central Mosque," *Anthropological Papers of the American Museum of Natural History*, vol. 52, no. 2 (1974), pp. 113–137.

9. The 1960 census is unreliable on the subject of northerners and aliens because it was taken a few months after the government issued a "quit order" to aliens. Many of them thereafter claimed to be from northern Ghana. Also, no ethnic breakdowns have been published at the time of this writing.

10. There is some debate on this point. See M. Fortes, *Kinship and the Social Order* (London: Routledge and Kegan Paul, 1969), p. 262; K. Poku, "Traditional Roles and People of Slave Origin in Modern Ashanti—A Few Impressions," *Ghana Journal of Sociology*, vol. 5, no. 1 (1969), pp. 34–38; Rattray, *Ashanti Law*, p. 40; and I. Wilks, *Asante in the Nineteenth Century*, African Studies Series No. 13 (Cambridge: Cambridge University Press, 1975). The question remains whether or not a naturalized Asante could attain *full* jural rights when many of these were conferred through filiation.

northerners who continue to come to the region to work as agricultural laborers. Only 28 percent of the region's population including the urban areas was listed as Akan in 1960, indicating that in the countryside the proportion of non-Akans is even higher than in Kumasi city.

In rural areas most of the non-Akans are laborers on Asante cocoa farms. A number have their own farms, or engage in trade, but most migrate temporarily to Asante to earn money and return home. They work for Asante employers in a number of capacities—on yearly contracts, on short contracts for piecework on specified tasks, on a share-cropping basis, or as daily or weekly laborers. The dependence of the Asante farmer on northern labor is so great that in 1970, following the Busia government's order that all unregistered aliens leave the country, a delegation of Asante farmers requested that the government suspend the order in the case of cocoa laborers, on the grounds that the year's cocoa crop would be destroyed without the assistance of northerners.

In urban areas, such as Kumasi, northern men are engaged in two main types of activity: unskilled and semi-skilled labor, and trade. A small minority are craftsmen and skilled laborers, but most professional and white-collar jobs are held by Akans or southern Ghanaians. Some northern groups are almost exclusively engaged in either trade or labor, while others have members engaged in both. For example, most Hausa and Yoruba men are traders, while the majority of the Tallensi, Grunsi, and Dagati are unskilled or semi-skilled laborers.[11] The Mossi, Dagomba, and Mamprusi men are both traders and laborers. None of these divisions is absolute, however, as no northern or stranger group has a monopoly over any occupation or area of trade.

There are certain obvious cultural differences between northerners and the Asante which should be mentioned briefly. In both rural and urban Asante, northerners, particularly the men, are distinguished from the Asante by language and dress, except of course when people are wearing Western clothes or speaking English. While northerners as a whole speak many different languages, in Kumasi they communicate with each other in Hausa, the lingua franca. Very few of the immigrants, in most cases only those with rural experience as employees of Asante, know Twi, the Asante language. Even fewer Asante speak Hausa, which is the first language of many second-generation northern immigrants. Religion is another area in which the cultural contrast between Asantes and northerners has become greater as the population of the stranger

11. Among women, these ethnic categorizations are almost totally invalid, because women in general are not highly represented in skilled or white-collar labor, and women from almost every group engage in trade. It is significant that ethnic stereotypes about groups in general are based on the behavior of men. The behavior of women enters only into those stereotypes that deal specifically with female sexuality. This may be a nearly universal phenomenon, and is worthy of much fuller treatment.

community has grown. Although there are an increasing number of Asante Muslim converts, they are still a small minority compared to the number of northern Muslims. Similarly, the number of northern Christians is negligible, while many Asante belong to one Christian denomination or another. In both communities, cultural change is obvious, but the direction of acculturation is very different: as the Asante increasingly become Westernized, the northerners become more thoroughly assimilated into a Hausa version of the Islamic tradition.

North-South Relations in Historical Perspective

The Asante had basically two types of relations with northerners in the precolonial period: they knew them as slaves and as traders. Although the political and economic context of these relations has changed in the twentieth century, one can still discern continuity—not, obviously, in continuance of the institution of slavery, but in the economic activities of northerners in Asante and in their position in the regional economy.

From the late seventeenth to the early nineteenth century, Asante was an expanding polity, conquering and governing a large area which extended northwards almost as far as what is now the northern boundary of Ghana.[12] Asante relations with the north had two main purposes: the exaction of tribute in the form of slaves, gold, cloth, livestock, and other commodities; and the control of trade between the savannah and the coast. Until the early nineteenth century, when the European slave trade was abolished, it was to Asante's advantage to exact in tribute as many slaves as possible, for these could be sold to Europeans for firearms and other goods. However, even before abolition, and to a greater extent after it, slaves were used in metropolitan Asante as agricultural laborers.[13] They were also used in industry, particularly gold mining, an activity fraught with taboos for the Asante but permissible to slaves; and they were also employed as soldiers and engaged in the manufacture of bullets.

Asante's requirements for labor were sufficiently great, due to migration to urban areas and military conscription, that she was almost always able to absorb large numbers of slaves, and even demanded in-

12. K. Arhin, ed., "Ashanti and the Northeast," *University of Ghana Institute of African Studies Research Review*, Supplement No. 2 (Legon: 1970). J. Goody, "The Mande and the Akan Hinterland," in Vansina, Mauny, and L. V. Thomas, eds., *The Historian in Africa* (London: Oxford University Press for the International African Institute, 1964), pp. 193–219. J. Goody and K. Arhin, eds., "Ashanti and the Northwest," *University of Ghana Institute of African Studies Research Review*, Supplement No. 1 (Legon: 1965). I. Wilks, "Ashanti Government," in Forde and Kaberry, eds., *West African Kingdoms in the Nineteenth Century* (London: Oxford University Press for the International African Institute, 1967), pp. 206–238; and Wilks, *Asante in the Nineteenth Century*.

13. K. Arhin, "Market Settlements in Northwestern Ashanti: Kintampo," in Goody and Arhin, eds., "Ashanti and the Northwest"; and Wilks, *Asante in the Nineteenth Century*.

creases in the tribute in slaves in the late nineteenth century. Given this regular and large influx of foreigners, the Asante rulers adopted policies specifically designed to prevent the emergence of an ethnically distinct servile class and at the same time maintain the productive use of unfree labor.[14] Bowdich observed in the early nineteenth century how the Asante distributed slaves throughout the country, using them "to create plantations in the more remote and stubborn tracts."[15] Some late nineteenth-century writers estimated the slave population as being half that of the total of the Kumasi area.[16] But accurate statistics on the number of unfree subjects in Asante were never obtainable, because of the official policy of dispersing and incorporating northerners into the general population.

After several generations, slaves were invariably assimilated into local kinship groups, and a taboo on mentioning the origin of another obscured slave ancestry even further.[17] Intermarriages between slaves and free Asante are said to have been common, and the children of such marriages were free. The children of Asante men and unfree women had an adoptive matriclan (*abusua*) affiliation, in that they usually joined the *abusua* of the father, in contrast to the usual matrilineal pattern. They were known as *kanifa* (half Akan) and "grew up to consider themselves Ashanti."[18] The children of free Asante women and male slaves were free and became members of their mother's *abusua* in the normal way.[19]

In the first generation slave status was difficult to hide, but it was not necessarily a greater liability than being born into the lower classes (*ahiafo*) of Asante society.[20] As Rattray emphasized, the notion of being subject (*akoa*) to the authority of another is intrinsic to many Akan institutions, and it can be used to describe the hierarchy of power within the family and within all levels of the political system.[21] Masters had the same responsibilities for their slaves as they did for their relatives, so that dependence also implied protection.

Despite incorporation into local kinship groups, first-generation slaves still stood out because of their foreign origins.[22] One connotation

---

14. Wilks, *Asante in the Nineteenth Century*, pp. 66, 84, 708.

15. T. E. Bowdich, *An Essay on the Superstitions, Customs, and Arts Common to the Ancient Egyptians, Abyssinians, and Ashantees* (Paris, 1821), p. 18.

16. Wilks, *Asante in the Nineteenth Century*, p. 674.

17. Rattray, *Asante Law*, p. 40.

18. *Ibid.*, p. 39.

19. *Ibid.*, pp. 38ff.; Poku, "Traditional Roles and People of Slave Origin . . . ," pp. 35ff.

20. Wilks, *Asante in the Nineteenth Century*, pp. 86, 443, 706; T. E. Bowdich, *Mission from Cape Coast Castle to Ashantee* (London, 1819), pp. 120ff., 250, 318, 376.

21. In *Ashanti Proverbs* (1916) Rattray translates the word *akoa* as slave, with a long note on the beneficence of the Asante institution of slavery.

22. Asante could also be reduced to slave status through capture in civil war, in voluntary search for protection, or through the non-redemption or outright selling of pawns (Rattray, *Ashanti Law*, pp. 37, 53). Fortes disagrees that Asante could sell each other into slavery (*Kinship and the Social Order*, p. 263).

of the general term for slave (*odonko*, pl. *nnonko* or *nnonkofo*) was "outsider" or "non-Asante and bought"—in contrast to those who were born into an Asante lineage or who were Asante but who had been pawned (*awowa*).[23] Rattray notes that the term *odonko* "was even once loosely used to describe all the inhabitants of the Northern Territories of the Gold Coast, who were once considered as being the potential slaves of the powerful Southern Kingdom. The main characteristic of an *odonko* in the Ashanti mind is summed up in the fact of his bearing tribal marks."[24]

He also reports that among the *odonko* much time was spent trying to rub out the marks. The children of slaves were not marked and were considered to be *akoa* rather than *odonko*.[25] (The Asante themselves do not practice facial scarification except for a small cheek incision in which medicine is inserted.)

Slaves in Asante had clearly defined rights which not only promoted their incorporation and assimilation but also protected them. An Asante proverb says, "gold dust is like a slave, if you do not look after it well it runs away."[26] Included in these rights were the right to own property, including other slaves, to be a witness, to swear an oath, and ultimately to inherit the property of a master. Slaves reached important political positions in the courts of chiefs at various levels. The major liability of an *odonko* lay in the fact that he (or she) had no kin. The *odonko* could be sacrificed in the Asante funeral custom under the supervision of an Asante chief, although this fate generally awaited only those who had committed a crime. A slave was not supposed to mix too familiarly with free men; he might not go to a chief's house unless he were the slave of the chief. Slaves usually wore distinctive dress, consisting of a shirt of blue-and-white woven material, drawers, and a metal (but never gold) or stone bangle on the right upper arm.[27] They were expected to work harder than free men, and were given work that was considered unclean. A slave would not be given an Asante burial, could not perform sacrifices to Asante ancestors, and could not succeed to lineage offices. In the

23. The Gonja were known as *ntafo*, although this is now a term used for all northerners. It is said to refer to people from the Northern Territories. The Dagomba were known as *anwafo*. *Odonko* described northerners who were not otherwise readily identifiable.

24. Rattray, *Ashanti Law*, p. 35.

25. If an Asante went south and returned with Fanti, Akin, or Accra marks, he was liable to be killed by the king, according to Rattray (*ibid.*, p. 35 n.) "for introducing a foreign fashion." However, an interesting exception to this prohibition on alien marks existed in the case of the *begyina 'ba*, the "come and stay child." After a succession of infant deaths, parents would give their next child a northern name or add the suffix *donkor* to the child's name, and give him northern markings, on the supposition that the malevolent spirit who had stolen the previous children would either be deceived or disinterested in the child. See Rattray, *Religion and Art in Ashanti* (London: Oxford University Press, 1927), p. 65; and *Ashanti Law*, p. 35n.

26. Rattray, *Ashanti Law*, p. 163.

27. *Ibid.*, p. 43.

first generation, the status of slave was in some ways equivalent to that of any jural minor.[28] The use of the metaphor of age to express relative incorporation into the society is also suggested by the proverb, "among royalty no one is a child."[29]

The Asante held notions of superiority vis-à-vis northerners even though they admired them and perhaps feared them in certain ways. Rattray quotes an Asante as saying that unlike an *odonko*, an Asante war captive would probably eat with his master "because he would know how to wash his hands."[30] Osei Bonsu, the Asantehene in 1817, alluded to the "insolent disposition of the lower orders of Asantes," many of whom were drawn from non-Asante groups; they were, he said, "the worst people existing, except the Fantees."[31] On another occasion, he made an even more revealing comment. When Bowdich was attempting to convince him of the altruistic "civilizing" mission of the British in conquering Asante, he told Bowdich:

> This motive cannot be the real one. I well see that you are much superior to the Asante in industry and the arts; for in [your] fort of Cape Coast itself, which is only a small establishment, you have many things which we do not know how to make: but there exists here, in the interior, a people, those of Kong [in Gonja, then Asante's northernmost outpost] who are as little civilized relative to us as we are relative to you. They do not know how to make ornaments of gold, to build comfortable houses, or to weave garments. However, there is not a single one of my Asantes, not even the poorest, who would leave his home for the sole purpose of going to teach the people of Kong.[32]

Muslim traders and teachers constituted the second category of northerners with whom the Asante interacted in the nineteenth century. Relations with northern Muslims developed out of the centuries-old trans-Saharan trade, which linked the forest and coastal polities with those of the savannah and North Africa. Asante policy in the precolonial period was directed toward expanding and preserving trading relations with the north, and at the same time controlling the influx and influence of northern traders in metropolitan Asante. Throughout the eighteenth and nineteenth centuries, the government of Asante exercised control not only over external trade but also over the status and activities of foreign traders in Asante, and over immigration policy into metropolitan

28. According to Fortes, "It was only if he [the slave] was granted quasi-nepotal status in his owner's family and lineage that he acquired the limited jural autonomy of a lifelong jural minor" (*Kinship and the Social Order*, p. 263).

29. Rattray, *Ashanti Proverbs* (Oxford: Clarendon Press, 1916), p. 118.

30. Rattray, *Ashanti Law*, p. 37.

31. Other revealing comments about northerners made by nineteenth-century Asante kings are quoted in Wilks, *Asante in the Nineteenth Century*, pp. 177, 706.

32. Anonymous review of Bowdich's *"Mission from Cape Coast Castle"* (1819), in the *Journal des Savants*, 1819, quoted in Wilks, *Asante in the Nineteenth Century*, pp. 308ff.

Asante. While foreign traders were encouraged under a succession of Asante kings in the early nineteenth century, Asantes themselves, except those employed by the government, were discouraged and even prohibited from actively engaging in trade.[33] The Asante, remarked the Asantehene to Dupuis, were a warrior people and did not understand about trade.[34] Foreign traders were courted and encouraged; rather than being taxed, they were given gold and provisions by the King.[35]

Given this policy, in the course of the eighteenth century a community of northern Muslim traders developed in Kumasi. There were perhaps a thousand permanently resident non-Asante Muslims settled in Kumasi in the second decade of the nineteenth century,[36] besides many more transient strangers who came to trade. Under three successive Asantehenes in the late eighteenth and early nineteenth centuries, the Muslims in Kumasi and in the Asante hinterland prospered. They had considerable influence on the court, and gradually succeeded in establishing a footing for Islam in Asante, at least in the capitol.

The position of the Muslims in Kumasi was at its best during the reign of Osei Bonsu, from 1800 to 1823. The King protected the Muslims, learned what he could about their religion, and encouraged them to proselytize throughout the Kumasi community.[37] The Muslims gained prestige and wealth by teaching the Qu'ran and making and selling protective medicines and amulets. They monopolized certain areas of trade—cattle, in particular, and much of the distributive trade in gold, kola, slaves, and salt. A number of the Kumasi Muslims became advisors to the King and served as secretaries in the administration, for they were the only ones who were literate. Some were appointed to offices as commissioners and ambassadors in the outlying Asante provinces. They also performed military services for the Asante ruler and provided him with a personal bodyguard.[38]

The Muslim influence in Asante government declined suddenly in 1818, however, when a contingent of the Asante army in Gyaman re-

33. Wilks, *Asante in the Nineteenth Century*, pp. 268, 684–688; and Wilks, "Asante Policy Towards the Hausa Trade in the Nineteenth Century," in C. Meillassoux, ed., *The Development of Indigenous Trade and Markets in West Africa* (London: Oxford University Press for the International African Institute, 1971), pp. 132–134.

34. J. Dupuis, *Journal of a Residence in Ashantee* (London, 1824), p. 167; quoted in Wilks, *Asante in the Nineteenth Century*, p. 686.

35. Wilks, "Asante Policy Towards the Hausa Trade," in Meillassoux, ed., *Development of Indigenous Trade*, p. 133; Dupuis, *Journal*, p. 167.

36. Wilks, "The Position of Muslims in Metropolitan Ashanti in the Early Nineteenth Century," in I. Lewis, ed., *Islam in Tropical Africa* (London: Oxford University Press for the International African Institute, 1966), p. 319.

37. Wilks, *Asante in the Nineteenth Century*, p. 257; and Wilks, "The Position of Muslims . . .," in Lewis, ed., *Islam in Tropical Africa*.

38. Wilks, "The Position of Muslims . . .," pp. 326ff., 330; and *Asante in the Nineteenth Century*, p. 260.

fused to take arms against Muslims from the north.[39] By the middle of the nineteenth century the open-door policy had changed, and not until after the British conquest in 1874 did Muslims again enjoy free access to trade between the coast and the savannah. At the time of the British conquest, resentment against the Asante had built up among the Muslim traders, who were prevented from trading freely within metropolitan Asante. The trade was carried on in Asante-controlled markets in the north, such as Salaga, and regulated by Asante government officials and a growing Asante bureaucracy. As a result of these events, when the British attacked Asante in 1874, they were able to enlist the support of Muslims and northerners anxious to throw off the Asante yoke. Even though, at that time, the Asante still recruited Hausa soldiers to fight against the Europeans, they faced many more northerners on the opposite side who welcomed British promises to open the trade between the north and the coast.

The relations between Asante and northerners in Kumasi itself, and in the Ashanti Region, evolved in the twentieth century under the direct control of the colonial government. I have recounted the changes in these relations elsewhere,[40] and can only summarize here (see also Sudarkasa, Chapter Eight). In the first two decades of the century, the British welcomed northerners into Kumasi and other Asante towns as traders and laborers. In many respects, the recruitment of labor for the colonial government and for European firms replaced the slave trade of the earlier period. In rural areas, the Asante cocoa industry developed rapidly and from the beginning relied heavily on northern labor. The development of mines also attracted northerners and, as in precolonial times, it was northerners rather than the Asante who provided most of the labor.

Politically, British policy changed during the course of colonial rule. Having conquered Asante and deposed the King, the British encouraged the growth of political power among northerners settled in Kumasi. This policy was pursued until the early 1930s, when the British attempted to implement the policy of indirect rule. Thenceforth the northerners in Kumasi formally fell under the authority of the reinstated Asantehene, although all Africans obviously lived under the umbrella of the colonial government.

After independence the situation again changed and remained unstable for some time, as aliens (non-Ghanaians) and strangers (non-Asantes), who were now numerically more significant in Kumasi than the Asante themselves, competed for power. Just over a decade after independence

39. Wilks, "The Position of Muslims . . .," pp. 335ff.; and *Asante in the Nineteenth Century*, pp. 267ff.

40. Schildkrout, "Strangers and Local Government in Kumasi," *Journal of Modern African Studies*, vol. 8, no. 2 (1970), pp. 251–269; "Ethnicity and Generational Differences," in Cohen, ed., *Urban Ethnicity*; and *People of the Zongo: the Transformation of Ethnic Identities in Ghana* (Cambridge: Cambridge University Press, 1978).

the expulsion orders of the Busia government were proclaimed, confirming the strangers' fears about the tenuousness of their position.

The opening of Asante to northern migration and the relatively strong political position of strangers vis-à-vis the Asante in the early colonial period must be viewed in the context of the economic changes occurring in the area as a whole. In this light the "advantages" of free migration are less clear, just as the relative political strength of northerners under the British became a liability after independence, when strangers were increasingly viewed as a threat to local interests.

There are two crucial aspects of economic change which must be considered: first, the differential development of the north and south, including the Ashanti Region; and second, the unequal distribution of educational opportunities. The growth of the cocoa industry in Ashanti, the development of gold mining, and the placement of most industry in the southern part of the country occurred at the cost of development in the north and created an intensified demand for northern labor in the south. The volume and seasonality of this demand was such that the traditional social bonds between northern laborers and Asante employers were never recreated. Whereas the *odonko* had been incorporated into an Asante family and eventually lost his alien identity, the migrant laborer of the twentieth century remained a stranger, whether he moved from farm to farm or lived in one of the many stranger communities, or *zongos*, which mushroomed all over the area.

The distribution of educational opportunities in Ghana also affected the status of northerners in the country as a whole. Although schools were opened throughout the country, the number of institutions above the primary level in the south far exceeded the number in the north. This, as well as the long tradition of Islamic education among northerners, meant that it was not long before southerners surpassed northerners in Western educational achievements. This had obvious repercussions on the distribution of occupations, opening up managerial and professional jobs to southerners and relegating manual and unskilled work to northerners. Northerners continued to control much of the long-distance distributive trade, but it was not long before this caused resentment.[41] Without political power, control over this or any economic niche meant little—for as strangers, and often as aliens, the traders remained vulnerable.

Thus the development of the southern economy, and the relative stagnation of the north, provided enticements for northerners to migrate south in large numbers. But because of their number and because of the altered political context of colonial rule and independence, the possibility of assimilation into Asante society decreased and the structural stability

41. It also caused increasing competition, and sometimes conflict, particularly with Asante women. See J. Rouch, *Migrations au Ghana* (Paris: Centre National de Recherche Scientifique, 1956) for a brief discussion of the longstanding dispute between Asante women and northern men over the yam trade.

of the stranger category was intensified. With the exception of the small community of Muslims in Kumasi in the nineteenth century—whose growth, we have seen, was controlled and limited by the government—most northerners in precolonial Asante had no stake in preserving their identity as strangers or as members of non-Asante groups.

Today northerners in Asante form stranger communities which, whether dispersed in rural areas or localized in towns, provide a source of protection and identity. Northerners themselves, except an occasional isolated rural laborer, generally make efforts to preserve their identity as Muslims and as northerners, and Asantes no longer pursue a vigorous assimilationist policy.

Regional Stereotypes of Southern Ghanaian Children

From the preceding discussion of the historical development of regional identities, it is obvious that relations between the peoples of the savannah and those of the forest have changed considerably in the past few hundred years. Nevertheless, the ideology of regionalism today exhibits some striking parallels with that described above for the nineteenth century.[42] This is not surprising, given the genesis of attitudes in both periods, at least in part, in the elaboration of ecological variations into a system of economic and social inequality. In the modern nation-state, the cleavage between north and south has taken on added significance, given the dependence of all regions on the national government for an equitable distribution of economic growth.

Research in Ghana, conducted between 1965 and 1967, on the transformation of patterns of ethnicity among northern migrants in the Ashanti Region, enabled me to conduct a limited study of the cognitive content of the ideology of regionalism, based on the use of projective "tests" on a sample of Ghanaian school children. The data analyzed for this paper consists of essays and "tests" given to eighty-one children in primary school and sixty children in Forms III and IV of middle school. The children were asked to write essays on the "differences between northerners and southerners." They were told that they could write about their personal experiences. The Form IV middle school children were also given a questionnaire which attempted to ascertain their knowledge of northerners, and one Form III class was asked to list two good and two bad traits about four groups, including Asantes.[43]

42. This refers to the period of fieldwork, in the mid-1960s. There is some evidence that government efforts at re-education through the schools, and attempts to develop the economy of the north, are making gradual but significant changes in the attitudes described here.

43. A similar test was given by Nelly Xydias in 1952 in Stanleyville to determine African attitudes toward whites. See Pons, Clément, and Xydias, "Social Effects of Urbanization in Stanleyville, Belgian Congo," preliminary report of the field research team of the International African Institute, in *Social Implications of Industrialization and Urbanization in Africa South of the Sahara* (UNESCO, 1956), pp. 362ff.

The school population becomes ethnically more homogeneous as the children get older. In the primary school sample, drawn from the sixth form of several schools in Kumasi, the children ranged in age from ten to fourteen (median twelve), and fifty-nine of them, or 73 percent, were Akan (Fante or Asante). Five children were from other southern Ghanaian groups, fifteen were northerners and Nigerians, and the ethnic identity of two was not ascertained.[44] In the middle school group, children ranged in age from twelve to seventeen, the median age being fifteen. By this age, few of the non-Akan children are in English school, although most attend Arabic schools. There were only four children in the middle school group who did not say that they were Akan, and one whose identity was not stated.

The school setting allows the repetition of a great deal of learned information, much of it bearing little or no relation to what the children have ever perceived. The setting also may eliminate some censuring which might take place where the children are actually interacting with northerners. The school situation is one in which Ghanaian identity is emphasized, and the children use the occasion presented here to define their own values, in contrast with outsiders, and to assert their relative superiority in a national context.

A comparison of the primary and middle school essays reveals much about how stereotypes develop among children.[45] The primary school essays are almost all structured in terms of simple oppositions or contrasts between northerners and southerners on a limited number of themes. These themes refer to objective conditions such as climate, house style, and clothing; they do not refer to behavioral differences, except for the most obvious ones of language and occupation. Although almost half of Kumasi's population consists of northerners, the primary school children are not describing the relations between northerners and southerners in Kumasi. They are describing the difference between the northern and southern parts of the country. They focus on ecological differences between the regions—notably the climate, and its role in determining differences in occupations, foods, clothing, and house construction. Very

44. A comparison of the content of these essays reveals that at this stage, when value judgments are infrequent, ethnic differences are not very apparent.

45. A consideration of the relationship between cognitive and chronological development has not been undertaken here because of the wide range in the children's ages, and because of limitations in the methodology of the study—particularly the reliance on English. It is instructive, however, to compare these results with those reported in the literature on the cognitive development of children's concepts of nationality. While Piaget and Weil maintained that children's concepts of nationality progress from "spatial" to "national" ones, and from a stage of egocentricity to reciprocity, Jahoda has argued that children's difficulty in comprehending nationality is due to the highly abstract and complex nature of the concept itself. S. Piaget and A. Weil, "The Development in Children of the Idea of the Homeland and Relations with Other Countries," *International Social Science Bulletin*, vol. 3 (1951), pp. 561-578.

few of the essays reflect personal experiences, although many of these children have relatives who employ northerners as laborers on cocoa farms outside Kumasi. Very rarely do the primary school essays contain value judgments. Only 81 out of 96 items mentioned (12 percent) are explicitly negative.[46] Compared to the middle school children, the primary school children seem unaware of status and stratification. Many of them seem to be repeating information they have learned at school, and few seem to test this against their own perceptions. Since the essays contain little description of character, behavior, customs, or even of the role of northerners in the social system in which the children live, it is difficult to call these descriptions stereotypes. But they contain information which later forms the basis of stereotypes. Some of this information is correct, though often overstated; some of it is simply wrong. One student, for example, discussed Zulus as northern Ghanaians and described their houses as kraals, an Afrikaans word. Although not many primary children use words such as "primitive" or "civilized," they have information which is later incorporated into a stereotype based on this distinction. They do not say they are better, but they specify how they are different. Overstatement of oppositions and contrasts seems to be an early and important part of defining distinctions between "us" and "them," "our place" and "their place."

The primary school children emphasize ecological explanations. They say that because it is hot in the north, northerners are darker skinned, live in round mud and straw houses, and wear light clothes; and that they are hunters, eat mostly grain, and travel by bicycle or on foot. In contrast, they say that Asante people live in rectangular concrete and iron-roofed houses, wear fine heavy clothes, are doctors and lawyers, eat a greater variety of food, drive in cars and fly in airplanes, and have lighter skins. These characteristics are frequently related to the lower temperatures and greater rainfall of the forest, and occasionally to the presence of the sea.

There is a very marked change in the content of the middle school children's essays. They are not as frequently built around simple contrasts relating to geography, climate, and other physical features. There are long descriptions of northern people, their behavior and customs. While the primary school essays seem to include only two kinds of linguistic elements—names of groups and places, and juxtaposed lists of traits—the middle school essays contain many evaluative expressions which can be linked to the groups or to the traits. These three elements (group and place names, traits, and evaluations) are variously combined

46. Many which may be implicitly negative by comparison with beliefs about southerners were counted as neutral in view of the difficulty of not imposing my own judgments. Comments such as "they are dark-skinned," "they wear light clothes," "they live in round houses," were all taken as simple statements of fact.

among the middle school children, giving rise to many of the incorrect attributions. Whereas primary school children will say that northerners have big marks on their cheeks, and southerners have small marks, the older children may say that "northerners have some very wonderful big marks." The younger children overstate oppositions and describe northerners as non-southerners. Opposition is not absent in the older groups' essays, but there is much more elaboration of cultural symbols: contrasts between the north and south are now expressed through the valuations linked to descriptions of northern traits.

The older children mention and emphasize different characteristics, reflecting in part their own interests at this stage. They are particularly concerned with hygiene, possibly reflecting a subject emphasized in their school curriculum. They often state that northerners' food, clothing, housing, personal hygiene, and so on, is dirty or poor. They have a great interest in marriage customs, and marriage and women are among the most frequently discussed topics. The treatment of children also becomes a focus of interest. It is apparent that these children are learning the rules of their own culture; defining different and unacceptable ways of doing the same things helps them learn and value their own ways.

The older children more frequently and freely express value judgments. They discuss northerners in Kumasi more often than they discuss the northern region, and they describe their own perceptions, experiences, and prejudices. Still, there is sufficient repetition of themes to indicate that we are dealing with cultural values and not simply individual observations. The middle school children are clearly aware of status differences and stratification, and more often make overtly disparaging comments about northerners. On a very conservative count, among the middle school children 37 percent of the comments were negative, compared to 12 percent of the primary school comments. Only 13 percent of the middle school childrens' statements were clearly positive. The interest in hygiene is one of the main ways in which the children express this, but it comes out in all the descriptions of cultural differences. For example, whereas the primary school children simply named different grains and root crops that could be grown in the north, and made the distinction between meat-eaters and fish-eaters, the older children specified that the animals eaten in the north are ones which are considered inedible and unclean by Asantes, such as snakes, rats, dogs, and dead hens.

Many of the comments, particularly those about character and work attitudes, refer to the role that northerners play in the economy of Asante. Remarks such as "they come to work on our farms," "they are hard workers," "they are lazy," "they carry our dirty things out of the country," "they provide us with yams," are common. This emphasis on work supports the hypothesis presented by LeVine and Campbell that in nation-states, stereotypes develop which reflect institutionalized role relations.[47] The stereotypes refer to the contexts in which interaction occurs, and express role expectations in these areas. It is important to stress, however, that the stereotypes tell us what the Asante expect from northerners, not what northerners are necessarily like. The element of symbolic contrast is important. As with the topic of marriage, the Asante children are defining and justifying their own cultural values by creating a negative stereotype of another set of values: Asante do not or cannot marry northerners because their marriage customs are different; they also need not do physical work because, they are claiming, northerners are ready and willing to do this for them.

Among the older children the tendency to overgeneralize is even more marked, and the "grain of truth" is often much smaller. They write as if they are describing things they have observed, but they dwell on the most exotic customs, since these are most useful in differentiating themselves. For example, sixteen Form IV children mentioned that the mouths of northern women were locked by men to stop them from talking to other men. Many children attributed this to all northerners, and some to specific groups such as Mossis or Dagombas. In fact, only a small number of Lobi people have any custom that resembles this: women wear lip plugs. Many children noted that northerners "use cows" or "use meat" in marrying, referring to bride-price and contrasting this with the Asante custom of using money. In Kumasi, of course, northerners also use money, but this was not noted. The emphasis here is an attempt to justify an avoidance of intermarriage. The comment that northerners rarely if ever bathe was also related to the undesirability of marriage, as were statements about childrearing, such as "they lock children's mouths to punish them" or "the Dagombas carry their babies in bags." Much more often than in the primary school essays, facts were stated that had little relation to reality. Some of the most extreme examples include references to cannibalism and human sacrifice. There were many references to aggressive behavior on the part of northerners—both physical and mystical—some with interesting explanations, such as that "the Mossis get mad when the sun heats them." The description of cultural differences which emerges in the middle school essays is linked to an awareness of status differences and is an attempt to define areas in which interaction is permitted and areas in which it is discouraged.

As among the primary school children, much of the information has been learned from adults rather than from empirical observation. This accounts for the frequency with which certain misattributions occur, and also suggests that re-education could be achieved through the schools. Many of the stereotypes are strikingly reminiscent of European writings

47. R. A. Le Vine and D. T. Campbell, *Ethnocentrism: Theories of Conflict, Ethnic Attitudes, and Group Behavior* (New York: Wiley, 1972).

on Africa in the last century. The Asante are described as civilized, edu-cated, clean, and intelligent, whereas the northerners are portrayed as dirty, uncivilized, uneducated, stupid, childlike, hard-working, and dangerous. Such stereotypes are common in situations of differential modernization,[48] and as we have seen, they were not totally lacking in precolonial Asante. Nevertheless, some of the essays could have been written—with the names of groups changed—by some of the less chari-table European writers who described the colonies in the nineteenth century.

Despite the frequency with which such ideas are expressed, experi-ence may positively modify stereotypes. One little girl said that there were Frafras in her house and she noted that they kept their rooms clean, played nicely with her, and cooked good food which she ate. There are a few essays like this, and in all but one case where real experiences are described, the stereotypes are positive. Some children alter their stereo-types by differentiating between northern groups, attributing their posi-tive experiences to one specific group and their negative experiences to another. In one essay a child described his Mossi friend as neat, kind, hard-working, and obedient, while he claimed that the Frafra have all sorts of negative and distasteful characteristics.

One further indication of the distribution of attributes for each group was provided by a good and bad trait "test". Form III children were asked to list two good and two bad traits for each of four groups: the Asante, the Hausa, the Mossi, and the Frafra. For the Asante, the category of "character" provided the largest number of good traits. Most of the good traits attributed to them involved kindness, honesty, politeness, and responsibility to others; the bad traits mentioned for the Asante were selfishness and greed. In this there seems to be a reference to intra-group status competition, something rarely noted when more socially distant groups are described. The good traits mentioned for the strangers most frequently referred to work. This is the area in which they perform the most important role vis-à-vis the Asante, and it is clear that their contribution to the economy, and even Asante dependence upon them, is noted and appreciated by the children. The bad traits noted most frequently referred to aggression, both physical and mystical. For the Frafra, if one combines the categories of aggression and antisocial behavior (which includes thievery, misbehaving in public, and "making unnecessary noise"), this ranks highest. Hygiene is mentioned, but it is by no means the most important "bad habit." Rather, the bad traits which concern the children most are those that relate to their interaction with northerners—their fears of a northerner's aggressive or hostile (retaliatory?) behavior. It is interesting to note, however, that the most frequently expressed stereotype of the Asante among northerners is that

48. *Ibid.*

the Asante, though often kind and good employers, can suddenly turn against a northerner and kill him.

While it is clear that the children have very clear and definite ideas about the north and about northerners, it is instructive to look at their answers to several questions which attempted to ascertain their factual knowledge of the north. These questions were asked only of one group of the oldest children, those in Form IV, the majority of whom were fifteen and sixteen years old. In a number of questions it is clear that names of groupings, towns, and countries are confused, and that the children have only a vague idea of northern geography and ethnography.[49] The children had a better idea of the names of peoples from Nigeria than they did of those from the francophone countries or northern Ghana. When asked who they considered to be strangers in Asante, the category mentioned most frequently was Europeans, including whites, English, French, and occasionally Asians. The Mossi, Frafra, and Hausa were mentioned next, followed by the Fante, the Kanjaga, Ewe, Dagate, northerners in general, and Nigerians.

Despite their generally scanty knowledge of the geography and ethnography of these groups, they are able to rank the groups they have heard of very precisely. This is not surprising in view of the function of stereotypes, as discussed earlier. When asked which group ranked highest or lowest on a number of characteristics such as intelligence, ability to work hard, temperament, honesty, beauty, and so on, some groups about whom there seemed to be very definite stereotypes were mentioned very frequently, and others were mentioned only a few times. Europeans were never ranked negatively, and were consistently given the highest rankings.[50] The Hausa received the most positive rankings but also received the second highest number of negative rankings—expressing perhaps, the ambivalence one would expect in stereotypes of strangers. The Mossi were the third highest in both positive and negative rankings. The Frafra were the fifth highest in positive rankings, primarily because of being ranked highly as hard workers; they also received the greatest number of negative rankings.

These results suggest that the children hold both positive and negative stereotypes about members of all groups except Europeans, about whom they seem reluctant to express negative attitudes. It is interesting that when northerners are asked directly, in an interview situation, to

49. This is not surprising in view of the way in which such concepts are learned. Jahoda argues that in order to understand this, one "has to abandon the exclusive concern with purely cognitive aspects" and study the symbolic environment in which the children are growing up. G. Jahoda, "The Development of Children's Ideas about Country and Nationality: I. The Conceptual Frame. II. National Symbols and Themes," *British Journal of Educational Psychology*, vol. 33, no. 2 (1963), p. 152.

50. At this point the children did not know that the researcher was white, because the tests were administered by their Ghanaian teacher.

express their opinions of the Asante, they generally offer very positive opinions and claim that because they are strangers (and generally in a structurally inferior position as employees), they must respect and defer to their hosts. In conversation, on the other hand, negative stereotypes are more fully and frequently expressed, although this may be because the occasion for commenting on any group at all is usually a negative one. In any case, in direct questions the same slightly subservient attitude characterizes the attitudes of the Asante children to Europeans, and northerners to Asante. Although political independence was attained in Ghana in 1957, attitudes obviously take much longer to change.

In general, one can conclude from their answers that the children are ranking groups according to the type of occupation they associate them with, and that it is the occupational categories which are ranked. The Frafra, often associated with unclean occupations, are evaluated negatively on a number of characteristics including beauty, neatness, and so on. The Hausa, associated with trade, and the Europeans, associated with managerial positions, are ranked most favorably. The category of "hard work" proved to be ambivalent, for it is hard to tell whether it is a positive or a negative trait: both the Frafra and the Hausa were described as both lazy and hard-working, by different children. Here are a few of the essays.[51]

Sixth Form Primary School
Asante male

The difference between the northerners and the southerners is that the northerners are black and the southerners are copper coloured. Because of the hot sun the land becomes hot, so when [they] plant the crops they cannot germinate, so they find it difficult to get food. Because they get [little] food they always grow unhealthy. The southerners also have land for food farming. So when they plant crops they can easily germinate so they find it easy to get food. Because of food they grow healthy. And also southerners can speak French. And the Northerners can also speak Asante, Hausa. The northerners are the people in the northern part of Ghana. The southerners are also the people on the southern part of Ghana.

Sixth Form Primary School
Fante male

There are differences between the northerners and the southerners. I am a boy of the Fante tribe. The northerners are mostly farmers, shepherds and skillful hunters as well. Most of the northerners live in huts while others live in Swiss [swish?] houses and

51. The original version of this paper included an appendix consisting of a small selection of the essays—four more than presented here—and the results of the other interview schedules, compiled in five tables. For reasons of economy these have been omitted from this volume, but the author will be glad to provide them on request.

they live chiefly on yam, maize, corn and meat. The Southerners are mostly fishermen, businessmen, government officials, lawyers and doctors. Southerners live in big and nice houses and they live chiefly on plantain, cassava, corn and fishes. And beside all things they enjoy the breeze of the sea. The religious denomination of both northerners and the southerners, has slight difference for the Northerners have adored Mohammedanism as their religious sect, while the Southerners are mostly Christians. The Northerners feel the heat of the sun more than the Southerners, for the heat of the sun reaching them seems to be [illegible]. It therefore seems to me that the Southerners enjoy life more than the Northerners but they show hospitality to anyone from all aspects of life.

Sixth Form Primary School
Asante female

There are many things which separate the northerners from the southerners. The most common difference is their building. The northerners do not eat good foods. They eat food made of cereals and vegetables and drink home made wine. Their clothes are some-times made of animal skins and bark of trees. They live in very poor buildings built with mud and straw. Above all the northerners are poor and cannot provide themselves with all their needs. But the southerners are much better than the northerners. They are rich and can provide themselves with almost all their needs. They eat good foods made of cereals, vegetables and fruits and drink good wine. They wear good clothes made of cotton, silk and other fibers. Their buildings use stones and all materials. The southerners are more civilized than the northerners.

Third Form Middle School
Asante male/age 14

The northerners are able to work on farms, but the Ashantis are not like that. A tribe like Moshies, they can work very well and they are kind to anybody and obey their Masters. These people are neat and if you teach them anything they would know it. They are hard workers and you will always see them in nice clothes and food. [The teacher, in correcting this essay, wrote "No" in red pen in the margin here.] I have one Moshie friend at New Tafo. When I was walking with him and my purse fell down. I did not see it, it was the boy who saw it and gave it to me.

The Frafra people are the bad people. They are lazy and thieves. If you do any bad thing to them they will become annoyed, and if you do not keep protection he will do something very bad to you. They are dirty in clothes and food. Every weekend you will see these people intoxicated and disturbs in the streets. These people always want to work in chop bars because of food. They treat their children very bad, you will always see them in a dirty uniform. They do not want to educate their children. They like gambling so if you hand anything to them to look after it, they will spend all the money on it. They always want to make a small okro farm. And they like selling tea and bread in the streets. [Teacher adds "in the night."]

Middle School Form IV
Asante male/age 15

The northerners have got big big marks on their cheeks so that the one who sees them may know they are northerners. The people such as the Dagombas, Moshies, Gonjas and others do not wear clothes but rather wore leaves around their waist. The people such as the Dagombas even carry their babies in a bag. Their women have got some big hole on their mouth with stick in it. The northerners are very wicked people that hate other tribes. When this people are to be married they would make something like a party and invite many people to it. Some dance and others beat drums. These people are almost all Mohammedans. They love human sacrifice. The Asante are very civilized people and also neat. The Asante wear clothes. They love each other. They do not like human sacrifice. Their character or manner is different from that of the northerners. They love education and the northerners do not know anything about education. Only about one fourth love education in their affairs.

Some of the customs of the northerners are that they use cows to marry. The girls of the northerners keep a long time to marry. If a girl has not reached the stage and she conceives she may be sacked off from the family. These people even do not take their bath for about a month. People such as Dagomba women have got a lock on their mouth so that they may not be able to talk to any men except her husband only. The official food of the people is kola nuts. People such as Dagombas eat snakes and dogs.

Fourth Form Middle School
Asante female/age 15

The difference between northerners and southerners are very difficult to describe. The Frafras who are very common in Ashanti speak languages that the Asantes cannot understand. When an Asante woman or man speaks Akan a Frafra person can understand. But when a Frafra speaks, Asantes cannot understand. Some of the Frafra peoples have got so many tribal marks on their faces. Their aims in coming to Ashanti are to help us to weed our farms and to sweep the street. It is through Frafras that our dirty things are carried out of the country. They wear dirty clothes while the Asantes wear beautiful clothes. Their foods are not clean for an Asante person to eat. They use snakes and dead hens to prepare their meals. A Frafra man could not marry until he becomes a sanitary inspector. The children of the Frafra are primitive and backward. They do not attend school as the Asantes do.

They do not understand things. The food they like best is *abetee*. The young Frafra girls keep long time to marry. But if she conceives she is driven away from the family. They do not take their bath usually [often]. When one is about to marry she is given a cow or sheep where as in Ashanti the one is given some amount of money say 72 cedis. Their main food is kola-nuts and ground-nuts. The young ones who are about to marry their mouths are shut with keys. Simply because when her mouth is not shut she will converse with another man.

Conclusion

Among the many ways in which strangers may be and are defined, one of the most persistent dichotomies between strangers and hosts is based upon the distinction between different regions. I have argued here that regional distinctions, and the stereotypes which develop out of them, are more persistent than many other types of ethnic distinctions and stereotypes because they are based on relatively fixed ecological or environmental variations. Other authors have noted the wide distribution of such stereotypes and the striking similarity of regional stereotypes in many parts of the world.[52] On a cognitive level, as the children's essays demonstrate, ecological explanations provide the basis for the elaboration of stereotypes. Cultural differences are "explained" in ecological terms. These ad hominem explanations, to those who accept them, seem to be as self-evident and unchallengeable as nature or the weather itself. They are, in some ways, very similar to explanations of cultural differences based on the notion of race: both attempt to explain culture in terms of nature. Moreover, it is highly probable that ecological explanations of cultural differences abound precisely in those situations where race is absent, or unavailable, as an explanatory mechanism.

The question now arises as to how the basic observation of environmental variation gets translated into the sorts of stereotypes described here. What are the social structural correlates of the formation of these stereotypes? What realities, if any, do they reflect?

Within a territorial unit where ecological variations are present, a differential distribution of resources "on the ground" very often leads to differential control over resources, as well as to a skewed distribution of socioeconomic roles. Within the context of a bounded political unit such as a modern nation-state, this differential access to and control over

52. U. R. Ehrenfels has studied north-south stereotypes in twenty countries above the equator and noted that northerners are universally seen as industrious and powerful, while southerners are described as indolent, lazy, temperamental, and artistic. Ehrenfels, "North-South Polarization: A Study in the Typicality of Attitudes," *Centenary Volume*, University of Madras, vol. 28 (1957), pp. 85–103. It has been suggested that south of the equator, the stereotypes are reversed. Le Vine and Campbell, *Ethnocentrism*, p. 162.

resources leads to the development of stereotypes which reflect a situation of regional inequality. Particularly in a colonial situation, where an alien value system intrudes, stereotypes develop which rank regional (or ethnic or racial) groupings according to their degree of control over resources, which is often expressed in the notion of "occupation."

This concept of "occupation" is used as a kind of symbolic shorthand to describe relative social status in a national context. The school children whose views are presented here described southerners as modern and civilized, and northerners as traditional and primitive; they were translating cultural differences (such as the type of houses people live in, or the sort of clothes they wear) into status evaluations based on Western concepts of socioeconomic status. The older children took what they believe to be elements of traditional northern culture, combined these with the notion of low occupational status, and translated the combination into a set of negatively valued cultural attributes. One distressing feature of this—which may be an inevitable concomitant of modernization and the imposition of a colonial value system—is that the adoption of foreign, in this case, Western, values seems inevitably to lead to the denigration of traditional culture.[53]

The stereotypes held by adults, although not discussed here, are focussed to an even greater extent on work. This is, in fact, the major context for interaction between northerners and southerners, and the stereotypes describe the rules of this interaction. This is why they implicitly or explicitly present contrasts between "us" and "them." They describe both parties to any interaction and set out the basic premises underlying the relationship (premises being such evaluations as relative inferiority and superiority or strength and weakness). Children are much less concerned than adults with the roles of employers and employees, and they use the stereotypes to define different aspects of their own roles; but as one follows the development of stereotypes, by comparing the primary and middle school responses, one can detect an increasing concern with this aspect of behavior.

Although stereotypes are not accurate descriptions of cultural differences, one can see in them certain preoccupations which reflect the structural relations between the groups in question. This partly accounts for the similarity between European stereotypes of Africans and southern Ghanaian stereotypes of northerners. Such stereotypes have, in fact, a great deal of universality. According to Le Vine and Campbell, one frequently finds the following causal chain: from a "superordinate

53. It is important to note, however, that in the case of Ghana, reference group theory, which would predict that northerners adopt this stereotype as their self-image, does not apply. As described elsewhere, cultural variations are still sufficiently significant so that the strangers use an entirely different scale of values, based on Islamic rather than Western values, to evaluate themselves (Schildkrout, "Government and Chiefs in Kumasi," and *People of the Zongo*).

socioeconomic system embracing several ethnic groups [to] institution-alized role relations between ethnic groups [to] perceptual sensitization to role-relevant attributes of out-groups [to] generalization of role-relevant attributes to unobserved behavior of out-groups." They add that this hypothetical sequence appears to "produce a transcultural set of socially structured biases in intergroup perception centered around ur-banism, occupation, and political-technological dominance." They also note that these stereotypes, while universal in many respects, are given local ethnic content.[54] Where ethnic distinctions of the sort meant by Le Vine and Campbell—namely, those based on cultural differences—are too subtle or too numerous to be relevant for defining distinctions in socio-economic roles, regional categories develop. Sub-regional ethnic distinctions become relevant only when they correspond to distinctions in socio-economic roles—for example, when a distinction can be made between Hausa traders, Mossi laborers, and Frafra sanitary inspectors. To an Asante in southern Ghana, the distinction between the Kusasi and the Dagate, two northern Ghanaian peoples, is no more relevant than the distinction between a Neapolitan and a Sicilian is to a northern Italian.

The concept of regional identity, then, has a much greater saliency, historical depth, and importance in a national context than many of the ethnic identities which are based on local cultural variations. When regional ecological variations, such as those between the forest and savannah in Ghana, benign in themselves, become congruent with a sys-tem of economic and social inequality, stereotypes develop which reflect this. The definition of the stranger in regional terms represents an attempt to define the relative statuses and claims to resources of various segments of a national population.

54. Le Vine and Campbell, *Ethnocentrism*, pp. 159, 160.

Part IV

Special Studies: Uganda

11

White Strangers and Their Religion in East Africa and Madagascar

Aidan Southall

I should like to compare, in this chapter, the confrontation between stranger and native in two coastal and two hinterland areas of Africa, focusing on specific individuals: the missionary Ludwig Krapf and the coastal peoples of East Africa; the missionary Luis Mariano and the coastal peoples of southeastern Madagascar; the journalist-adventurer Henry Stanley and King Mutesa I in the East African hinterland of Buganda; and the British agent James Hastie and King Radama I in the Malagasy inland state of Imerina.

All four cases are examples of reaction to white strangers who were important early carriers of Western influence. The coastal cases are primarily concerned with religious influence, the hinterland cases with political and personal influence leading to widespread change. These cases have been chosen because of their beguiling similarities; but the more closely they are studied, the more the details differ. There are, first of all, significant chronological differences. Krapf worked on the East African coast in the early nineteenth century, and Luis Mariano worked on the coasts of Madagascar in the early seventeenth century. This is important for what it implies about the contemporary technological situation and the particular phase of the global process of colonialism which was involved in each case. The same points apply to the encounter of Stanley and Mutesa in the 1870s, which was sixty years later and hence in a significantly different technological and historical context from the encounter of Hastie and Radama.

I shall be concerned not only with the general problem of stranger and native, but more specifically with whether the stranger can exert religious influence without effective political support, and with the role of great men in contexts of fundamental change. It would seem that when

I wish to express my gratitude to the National Science Foundation, whose grant no. GS–1301 enabled me to carry out field work in Madagascar during 1965 and 1966, and also to the Rockefeller Foundation and the Wenner-Gren Foundation for Anthropological Research, from both of which I received assistance which enabled me to work in Madagascar during April, May, and June 1973.

211

no dramatic changes are taking place, there is considerable justification for looking at events in structural-functional terms, under their new guise of general systems theory. But when dramatic changes do occur—in wars, conquests, revolutions, and mass conversions—certain individuals seem to force themselves upon our attention as especially significant. To say that such prominent figures are thrust into prominence by events is to say that they are still the products of systemic processes. But are they, and in what sense? This is the heart of the debate between social anthropology and history, a debate not likely to be concluded here, and with which I have recently wrestled in another context.[1]

Ludwig Krapf in East Africa

Krapf arrived on the East African coast in 1843 after having been refused permission by the Ethiopian authorities to return to Shoa; he blamed this refusal upon the machinations of a Frenchman whom he had helped in Shoa. He and his companions gradually developed the idea of visiting the southern Galla, who he had heard extended as far south as the equator. And so he traveled by boat to Zanzibar and Mombasa, the great East African port cities, and eventually chose Rabai, only a few miles from Mombasa, as his mission headquarters. He and various companions worked there, on and off, from 1846 to 1850. During this period they also made journeys to the Kamba, Shambaa, and Chagga countries looking for people and places favorable for the establishment of mission stations. As in many similar epics of missionary effort, these men endured sufferings and privations almost beyond belief: they were racked by fever to the brink of death, thrown in prison, robbed of all their possessions, and narrowly escaped murder many times. There can be no doubt of their extraordinary courage and devotion to their cause.

Krapf was a purist, who insisted that the Christian mission must not be contaminated by its dealings with the powers that be. But could it be avoided? Krapf enjoyed, and doubtless owed his life to, the assistance and hospitality he received from the Sultan of Zanzibar and other local rulers, from British and French consuls and agents, and from the British Navy. More important, he took sides on the political question of slavery, stressing the connection between English efforts to suppress the slave trade and the process of Christian evangelization. He believed that the establishment of a chain of mission stations would help eradicate slavery more quickly, for slavery would continue until Christianity became the ruling faith of Africa. He even considered the desirability of England establishing a liberated slave colony in East Africa similar to Sierra Leone.[2]

1. A. W. Southall, "General Amin and the Coup: Great Man or Historical Inevitability?" *Journal of Modern African Studies*, vol. 13, no. 1 (1975), pp. 85–105.
2. Rev. Dr. J. L. Krapf (1860). *Travels, Researches and Missionary Labors, during an eighteen years' residence in Eastern Africa; together with journeys to Jagga, Usambara, Ukambani, Shoa, Abessinia, and Khartum; and a coasting voyage from Mombaz to Cape Delgado* (Boston: Ticknor and Fields), p. 110.

Indeed, it was by this very process that his own mission, long after his time, finally succeeded in building up a community of adherents.

When Krapf first visited Rabai, the people were full of welcome and rejoicing.[3] He realized that this was partly because he was being accorded the same honors as "any great man from Mombaz." He introduced himself not as soldier, merchant, or government official, nor as traveler, physician, or exorcist, but as a teacher, a man who would give them everlasting joy, and save them from the worst of maladies, sin. "The Wanike [Nyika] had made a favorable impression on me; for they were both quick and well behaved, but wore extremely little in the way of clothes, even the women not being sufficiently clad." He remarked that some of the people looked very intelligent. In return, their leaders said winsomely, "our land, our trees, our houses, our sons and daughters are all thine."[4]

But disillusion soon set in. Building materials had to be bought, and although help was offered, it was always delayed. The white missionaries did much of the hard work themselves, fever-ridden though they were, because "all that the Wanike would have done would have been done wretchedly and superficially."[5] At first, people came to meetings and listened, or a group of children could be gathered for instruction; but as time went on, they dispersed. On the great day when the new church building was consecrated, the missionaries were informed that people would not come regularly unless they were given food and drink. After some time Krapf was "grieved at the drunkenness and sensuality, dullness and indifference" of the people.[6] After a year's preaching, he wrote, "The darkened and worldly minded people remain deaf to all exhortation."[7]

His ten years in Africa apparently resulted in the conversion of only one family: "the wife of Abbe Gunje begins to pray, and he himself is diffusing Christianity among his countrymen. A single Christian family among a heathen people is of signal value."[8] Perhaps, then, the incredible journeys to Kamba, Chagga, and Shambaa were something of a relief. At the end of it all, there was still insistence on the certainty of ultimate spiritual victory; but humanly and materially speaking, it is hard to see the results as other than a failure.

This was not the first Christian effort on the coast, for the Portuguese had tried hundreds of years before, but as Krapf remarked, they had "left nothing behind them but ruined fortresses, palaces, and ecclesiastical buildings."[9] Although Krapf wanted to keep his work quite independent of local politics, and evidently believed that he was succeeding, he realized that it was impossible to work without protection and approval from some kind of government. Thus he was keen to get work

3. *Ibid.*, p. 111.   4. *Ibid.*, p. 113.
5. *Ibid.*, p. 128.   6. *Ibid.*, p. 115.
7. *Ibid.*, p. 151.   8. *Ibid.*, p. 394.
9. *Ibid.*, p. 428.

started among the Kamba, Masai, and Kikuyu, but when he learned that these were all stateless societies without any central government, he wisely postponed this plan. He was enthusiastic about Sambaa precisely because the king there seemed to be in firm control; he went so far as to compare him to the King of Shoa in this respect.

Krapf was scathing in his comments on the Muslim practice of combining religion, politics, and trade. He saw the Muslim Arabs monopolizing the trade in gum copal, getting ships' timbers from the forests, and setting up communities of their own slaves to gradually gain control of the coastal territory. The Nyika became Muslims in time of famine to beg for food, but dropped the religion after the famine was over. And yet, Krapf also remarked, the Nyika "bring in a Sheikh who deals with [their] religious wants."[10] Perhaps, indeed, this is the only way that a new religion can be spread without a political umbrella of some sort. In fact, both the sheikhs and Krapf were under the protection of the Sultan of Zanzibar, enjoying the reflection of his influence whether they liked it or not; and Krapf himself was also under the paternal and increasingly influential eye of the English consul in Zanzibar.

Luis Mariano in Madagascar

Between 1613 and 1620 the Portuguese Jesuit Luis Mariano and several other Jesuits endeavored to establish missions at various points round the coasts of Madagascar. Their efforts were precipitated by the fact that the King of Portugal had ordered an investigation into reports that there was a community of shipwrecked Portuguese sailors and their descendants living somewhere on the island. The captain of the ship commissioned for this task asked for some priests to be sent with him. The priests intended both to minister to the spiritual needs of their fellow Portuguese and to gain their assistance in the general conversion of Madagascar. They made treaties of friendship and peace with a number of local rulers, some of whom welcomed the idea of the priests staying in their country and teaching them.

Their first serious effort was in the country of the Antanosy, near the present port of Fort Dauphin in southeast Madagascar, because that was where they were led by the strongest rumors about the shipwrecked sailors. The sailors never were found, but the effort eventually led to much ill feeling because the missionaries suspected King Tsiambany of Antanosy of trying to obstruct their search, and became more and more convinced that he had their countrymen. It is worth unraveling the tangled skein of events in Antanosy because it is typical of the initial embroilments of the Portuguese all round the coasts of Africa.[11]

---

10. *Ibid.*, p. 114.

11. Of course, the Portuguese account is the only one we have. The letters of the Jesuits convey the impression that they were truthful men, though they may sometimes have deluded themselves and there are many nuances subject to different interpretations; and their

At first everything seemed friendly on both sides. King Tsiambany signed a treaty, writing Malagasy in Arabic characters, in which he bound himself to give his eldest son to the Portuguese to take to Goa, to be educated in Roman Catholicism and Portuguese culture; his price was that they leave the Jesuit priests themselves as hostages. He also gave the priests the island of Santa Cruz (Fanjahira) for their mission station, an act ratified by the eldest son, who accompanied them there and symbolically gave them a handful of earth from the island. The priests and some Portuguese from the ship spent two weeks building their station, and soon became disappointed because all the help they had been offered, including the personal assistance of the king and his family and the labor of his slaves, was not forthcoming.

By the time the ship was ready to leave and the Portuguese went to bid farewell to the king, they found his mind completely changed.[12] He said he could not possibly let his eldest son go, and would have to think further about sending even his younger son; later he offered to compromise by sending another young man with them. The Portuguese were deeply insulted and overcome with anger at this. At a farewell ceremony in which both sides were drawn up in force on the beach, Portuguese sailors managed to seize the prince and rush him to the ship. The ensuing Antanosy attack was dispersed by muskets and the thunderous firing of the ship's cannons. Doubtless the Antanosy were afraid that their prince was being taken into slavery. They offered to buy him back, to no avail.

It must be noted that the Portuguese had done this kind of thing many times before. When they stopped at Sadia on the west coast of Madagascar on their way to Antanosy, the ruler gave them his son to go with them as guide. So he accompanied them and was taught Portuguese and Christianity. Six months later, after the events in Antanosy, they did return him to his native land as "Dom Jeronymo," where he was received with much rejoicing. This gave the Portuguese a good name in Sadia.

The kidnapped Antanosy prince was treated with honor in Goa and also brought back home, some two years later, as "Dom André"—but he rejoined his people only after a stormy affair in which the Portuguese tried to make his release contingent upon the signing of a new treaty of peace with the king.[13] Several Jesuits and a few followers then spent a whole year on the island endeavoring to get their mission started. But the relations between stranger and native had already been thoroughly poisoned by this time. Dom André, on whose assistance their hopes had

major prejudices are fairly obvious. *Collection des ouvrages anciens concernant Madagascar*, publiée sous la direction de MM. A. Grandidier, de l'Institut, Charles Roux, Cl. Delhorbe, H. Froidevaux, et G. Grandidier. Tome II: Ouvrages ou extraits d'ouvrages français (jusqu'à 1630), portugais, hollandais, anglais, allemands, italiens, espagnols et latins relatifs à Madagascar (1613 à 1630) par MM. Alfred Grandidier, de l'Institut et Guillaume Grandidier (Paris: Comité de Madagascar, 1904).

12. *Ibid.*, Tome II, p. 56.
13. *Ibid.*, p. 125.

rested for converting the country, was prevented by the king from coming to see them. The whole people were dissuaded from bringing them food or coming to listen to their preaching. They came only to beg for gifts. The people were accused by the priests of being Muslims after all, because they practiced circumcision, fasting, and polygamy. They were so attached to superstitions that they could never be converted. The Jesuits finally reported to their superiors that the people were evil, deceitful, liars, who broke their promises and did not wish to know their Creator. Not a single man or woman, noble or slave, paid attention or believed, showing themselves to be more savage than wild beasts.[14] The king and his people hated the Portuguese and would have killed them for their clothes had it not been for fear of the muskets they saw in their hands, and the thought that Portuguese ships would come to revenge them. The priests said, revealingly, "they wanted to kill us not because of our religion, but because they thought us thieves, stealing the land we occupied, [thinking] that Portugal first sends missionaries to countries it wants to seize."[15] This, they complained, was a wicked slander spread about by the Dutch!

Tentative efforts were made at other points on the east coast, but these also proved disappointing. By 1620 the mission was over, and the Portuguese plan to convert Madagascar was abandoned. Over fifty years later the French Lazarist priests tried again in the same area of southeast Madagascar, but their chances were ruined from the start by their connections with the French from Fort Dauphin, who were involved in a general ravaging of the country. Most of them perished, and once again the mission was abandoned. The mission of Father Luis Mariano, though a total failure by our lights, was the most successful missionary attempt on Madagascar for two hundred years.

These concrete accounts of the experiences of Krapf and Mariano, with their confusing detail, have to be taken on trust as representative, for the points intended, of a vast literature of similar encounters round the coasts of Africa. They show that in the early centuries of European colonial expansion attempts to establish Christian missions on the coasts failed. The failure was not due to the strength of Islam, although in the absence of any serious threat from Christianity Islam did spread among many coastal peoples. These early attempts at missions were not made under the benign protective umbrella of colonial rule, but all were prejudiced and many were ruined by involvement with political issues and activities. In all cases, the missionaries perceived themselves as nonpolitical. Krapf could not see that his status as a stranger was essentially a colonial status, the initial effects of which led him to deceive himself as to the prospects of his mission. Luis Mariano and his companions apparently could not see that their effective membership in royal ships' com-

14. *Ibid.*, p. 160.
15. *Ibid.*, p. 170.

panies, which were concerned with wider issues of empire and constantly involved in acts of violence, doomed their efforts from the start. Trade always and inevitably involved power struggles and politics. The coasts of Africa and Madagascar were ravaged during the early centuries of colonialism. The east coast of Africa and the coastal areas of Madagascar have remained relatively impervious to Western influences until this day, perhaps because of their devastating first experiences of it. By the nineteenth century, earlier in Madagascar and later in East Africa, an improved Western technology, matched with the strength of powerful kingdoms which had developed in the hinterland, led to quite different and apparently much more successful results.

Henry Morton Stanley and
Mutesa I, Kabaka of Buganda

There is a great difference in tone and quality between the encounter of John Speke with Mutesa in 1862 and that of Henry Stanley with Mutesa in 1875.[16] At the time of Speke's arrival, Mutesa had been on the throne of Buganda for about five years, but Kiwanuka insists that he was a weakling and one of the youngest and most insignificant of the sons of his father, Suna II.[17] When Stanley arrived thirteen years later, Mutesa was much more experienced, secure, and confident. He had a much broader conception of the world as well as a deeper side to him, as expressed by his serious study of the Koran and practice of the Islamic religion, apart from the insurmountable barrier of circumcision.[18] So it is likely that the Mutesa of 1875 was more impressive and sophisticated than the ruler of 1862. On the other hand, it does not seem that Speke was very successful in establishing a personal relationship with him, although he had much longer than Stanley in which to do so. Both explorers were extremely sensitive about their dignity as white men, but Stanley used this more as an instrumental survival technique when necessary, whereas for Speke it seems to have been a fixed trait which he could not transcend.

Speke, like every other foreigner, was profoundly impressed by the size, quality, and complexity of the Ganda capital, and he found Mutesa tall, well-built, and smartly dressed and everything about him light, elegant, and neat. But of anything which may have occurred on a more intimate, personal level during Speke's many visits to Mutesa and their shooting excursions together, we know little. Stanley himself exaggerates this contrast, crediting Speke with writing of "a youthful prince, vain

16. John Hanning Speke, *Journal of the Discovery of the Source of the Nile* (Edinburgh & London: William Blackwood and Sons, 1863).

17. M. S. M. Semakula Kiwanuka, *A History of Buganda: From the Foundation of the Kingdom to 1900* (London: Longmans, 1971).

18. The Baganda have a profound belief in the necessity of a man being *complete*, dramatized in the case of women by the elongation of the labia minora, which makes them *more* than complete.

and heartless, and a wholesale murderer and tyrant delighting in fat women," and adding: "Doubtless Speke described what he saw, but it is as far from being true of the state of things now, as white is from black."[19] Stanley found Mutesa "not a tyrannous savage, a wholesale murderer, but a pious Mussulman and an intelligent humane King reigning absolutely over a vast section of Africa, loved more than hated, respected more than feared, of all his subjects." The King of all Uganda, Usoga, Unyoro, Karagwe, Uzongora, Kamiru, and Uwya [Buhaya] was "a most intelligent, humane and distinguished prince, a man who if aided timely by virtuous philanthropists will yet do . . . for Central Africa and civilization what fifty years of gospel teaching unaided by such authority cannot do."[20]

While helping Mutesa to fight the Bavuma, Stanley began to translate the Bible for him. "The Lake begins to belch forth the dead in the late passage of the day. I have begun to translate the Scriptures for Mutesa in the intervals of war business. A cannon I aimed at the island has caused five deaths. Today I dropped two with a Snyder rifle."[21] This bizarre combination of Bible translation punctuated with carnage, each activity being pursued with equal verve, is characteristic of the period and of the man, illustrating the grave limitations of sensibility and understanding which accompanied the supposed detachment of the stranger, despite the genuine excitement aroused in Stanley by his interaction with Mutesa and the Baganda. Four days later he wrote: "The causeway is progressing, Scripture is being translated, and we touch now and then upon the wonders of nature, the Heavens, the air, the nature of rocks, etc., all of which is hailed with wonder by the Sultan and his people." By contrast, Speke had remarked, "The small talk of Uganda had much more attractions to his mind than the wonders of the outer world."[22] Stanley continues in his diary:

> October 8. The Sultan (Mtesa) asked his chiefs today which book they would accept to guide them in their duty to God. The chiefs with one accord said, "We will take the White Man's Bible." Sultan said he would also, as he could not understand the Mohammedan book.
>
> October 12. Sultan told me today that he renounced Mohammedanism and became a Christian.
>
> October 14. The Wavuma brought two young girls as tribute and the war is over.
>
> November 6. The church foundations were laid on the summit of a hill adjoining the Palace. Thus Mtesa begins his new faith with

19. Richard Stanley and Alan Neame, eds., *The Exploration Diaries of H. M. Stanley* ["now first published from the original manuscripts"] (London: William Kimber, 1961), p. 70.

20. *Ibid.*

21. *Ibid.*, p. 101.

22. Speke, *Journal*, p. 348.

ardor. Another church will be built at Rubaga, which will be the Cathedral.

November 8. Mtesa is the most intelligent African, who owes his intelligence to his own natural capacity, in or out of Africa I ever saw. . . . He is not averse to flattery, and herein is one weak fault, he is also too fond of women. . . .[23]

So Stanley left Mutesa after a brief but intense and, in its way, world-changing encounter. Mutesa's conversion to Christianity has not been taken seriously by students of the episode. He was never a practicing Christian to the extent that he had seemed, for a while, a devout though uncircumcised Muslim. He must be given credit for a genuine interest in the holy books of the Muslims and the Christians, as well as for a deepening appreciation of and apprehension about the implications of increased contact with Muslims from Zanzibar and Egypt, Protestants from England, and Roman Catholics from France. In this, does he compare so badly with Henry VIII?

The English Protestants of the Church Missionary Society arrived within two years of Stanley's departure, the French White Fathers two years later. So began the intense and competitive evangelization of the new elite, leading to the battles between the Muslim, Protestant, and Catholic factions after Mutesa's death. These battles, reflecting Anglo-French international rivalries, culminated in the establishment of the British Protectorate and its use of Buganda and its leaders as a principal instrument of colonial rule, which committed them in turn to the invidious role of obstructors of nation-building—a role which brought about their downfall in 1966. Thus Stanley's encounter with Mutesa I was pregnant with consequences.

James Hastie and King Radama I
of Imerina

The hinterland state of Imerina in the central plateau of Madagascar remained largely unknown to the outside world until late in the eighteenth century. The state of Buganda, by comparison, remained in obscurity until the early decades of the nineteenth century, for it was even further inland—some six hundred miles as the crow flies, but over a thousand by the route which the early Arab and European travellers had to follow; besides, it was in the midst of a massive continent, not an island, even such a very large island as Madagascar. Imerina was only one hundred miles from the east coast of Madagascar, but the extremely mountainous terrain of the eastern escarpment, the bandits in the forests, and the heat and fevers of the low-lying coastal plains approximated the hazards of disease, physical attack, and exhaustion faced by those who journeyed into the East African interior.

23. Stanley and Neame, eds., *Exploration Diaries of H. M. Stanley.*

While the state of Buganda seems to have developed slowly from very small beginnings some five or six hundred years ago, the Merina state emerged more suddenly from the conquest and amalgamation of a large number of petty principalities. Such unification had been attempted before but did not become lasting until the second half of the eighteenth century. While Mutesa I of Buganda came of a long line of relatively powerful kings, the story of the Merina state is primarily one of two reigns: that of Andrianampoinimerina, who unified the Merina themselves (and for whose name I shall use the French abbreviation "Nampouine"); and that of his son Radama I, who led the unified Merina people to conquer almost the whole island of Madagascar. Nampouine is credited with the famous assertion, "the ocean is the border of my rice field," which set the goal his son very nearly accomplished.

There are no personal accounts of Nampouine. The first well-attested visit by a white stranger to Imerina was in 1785 when Nicolas Mayeur, an agent of French trading interests on the coast, actually witnessed a battle between Tananarive and Alasora, two of the ancient twelve towns of Imerina, in which he counted 12,000 warriers on each side. This was two years before the accession of Nampouine, yet Mayeur made a prophetic assertion, which echoes Stanley's claims for Mutesa's Buganda: he said that thirty leagues away on the plateau was a people with arts and industry more advanced than any on the coast, whose inhabitants would receive with friendship and understanding any Europeans who would teach them practical arts, because they were most intelligent and adept at work.

By this time French and British merchants, adventurers, and semi-official agents were engaged in constant trading on the East coast, mainly in the port of Tamatave; few of them ventured far into the interior. Many of the coastal rulers were of mixed descent, from Malagasy royal lines, Arab traders, and European pirates and shipwrecked sailors. Because of the blood and treasure spent on their disastrous enterprises there, the French had a deep and possessive interest in Madagascar. Louis XIV had already claimed to be King of Madagascar with a theoretical annexation of the island, but as usual the local French entrepreneurs received poor backing from home, and after the abandonment of Fort Dauphin in 1674 there seemed little left of French claims, though they were never dropped. Deschamps describes the next half century as the Age of Pirates.[24] French interests centered upon the Mascareignes Islands, including Bourbon (La Réunion) and Ile Maurice (Mauritius), to which many of the survivors of Fort Dauphin had escaped. This sphere of interest received a severe blow with the territorial settlement after the Napoleonic wars, which handed over Mauritius to the British. They occupied Tamatave in 1811, and Governor Farquhar of Mauritius began

---

24. Hubert Deschamps, *Histoire de Madagascar* (Paris: Editions Berger-Levrault, 1965).

systematic plans to gain influence in Madagascar as a means of suppressing the slave trade in the Indian Ocean and opening channels of legitimate trade.

In 1816 Sir Robert Farquhar sent his agent Le Sage from Mauritius to make contact with Radama I. He left two British sergeants there to train the army and brought two of Radama's brothers to be educated in England. In 1817 the British agent James Hastie was sent with money, arms, powder, trade goods, and uniforms, to negotiate a treaty suppressing the slave trade and facilitating legitimate commerce. Radama's main resource for obtaining the arms he needed to extend his power was the sale of slaves. He took the very rational view that if the British could provide an alternative source of income and support, he would be happy to cooperate in suppressing the slave trade. The British were prepared to supply $2,000 a year, with arms and other trade goods, to train the army and bring missionaries to educate the elite. From 1816 till 1826, when he died in Tananarive (just two years before the premature death of Radama himself), James Hastie journeyed back and forth between Mauritius and the court of Radama I.

Hastie was not the only competitor in the field. Robin, a French citizen from Réunion, had already taught Radama French, and acted at various times as his commander-in-chief and governor of the port of Tamatave. He was not consistently supported by France (which was preoccupied with its own convulsions at the time) and worked for his own and Radama's interests more than for those of France. France was also handicapped by the fact that when she did show any interest, it was always with ulterior territorial ambitions; the British also wanted to use Madagascar and King Radama in particular to further their own policies, but they had no territorial ambitions and were naturally opposed to those of France.

Robin became intimate with Radama, as Hastie did also—they both, in turn, occupied the right hand place at Radama's dining table—but Hastie's influence prevailed because he had the official and material backing of Britain. We have no detailed account of Robin's personal experiences, but Hastie left a journal which gives vivid glimpses of his developing relationship with Radama and of the revolutionary transformation of the king and his country which accompanied it.

In 1816 King Radama was sitting on the floor, clad in a traditional loincloth of raw silk, eating off silver plates. A few years later he was presenting himself as a princely hussar, attired in a military hat, red tunic, blue pantaloons, and green boots, giving formal European dinners on silver and crystal, with courses of fish, flesh, fowl, and ham, accompanied by ale, porter, claret, champagne, and madeira, with dessert and coffee—liqueurs on one occasion having been served beforehand. A band played English and Scottish music, and afterwards European country dances were sometimes performed. His new palace of Soanierana, built in 1826 by French and Réunionnais architects, was a place of exquisite beauty; Napoleon was his hero and he read extensively in European history. Like Mutesa I, he was ambivalent in the face of the contradictory influences playing upon him, and in 1818 he asked Hastie, "Am I not becoming an English monarch?"

Hastie accompanied Radama I on several military expeditions and even, at his request, led some himself. When the treaty was at last implemented in 1820, Radama threw himself conscientiously into suppressing the slave trade and was even prepared to consider the suppression of slavery itself. On their military expeditions Hastie was constantly exhorting Radama to adopt what he considered civilized practices, tactfully reminding him of his honor and repute as a monarch bent upon achieving recognition in the Western world. Radama was also constantly exhorting his troops and his local rulers to obey the laws, to suppress the slave trade, to stop slaughtering excessive numbers of cattle for funerals, and not to kill children born on inauspicious days. He went round making treaties with local chiefs, supplying them with flags and certificates, for all the world like the European agents of the day.

By conventional Western standards of concern for human life, Radama had been as cruel as Mutesa was. Large numbers of people were summarily beheaded for suspected treason, or subjected to the poison oracle. When Jesus' sufferings on the cross were described to him, he said crucifixion seemed an excellent idea, one which he might adopt. When one of his officers sold a slave, he was put in irons, judged and condemned, and shot in public; he was then beheaded and his head stuck up on a pole, and Radama decreed the same treatment for anyone breaking the new anti-slavery law. But likewise, when a slave in irons killed a Frenchman and wounded another, Hastie says of himself and the local chief: "we decided to make an example—cut off the slave's hands with the same axe he had used and burned him alive before a large crowd, all having been told to send their slaves to see."

Radama used his army as an instrument of political development, establishing fortressed garrisons all round the country to enforce the laws, including the anti-slavery provisions; he also used it to start plantations. When he had the soldiers' hair cut short like that of the British soldiers, there was a great outcry from the women; and the army, so modern and Western-trained, was still accompanied by singers dressed in white and choirs of women.

Radama himself requested that the British send traders to establish themselves and stimulate the economy. (They had the legal right to reside in Madagascar by the terms of the treaty.) He never seems to have been so devoutly concerned with religion as Mutesa was at one stage, but the two kings had much the same cynical, almost anthropological, view of religion in society. Radama said to one missionary Bible teacher on his arrival, "I carry my bible in my heart!" After praying for rain to the national shrines at the people's request, in 1825, he said, "religions are political institutions, suitable for leading children of all ages." Nonetheless he encouraged and supported the missionaries, and by 1831 there were said to be two hundred Christians in Tananarive.

A number of French craftsmen, mainly of mixed descent from Mauritius and Réunion, had an important and probably the earliest influence on Imerina during the second decade of the nineteenth century. But with the arrival of the missionaries of the London Missionary Society, aided by Hastie's British Mission and encouraged by Radama's enthusiasm, there was an explosion of educational activity during the 1820s. In 1820 ten Merina men, most of them nobles, were sent to Mauritius to learn carpentry, goldsmithing, jewelry, ironwork, painting, and cobbling. Ten former slaves went there to learn music, and women were sent to learn house management. Fifty more Merina were learning navigation on British ships. One noble offered Radama 3000 piastres to have his son chosen for training—an indication of how much things had changed from the days when Europeans had to kidnap nobles for the same purpose. In 1821 nine Merina men, including a prince, were sent to England with the London Missionary Society, first to attend school in London, and then to be apprenticed in Manchester. During 1824 twenty-two schools were opened in and around Tananarive. Radama displayed a deep personal interest in them, often paying visits and once addressing 2000 pupils at a meeting which lasted from 9 A.M. until sundown. When holidays were given, some nobles complained of the interruption. By 1827 it was estimated that 4000 persons in the country could read and write. Schools continued to proliferate even after Radama's death, until in 1835 there were one hundred schools with 4000 pupils (slaves being excluded). By the time the last missionary was expelled in 1836, and the persecution began, it was said that ten to fifteen thousand persons had been educated, mainly within thirty miles of Tananarive.[25]

Comparing this with the situation in Buganda, Radama I seems to have become much more Westernized in a single decade than Mutesa did. The island itself offered to Nampouine and Radama a specific goal for military and political action which did not present itself to Mutesa. Mutesa was preoccupied with traditional concerns: improving his position vis-à-vis Bunyoro to the north and increasing his hold over the Haya kingdoms to the southwest and the Soga kingdoms to the east, to which was added the diffuse fear of Zanzibar and Egypt, together with the Europeans who began to appear from those directions. Thus Mutesa's

25. S. Chapus, "Quatre-vingt années d'influences Européennes en Emerina," *Bulletin de l'Académie Malgache*, nouvelle série, Tome VIII, pp. 1–350, 1925; G. Mondain, *Un Siècle de Mission protestante à Madagascar* (Paris: Société des Missions évangéliques, 1920); P. De la Vaissiere, *Histoire de Madagascar, ses habitants et ses missionnaires* (Paris, 1884).

distant coast constituted a threat beyond his reach, whereas Radama's coast was a protective barrier within his grasp. Mutesa never visited the coast, nor was he ever able to establish regular channels of communication with the economic or political interests there.

In addition, Radama never went through a period of deep intellectual and religious influence from Islam, as Mutesa did. Muslims had been on the Malagasy coast, and sometimes in the interior, for centuries, but they were, at the crucial moment, far removed from any powerful source of inspiration and Islamic initiative of the sort that Zanzibar provided on the East African Coast.

Radama's frequent personal presence on the coast enabled him to exercise direct control over foreign trade and gave him status in the eyes of foreign powers. The Anglo-French rivalry which was so important, and finally fatal, to Madagascar, also bedeviled Buganda, but there it remained largely an issue between the English and French missionaries until after Mutesa's death. Because of Britain's direct policy interest in Madagascar, potent material resources became available to Radama which never came Mutesa's way.

The very existence of an ancient and centralized social structure among the Ganda imposed constraints, even on a highly autocratic monarch like Mutesa. It almost seems as though the much more recent creation of the Merina Empire in Madagascar, on the basis of the strong father-son combination of Nampouine and Radama I, left Radama comparatively free of structural and traditional constraints. The Malagasy and the Merina conceptions of kingship, which shared a common origin in remote Indonesian antecedents, both defined kingship in absolute terms, but its application was ritual and symbolic, rather than in widely shared political institutions. Although Nampouine and Radama created an efficient system of administration in central Imerina, it was rooted neither in established tradition nor in the institutions of local groups. These groups were highly endogamous and hence rather isolated from one another, leaving the kingship with few strong institutional ties to the rest of society. This contrasts strongly with Buganda, where kingship was closely integrated with the exogamous clan system, and where the administrative system run by appointed, landholding chiefs was also of long standing. But, of course, this contrast does not mean that the Merina king confronted no powerful vested interests, vying with each other to impose their will on national policy—as amply proved by the aftermath of Radama's reign.

In 1827, only a year before his death, Radama told Lyall, who had taken Hastie's place: "My people even now ask me boldly why I forget the customs and manners of my ancestors—why I put on fine uniforms like white men, why I have my table set out after their manner, why I use knives and forks, why I ride on horseback and make use of gaudy trappings, why my soldiers are clothed and disciplined like Europeans, why I have foreign music—and then they pray me to relinquish them all, and to return to the days of yore."[26]

The forces of reaction had their revenge on both Buganda and Imerina after the deaths of Mutesa and Radama. In both, the Christian converts were persecuted and martyred. But just as the changes had been more sudden and spectacular in Imerina, so was the reaction. The missionaries, who had converted a whole new elite and taught it to read, were finally expelled in 1836, not to return for over twenty years. Perhaps, we might speculate, if Radama I had not died suddenly of fever before he reached the age of forty, he might in another ten years have been able to consolidate some of the radical changes he had made, and to develop vested interests which would have supported them; he might have gained effective control over the whole of Madagascar and been recognized as its legitimate ruler by all the nations of Europe except France; in that case Madagascar might have escaped the whole experience of colonial conquest, and the Merina state might have survived to this day. But it was not to be.

Conclusion

Luis Mariano and the Portuguese Jesuits failed on the coasts of Madagascar in the seventeenth century, and their French successors failed again later in the seventeenth and in the eighteenth centuries. During the same period, Portuguese Roman Catholic priests failed on the East African coast also, except as chaplains in the few strong posts which Portuguese arms were able to retain in Mozambique. Krapf and the early Protestant missionaries again failed on the East African coast in the first half of the nineteenth century, and indeed the Protestant missions in the coastal regions of Madagascar have been relatively unsuccessful to this day. But when the hinterland kingdoms were discovered by Europeans there was a great burst of successful missionary activity, under the protection of the monarchs concerned, and a whole new elite was educated in both cases.

Most autonomous African societies were small, with the entire political community consisting of only a few thousand people. Some of these small societies had centralized political institutions, and some did not. It was with such small societies that the white missionaries were dealing on the coasts of Madagascar and East Africa. But the hinterland kingdoms which attracted the white strangers in the nineteenth century were large and centralized societies, with hundreds of thousands of persons bound together in the same political community.

White strangers, or "red strangers," as the Kikuyu called them, according to Elspeth Huxley, were an important category of strangers in African societies. When they tried to bring new religions into the smaller

26. R. Lyall, *Journal of the Mission of Robert Lyall to Radama I, King of Madagascar*, 1827.

African societies, without political protection—whether imposed by
their own nation or lent them by local rulers—they failed. But when they
worked in the larger African societies, under the political umbrella of the
ruler, they achieved spectacular success. New ways, new knowledge,
and new power were introduced rapidly and whole new elites were
created. These larger societies were transformed, through the harnessing
of their own initiative and energies to the process, but they were not
thereby preserved from destruction. The Merina state ceased to exist in
1895 with the French conquest; the Buganda state ceased to exist in 1966
after being artificially preserved by the British for seventy years.

White strangers are particularly interesting as expressing the African
encounter with the colonial system. Ethnic strangers from within African
societies have become a more acute problem since that system's breakdown.

White strangers such as Ludwig Krapf and Luis Mariano, Henry
Stanley and James Hastie, were enormously important in setting the tone
of European relationships with African peoples, shaping the image which
Europeans had of Africans and Africans had of Europeans, and significantly influencing the course of events. They should not be dismissed
as conquering aliens or as *estrangers*, although they were harbingers of
this; for despite the superior technology they brought with them and the
aura of foreign power which hung around them, they were lonely and
isolated pioneers and adventurers still at the mercy of many perils, both
human and natural—to which, indeed, most of them succumbed. The
ones who helped to make history were the few survivors from a much
larger army in which the survival of the fittest was a very severe test.

While Simmel's paradox of nearness and remoteness certainly
applies to them, they seem to form a varied category which was not considered by Simmel or by subsequent commentators. They were certainly
not marginal in the sense of the Jews, who have understandably occupied
so much attention in the discussion of Simmel's ideas. Despite the fact
that they were physically detached from their home societies, and to that
extent free from its immediate pressures, they were by no means free
from its characteristic arrogance and prejudice. Nor can this diverse category be very fruitfully fitted in to elaborate typologies of the kind being
developed by Donald Levine, and it is doubtful whether this is the direction in which illumination lies.

We must conclude that this particular type of stranger who "comes
today and goes tomorrow," though excluded from consideration by
Simmel, was of enormous importance in setting the tone and direction of
externally induced change in African and Malagasy societies—whether
negatively, as in the early encounters on the coasts, or positively, as in
the later encounters in the interior. Perhaps, with the benefit of hindsight
and empirical data, this should be regarded as a significant modification
of Simmel's basic theory. There were, it seems, more things in heaven
and earth than he dreamed of.

12

Village Strangers in Buganda Society

Christine Obbo

L uganda, the language of the Ganda, has an impressive collection of
words designating different stranger statuses, and Luganda proverbs perpetuate stereotypes about different strangers. The Ganda have
often had to deal with strangers for a very long time. In the pre-colonial
period they engaged in wars with their neighbors, particularly the
Nyoro. The women and slaves acquired during the wars must have presented problems to the Ganda, and this chapter examines the different
methods used to assimilate these strangers.

Historical Background and the Research Setting

During the colonial period, the favorable stereotype created by
Speke and Stanley attracted European missionaries and British administrators. The existence of a recognizable political system consisting of a
ruler assisted by chiefs made the prospects of indirect rule feasible at the
time the territorial and political entity called Uganda was created. Ganda
chiefs assisted the British in spreading colonial rule over a much wider
area to the east, north, and west, so that the Uganda Protectorate came
to consist of four provinces, of which the Buganda Kingdom was only
one. Linguistically, Uganda is simply the Swahili form of Buganda.

Administrators were preceded by explorers, missionaries, and Asian
and Arab traders. The introduction of cash-crop farming created
employment for many different kinds of people. First of all, rural-rural
migration was stimulated from different parts of Uganda and Ruanda-
Urundi. Some migrants, such as the Lugbara and the Alur, came to
Buganda, rented land and grew cotton, and after selling it, returned to
their areas of origin until they needed money again, for something like
taxes or bridewealth. Other migrants, like the Ruandese, worked as agricultural laborers for Ganda farmers and landowners. They cleared the
ground, weeded crops, and picked cash crops. More Asians came to

My discussion of certain aspects of Ganda perceptual categories and social structure would
have been limited indeed without the enthusiastic assistance of Leya Namwandu and
Mikairi Mundu, who were born and raised before the colonial changes; and the intellectual
stimulation of Yayeri Gutabingi, Bowazi Waswa, Joseph Mukasa, Fere Muwala, and Maria
Nsubuga.

Uganda and opened up small shops (*duka*) in the rural areas. Soon cotton gins and coffee-curing plants were opening up. This created jobs for the villagers, but it also stimulated further migration into Buganda.

There was also urban migration and employment resulting from the introduction of cash crops. The railway line from the coastal part of Mombasa at first stopped at Kisumu in the Luoland. This meant that goods and supplies had to be taken by steamer across Lake Victoria to Uganda. The Luo performed the loading and unloading on both sides of the lake. Some migrated to Uganda and soon came to dominate in all un-skilled urban jobs in Kampala. They worked not only as domestic ser-vants and porters; when the railway was extended to Kampala, they even dominated the ranks of workers responsible for its day-to-day maintenance.

By 1920 people from the surrounding countries were being attracted to Buganda in large numbers. In my travels in Kenya and Tanzania I have met old men who have told me that their dream had always been to go to Uganda. Some elderly women told me stories about how their young men suggested eloping to Uganda when they were unable to accumulate enough bridewealth.

With this much for background, we may examine the cognitive skills the Ganda have employed to deal with the presence of foreigners. My data are drawn from personal experiences and research conducted in the two villages of Namumira and Kyetume, in Kyagwe county of Buganda. Kyetume village was a typical small, rural center and Namu-mira was an extension of it. It had an Anglican church with a primary school attached to it, four shops, six restaurants, and two market days per week. Observers remarked on how in the last twenty years the area should have developed into a township, or an urban center, but had not. Urban development was hindered by the fact that the area was essen-tially a dormitory for urban wage-earners. It accommodated the follow-ing types of workers: clerks who worked at the local administration headquarters at Mukono township; medical technicians and nurse-mid-wives; teachers; taxi-drivers, who made several trips daily between the capital city of Kampala and several townships and rural centers in Kyagwe county; charcoal-makers who peddled charcoal on their bicycles to Kampala; fishermen who cycled throughout the villages selling fresh fish; and tree-cutters who sold wood to the local carpenters.

The two villages were situated on a major road to Kampala. This meant that public transportation in the form of buses or taxis was easily available. But the majority of people walked, cycled, motorbiked, or drove cars to work. Altogether in the two villages, there were one hun-dred bicycles, five motorcycles, and ten cars.

The two villages had a total population of five hundred people, of whom about half represented migrants from some twenty ethnic groups.

The most interesting feature of these villages which concerns us immediately is how the migrants were received and categorized by their Ganda hosts.[1] Three cases which illustrate this process will now be presented.

Case I. The True Ganda and Those Who Remain Strangers

Musoke enjoyed making fun of non-Ganda persons (*munamawanga*).[2] But after he quarreled with two Hima herdsmen who were greatly respected throughout Namumira village, whispered rumors about his background began to circulate. He was not a pure Ganda (*muganda-wawu*). His father was a Soga, who had come to a nearby village and made a blood-pact with a local man. He married the daughter of his blood-brother's friend, from Buddu county. It was not clear whether she was an orphan or a captive taken in one of the Ganda wars against the Nyoro. It was known only that she was a "child of the calf-muscles" (*omwana-we'ntumbwe*), as children captured in war are called. Thus, the argument went, Musoke was a Ganda only by incorporation.

Discussion

There are Ganda stories, riddles, proverbs, and songs that advise one not to shut strangers out, but to give them food even if you yourself are starving. So in the villages hosts will try to persuade guests to stay on, and the guests are expected to take it as an honor. The Ganda argue that one never knows when one will be a stranger in a foreign place. Some of the strangers to whom you give water and food are likely to come to your rescue someday.

Until 1966, when the kingdoms were abolished by the Uganda government, everyone who settled in Buganda was at the village level a "chief's man" (*musajja wa mwami*) and at the societal level a "king's man" (*masajja wa kabaka*). All visitors had to be introduced to the chief as belonging to some relevant category. The visitor could be a guest (*mugenyi*), a traveler (*mutambuze*), a blood brother (*munywanyi*), a kinsman (*waluganda*), or a client (*musajja wange*). Should the visitors decide to stay in the village and acquire some land, they became settlers (*mutuze*). The visitors from this point on ceased to be strangers; they became fellow villagers (*munakyalo*), neighbors (*muliranwa*), and new tenant-subjects (*musenze mugya*). The tenant-subject category indicates that everyone was either a client or landowner. Some strangers could attach themselves to Ganda commoners (*mukopi*), who would undertake to care for them in all matters political and legal. Strangers could thus

---

1. In Luganda "to migrate" is *kuwanganguka*, as in going to another nation (*gwanga*); *kusenguka* means to change houses or villages, and in the past it referred to changing allegiance from one chief to another; *kufuluka* means to abandon the nest, as done by bees or termites.

2. All Ganda terms in parentheses are given in the singular form.

acquire usufructuary rights over some land and entry into Ganda society via the clans. But ultimately, protection of the strangers depended upon the local chiefs (*mutongole*). The Ganda have a saying that the chief does not rule the land, he rules people. Thus toward the turn of the nineteenth century it was not unusual for villagers to pack up and follow a chief to another part of the country, if he decided to move after retiring or being transferred.[3] If the chief died, some subjects would move out to try their luck elsewhere. What was important was not land per se, but the relationships between the people who occupied a given territory. The result was an open system which allowed the chief, as well as the subjects, to recruit new members who could be relatives, non-relatives, or non-Ganda. Recruitment took place through two institutions: the blood-pact and assimilation.

Before the twentieth century, when an ordinary Ganda or foreigner felt that his life might be endangered by his mission (as it might if he were a royal emissary in enemy territory), he could demand to make a blood-pact with the king. This meant that if he was killed, his death would be avenged, or that if the king himself were annoyed or dissatisfied with him, he could kill him only on pain of supernatural consequences or sanctions. This applied to the close relatives of the blood-brother as well.[4]

The chiefs made blood-pacts with each other and also with commoners. It is not clear whether the chiefs made blood-pacts with all their subjects, but informants stressed that the practice was widespread, and at least the heads of all households must have secretly entered the pact. Commoners, too, made blood-pacts with their neighbors or other friends. All this indicates that in Ganda society there must have been a lot of physical mobility involving individuals and families. The blood-pact institution made it possible, among other things, for people to settle in villages where they had no kinsmen or clansmen. As a Ganda adage puts it: "Distant or little kinship is better than great friendship." Making

3. For example, when the Chief of Buddu county, Nikodemo Sebwato, went to be the Chief of Kyagwe county, his people followed him. First they settled at Mukono village, the present-day township headquarters, but when he transferred his headquarters to Ngogwe Kiwologoma village, they moved with him. John Hall Martin, *Through My Spectacles* (London: Church Missionary Society, 1898), p. 75. Richards has noted that at the end of the nineteenth century control over land changed hands so rapidly that peasants on land either followed their old lord or changed allegiance. A. I. Richards, ed., *Economic Development and Tribal Change: A Study of Migrant Labour in Buganda* (Cambridge: W. Heffer and Sons, 1954), pp. 126–127.

4. King Kyabagu was possessed by the spirit of Dibongo, the blood brother of his brother, Namuzaala, whom he had ousted. He brought diviners from the Ssese Islands, but had them killed when he thought that the spirit had been destroyed. He ran to Busoga, a neighboring territory, to escape the spirit that was torturing him with itches every time he went out of the house. Sir Apolo Kagwa, *Empisa za Baganda* (Kampala: Kagwa Press, 1901), pp. 60–62.

a blood-pact involved splitting a coffee berry and having each actor dip one of the beans in the other's blood and chew it; this was performed in front of witnesses. A person who had thus drunk another's blood was known as *munywanyi*, a word which also refers to a great friend. Kinship and moral and legal relationships were established between the protagonists. This entailed observing the taboos concerning each other's major and minor totems, helping each other at important times (celebrating the birth of twins, marriage, death, or moving into a new house), defending and vindicating the innocence of one another if accusations of witchcraft or theft should occur; and taking responsibility for the other's family after his death, if necessary.

So important was kinship that even slaves were called children. Since they were usually captured in war, they were called "children of the calf-muscles." It was difficult to know who the slaves were, unless one was a member of the household; economic and status inferiority seem not to have been associated with slavery (*obuddu*), at least so long as the slaves were obedient. A Ganda saying stresses that an obedient slave "will keep his ears for a long time." But since it has been easy for foreigners to become Ganda, the Ganda make a further distinction between ordinary citizens and the pure Ganda, whose clans supposedly helped the first king of Buganda, Kintu, to consolidate the Ganda state at Kiwawu. However, the people belonging to the clans that supposedly came with Kimera, the third king of Buganda according to oral tradition, claim that the legend of Kintu is a just-so story and that the Ganda kingdom began with Kimera; thus it is their clans that are pure Ganda. But members of the clans that supposedly were in the area before the others arrived (*nansangwawo*) claim to be the truest Ganda of all because the land on which the kingdom was established was theirs. Still, some Ganda claim that the *nansangwawo* were bird hunters (*balasangeye*) scattered in individual families, and that Buganda did not exist; the hunters may have owned the land, but the Ganda kingdom or state was not established then.

The notion of pureness (*wawu*), then, remains a major point of distinction between the "pure" Ganda and those who have acquired this status. One of my informants was of the view that there must be few pure Ganda left because of population movements and intermarriage. He went on to say, tongue in cheek, that even some of the Ganda kings were of foreign origin. Kimera, for example, whom most people recognize as the founder of the Ganda kingdom, is reputed to have had a Nyoro mother; and since Ganda kings took their mother's clans, he must have been a Nyoro and not a Ganda. More seriously, this informant expressed the view that some of the most zealous of the king's ministers may have been assimilated foreigners. Girls and boys could be offered (*kusiiga*) to serve the chief or king. At first people used to offer slaves or orphans in preference to their own children. However, it soon became apparent that being in the king's service brought with it important privileges, such as the chance of marrying an important man in the case of the girls, or of being appointed to chieftainships for the boys. Another informant, a woman who had been offered (omusiige) in this way to one of the important men at the turn of the century, asserted that Ganda missionaries and chiefs, including her patron, usually returned with clever boys from other kingdoms in Uganda. The boys were groomed, given the name of the mentor or a name from his clan, and some were even sent to Budo, one of the earliest and most prestigious schools. The informant went on to say that the worst insult one Ganda can hurl against another is to insinuate that he is not true Ganda.[5] In my experience, people are ready to accept such suggestions about another with glee. For example, in the 1966 crises between the Buganda and central governments, rumor had it that two Ganda members of parliament had leaked out important information concerning a meeting the king had had with certain individuals. The populace quickly explained this betrayal by noting that the two men were not true Ganda—one was a Nyoro and another a Soga.

All non-Ganda are categorized as foreigners (munamawanga or munagwanga). The word gwanga originally referred simply to people of another nation, but as the Ganda absorbed the European stereotyping that they were superior to their neighbors, the word acquired derogatory connotations. Thus munamawanga in some cases now refers to someone who has refused to be assimilated, even after long residence in Buganda. But the application of the term is situational. People will state categorically that the term refers to people with different dietary habits (for example, "millet-eaters") or different linguistic styles (such as speakers of Sudanic and Nilotic languages). The food preferred by these strangers was "tasteless and liable to cause constipation"; their languages were "difficult" to speak and understand, besides sounding "loud" and "ungraceful." The foreigners were quite aware of these stereotypes, and although some spoke impeccable Luganda, a large number of them pre-

5. For example, in 1904 Puliti-Kajjubi, a sub-clan chief, denounced Apolo Kagwa, the Prime Minister, as a Soga by origin and therefore not a true member of the grasshopper (Nsenene) clan. Kagwa was supported by clan members and Puliti was stripped of his office and land. Ekitabo Kyekika Kye (Nsenene, Kampala: Kagwa Publication, 1904), and J. A. Rowe, "Myth, Memoir and Moral Admonition: Luganda Historical Writing, 1893-1969," Uganda Journal, vol. 33 (1969), p. 22. There were other attacks on Kagwa by Daudi Basudde, the newspaper editor of Munyonyozi (The Explainer) and Sekanyolya (Grey Heron). It was claimed that Kagwa was a Soga who secretly worshipped fetishes, also that he was a Mukedi (someone from Bukedi district) who worshipped Islam, that he had 51 wives and 493 children, and so on. Kagwa Papers, Makerere University Library, Kampala, 1926; and Rowe, "Myth, Memoir and Moral Admonition," Uganda Journal, vol. 33, Part II (1970), p. 219. The editor was sued and fined. This seems to have been an all-round attack to show that Kagwa was by no means an upright Ganda Christian.

tended to know only a few words of it. The Ganda could not understand why everyone did not learn Luganda. The foreigners expressed the view that because the Ganda made no effort to learn even the Bantu languages, which to them sounded similar to Luganda, and insisted on talking to everyone in Luganda, they would act likewise. They gave the impression of knowing only a few Luganda words, just enough to enable them to get by. They paid the various taxes and by and large kept to themselves; they resided in groups, either in existing houses which they rented or built themselves with permission from the landlords. One Lugbara said that they purposely kept the distance between them and the Ganda because they wished to avoid pressure to assimilate. In his words, "The Ganda are happy when they are sitting on you. Besides offering invitations to join various Ganda clans, they often give foreign names a Ganda version." A Ganda who was present agreed with these charges, but expressed the view that if foreigners wished to stay in Buganda, they had to expect some control; after all, as the saying goes, "one who does not wish to be ruled, dies a vagabond." This group of unassimilable foreigners included Alur, Acholi, Lugbara, Kakwa (from northern Uganda), Luo (from Kenya), and Adhola, as well as Teso (from the eastern province). Some had been in the villages for over twenty years, and had married Ganda women; two of them had held political offices, such as an assistantship (busigire) to the local chief (muluka).

Some Bantu foreigners, such as Soga or Nyoro (and to a certain extent Toro), were incorporated into Ganda clans, but the Ganda were fond of denying this fact.[6] The result was that the migrants who came in the late 1940s and the 1950s did not wish to be assimilated. From the two villages that were studied, assimilated foreigners were migrating to the urban areas in the hope of escaping Ganda "arrogance." For example, Bantu-speakers (Soga, Nyoro, Toro, Nyuli, Gisu, Gwere, and Samia) were easily referred to as banamawanga if they spoke "bad" Luganda or spat in public. It would seem that the Ganda associated unclean habits with an inability to learn Luganda or to learn other "refined" behavior.

The best example of a Bantu-speaking ethnic group that maintained the stranger status was the Nkole, whose society consisted of two strata: the upper, consisting of the Hima cattle-owners, and the lower, consisting of Iru agriculturalists. There was also an intermediate class of "half-caste" Bambari. The Hima were, on the whole, tall and slim; the Iru were sturdy and short. The Hima in the village had been there for over twenty years in some cases, but they insisted on wearing car-tire shoes and cloths (kikoyi) draped over their heads and waists. Although this style of dressing is comfortable for people who spend the whole day in the sun looking for pastures, the Ganda made disparaging remarks about balalo refusing to wear trousers. There had been no intermarriage between the

6. Richards, ed., Economic Development and Tribal Change, pp. 175–176.

Hima and the other groups. This is an important point, because from some Ganda songs one gets the impression that the ultimate symbols of female beauty are the noses and eyes of Hima women.

The Hima Nkole specialized in herding cattle (*kulunda*) and were referred to as *balalo*, a word that some Ganda informants said was slightly derogatory. The other word for herdsmen or shepherds is *basumba*, but it was rarely used to refer to Hima herdsmen. One got the impression that the word *balalo* had once indicated an occupation but now indicated an ethnic group—that of Hima Nkole. Some careless speakers referred to these people as *banamawanga*, which technically they were, but most Ganda in the village felt that *balalo* was adequate to indicate this particular type of foreigner who did not assimilate.

A Hima who worked for a Ganda was usually given a calf or supplied with dietary requirements in return for his services, which included herding the cattle, cleaning the stables, and sometimes peddling milk through the village. The Hima, it was alleged, subsisted on the customers' milk during the dry season, because that was when one heard the most complaints about milk being diluted with water and skimmed of cream.

The migration of the pastoral Hima was originally triggered by a tsetse fly infestation that forced them to move in search of grass. In 1948 there were 56,000 Nkole of both sexes and ages outside their home district, 26,000 of these being in Mengo district and 17,000 in Masaka district—the main part of Buganda. However, only 10,000 (14,000 in 1957) appeared in the official figures as wage-earners. This is due to the fact that they were unskilled workers earning low wages and employed on an informal basis by Ganda farmers.[7] Some Ganda also referred to the Hima as travelers (*mutambuze*) because of the ease with which they moved from one employer to another.

In the two villages studied, there were old and young Nkole men who had no families. The young men sent money or visited their families back in Ankole regularly, but the older men seemed to have settled on plots of land, after having worked as cattlemen in most parts of Buganda.[8]

7. A. W. Southall, "Population Movement in East Africa," in *Essays on African Population*, K. M. Barbour and R. M. Prothero, eds. (London: Routledge and Kegan Paul, 1961), p. 180.

8. A plot of land is known as *kibanja*. In the past it was of unspecified size, depending on what the individual family could cultivate. More recently the plots have been of various specified sizes. The *kibanja* buyer paid a specific sum in down payment to the landlord. The sum ranged between 100 shillings and 600 shillings per acre, depending on the crops and houses on it and whether it was far away from any main road or townships. The *kibanja* owner had also to pay 10 shillings (or 8 shillings in the case of elderly people) annually as a fee for renting the land (*busenze*). The fee was known as *busulu* because it enabled the buyer to live on the land. But in addition, the buyer gave the chief money for beer or a gown (*kanzu*), the sum depending on the current prices. For thorough discussions of the

Since the early 1960s Iru Nkole have been migrating to the area. Some worked as cattleherders, but the majority began to sell their labor for agricultural work (*bapakasi*) which had previously been performed by Ruandese and Rundis. Interestingly, the Ganda cultivators complained that the Nkole were weak and could not dig much—which was nothing more than stereotyping. The Ganda could not make the distinction between the cattle-keeping Hima Nkole and the agriculturalist Iru Nkole; they were all from Ankole. The few Ganda who could make the distinction, however, presumed the Iru to be Ruandese or Rundi because of similarities in stature. The fact remains that the Iru Nkole fulfilled their daily labor contracts as well as the Ruandese and Rundi did.

Another group of foreigners, who like the Hima Nkole merited a separate category, were the Ruandese. By the 1930s they were the largest group of foreigners, and appeared to be poor because they wore ragged clothes. Since they were constantly digging, their clothes, hands, and legs were soiled and so they were regarded as dirty. This was particularly true of the migrants or temporary residents, who were very frugal. Thus the Ruandese were known by their own name *banyarwanda*, which seemed to carry the same disparaging connotation as *banamawanga*.

Case II. The Ganda Are Born, Not Made

Nalwoga sat surrounded by her luggage. She breast-fed her baby girl as she waited for a bus to take her to Kampala, where she hoped to stay with a friend until she could find employment and lodgings. Nalwoga was deserting her husband after one year of marriage. It was obvious to everyone that they were incompatible. The night before, she and her husband had had a violent quarrel which attracted a large number of spectators. He accused her of tricking him into marrying her. He claimed to have been made the laughing-stock of the village since everyone knew that he, a Ganda, had married a Nyoro.

Nalwoga's father had come from Ruanda as a teenager to seek employment. He had worked for a Ganda landowner in Buddu county. For faithful service, the landowner had adopted him as his own son, and he became a Ganda, a member of the Lungfish (*mamba*) clan. The landowner allotted a piece of his land to him and found him a wife from among his relatives. According to Nalwoga, her father was totally assimilated except for his accent. His children spoke impeccable Luganda, but he remained the obvious stranger. He did not wish to associate with other Ruandese who worked on the Ganda farms, and yet his Ganda associates constantly reminded him that although he was a Ganda, he was different. He became an alcoholic and his wife took the

land tenure system and the rents involved, see particularly A. B. Mukwaya, *Land Tenure in Buganda*, East Africa Studies No. 1 (Kampala: The Eagle Press, 1953). Also Richards, ed., *Economic Development and Tribal Change*, pp. 126–131.

children and left him. They stayed with her mother's brothers at Namumira, one of the villages studied.

The Ganda spectators at the quarreling, when asked about the ethnic identity or clan affiliation of the baby, asserted that the baby was Ganda. Several people quoted a proverb that says, "Your mother may be a Nyoro as long as she begets you in the clan." When I reminded informants that Nalwoga was a Ruandese, not a Nyoro, they assured me that the Ganda were well aware of the distinction between Nyoro and Ruandese. The word Nyoro was used to refer not only to people from Bunyoro, but to anyone who was a foreigner. As one informant put it, "calling people Nyoro, as a form of abuse, is a leftover from our wars with Nyoro, and particularly ones in which the Ganda sustained great losses."[9]

Discussion

The Ruandese are the best known of all strangers in Uganda. They have settled in Kigezi, the most overpopulated district of Uganda, and either have retained their ethnicity or have claimed to be Kiga. In the 1920s land shortages began to force Ruandese and Rundi to migrate to Buganda province as agricultural laborers. In 1927 it was estimated that 46,000 immigrants entered Uganda by the southwest route. The numbers involved always fluctuated between forty and sixty thousand people, depending upon the relative prosperity of the areas of origin and destination in different years.[10] The number of men migrating far outnumbered women. But the women tended to stay longer in Uganda; it is estimated that they stayed from 48 to 50 months, while the men stayed for only 8 to 14 months. Also, 86 to 98 percent of the women expressed the intention of settling in Buganda, but only 28 to 36 percent of the men did so.[11] The majority of male migrants were first employed at the Lugazi and Kakira sugar estates. This was erroneously referred to as the Kasanvu system—

9. In the two villages studied, it was observed that children were trained by being told not to be like foreigners. A few examples will suffice to illustrate the point. Mothers would tell their children not to have a Soga's stubbornness (*emputtu yo musoga*). Peer group members would discipline an obnoxious individual by saying his head was like that of a Nyoro (*omutwe gw'omu nyolo*). This often resulted in withdrawal from the group or a fight. Greedy children would be told that they possessed Gisu greed. Children who dressed in slovenly fashion were asked, "Where has this munyarwanda come from?" Girls who walked in ways that were thought to be ungraceful were called Luo (*bajaluo*). Children who were constantly hot-tempered and wanted to fight were referred to as Lugbara (*balugwala*) or Alur (*balulu*).

It is also worth mentioning that the most popular plays on the radio in the late 1960s and early 1970s featured people speaking Luganda with foreign accents. The families I knew well used to listen to the radio broadcasts after dinner; hysterical laughter from young and old always followed the Ruandese and Gisu accents, in particular.

10. Southall, "Population Movement in East Africa," pp. 176–177.

11. Richards, ed. *Economic Development and Tribal Change*, pp. 265, 267.

erroneously because compulsory paid labor was abolished in 1922.[12] Until the late 1950s prospective employers (Asian plantation owners) continued to send lorries to Ruanda or met migrants at the border. However, a considerable number of migrants ended up as *bapakasi* (hired agricultural laborers) for Ganda cotton and coffee-growers. Buddu and Kyagwe counties, which were for some time tsetse-fly infested, had at the beginning of this century plenty of land, on which some of the migrants settled as tenant farmers (*basenze*) and became prosperous.

Richards noted the superficial assimilation of Ruandese migrants into Ganda village life, as they took on Ganda names, wore loose cotton gowns of Arab origin (*kanzu*) and tweed or woolen jackets and shoes, and adopted the general spending pattern of their hosts. They even built square or rectangular mud-wattle houses, with corrugated iron roofs which cost 100 to 150 shillings, instead of the grass huts which most short-term Ruandese migrants constructed and still construct in a day or so without incurring expenses.[13] Richards believed that meaningful structural incorporation would be difficult to attain so long as both groups, the Ganda hosts and the Ruandese strangers, remained vividly conscious of their own origins and felt a need to maintain ethnic boundaries. We have already mentioned that a Ruandese migrant could attach himself to a Ganda peasant who would then undertake to take care of him in all matters political and legal. According to one of my informants, the incorporated Ruandese were informed about the minor totem but were kept ignorant about the major totem and its area of origin (*obutaka*). This particular informant had incorporated five Ruandese in his own clan, and he appeared to know what the common practice was.

The Ruandese was all right so long as he remained submissive— *akasajja kaffe* (our little man). Sometimes, if a migrant stayed with a family for a long period of time, the patron-host would find him a wife from among his poor relatives or friends. If the couple had children, they would be given names from the host's clan. But the arrival of children was usually received with mixed feelings on both sides. For some reason, the host's relatives often felt that they had been let down. The client-migrant realized that he would have to endure being patronized all his life, and would always have to defend and justify his acquired identity. This would seem to be a case of a stranger who is supposed to be inside and yet outside, especially since one can always tell the assimilated Ruandese because they have an accent and the Ganda accuse them of "murdering" their language, Luganda. The Ruandese speak a Bantu language,

12. Between 1908 and 1922 in Uganda, chiefs were required to induce their people to work for the government "for at least one month a year." This was known as the *kasanvu* system. Construction and road work was the labor extracted from taxpayers by the colonial government, and the system was greatly resented.

13. Richards, ed. *Economic Development and Tribal Change*, pp. 161–193.

and it is a great mystery why they do not master Luganda, since some Nilotic speaking people do.

In the villages studied, only five Ruandese out of forty had been assimilated. They had Ganda names and claimed affiliation to certain clans.

However, the Ruandese migrants who have been coming to Buganda since the late 1950s have not been interested in settling: they are what we may call target-circulatory migrants. This is partly because there is a shortage of land in Buganda, and partly because their fellows who have settled in Buganda are treated like "rotten tennis shoes" (lusejjera envundu), in the words of one Ruandese. Among the target-circulatory migrants were teenage males or men in their twenties who had left their families in Ruanda, and men in their thirties who brought their wives to work with them so that the families could obtain two incomes. They stayed in the villages for a year or two and then returned home. During each tour they accumulated money for a specific purpose: sending children to school, building houses, paying bridewealth, buying land, or expanding agricultural production. On returning to Buganda they resided in the same villages or moved to others, depending on whether they had relatives or friends there. In 1972 the Ruandese migrants still wore tattered and patched clothes, as Richards reported (1954). They smoked and spat. They spent very little money in Buganda except to purchase (previously from Indian shops) saucepans, beds, and the khaki clothes they wore. For accommodation, they either put up grass or banana-leaf houses, in banana and coffee gardens, or they are offered empty rooms which are usually adjacent to the kitchen. For this free accommodation they help out with fetching water, cutting and chopping firewood, and sometimes digging or harvesting crops.

Case III. The Wayward Stranger

The case before the parish (muluka) chief concerned two Kenyan students (basomi) both men—Ngethe, a Kikuyu, and Musau, a Kamba. An old woman was officially complaining that Ngethe had put her fif-teen-year-old granddaughter in the family way, and that Musau had not been paying his rent for the last twelve months.

In the arguments that followed, the chief and the court, consisting of spectators who had wandered in, decided that this was a difficult situa-tion on which to pass judgment. While it was agreed that foreigners (bagwira) should not be encouraged to "spoil" the children, it was also pointed out that the granddaughter in this case was promiscuous (mwenzi), and therefore it was difficult to decide who was responsible for her pregnancy. With regard to rent, Musau claimed that he had helped teach three children mathematics and English for two hours every evening; in addition, he had helped with homestead chores like fetching water and chopping firewood. The court decided that his role seemed to have been that of a lodger (*musuze*) and not a renter (*mupangisa*).

The court adjourned because the chief said he needed to think the matter over. But everyone knew that there would be no action taken by him. The students went home, packed their things and sought new residences. The old woman went to the shopping center and complained to everyone how foreigners always take advantage of people who treat them decently.

Discussion

In the 1950s private schools mushroomed in many parts of Kyagwe district. Ganda entrepreneurs started these non-official schools to meet the needs of students who were not bright enough or had not been lucky enough to enter the government secondary schools. As time went on, these schools began to attract students from all parts of Buganda province, and from Uganda as a whole; they even received Kikuyu, Luo, Kamba, and Luyia students from Kenya, and Chagga and Sukuma students from Tanzania. The students rented rooms in pairs in the villages near the schools, or as far away as three to five miles. Soon, villagers were building houses specifically for renting. Some students lodged free of charge with old people who wanted companionship. Thus the students were either renters or lodgers. The categories were determined by the relationship of the foreigner to the Ganda host.

The last category of strangers or foreigners were the *bagwira*. This group included Arabs (*bawarabu*), Asians (*bayindi*), and Europeans (*bazungu*). But sometimes Africans from distant places were categorized in the same manner. The category refers to the manner of arrival: no one knew that they were coming, nor where they came from. The word comes from the verb *kugwa; kugwira* is, therefore, to fall upon unexpectedly. Although they created the impression that their stay was to be temporary, they normally seemed to stay for a long time. Individuals came and left, but their communities appeared permanently established in Uganda. Villagers worked as cooks, gardeners, cleaners, and house attendants for European expatriates at nearby Catholic and Anglican missionary schools and hospitals. Other villagers were employed as sweepers, house servants, and porters by Asian shopkeepers and coffee-store owners at Mukono township. One Arab owned a shop, another owned a restaurant, and a Somali also owned a shop. The Arab and Somali were liked not only because they stocked the clothing in their shops that women loved wearing, but because they peddled it in the villages, on foot, bicycles, and by 1972 on motorcycles. The villagers claimed that the Somali and the Arabs usually sold better quality cloth and charged lower prices than the Asian shops. This was true, but the Asians could always be persuaded by bargaining to lower the price on their merchandise.

At Kyetume, there were two Asian families who owned small shops. Each family employed a Ruandese as a laundryman. The villagers felt that these Asian families were not as arrogant as those at Mukono. In fact, one Hindu was married to a Ganda woman. She was Protestant but her children were Catholic as a result of having attended a Catholic school five miles away. In 1972 when the Asians were expelled from Uganda, while the other family returned to India, the Hindu refused to go to Britain or India or any other country. He claimed that his roots were in Uganda. In fact, some of his relatives who resided at Mbale did not leave either. In 1974, he had abandoned shopkeeping and concentrated on running his lumber mill.

There were three coastal Arab families who owned restaurants, at which they sold Arab bread and cookies as well as such local foods as potatoes and bananas. They did not hire labor because the businesses were too small to need it. They were attracted to Kyetume by the rail station and the market, to which merchants from the city brought their goods, butchers from all parts of Buganda came to buy cattle cheaply, and Teso and Lango cattle-sellers disposed of their stock. The market was held twice weekly, and needless to say the restaurants made their greatest profit on market days. The relatively rich Arab was married to a Toro woman who was a land tenant. They cut their costs by growing most of the food and vegetables they required.

Conclusion

Peaceful ethnic interaction in East Africa has often been associated with the British colonial administration. For example, the British imposed a peace agreement between the Nyoro and the Ganda; and as shown above, the constant warring between these groups is probably reflected in the disparaging way the word "Nyoro" is used in Luganda. Individuals like Stanley helped the Ganda capture the Buvuma Islands. Consequently, "the Bavuma are Ganda, but not quite."

Buganda was the first area of contact for the Europeans, and it is therefore not surprising that Europeans established schools, hospitals, and the capital city there. Thus the rest of the Ugandans had to come to Buganda for schooling, medical care, and most urban-type jobs. This essay, however, has concentrated on rural-rural migration, which has been stimulated particularly by coffee and cotton farming. Famine and disease have forced individuals from Uganda to migrate and settle in Buganda. Differing resources of physical environment in relation to human needs forced Hima Nkole, and Ruandese and Rundi, Lugara, Alur, and Luo to migrate in search of cash incomes. Asian and Arab traders, with their small shops and restaurants, helped spread industrial goods to rural areas and thus exposed the Ganda villager to more urban influences than other Ugandan villagers.

We have paid considerable attention to the pre-colonial movements of individuals into Buganda. It has been shown that the Ganda have linguistic categories and special institutions for dealing with strangers. This indicates fluidity of both physical and social boundaries.[14] Ganda oral tradition also shows population movements in the interlacustrine region. We have already mentioned the Nkole, Nyoro, and Soga; and there was another group of people, collectively referred to as the Ziba, who came from the then Karagwe Empire to the south of Lake Victoria.[15] In precolonial days it was imperative for strangers in Buganda to be assimilated into the kinship by clan, and consequently brought into the political structure.[16]

After the imposition of colonial rule, however, strangers in Ganda villages could either assimilate or remain strangers. However, as we have shown, particularly in the case of the Ruandese, total assimilation was often difficult—particularly if the individual failed to master the linguistic skills that were felt to be the key to social skills. Because some people could be totally assimilated, the Ganda make a further distinction between the Ganda and pure Ganda. There was fear that the assimilated Ganda might one day dominate the political structure. This comes out clearly in the proverb, "A brazen, bold-faced Nyoro will divide meat for the Ganda." "Meat" in this case refers to power and privileges. The host is supposed to carve the meat and distribute it. But if the host is lazy or slow, a brazen stranger can easily do the job for him, thus causing embarrassment. This perhaps accounts for some of the fears that some high office-holders serving the king may have been of foreign origin.

14. Southall, "Population Movement in East Africa," p. 157.

15. L. P. Mair, *An African People in the Twentieth Century* (London: George Routledge and Sons, 1934), p. 266; Kagwa, *Empisa za Baganda*, p. 60.

16. Other East African societies have had to deal with the presence of strangers. For example, the Luo had the Jodak stranger clans and individuals, with whom wives could be exchanged (G. M. Wilson, "The Luo Homestead and Family," 1955 mimeograph, p. 24); the Ndu, who lived among the Lugbara but resisted assimilation (John Middleton, "Political Incorporation Among the Lugbara of Uganda," in R. Cohen and J. Middleton, eds., *From Tribe to Nation in Africa* [Scranton: Chandler Publishing Co., 1970], pp. 157–192); and the *jopath* or *jowiloka* strangers, who obtained usufructuary rights over land among the Adhola (A. W. Southall, "Padhola: Comparative Social Structure," East African Institute of Social Research Conference Paper, 1957; B. A. Ogot, *History of the Southern Luo*, Vol. I [Nairobi: East African Publishing House, 1967], p. 86).

13

"Goan" and "Asian" in Uganda: An Analysis of Racial Identity and Cultural Categories

Jessica Kuper

I n August 1972, President Amin of Uganda ordered all non-citizen Asians in the country to depart within three months. The decree was then extended to include all Asians, but after considerable protest from various quarters, Asians who were citizens were permitted to remain. Most of them, however, took heed of the earlier order and left, so that by November of that year there were only about a thousand Asians remaining in Uganda—out of the 80,000 who had lived there in the mid-1960s. Their sudden departure had an immediate and dramatic impact in the urban areas, where they had dominated the retail trade.

Stranger communities in Africa, occupying the intermediary position between the colonial European rulers and the indigenous populations, have been called the "hyphen" between Africans and Europeans.[1] After independence, they continued to be wedged between the two, at least in economic terms. They were usually traders—although the community I have studied, the Goans, had few traders among its members. "Stranger" or "hyphen" may be evocative and expressive terms, but they do not particularly help to direct attention to the structural essence of the situation, the typical plural society which generates the relevant political constraints. In this chapter, I shall argue that the development and the fate of the Goan community—one of several communities which made up the "Asian" sector in Uganda—was pre-eminently determined by the racial identity of its members.[2] Goans were mainly clerical employees, in the civil service and the private sector, and low-grade artisans, notably tailors and cooks. They were thus occupationally distinct from the majority of the Asian communities, as well as differing fundamentally in

---

1. L. A. Fallers, ed., *Immigrants and Associations* (The Hague: Mouton, 1967), p. 13.

2. My fieldwork was carried out between January 1968 and September 1970. For part of this period, I held an assistant research fellowship at the Makerere Institute of Social Research.

religion, language, and general cultural orientation.[3] Nonetheless, their distinctive economic and cultural circumstances have been ignored by European rulers before independence and by African rulers afterwards. From the point of view of class analysis, it can be argued that after independence they had more in common with African white-collar workers than with Asian traders. However, regardless of class position or culture, and despite whatever attempts some of them may have made to become Ugandans (by adopting citizenship and identifying with the aspirations of the new nations, or even by marrying Africans), their fate has been determined by the color of their skins. Their exclusion and ultimate expulsion, though certainly not inevitable, was inherent in the plural structure of society in Uganda.

The discussion here will be concerned largely with Asians in general, since "Asian" was the foremost identity imposed from the outside on the Goans—who accepted it, while simultaneously arguing for their separate recognition as a culturally distinct sub-group. I have also attempted to view the Goan community in relation to the other Asian communities, in order to show that while cultural differences fostered their alienation from the rest, they could not expect to be treated differently from other Asians by most members of the society. The Goans were peculiar both for being "Asians" in a predominantly African country, and for being "Goans" who were different from other "Asians." These two features of their situation will be the main subjects of my analysis.

The point has frequently been made that the Asian population of Uganda in no sense represented a community.[4] "Asian" was merely a racial category imposed upon several communities originating from the Indian subcontinent and broadly differentiated from one another by language, religion, and area of origin in India and Pakistan, with still further divisions according to caste or sect. The first large group of Asians had been brought out to East Africa by the British at the turn of the century as indentured labor for the construction of the Uganda Railway. Most of them returned home after their indenture period,[5] and the Asian population in the mid-twentieth century could trace its more recent origins to the opportunities for trade and employment which were created with the establishment of British rule. (Uganda became a British Protectorate in 1893.)

3. According to the 1959 census of Uganda, the (then) 72,000 Asians included 47,469 Hindus, 22,176 Muslims, 3,047 Sikhs, and 3,000 Goans: *A Report on the Census of the Non-Native Population of Uganda Protectorate, 1959.*

4. See, for example, H. S. Morris, *The Indians in Uganda* (London: Weidenfeld and Nicolson, 1968), and D. P. and Y. P. Ghai, eds., *Portrait of a Minority: Asians in East Africa* (Nairobi: Oxford University Press, 1970, rev. ed.).

5. Of the 32,000 indentured laborers, only 6,700 chose to stay on in East Africa. See Morris, *The Indians in Uganda.*

Goans constituted 3.5 percent of the total number of Asians in East Africa. They originated from the enclave on the west coast of India which was colonized by the Portuguese in the fifteenth century and remained under Portuguese control until 1961, when Goa was occupied by the Indian army and incorporated by India. The first Goan settlers in East Africa came to Zanzibar in the mid-nineteenth century; they were a mere trickle, mainly traders, clerks, and cooks. Their recruitment as clerks was encouraged later by the British rulers. In general, like the other Asian immigrants, most of the early Goan settlers in East Africa had no intention of making it their permanent home. It was simply a convenient place in which to find relatively remunerative employment, or where the hazards involved in setting up small trading businesses were not great, while the rewards were sufficient to ensure a comfortable retirement "back home" in Goa. Moreover, in Uganda, Asians were not encouraged by the colonial authorities to put down permanent roots. Uganda was regarded as a country to be developed for the benefit of Africans—unlike Kenya, where some of the best areas were appropriated by white farmers.

On the other hand, fear of competition from Asians encouraged their exclusion from the more fertile highland areas of Kenya, which, the British considered, were climatically better suited to white settlement. Indeed, they were encouraged in their commercial and other enterprises only in those spheres where Europeans were less inclined to work and in which Africans were not yet capable; and even then, they operated in the face of disadvantages and growing prejudice. In Uganda, for example, Asians could not obtain freehold land in most areas, nor was there adequate provision made for their education, which meant that those parents who could afford to do so sent their children to boarding schools in India or Goa. This, together with the fact that Asian government clerks and their families were given six months paid home leave every four years encouraged a continued attachment to "home." In the first generation, men often worked in Uganda while their wives and children remained in Goa, dependent on the remittances of the breadwinner in the "bush."

In later years, however, the cities grew, as did the Asian communities, special schools were opened for them, and wives and children came out to join the men. In the Uganda-born generation of Goans, feelings of closeness to Goa were somewhat modified. Younger Goans, for example, might still have been connected with Goa through family ties, or by a sentimental allegiance to their villages of origin, whose saints' days were occasions for lavish feasts and celebrations among the descendants of the villages living in Uganda; or they might have had a share in some land or property in Goa. But most did not relish the prospect of a permanent return to Goa, and when they were expelled most younger people moved elsewhere. Even many of the older people who returned to Goa or India after retirement found that the experience of living away from Goa for many years had alienated them from those Goans who had never embarked on an African odyssey.[6]

From early on, most of the junior clerks employed by the British in East Africa were Goans; these were the "Indian Baboo-clerks" who were the envy of German officials in Tanganyika.[7] Various past governors had paid them tribute, pointing to "their fine reputation for loyal service," and to the fact that the "most trusted member of the district staff was the senior Goan clerk."[8] Goans prided themselves on this image and believed, with some justification, that they were the favorites of the British.[9] In addition to the clerks, there were several Goan trading families who catered mainly to the European market, but their prominence declined later on. Finally, a steady supply of artisans from Goa provided the territory with cooks, butlers, and tailors. These were lower-class and lower-caste Goans, who remained fairly isolated from the others and who could almost be described as forming a sub-community within the Goan community.[10] However divided they may have been, and despite occasional periods of acute tension and factional conflict, they nevertheless all identified themselves primarily as Goans. As a community, then, the Goans had a distinctive occupational profile, which

6. On their return to Goa, Goans who had spent their working years in East Africa would emphasize their differences and their marginality in terms of their "Africanness." Stories were told in Kampala of the ex-"Africanders" who sat around idly in village bars in Goa, talking Swahili together (which they never did in Uganda) and enjoying reminiscences of life in Africa. A cartoon in a Goan magazine depicted such a character being reprimanded by a stay-at-home: "What, can't you get employment here? Perhaps because of your experience in drinking Scotch whiskey, German beer, and eating Dutch cheese, they find you too highly skilled to be of use in Goa" (*Goa Today*, Bombay, February 1970).

7. J. S. Mangat, *A History of the Asians in East Africa, c. 1886–1949* (Oxford: The Clarendon Press, 1969), p. 46.

8. Sir Evelyn Baring, and Sir Frederick Crawford, quoted in *The Goan Voice*, Nairobi, June 1, 1957.

9. The report from the district of Malindi, a coastal town in Kenya, for the year 1911, lists the following members of the clerical staff: Fernandez, district clerk cashier; Braganza, assistant district clerk; and four other men all with Goan (or Mangalorian) names. The report comments: "It speaks well . . . for the reputation and standing of our clerical staff that after 14 years of District work in five provinces, I have never known one's confidence in the members to be misplaced or have had any reason to regret the extent to which one has trusted them." Cited in Mangat, *The Asians in East Africa*. p. 6.

10. Though converts to Catholicism for about 450 years, Goan Catholics preserved some forms of the Hindu caste system. Everyone was assigned to one of four named castes—Brahmin, Chardo (Kshatriya), Sudir (Sudra), and Gauri. There was no concept of pollution but endogamy persisted, even in Kampala, and the position of one's caste in the hierarchy affected one's status crucially. Wealthier and occupationally more prestigious Goans were generally Brahmins or Chardos. It is a fascinating paradox that despite Christianity and their European self-image, the Goans had perhaps the most highly developed caste structure in East Africa. See Jessica Kuper, "The Goan Community in Kampala, Uganda" (Ph.D. dissertation, London University, 1973), and J. S. Montemayor, "A Sociological Analysis of a Goan Village Community" (Ph.D. dissertation, University of Delhi, 1970). See also Donna Nelson, "Caste and Club: A Study of Goan Politics in Nairobi" (Ph.D. dissertation, University of Nairobi, 1971).

altered little over the years.[11] The local inhabitants, however, ignored the special nature of their economic niche and tended to identify them in most contexts with the other Asians, who were predominantly traders.

Occupational specialization was merely one distinguishing factor. There were others. For a start, Goans formed the only numerically significant community of Christian Indians in Uganda. (Goa itself had a slight preponderance of Hindus, but only Catholic Goans emigrated to East Africa.) Mangalorians and "East Indians" were also Catholics from the Indian sub-continent, who also worked mainly in clerical positions and were culturally similar to the Goans; but they constituted no more than about twenty families. Goans were also the most Westernized of the Uganda Asians, being immediately distinguishable from the others by a combination of factors: their Portuguese surnames (de Souza, Fernandes, and so on); their dress, for most other Asian women wore the *sari*; and the fact that English was the first language in most households. The Goan language, Konkani, was spoken by some of the older people and understood by nearly all Goans over thirty, but most interchanges in the community were in English. As these factors suggest, the Goans tended to regard themselves as culturally European rather than Indian.

Goans as a Cultural Category

The communities which made up the Asian sector asserted their special identities mainly in terms of cultural and religious differences, and every community insisted that it was superior to the others on the basis of whichever criteria it favored.[12] At the beginning of colonial rule, the British were disinclined to recognize these differences and to cater separately to each community. It was only as a result of pressures from the Asians themselves to be provided with separate schools, cemeteries, and places of worship that official recognition of such differences was ultimately granted.[13] Once communities were better organized, and had with increased numbers become more self-sufficient, Asians were left with even fewer possibilities of acting in concert on certain issues which affected them all. Greater interaction between members of different groups remained characteristic of the minor centers throughout East Africa where the Asian population was small; but even there, endogamous sub-community marriages were the norm, and distance was maintained at more intimate levels of social interaction.

11. In 1970, 61 percent of Uganda's Goans were clerks, half of them in the civil service; 13.6 percent were in service occupations, 4 percent were businessmen and small shopkeepers, and less than 1 percent were owners of bars and restaurants; 1.7 percent were salesmen; and the occupations of the rest were unknown.

12. See D. Pocock, "'Difference' in East Africa: A Study of Caste and Religion in a Modern Indian Society," *Southwestern Journal of Anthropology*, vol. 13, no. 4 (1957), p. 292.

13. See Morris, *The Indians in Uganda*, p. 34.

Goans can thus be described as the stranger group within the broad, racially defined category of Asians. As compared to the other communities, they had few cross-cutting religious or cultural ties with their fellow Asians. They spoke mainly English, which the others did not, and Konkani was not spoken by other Asians. Gujerati, by contrast, was the language of Lohanas, Patels, many Ismailis, Ithnasheris, and Sunnis, thus cutting across religious cleavages. The fact of being Christian, with the concomitant lack of dietary restrictions and fears of pollution, set them further apart from Hindus and Moslems, who regarded them as unclean for eating beef and pork. Some of the other Asians referred disparagingly to the Goans as *mesticos*, equating them with Anglo-Indians in India, an identification which carried implications of being "half-caste" and illegitimate. Goans, however, vociferously denied any imputations of mixed ancestry, particularly the stereotype of descent from a rough Portuguese sailor.[14]

Goans themselves wanted to be thought of as quite different from other Asians. They would accept being called "Asians," but they used the term "Indians" to refer to all the others. Through religion, language, and ties to Portugal, Goans felt that they belonged culturally more to the West than to the East. The British distinguished the Goans only for census purposes, probably because many of them were Portuguese nationals. They had to use the same "Asian" health clinics and secondary schools (all communities had their own primary schools), they had to live in "Asian" residential areas, and their job ceiling in the public sector was the same as for all other Asians.

Nor were Goans entitled to separate representation in the pre-independence legislative councils and other councils which had representatives from the different communal (racial) groups. One Goan was appointed to the legislative council in the 1950s, but as an all-Asian representative; he assured his own community, however, that his particular unofficial concern would be to represent the interests of the Goans. Goans protested in their weekly newspaper, published in Kenya, that they, as an important section of the general community, had not been given due recognition in these councils. They wanted to be treated as a separate and distinct group—a desire expressed in several quasi-political associations which they established over the years, all of which aimed at creating greater unity within the community but never with the other Asian communities. They did, however, field their own team in the annual inter-communal cricket tournament (the Pentagular), competing against the "Asians" (in this case, meaning the Hindus), the Moslems, the Africans, and the Europeans.

14. A Goan friend who in Uganda had told me that she was offended at being taken for part-white, began, in England, to pretend that she was Portuguese. A highly educated schoolteacher, she rebelled against the English implications of the labels "immigrant" and "Asian," with their connotations of being uneducated and working-class.

The invasion and subsequent takeover of Goa by India in 1961 presented Goans with an emotional crisis which was felt even by those who had strongly opposed Portuguese domination. They felt that being part of Portugal, whose policy was to encourage cultural assimilation in Goa between different ethnic groups was a vital point of difference between themselves and the Indians, and they doubted whether their unique culture could be maintained within an Indian-controlled Goa. The attitude of both the Ugandan and Indian governments forced them to play down their sympathies, but they privately expressed their reservations. As one Goan put it, at the height of the crisis, "the whole Goan outlook and culture is the result of what Portugal has been able to impart, and it makes us so different from the others."[15]

Of course, every Asian sub-community employed criteria which established its distinctness and superiority vis-à-vis the other Asians, and they all valued their separate institutions. The values or criteria which they used, however, varied considerably. Goans stereotyped Hindus as traders, implying that they were exploiters, lacked education (specifically, fluent English), and were isolated and behaved in a foreign way; by Western criteria they were inferior. But Hindus reversed the evaluation and ranked Goans below themselves. The service-type occupations of the Goans implied a low caste position in Hindu terms, the lack of wealth implied low rank in terms of African values. Their dietary habits and the liberty allowed their women were also sources of disrespect. Ismailis used different criteria to distinguish themselves, stressing their commitment to independent Uganda. In claiming superiority on the basis of their Ugandan citizenship, which most of them had taken out on the advice of the Aga Khan, they were making a statement about their modernity, their foresight, and their willingness to adjust to changing situations; but the others, in turn, despised them for political opportunism and spurious commitment. (It should be emphasized that while the Ismailis wanted to belong to Uganda, they were just as determined as the others to maintain their communal boundaries.)

Goans were the only ones to emphasize cultural remoteness from Indian ways. It is true that they maintained a caste system and retained other "Indian" customs, including arranged marriages, but they deliberately played down the significance of anything which smacked of "Indian-ness." They might once have expected that their Westernization would have given them some of the privileges of the Europeans in the colonies, but they had long ago come to realize that this was not a factor in British colonial policy. Like the others, the Goans were able to influence their relationships only with other Asians. Moreover, they were forced to recognize (as were the Ismailis in 1972) that their fate was bound up with that of the other Asians. They were inevitably closer to

15. *Goan Voice*, Nairobi, December 30, 1961.

them than to Europeans (in the case of the Goans) or to Africans (in the case of Ismailis). In practice—seeking favors, for example—they found it easiest to use Asian channels; and in this situation the Goan clerk, working in government offices with access to files and to senior officials, might be a key figure. Goans themselves were forced to accept the fact that in a racially divided society they could not escape from their ascribed position in the middle. No acquired characteristics could ultimately override racial ascription. "I may be Westernized, but I was born on the wrong side of the Atlantic," a sophisticated Goan wryly remarked, summing up the predicament of his community in Uganda.

In an interesting paper on joking relationships in a small town in Uganda, R. Desai has demonstrated how the different Asian sub-communities, which he describes as "identical yet independent social units," are drawn together in leisure-time activities such as sport, conversation, and drinking. In these situations, joking is common. Desai argues that this sort of joking does not use true racial stereotypes, which imply a great social distance that is not reduced at all by the joking. But in joking relationships, "The situation is too close for comfort. Hence the stereotypes in fact are based on trivialities and therefore reaffirm an overall identity. Thus Patels are thieves, Lohanas are tortuous, Ismailis are untrustworthy, Sikhs are brainless, Goans are brown Europeans." Or differences may be expressed in unflattering names, Goans being referred to as Machli Khan (fisheaters), or Goula or Govindjibhai, both terms referring to Lord Krishna and alluding to the Goans' desire to be separate and their feelings of superiority. Finally, a set of proverbs about Goans have evolved in East Africa, one of them being, "Three things should be avoided: a swelling in sickness, a Khoja (Ismaili) in friendship, and a de Souza (a Goan) in the neighborhood"[16]

Desai explains that jokes of this sort have emerged because pressure from the wider society has frequently forced a man to act as an Asian rather than as a Lohana, a Goan, or whatever. The communities being similar but distinct, people have wanted to cling to their distinct identities, which are the focus of the joking stereotypes. These have helped relieve the tensions of being viewed merely as an "Asian." The relationships Desai describes were more characteristic of the smaller centers, but where interaction between Asians of different communities did occur in the cities, it was qualitatively similar.

Desai found it striking that when the others referred jokingly to Goans as outsiders, they included them in the joking circle. This was, of course, due to their common racial status. So, in a sense, Goans were in the dual position of being different but equal, though not quite so much

16. R. Desai, "On Joking Relationships among Asians in East Africa," paper presented to the Puberty and Joking Conference, Makerere University, Kampala, in December 1966. Cyclostyled.

part of the wider Asian community as the others. The reasons were cultural, in that their cultural differences from the other Asians and their similarity in many ways to the Europeans made it that much more difficult for them to adjust to their enforced membership of the "Asian" category, and to accept this broad and undifferentiated identity. When they stereotyped other Asians there was certainly a joking element, but at times there was also something approaching racial stereotyping. In fact, they often voiced the same prejudiced opinions as many Africans.

Here are some examples that illuminate the ambiguous status of the Goans. In February 1968, several crucial political decisions were taken, by both the British and Ugandan governments, which placed the already dubious security of the Asians at great risk. The British government decreed that certain categories of British citizens living outside Britain, who could not claim descent from British citizens resident in Britain, would be debarred from entering Britain unless they possessed a special voucher. This move was a response to a racist campaign in Britain. It soon became clear that vouchers would not be readily granted. Simultaneously, the Obote government stepped up its campaign to rid the country of Asians by withholding trading licenses and work permits from noncitizens. Asians who were citizens were discriminated against in promotions in the civil service, their access to medical schools and other facilities was impeded, and in some cases citizenship was withdrawn on the basis of flimsy technicalities. Goans were particularly vulnerable in this situation, since about half of them were British citizens though not of British ancestry, and only about 10 percent were Ugandan citizens.[17]

Before the British government decree could take effect, British Asians throughout East Africa, Goans included, were jamming the international airports trying to reach Britain. At the height of the crisis, the Goans at the Kampala Institute (the more prestigious Goan club) celebrated their annual pre-Lent carnival day. A group of parents had dressed up their children for the fancy-dress parade as "Indians" queueing up at Entebbe airport; laden with pots and pans and tattered boxes and suitcases, they were meant to typify the local "Patels" (Hindus) rushing off to the United Kingdom. People at the gathering were clearly amused by the portrayal, and in mocking the Indians they passed remarks which left little doubt that they were adopting the same attitude toward their plight as that of most Europeans and Africans. This was despite the fact that at the same time many Goans were also hurrying to get to Britain before the deadline.

"But why should the British take in the Indians?" one Goan asked. "After all, the Indians never showed them any respect when they ruled out here. Like you would go to a cinema and none of them even bothered

17. This estimate is based on a survey I conducted in Kampala and Entebbe in 1969. See Jessica Kuper, "The Goan Community in Kampala, Uganda."

to stand up when 'God Save the Queen' was sung." However, insofar as it affected the Goans, the decree was a different matter. Goans were the loyal camp-followers, the closest companions to the district officer in up-country stations (where there were no other Europeans), with whom the European could drink and let his hair down. Goans had never caused any trouble, and needless to say they felt deeply betrayed. Still, many of them projected all of their hostility onto the Indians: the Indians were really responsible for the British decision, because were it not for their foreign and unsavory ways, Goans would not have been penalized—and it was understandable that Britain should not want to extend her hospitality to that kind of immigrant.

But the situation was not all that clear-cut. One can also find illustrations of another viewpoint and different attitudes. In one such incident, which also occurred during the 1968 crisis, an argument flared up in a Kampala street between an "Indian" and a European over a parking space. Goan friends told me how they had cheered when the "Indian" finally gained the upper hand. In this context they were united as "Asians." The point is that the Goans were subjected to the same racial discrimination as the other "Asians," even though they were loath to accept the fact that their racial identity placed them on the same level as the rest. In such a situation, one can understand why they were ambivalent about their relations with Europeans and other Asians.

The conflict between aspiration and reality came out very clearly when, after Uganda became independent, the Kampala Institute was faced with a government order forbidding communally exclusive associations. They opened their doors and hoped to attract Europeans, members of a community with whom they felt they had much in common, and a few Africans, who would symbolize their public willingness to integrate with Ugandans. But the consequence, inevitably, was an influx of other Asians, who were viewed with suspicion and occasional hysteria by Goan members, who feared that they were trying to take over the club, and take liberties with their women, while keeping their own wives in traditional subservience at home and neglecting the responsibilities of members. The fear that the "Patels" were taking over was expressed by many Goans, although in fact there were only about 25 Hindu members out of a total of 300. The real trouble was that the Goans wanted to remain apart, to preserve their distinctive image, and here were traditional "Indians" joining and lowering the status of the club. Similarly, the influx of lower-class Goan tailors, previously excluded on the grounds that they were not able "to conduct themselves in society," threatened the European-like self-image of the club members.

Goans as "Asian" Strangers

At this point it will be useful to disregard the distinctive cultural identity of the Goans and to consider their position as "Asians" within a racially structured society, for the establishment of which Britain was responsible.

From the beginning of the colonial period, the various "racial" groupings in East Africa were deliberately isolated from one another as well as internally divided. In the absence of any significant interaction beyond the market place, members of the various racial categories viewed one another in terms of stereotypes.[18] Asians, placed precariously between white rulers and black subjects, were ideally situated to act as scapegoats, and from early on they became a target for hostility and criticism from above and below; indeed, it could be argued that it was in the interests of the British rulers to encourage the displacement of all negative feelings onto them. (After independence, racist Europeans found that by attacking "Asians" they could even win African acclaim.) There was, of course, a contradiction between the views of high officials, who valued their services, and those of white settlers, who feared their competition and claimed that they had a deplorable influence on the local Africans.[19]

In 1929 the Kenyan government was pressed into setting up a commission to investigate charges of unscrupulous dealing by Asians. In its conclusion it presented the official view, which was that such charges "are brought against middlemen all over the world and no doubt the ignorance of the African offers special opportunity to the unscrupulous. But . . . it must be recognized that the Indian middlemen are doing useful work for which no other agency is at present available."[20] Britain had secured for the Asians a protected economic niche which reinforced racial separation with a class differential, thereby enhancing the antagonism between Asians and Africans, and thus encouraging the probability that they would one day serve as scapegoats.

Another relevant legacy of colonial rule was the way in which the British taught others to judge local cultures. The Goans in particular eagerly adopted many traits of the dominant British, and the Asians as a whole readily acquiesced in the British view of the Africans as remote, backward, and "primitive." When independence came they were unprepared for the revolution (perhaps more apparent than real) in the evaluation of "African-ness," or for the new demands that the boundaries between the various racial groupings should be reassessed. Tom Mboya, in a speech to a conference of African nationalists in Kenya, said: "Cocktail integration is not enough: you must be prepared to examine some of your long-established conceptions; for instance, an integrated community can lead to intermarriage between the members of that community— and why not?"[21] Why not indeed, when Goans would not only refuse

18. I am, of course, echoing Furnivall's famous description, in *Colonial Policy and Practice* (London: Cambridge University Press, 1948).

19. See, for example, Mangat, *The Asians in East Africa*, p. 105.

20. *Ibid.*

21. See the report of the speech, and the highly emotional Goan reaction, in *The Goan*

marriage with other Asians (who were all organized in endogamous communities), but Goan Brahmins would unhesitatingly reject marriage with Goan Sudirs.

In colonial East Africa, Asians were not the only strangers or outsiders: what marked them off was their position in the racial, occupational, and cultural hierarchy. The European rulers were of foreign origin, and in Uganda they were also only temporary residents who ultimately intended to return home. But they were in power, and in fact provided the cultural model for the emerging African elite. The local Africans, separated by tribal differences which were carefully preserved by the colonial power, remained at many levels "strangers" to one another; and though indigenous to the country, they were the furthest estranged from the dominant political, economic, and cultural institutions. It is worth noting that when Uganda became independent, and African politicians took control, the large number of foreign Africans who came, often as refugees, from neighboring territories were the only outsiders who achieved general acceptance as citizens purely on account of their race.

The racial structure established by the British did not melt away with independence. Many British administrators did leave, and key civil service posts were gradually Africanized, but most of the Europeans stayed on, or were replaced by other Europeans, and they continued to fill their previous posts as contract teachers and technical assistants, or as managers of large businesses. The national composition of the European category changed, as Americans, Canadians, Scandinavians, and Eastern Europeans were brought into Uganda, mainly as aid personnel, but the high prestige and relative isolation of the European community was maintained for many years. The Asians, for their part, continued to trade, despite increasing harassment, and to perform their skilled clerical and service tasks. Their very visible position, midway between the Europeans and the new African elite, on the one hand, and the majority of Africans on the other, made them appear an obvious barrier to the economic and occupational advancement of the majority.

The leaders of independent Uganda were opposed to the idea of a racial hierarchy, and were determined to dislodge it, but at the same time they fostered a fundamentally racist, "Africanist" ideology. They were intolerant of imported customs, and sought to establish a distinct African identity as well as visible African control of the bureaucracy and the economy, although there was a certain ambivalence toward British culture, particularly among the elite.

Ideological developments in independent Uganda—in contrast, say, to Tanzania—appear to have had some effect on the toleration of Asian strangers. Both countries had the same constituent racial elements, but

---

Voice, Nairobi, February 2, 1962. Some Goans cited this speech as their reason for leaving East Africa, even many years later.

they approached their non-African inhabitants differently, at least on paper. During the 1960s, Uganda (and Kenya too) pursued a policy of "Africanization" while simultaneously offering Asians and Europeans the chance to become local citizens. In Uganda after 1962, this was illusory in practice, for deliberate bureaucratic obstructionism prevented more than a tiny handful of Asian or European applicants from acquiring citizenship. Even citizen Asians were painfully aware of the fact that their color was a major handicap, and it soon became obvious that they had little chance of gaining equality of treatment as full citizens.

Specifically, Asians who were not citizens of Uganda were steadily deprived of work permits, trading licenses, and the like; but what was perhaps more poignant was the helplessness experienced by the Asian citizen, who was made to feel that his citizenship certificate might at any time be declared invalid. A number of Asians were deprived of their Ugandan citizenship because, through no fault of their own, the British authorities had not canceled their previous citizenship quickly enough; suddenly, several years after obtaining local citizenship, they found themselves stateless. Thousands of others who applied for citizenship before the deadline (a couple of years after independence) were forced to play a humiliating and useless game by the authorities, who would periodically order all of them to reapply, fill in new forms, pay new fees, and then, once again, simply not process their applications.

Thus Asians in Uganda were made well aware of their uncertain future, and of the importance of race in defining a man's public identity, and in the distribution of favors. Tanzania, by contrast, was a better place to be in—though not free from racism, a non-racist ideology had developed there. She was a country moving along a socialist path, and though her ideology emphasized the equitable redistribution of wealth, it did not continually stress racial disparities. Thus, although her policies were bound to be hard on the many successful Asian traders, the Asian citizen felt that on balance he was being given a better chance to lead a decent life.

It is clear enough why most Asians in Uganda decided against applying for local citizenship at the time of independence; by that time it was too late. They were anxious about their future in the country, and foresaw the possibility of being treated as scapegoats, or at least of being the victims of discrimination.[22] Europeans were more secure. They controlled important financial resources, held highly skilled positions, and were protected by powerful foreign states.

22. A novel by a Uganda Goan, Peter Nazareth, accurately expressed the point of view of the rulers: "Whereas the Asians were nonexistent politically, physically they were all too real. They were the customs and immigration officials, the desk clerks and managers, the shopkeepers, landlords, etc. There were African businessmen and landlords, but they were invisible. [The Government's] task was to turn the towns of Damibia into visible African areas only speckled with Asians and Europeans." In a Brown Mantle (Nairobi: East African Literature Bureau, 1972).

Even those Asians who did commit themselves to Uganda by becoming citizens were disinclined to forego their separate communal identities and social ties. Marriage was still largely sub-community endogamous, with a slight increase of Asian-European marriages as younger Asians became more Westernized; and social life continued within the old recreational clubs. This was equally true of most of the Europeans.

The residential geography of Kampala also fostered the continued separation of Asians and Africans. Residential segregation continued more or less as in colonial times, except in the few elite suburbs, where Europeans and well-to-do Asians and Africans lived alongside one another but rarely mingled socially, and in predominantly African areas, where some very poor Asians were to be found. In general, however, Asians living in African suburbs formed distinctive pockets, and even their "Asian" houses set them apart.

The integration of Asian businesses was not easily achieved. Most of the traders operated small-scale concerns, sometimes in partnership with other members of their family, affines, or members of their sub-community, and they were assisted in the daily operation of their businesses by their wives and children. The turnover was not usually substantial. The Africans who were employed in such businesses tended to be in menial positions. In the more successful and prestigious Asian businesses, prominent Africans were offered directorships by insecure Asian owners hoping to win protection. There were, however, very few effective working partnerships between Asians and Africans.

Feelings of superiority toward Africans persisted, while at the same time Goans, like all Asians, made some attempts to come to terms with the new situation, hoping that good behavior and some modification of their attitudes would assure them security. Important Goan businessmen, besides giving directorships to Africans, sought the company of prominent Africans on social occasions. When a Goan friend celebrated his fiftieth birthday, his wife boasted about the many important people who had attended—the European boss, and "so many Africans in their Mercedes Benzes!" President and Mrs. Obote and other African ministers were invited to attend special events at the Kampala Institute, and if one had access to a well-known African he would invite him to propose the toast at a wedding or other important family occasion. However, there was an underlying and privately expressed feeling among most Goans that Africans in positions of power were often rogues and clowns, and loyalty to the former British rulers died hard. Among the young and educated Goans there were many with a strong ideological commitment to the new state—the novelist and civil servant Peter Nazareth is a notable example—but given the general situation they made little impact on majority opinion in the Goan community.

Beneath such public interaction there was usually a private disinclination to have intimate social contact with Africans. After one well-known Goan lost his money and served a term in jail, he was described disparagingly as having "resorted" to the company of Africans, even though his African companions were members of the elite. In another instance, a Goan shopkeeper, a member of the Brahmin caste, treated one of his employees, a low-caste Goan, very shabbily. Goans said he was "proud" because he was a Brahmin, and enjoyed relating how he had got what he deserved when his daughter went off with an African. When another Goan Brahmin married an African, his friends found it particularly difficult to reconcile his action with his previous, and much more conventional, refusal to date a non-Brahmin Goan girl. Finally, an extremely poor Goan family, who lived in isolation from the rest of the community in a predominantly African suburb, in a typical African mud and wattle home, were talked of with embarrassment. Members of their own extended family virtually ostracized them. As one of them told me, "They don't count—they're just Africans."

The counterpart to Asian prejudice toward Africans was African discrimination and prejudice toward Asians. I have dealt with the difficulties created for Asians wishing to become Uganda citizens. Asians in general—except for a few useful individuals—were excluded from the army, the police, and the ruling political party. Anti-Asian prejudice, strong for some time, was fostered after independence by the politicians. It was particularly evident among educated Africans, and was deeper than the reciprocal prejudice of the Asians. Goans, however, were slightly less unpopular than the rest.[23]

Pierre van den Berghe has aptly summed up the predicament of the Asians in East Africa:

> To be Asian in Africa means that one is always wrong. Hopes that this state of affairs might change after independence in East Africa have not materialized. In politics, where Asians collaborated with Europeans, they were blocking African aspirations. When they sided with Africans . . . they were being opportunistic in anticipation of independence . . . those Asians who did not opt for local citizenship were accused of disloyalty; those who did were suspected of opportunism and were still discriminated against on racial grounds.[24]

In short, "strangers" in Uganda were defined primarily by their race, so that a Goan born in Uganda, and a citizen of the country, was still

23. Ghai and Ghai, eds., *Portrait of a Minority*, p. 185. P. Fordham, "Out-groups in East African Society," in *Racial and Communal Tensions in East Africa* (Nairobi: East African Publishing House, African Contemporary Monographs No. 3, 1966).

24. P. L. van den Berghe, "Asians in East and South Africa: a Comparison," in Ghai and Ghai, *Portrait of a Minority*.

generally looked upon by the majority as a stranger, while a more recent black immigrant from Ruanda or the Sudan would be more readily accepted and treated as an "honorary citizen" or a "guest."[25] In addition there was the occupational stereotype of the exploiting trader, which was applied to all Asians. At the level of day-to-day interaction, a small minority of Africans might distinguish between the Asian sub-communities, and perhaps even express a preference for the "MuGoa" (a Swahili term for a Goan, which was commonly used), but the final and sad outcome, in 1972, revealed that crude racial classifications overrode all else, at the expense of finer distinctions.

Conclusion

I have used the term "stranger" in several different ways. Simmel's stranger, the outsider who was nevertheless part of the society, would correspond to the whole Asian sector in Uganda; but at another level, one can use the notion to explore relationships within the broad "stranger" category itself. Goans, by virtue of their relative cultural remoteness from other Asians, perceived themselves, and were generally perceived by the other Asians, as the strangers within, the "brown Europeans." In this context, however, the identification of Goans as strangers does not imply the counterpart of envy and feelings of exploitation which is central to Simmel's definition; it is merely a way of stressing cultural distinctness. In another sense, structurally related to the first, the plural society made the constituent communities seem strange and foreign to each other, defined in terms of stereotypes, so that everyone was an enigma to others belonging to different sub-groups.

One may ask to what degree being a "stranger," in the Simmelian sense, is a self-imposed identity. It is clear that both before and after independence, in Uganda, Asians were always excluded from full participation in public affairs. Before independence, they were straightforwardly assigned to a racial category with its attendant privileges and disabilities. Afterward, when some of them did attempt to become "committed" by taking out local citizenship, they still could not bypass certain levels in the hierarchy of identity—they were still ranked as Asian, and to a lesser extent as Goan. Despite the claims made from time to time by the ruling party, the Uganda Peoples' Congress, that it was firmly opposed to racism, racial identity remained crucial. On the other hand, the majority of Asian citizens saw their attachment to the nation only in political and instrumental terms. They did not want to become socially

25. Fortes draws this distinction, and contrasts the "internal stranger" who is "from the same cultural and political community in the widest sense as the host group, and the external, foreign, or alien stranger who may be left to live in peace segregated from the host group but is not permitted to become assimilated into the host group even in a client or other dependent status." M. Fortes, "Strangers," in M. Fortes and S. Patterson, eds., Studies in African Social Anthropology (London: Seminar Press, 1975).

integrated with Africans, nor, for that matter, with members of other Asian subcommunities or with Europeans.[26]

Simmel argued that the stranger is an ethnic type. But in Uganda ethnicity was not crucial, for a man's race was far more important than what he ate, believed, or did for a living. The Goans exemplify this quite clearly. Ethnically they were similar to the Europeans, but this cultural affinity did not place them structurally within the European sector, because their identity was fixed by racial criteria as "Asian."

The ideology and practice of "Africanization" defined the stranger citizen unequivocally in racial terms. There was a political purpose behind this, perhaps more than one purpose. So long as the Asians remained in Uganda, anti-Asian feeling helped to unite divergent black tribal groups, with Asians serving as a lightning rod for black hostility, as if they were to blame for all the disappointments of independence. After they departed, blame shifted to the British foreigners, or to Tanzania, or to various tribal groups within the country. So long as things were going wrong, the creation of new stranger categories to take the blame seemed to be a structural necessity.

The rhetoric of anticolonialism and "economic war" was often used by African leaders in Uganda, but the racist bias of their anti-Asian policies was clear. Class labeling was frequently used as a convenient, indeed an intellectually respectable, way of expressing racial intolerance, but the pseudo class idiom was as foreign to socialist policies as the problem was recalcitrant to Marxist interpretation. The Goans are once again a clear case in point, for their members were not rich and were seldom traders, but racial criteria placed them in the same category as the trading communities. Race was the crucial attribute at the political level, the level at which Goans were all "Asians." Cultural factors were vital within the "Asian" category, in fixing the identity of the sub-communities. Class factors were important mainly within the Goan community itself, serving, together with caste, to divide the Goans into two major groups.[27] As Leo Kuper has observed, "The racial conflicts in plural societies are not to be equated with the class struggle. . . . Classes act within the context of racial conflict and tend to be subsumed under it, classes themselves being appreciably divided along racial lines."[28]

26. Ghai and Ghai, *Portrait of a Minority*, p. 226.
27. See Jessica Kuper, "The Goan Community in Kampala," in M. Twaddle, ed., *The Expulsion of a Minority: Essays on the Uganda Asians* (London: Athlone Press, 1975).
28. Leo Kuper, *Race, Class and Power* (London: Duckworth, 1974).

14

Casualties of an Underdeveloped Class Structure: The Expulsion of Luo Workers and Asian Bourgeoisie from Uganda

Ali A. Mazrui

L uo workers from Kenya and other unskilled black East Africans from outside Uganda were expelled from Uganda in 1970 by President A. Milton Obote. Asian businessmen, professionals, and petty bourgeoisie were expelled from Uganda in 1972 by Obote's successor, President Idi Amin Dada. Obote was expelling proletarian strangers as part of his highly publicized socialist "Move to the Left"; in contrast, Amin was expelling bourgeois and petty bourgeois strangers as he was about to inaugurate a new "economic war" in favor of private enterprise and against socialism. Obote's strategy for creating what he called "the new political culture" chose for its first casualties ordinary workers from across the border, whereas Amin's economic war uprooted the most efficient capitalists Uganda had ever possessed.

Clearly, these were not cases of class solidarity, for they pitted socialist against worker, and bourgeois against businessman. In this chapter I shall examine how the expulsions of the Kenya Luo under Obote and of the Asians under Amin reveal the implications of structural underdevelopment for class relations. The expulsion of Luo and other black workers will be given more attention, mainly because the Asian case received much greater international publicity at the time and has since been given more extensive scholarly analysis. Our thesis is that racially and ethnically distinct strangers are at their most vulnerable in situations of inchoate class formation.

An underdeveloped class structure has five major attributes. These are, first, a trans-class ambivalence and fluidity; second, a low level of class consciousness; third, a high level of class masochism; fourth, diffuse ideological orientation; and finally, a potential for primordial militancy. Let us examine each of these attributes more closely before we relate them to the expulsion of Luos and Asians from Uganda.

The trans-class ambivalence arises in a situation of rapid structural change, characterized by a high degree of social mobility; the class structure is in a state of formation or transformation. Partly because of transclass ambivalence, class consciousness is at a low level. The sense of solidarity among members of the same social class, or the perception of shared interests as a class, tends to be weak.

A low level of class consciousness, in turn, often results in a high level of class masochism—which occurs when members of a class behave in a manner detrimental to their own class interests. Sometimes this behavior takes the form of acute internal cleavages within the class, animated by sub-class loyalties based on ethnicity and village ties, or by supra-class loyalties such as patriotism or affiliation to a universalistic religion. The fourth attribute of an underdeveloped class structure is a diffuse ideological orientation. The diffuseness can be inherent in an ideology, resulting in vagueness and relative incoherence; or it can inhere in the attitudes of those who profess the ideology, resulting in a weak commitment to the ideals and purposes of the body of thought.

Finally, the competing values of primordial loyalty may acquire precedence. A Kikuyu worker or peasant may decide that he has more in common with a Kikuyu businessman than with a Luo worker or peasant. And if ethnic fears are aroused, primordial militancy comes to the fore at the expense of class solidarity. Militancy expressed in primordial symbols such as kinship solidarity or religious ties is the fifth attribute of an underdeveloped class structure.

Let us now examine more closely the specific episodes of the expulsion of Luos and Asians from Uganda, and assess how those expulsions related to the country's underdeveloped class structure. We shall focus here on the Luo, using the Asian exodus mainly for comparative purposes.

1970—The Black Exodus from Uganda

Beginning in July 1970 the issue of migration of labor between the three members of the East African Community—Tanzania, Uganda, and Kenya—exploded into a heated regional controversy. The controversy arose from the Uganda government's decision to "Ugandanize" unskilled positions in the national economy as rapidly as possible, with September 1, 1970, as the official deadline. On July 10, 1970, the country's Minister of Labor explained the Uganda government's position. Out of 295,000 people employed in the wage-earning sector in Uganda at the time, 80,000 were non-Ugandan. The largest single group of these non-Ugandans were Kenyans, among whom the Luo were heavily preponderant. Their precise number was not easily ascertainable, but one popular estimate at the time was that there were more than 20,000 Kenya Luos in the country.

The Luo of Kenya have been exceptionally mobile as a labor force, crossing boundaries and establishing their presence in important fields of employment outside their homes. Although the Luo, like the Kikuyu, are basically a rural people, their role in the history of both urbanization and labor organization in East Africa has been noteworthy. Their impact on trade-unionism in Kenya and Uganda has been impressive. The mobility of the Luo community across national frontiers has given it a cosmopolitan dimension rooted in relative urbanism. The late Tom Mboya, a Luo, emerged as a founding father of African trade-unionism in East Africa as a whole, and as a great fighter for fair wages in the towns before he became a major fighter for political independence in Kenya. Partly because the Luo were conspicuous in certain urban areas of employment in Uganda, they became the single most visible community affected by the Uganda government's policy on labor in 1970.

In the course of September and October 1970, many of them began migrating home—pensioned off, retired, or sacked by nervous or overzealous employers in Uganda. The number of those who left was often exaggerated in the press, but there were enough of them to put a serious strain on relations between Uganda and Kenya. Trade-unionists in Kenya threatened not to handle Ugandan goods arriving at the port of Mombasa; and since Uganda is a landlocked country, and depends upon Mombasa's port facilities for the bulk of its imports from abroad, this threat had important regional implications.

The Ugandan authorities implied that such a boycott could not really be put into effect. A high proportion of the goods which finally found their way to Uganda were initially imported as goods for Kenya; in other words, Kenyan firms and companies imported certain commodities into Kenya, and later distributed these to their branches elsewhere in East Africa. A boycott at the Mombasa port of entry could not really cope with the problem of distinguishing what was and what was not ultimately destined for Uganda. Only an initiative by the Kenyan government itself to close the border between the two countries could effectively cut off Uganda from the Mombasa port facilities, so the argument went.

Nevertheless, the sense of an impending economic war was aggravated by a rejoinder from trade-unionists in Uganda, some of whom threatened to cut off that part of Kenya's electricity which emanated from the dam on the River Nile in Jinja. As the situation seemed to be warming up in an ominous manner, the two governments began to reassert control over their labor unions. In the case of Kenya, there was ambiguity at first, as the labor minister of Kenya appeared to be on the side of those who threatened to boycott Ugandan goods at Mombasa harbor. But the minister retreated from his militant position, presumably on the advice of President Kenyatta or the Kenyan Cabinet as a whole.

A proposal was made in the Kenya parliament to send Kenya's Minister of Labor to Uganda, heading a delegation which would seek to understand the background of the Ugandanization policy. President Obote of Uganda discouraged this idea, however, by suggesting that the real problem lay in Nairobi rather than in Kampala—meaning, presumably, that it was up to the government of Kenya to solve the problems of its own citizens who were no longer welcome in a neighboring country. Instead, an alternative strategy was adopted: President Kenyatta would use his impending visit to Kampala (for a ceremonial occasion at Makerere University) as an opportunity for an exchange of views with President Obote. Obote himself was being installed at Makerere as Chancellor of the newly nationalized university, and the atmosphere of ceremony and comradeship seemed potentially conducive to amicable discourse between the two presidents. Obote later denied that any extensive discussions had taken place between himself and Mzee Kenyatta on the problem of labor. Kenyatta, he said, had simply mentioned that his labor minister was interested in coming to Uganda to discuss the matter further.

Although a lot of Kenyans did in fact leave Uganda, Obote later decided to soften the implementation of his Ugandanization policy. The policy had stipulated that skilled workers were not subject to the same speed of Ugandanization as semi-skilled workers; and semi-skilled workers would not be subject to replacement as speedily as unskilled laborers. A partial reinterpretation of what constituted "semi-skilled labor" enabled a significant number of Kenyans to remain. What was a lorry-driver, unskilled or semi-skilled? Indeed, was the chef in a major hotel unskilled, semi-skilled, or skilled? The implementation of the policy in the latter part of Obote's presidency tended to give the benefit of the doubt to the workers. But in any case, many had lost their jobs by then, and returned to their homes. Let us now examine more closely how this episode in the history of "strangers in Uganda" relates to the whole problem of class formation and fluidity.

Male Proletariat and Female Peasantry

One of the chief weaknesses of certain schools of Marxism is the assumption that man can belong to only one class at a time. Marx allowed for social mobility, and even for the merger of classes, as the historical process approached the polarization of class conflict. What Marx did not adequately allow for was the phenomenon of the person who, in a situation of great structural fluidity, is compelled to belong to more than one class. In such a situation, a dual or even a poly-class personality becomes conceivable.[1]

1. The concept of the trans-class man was first developed in Ali A. Mazrui, "Political Superannuation and the Trans-class Man," *International Journal of Comparative Sociology*, vol. 9, no. 2 (1968), pp. 81–96.

In an African situation, the trans-class ambivalence arises partly out of the coexistence of the old traditional system of stratification (often with special emphasis on age) and the new universe of educational and monetary ranking. The dual system is fraught with possibilities of trans-class ambivalence. A person of lower status in the traditional gradation could be a member of the modern elite in terms of monetary or educational achievements. If his clan or tribe is unsure which gradation should prevail, the man may have to retain a trans-class identity.

Linked to this dual system of stratification in much of East Africa is the duality of African economies. The traditional sector, with its tendency toward a subsistence economy, still has to exist alongside the modern sector, which has a market economy.

Third, there is the phenomenon of the rural-urban continuum. If the landholding peasant, on the one hand, and the wage-earning urban worker, on the other, are normally classified as belonging to two distinct classes, then African experience has often bridged the gap of class identity. The peasant-proletariat identity, when merged in the same person, is connected with the phenomenon of the rural-urban continuum. The connection between the urban worker and his rural roots is not yet completely broken; the bonds of the countryside affect much of the style of life in the city. "In the Marxian sense of class, peasants who own their land and artisans who own their workshops belong to a different class from landless laborers and factory-workers. . . . People whose incomes consist mostly of rent or interest belong, in the Marxian sense, to a different class from people whose income consists mostly of wages or salaries."[2] But the striking thing in much of Africa is that a person could be an urban worker laboring for wages for part of the year and a peasant farmer for the rest; or an artisan who owns his workshop during the day and a hired night-watchman working for wages in the evening.

What was particularly intriguing about the Luo experience was very often an emerging class differentiation between the men working for wages in Kampala, or Nairobi, or Dar es Salaam, and the wives engaged in peasant agriculture at home. The situation could be compared with that in many other parts of the continent, and especially in southern Africa, where many men traveled to the cities or to the mines to work, leaving their wives to maintain their small farms. What was emerging was a distinctive duality: a male urban proletariat and a female peasantry.

This particular division of labor between husbands and wives came to have a bearing on the fortunes of the Luo in Uganda. The Luo inclination toward urbanization was connected with their attitude toward the land. In the words of B. A. Ogot,

> This was concrete, matter of fact, and utilitarian. Such mystic categories as Earth cult, Goddess of Fertility, or the mystic connection

2. John Plamentaz, *Man and Society*, vol. 2 (London: Longmans, 1963), pp. 296–297.

between the Mother soil and the man working it—so often attributed to the peasantry wherever they may be—was singularly
absent from their minds and civilisation. . . . The people had thus
no great love for the land on which they lived, as long as there was
enough of it for their cattle and their crops. A man would readily
leave his father's grave and build a new home several miles away, if
the land in the latter place was better, and enemies fewer.[3]

Ogot goes on to observe, however, that some important changes in Luo
attitudes toward land had taken place as they moved south. The Luo migration from the north had taken them to areas where rearing cattle was
not quite so profitable, and where the agricultural economy had begun to
foster some attachment to settlement living. The acute shortage of land
in western Kenya had accelerated this tendency, and had given land a
more important place in the Luo complex of values than it had had
before.

But the relative depastoralization of the Luo also resulted in increased female participation in the work of earning a living. Looking
after the cattle had always been pre-eminently man's work. What cultivation had taken place before the major Luo migration southward had
always been supportive of a primarily pastoral style of life. But over the
generations, as cultivation increasingly became the mode of production
among the Luo, the female contribution to the economy acquired additional importance.

After the Europeans came, working in the city increased, and
became a long-delayed functional male equivalent of the nomadic pas-
toralism of earlier ages. The men once again were on the move. There
was still enough of a hard-headed attitude toward land to make a departure for Mombasa or Jinja psychologically acceptable, provided the
women carried on the cultivation at home. The consolidation of a female
peasantry in active partnership with a male proletariat seemed to be
underway.

But the partnership also required that the men send some money
home every month from whatever city they were working in. It was in
their efforts to meet their responsibilities in this partnership, and send a
portion of their earnings home, that the Luo became prominent in Uganda
after May 1970. In his May Day Proclamation in that year, President
Obote not only nationalized the export and import trade, and took over
60 percent of all the major industries in Uganda, but also imposed some
of the strictest currency controls ever applied in Uganda. Even the relatively limited amounts of money which Luo workers sent to their families
became subject to cumbersome limitations. Obote's Move to the Left,
and the sudden implementation of a wide range of nationalization mea-

3. B. A. Ogot, *History of the Southern Luo* (Nairobi: East African Publishing House,
1967), vol. 1, *Migration and Settlement*, pp. 38–39.

sures, had made the movement of currency a matter of high political sensitivity. Until then, Uganda's paper money was negotiable at par in Kenya, and Kenyan money was negotiable on the same basis in Uganda. Kenyan workers within Uganda could therefore send Ugandan notes home without converting them. The notes were negotiable in Kenya, and the rural female peasantry could thus take advantage of contributions from their husbands and families working in distant cities.

It is true that Uganda paid a price for this mutual negotiability of currencies. Each year Kenya and Uganda exchanged each other's shillings, but whoever had a surplus of the other's currency could expect that surplus to be met with sterling in exchange. Because there was more Ugandan money going to Kenya from the unskilled earnings of Kenyans than Kenyan money flowing to Uganda from a similar category of workers, it was indeed understandable that Uganda should have begun to worry about the amount of sterling she had to provide each year for the surplus in Kenya's banks.

Until 1970 this issue had not been elevated into a major policy quarrel. After all, it was understood that each of the partner states of the East African Community had to sustain certain economic costs in return for benefits in other spheres of interaction. On balance, Kenya continued to be the greatest single beneficiary within the Community, but the others benefited enough to want to remain members.

From May until July 1970 the problem was dramatized at the proletarian level. Long queues of non-Ugandan workers formed outside the Bank of Uganda waiting to complete the formalities which would allow them to send the equivalent of $10 to $20 in East African shillings to their families across the border. Some observers were disturbed that people with such simple earnings should be subjected to so much regulation. Many of those who went to the bank had to forfeit a day's wage, standing in line from very early morning in order to have the exchange regulations formalized. The Ugandan press was influenced less by compassion for the workers standing in queues than by alarm at how much money was leaving Uganda. There was a calculated attempt by the party press to stir up hostility among Ugandan workers toward their immigrant counterparts. What emerged was an illustration of low class consciousness and high class masochism. Let us now turn to this interplay.

Collective Consciousness and Class Masochism

It is worth noting, to begin with, the dialectical roles of conflict and integration in class formation. Internalized class conflict arises when opposing tensions related to important economic issues exist within the same socioeconomic group. Externalized class conflict, on the other hand, is conflict between two or more different socioeconomic categories of people. Marxists might argue that only this is true class conflict. But it is certainly arguable that an underdeveloped class structure, given the five attributes mentioned above, has a high propensity for the internalization of class conflict, for pitting worker against worker, bourgeois against bourgeois.

We have noted that the first major response to the decision to expel Kenyan workers from Uganda came from fellow Kenyan workers in Mombasa, who threatened to boycott the handling of Ugandan goods arriving at the port. Was this an instance of class solidarity, with port employees in Mombasa coming to the defense of migrant laborers in Jinja? To some extent, of course, this reaction of the Kenyan trade unions was a form of class solidarity. But was the support coming mainly from the Luo section of the union leadership in Kenya? If so, it seems more likely that the affirmation of support for fellow Luo expelled from Uganda was a case of sub-class loyalty based on ethnicity. On the other hand, the support may have been primarily because those expelled were fellow Kenyans. In that case, the threat of boycotting Ugandan goods was an instance of supra-class solidarity of all Kenyans, implying a sympathy for the expelled workers from Uganda not because they were workers but because they were national compatriots.

The counter-response of the Ugandan trade unions re-emphasized that the relevant level of solidarity in this case was national rather than class-based. The ruling elites of the two countries were for a while less vocal than their trade unionists. To the extent that the ruling elites were sometimes benefiting from their positions of power at the expense of ordinary workers and peasants, those confrontations and reciprocal threats between Kenyan labor unions and Ugandan ones were clearly an instance of class masochism.

What ought to be borne in mind is that there is often an advantage as well as a cost in such behavior. Many African societies are more deeply divided by ethnic cleavages than by class antagonisms. The mitigation of ethnic conflicts is a slow process. But sometimes internalized class conflicts across territorial frontiers—such as the one which afflicted Ugandan and Kenyan workers—can be mobilized to serve the process of national integration. Once again, different levels of conflict can serve either integrative or divisive purposes. The dialectic between conflict and integration is a complicated one. The theory of cross-cutting loyalties as a method of achieving national cohesion becomes relevant here. Where ethnic groups are divided too neatly, without overlapping affiliation, the danger of ethnic or tribal confrontation is acute. But when, for example, a Muganda finds a religious tie with a fellow Catholic who is a Munyoro and an economic tie with a fellow coffee-grower originally from Lango, the situation is one in which people are divided in some matters and united in others. They might be divided as members of different ethnic communities and united as members of the same socioeconomic class or the same religious denomination. The danger of a sharp ethnic confrontation is strongly reduced when there are alternative areas of alliance.

In the East African situation there is also an interstate cleavage, an area of conflict which may divide laborers or the intelligentsia across territorial boundaries but may nevertheless unite them within each of the nations. At this interstate level, the main cleavage in 1970 concerned Uganda's relations with Kenya, as we have indicated. But what was the attitude of Tanzania to Uganda's policies under Milton Obote? Here a distinction needs to be made between the two parts of the United Republic of Tanzania. Mainland Tanzania, under Julius Nyerere, was cautious in its response. On the one hand, Nyerere was a friend of Dr. Obote, who sympathized with Obote's Move to the Left and preferred to give Uganda under Obote the benefit of the doubt in any apparent altercation between Uganda and Kenya. On the other hand, there were individual Tanzanians working in Uganda who were seriously affected by Obote's policy, and whose expulsion from Uganda could arouse feelings among their relatives in Tanzania.

At a meeting with students at the University of Dar es Salaam in 1970, President Nyerere said that it could serve no good purpose for each partner state of the East African Community to drive non-citizens out of useful employment. He preferred to understand Uganda's policies as an effort to avoid undesirable effects of seasonal labor. After all, he said, people from neighboring countries went to work in sugar plantations during harvest seasons, but they had to return to their own countries when the harvest was done. Nyerere was reported to have asked why, if the policy of the Uganda government was "what the newspapers claim it to be," not a single Tanzanian had been expelled from Uganda. President Nyerere's information at the time was less than adequate; there were in fact some Tanzanians who had been affected by the Ugandanization of unskilled labor. But the main thrust of his argument was that the sacking within Uganda was being grossly exaggerated, and that there should be more sympathy shown for the Ugandan government than was being accorded to it by the Kenyan press. It was quite clear that mainland Tanzania's policy, at least as represented by Julius Nyerere, was cautious and ambivalent on the labor question.

Curiously enough, the other partner in the United Republic of Tanzania, Zanzibar, adopted a different position. Although foreign relations were supposed to be conducted from Dar es Salaam, the Revolutionary Council in Zanzibar decided to send a telegram of support to Uganda's President Obote. The telegram read: "The Zanzibar Revolutionary Government supports the Uganda Government in employing its citizens in place of non-citizens. It is the duty of every leader of every nation to ensure that their citizens enjoy their rights. Please do not allow people from Tanzania or Zanzibar to usurp the rights of Uganda citizens by offering them employment." The telegram was signed by the Chairman of the Revolutionary Council, Mr. Abeid Karume, who was at the time Tanzania's First Vice-President.[4]

A continuation of class masochism seemed to be at play here. Mr. Abeid Karume was himself an immigrant in Zanzibar from Malawi, although he had arrived there much earlier as a child, with his parents. He himself had grown up in relatively poor and underprivileged conditions, and had later earned a living as a fisherman. His parents had sought economic opportunities elsewhere, and had found economic asylum in Zanzibar.

It is even arguable that the Zanzibar revolution itself would not have taken the form it did but for the tradition of free migration of labor within the old East Africa. John Okello, the man who was destined to spearhead the Zanzibar revolution, was in fact an adult Ugandan immigrant residing in Zanzibar. As fate would have it, Okello was in fact from Obote's own ethnic community, the Langi. Okello had migrated from one part of East Africa to another, and had settled in Zanzibar for a while. He had even worked in the police force there, and had acquired a good mastery of Zanzibari Swahili; but he remained a Ugandan citizen, and was expelled from Tanzania not many weeks after he had helped to spearhead the Zanzibar revolution. What was even more ironic was that Milton Obote himself had once been a migrant worker in Kenya during the colonial period, had dabbled in Kenyan politics and Kenyan trade unions, and later considered migrating to the Sudan in search of further education; and yet here was Obote—now president—ordering the expulsion of immigrant workers from neighboring countries.

This was indeed a far cry from British policy during the colonial period. The British had recognized the artificiality of the boundaries in East Africa, and had allowed the movement of indigenous Africans between the four colonial territories—Kenya, Uganda, Tanganyika, and Zanzibar—to take place without any special immigration or customs formalities. East Africa entered the independence period with a system of free indigenous migration—except for the restrictions imposed on the Kikuyu during the Mau Mau insurrection in the 1950s, restrictions which the independent state of Tanganyika decided to uphold.

Nor was easy migration across territorial boundaries limited to these four British colonial areas; colonies bordering Uganda, Kenya, and Tanganyika also permitted a considerable amount of movement across their borders. In some cases the movement was seasonal, depending on harvests. In the case of the Somalis of northeastern Kenya, the movement was nomadic in the more classical sense, as the herdsmen moved between Somalia and Kenya according to the needs of their animals.

4. See *Standard* (Tanzania), October 7, 1970, and *East African Standard*, October 8, 1970. Mr. Karume has since been assassinated, and has been succeeded as ruler of Zanzibar by Mr. Aboud Jumbe.

There were also occasions when particular immigrants became assimilated, and settled down fully as citizens of their countries of adoption. What these examples show is that there was a firm tradition of migrant labor in East Africa, which had helped the less privileged sectors of the different countries to broaden their economic horizons as they sought jobs elsewhere.

To repeat the main point here, trans-class ambivalence in conditions of structural fluidity and high social mobility eroded the relatively limited proletarian consciousness which Obote had had when he participated in trade unionism in Kenya, or which Karume had had as a struggling fisherman. Low class consciousness, combined with a determined refusal to remember harder times as fellow migrant laborers, inclined them toward class masochism.

Ideology and Primordial Culture

On balance, the issue of ethnicity and the primordial culture of the Luo was never a factor behind Obote's policy. Indeed, although the people of Lango were, by the second half of the twentieth century, a very distinct group from the people of Nyanza, the Lango and the Luo were ethnically, culturally, and linguistically linked. And Obote himself was, in any case, less deeply influenced by sub-class ethnic considerations than many of his countrymen were, in spite of his strong and uncompromising policy in Buganda's relations with his own government.

The popularity of his policies among ordinary Ugandans certainly included such ethnic sentiments. The Baganda looked down on the Luo, not simply because they were Kenyans, and not merely because they were migrant laborers, but also because their culture was regarded as distinctly inferior to Kiganda culture. Many Luo had settled in Buganda, and not always as laborers; on the contrary, many Luo small shopkeepers and artisans were scattered around different parts of Buganda. Many of these survived the expulsion order, either on the grounds that they were not unskilled or on the grounds that they were not engaged in paid employment. But on balance, the acclaim which greeted Obote's policies regarding Luo and other non-Ugandan blacks included as an undercurrent the usual ethnic prejudices of East African societies.

President Obote in fact was somewhat embarrassed by the whole issue when it first arose. When I interviewed him in August 1970, he claimed that his own Minister of Labor had not really involved him in the formulation of the policy of Ugandanizing unskilled employment. Indeed, Obote claimed that the matter had not even come before the Uganda Cabinet, although by that time it was already an issue of passionate debate between his country and Kenya. He appeared to have strong feelings about certain aspects of Kenya's economic policy and ideology, and he was certainly not enthusiastic about rescuing Kenya from the effects of its own economic policy by keeping Uganda's doors open to unemployed Kenyans. He implied that Kenyatta's government was disguising the employment costs of its capitalist strategy by exporting Kenya's surplus labor to neighboring countries. At the time I interviewed him, Obote was still cautious in how he formulated his views, and tended to attribute Uganda's policy to a decision by his Labor Minister. But as the denunciation of his policy in the Kenya press and the Kenya Parliament became stronger, he reacted by becoming a more militant supporter of the Ugandanization policy. His concern about not letting Kenya get away with exporting its surplus labor was never publicly articulated in those terms, but I am certain that he nourished a profound ideological distrust of Kenya.

What Obote overlooked was that an overwhelming proportion of the people who had been expelled had not come to Uganda recently, nor were their reasons for being in Uganda necessarily connected with Kenya's ideological policy. For the people of the lake area in Kenya, Kampala was a more convenient city to migrate to than Nairobi. It was certainly nearer for most. And since for a long time under the British the option was there, whether to work in Kampala or in Nairobi, it was sociologically unsound to attribute their presence in Uganda to Kenya's choice of a capitalist mode of production.

Besides being sociologically unsound, the expulsion seemed to be an instance of ideological diffuseness. Here was Uganda, declaring a Move to the Left, committing itself to the protection of "the common man" and the promotion of socialistic solidarity. Obote had just issued his Common Man's Charter and proclaimed several new nationalization measures in May 1970. The new political culture seemed to be defined in terms of caring for the underdog and the underprivileged. Yet Obote's government was reacting strongly because a few thousand laborers, earning less than $30 a month each, wanted to send home an average of $10 a month each. By contrast, Kenyans and Tanzanians who were skilled workers continued to work in such places as Makerere University, the police force, and Mulago hospital. These elitist immigrants put a much greater strain on the foreign reserves of Uganda, and yet procedures had been worked out by which they could avail themselves of more money for international travel, or allowances to their families, or annual holidays. For every day that I, as a Makerere professor, chose to spend outside Uganda on a lecturing or conference assignment, I was eligible for an allowance of more dollars than a Luo railway porter could afford to send out to Kisumu for the whole month. Uganda was thus moving toward socialism partly at the expense of its poorest immigrants.

Uganda under Obote seemed to speak with the rhetoric of Kwame Nkrumah—radical and hospitable to immigrant dissidents—and yet the country was pursuing policies reminiscent of Kofi Busia, Nkrumah's more conservative successor. Nkrumah had maintained a relatively open-door policy for those who scrambled to Ghana from neighboring countries, but Dr. Busia, upon being elected to power in Ghana, proceeded to expel thousands of Nigerians and other non-Ghanaian Africans from Ghana. Obote was handling his country's unemployment problems as Busia might have. The tensions of ideological diffuseness and inconsistency were more manifest under Milton Obote than they had been under either Kwame Nkrumah or Kofi Busia in Ghana.[5]

Some of the ideological factors had relevance for East Africa as a whole. Certainly East Africa's experience has tended to reveal a tense relationship between local socialism and regional integration. In Tanzania, for example, a growing desire to control the internal economy had produced impatience with factors of production over which Tanzania had no control. Clearly, it could not be a member of a Common Market or an East African Community and still control, on its own, each factor of production. Socialist Tanzania, by insisting on central planning and central control of the economy, became intolerant of the free flow of goods from Kenya and the free flow of currency to and from Tanzania. The common currency of East Africa was an early casualty of socialistic change in Tanzania. Then the Kampala Agreement of 1964, though never fully ratified, began with the erection of de facto customs barriers between the East African states. Socialistic experimentation in conditions of ideological diffuseness made it hard to distinguish between the broad goals of genuine socialism and the narrower goals of territorial economic nationalism.

When Uganda also began to turn to the left in 1969 and 1970, the relative incompatibility between militant internal protection of the Ugandan economy and the promotion of regional integration in East Africa became clear. In East African conditions, diffuse socialism has often camouflaged economic nationalism in the narrow sense. And so in Uganda under Obote the socialist rhetoric about workers' solidarity across national boundaries had a hollow ring, for at the same time workers in Kilindini harbor in Mombasa were exchanging economic threats with workers in Jinja at the dam. Nor could rhetoric disguise the hard fact that to the immigrant workers in Uganda, the Common Man's Charter was a charter of expulsion and degradation. In the wake of the Move to the Left, proletarian solidarity had deteriorated into militant proletarian parochialism.

I expressed some of these anxieties in a lecture I delivered in Kisumu, in the heart of Luoland, in October 1970. The lecture was in part a protest at what was happening, and I was aware that the protest might result

5. For a comprehensive discussion of ideology in Uganda since independence, see James H. Mittelman, *Ideology and Politics in Uganda: From Obote to Amin* (Ithaca: Cornell University Press, 1975). See also A. G. G. Gingyera-Pincywa, "Political Development and Ideological Void," a paper presented at the Ninth World Congress of the International Political Science Association, Montreal, August 1973, and at the Third International Congress of Africanists, Addis Ababa, December 1973.

in another crisis in my own relations with the authorities in Uganda. After the event, I waited with some concern for the reactions of the authorities, since the lecture had been prominently publicized in Kenya. But there was no public or overt reaction. Obote, who had been known to react strongly to a cautious criticism of the Common Man's Charter, seemed supremely self-controlled over my speech in Kisumu. Was he waiting for an opportunity to take more severe action? Had he changed his tactics in handling my social commentaries? Or was there a genuine difference in his reaction to this particular speech, however provocative it might have sounded compared to other speeches I had given?

I shall never know for certain. What I do know is that he believed in Ugandanizing unskilled work in Uganda as rapidly as possible, and that he was reluctant to help the government of Kenya mitigate the social costs of its capitalistic policies by allowing Kenya to export some of its unemployed workers to Uganda. On the other hand, Obote was a genuine East African in some of his broader sympathies, and so the labor question may have hit him in a most sensitive area: he must have been aware, to some extent, that he was sending home people in whose country he himself had once found employment and social hospitality, and that he was helping to weaken the East African spirit at a time when he was just gaining respect as a pan-African in continental affairs.

1972: The Asian Exodus from Uganda

On January 25, 1971, Milton Obote was overthrown in a military coup and Idi Amin Dada and his fellow soldiers assumed supreme political authority. As with all military coups, a series of grievances against the government which was overthrown were articulated. The soldiers did their best to mobilize all sectors of opinion, as well as to influence opinion in the member states of the East African Community. The soldiers asserted that Obote's policies, both on labor and on the flow of East African currencies, had had the effect of weakening the East African Community. The expulsion of workers from Uganda back to Kenya and Tanzania was inconsistent with the spirit of the community, they said, and the difficulties of converting Ugandan money into Kenyan or Tanzanian currencies, and vice versa, had considerably reduced economic interaction among the member states at the grass-roots level. It was not immediately clear whether the soldiers would in fact improve the situation, but the atmosphere after the coup was sufficiently congenial that many Luo workers who had already left the country drifted back; some of them returned to their old jobs, others found new opportunities.

By the end of 1971, however, another community in Uganda, the Asians, began to feel insecure under the new regime. The Asians had not been secure under Obote either, but at least those who were already citizens of the country had enjoyed relative respectability and security in Uganda for the first eight years of the country's independence. By the mid-1960s there were approximately 80,000 Asians in Uganda. At the time of independence they had been given a choice between becoming Ugandan citizens, becoming British subjects, or re-establishing affinities with the Indian subcontinent. The largest single group in Uganda, estimated at 50,000, had chosen to become British subjects; 23,000 chose Ugandan citizenship, and the remainder were immigrants from India, Pakistan, and Bangladesh.

Even under Obote the British Asians had felt unwelcome pressure in the form of new laws concerning trade licensing and immigration. But under Amin, all Asians, citizen and non-citizen alike, began to be attacked on a variety of grounds, ranging from their relative sexual exclusivity and endogamy to their disproportionate share of the import and export trade of Uganda. By August 1972, General Amin had decided to push the logic of Indophobia to its extreme and create a black ethnocracy. On August 8 he ordered the departure of all remaining Asians from Uganda. (The peak population of 80,000 had already been diminished considerably.) At first, Amin made no distinction between citizen and non-citizen. But after vigorous expressions of concern by his Cabinet Ministers, by students at Makerere University, and by one or two of his trusted civilian friends, he decided not to enforce the order against Asians who were citizens of Uganda, and contented himself with driving out only the Asians who were not nationals of the country.[6] But so much insecurity had by then been created that many Ugandan nationals also left.

To what extent was the fate of the Asians a product of the underdeveloped class structure of Uganda? Certainly all of the five attributes of class underdevelopment mentioned earlier were operative in the general situation which culminated in the Asian exodus from Uganda in 1972.

Idi Amin Dada was himself an example of the trans-class man. Like most other soldiers in the Ugandan army, he was recruited from among the least educated and least privileged sections of Uganda's society before the military coup—the Nilotic and Sudanic people. (Amin himself comes from the Kakwa, a small Nilotic group.) He remained a trans-class man for much of his life after he became an officer in the King's African Rifles, preserving connections of a relatively intimate kind with the more rural and less sophisticated elements of Ugandan society. In temperament and orientation, in style of thinking and cultural leaning, and in his personal

6. Among the scholarly works on the Asian exodus are the following: Michael Twaddle, ed., *Expulsion of a Minority: Essays on Uganda Asians* (London: Athlone Press, University of London, for the Institute of Commonwealth Studies, 1975); Mahmood Mamdani, *From Citizen to Refugee* (London: Pinter, 1972); Justine O'Brien [pseud. for Yashpal Tandon], *Brown Britons: The Crisis of the Uganda Asians* (London: Runnymede Trust Publication, 1972); Hasu H. Patel, *Indians in Uganda and Rhodesia: Some Comparative Perspectives on a Minority in Africa* (Denver: Center on International Race Relations, University of Denver, 1974); Selwyn Ryan, "Economic Nationalism and Socialism in Uganda," *Journal of Commonwealth Political Studies*, vol. 11, no. 2 (1973).

response to political issues, he was much more like a peasant than a member of the bourgeoisie.

His response to the Asians was in some ways characteristic of the less educated sections of Ugandan opinion. Prejudice against Asians in Uganda cut across all sections of society; but Amin's relative inability to disguise the racism involved in those attitudes, and his incapacity at first to distinguish between those Asians who were Ugandan citizens and those who were aliens, were symptomatic of the styles of thought of the peasantry and the proletariat in Uganda rather than of the bourgeoisie.

Curiously enough, the very history of the Asians in Uganda is an instance of trans-class ambivalence. There was a widespread belief that their origins in East Africa lay in the building of the railway line by the British from Mombasa to Lake Victoria, in the late nineteenth century. It was part of the style of imperialism in that age to transfer labor when needed from one colony to another, sometimes across continents. That was what had led to the export of slaves to the West Indian and American colonies much earlier, and also to the importation of Chinese and Indian laborers into Southern Africa. Because Indian workers were indeed imported to build the East African railway system, it was therefore believed throughout East Africa that the Indian community in Kenya, Uganda, and Tanzania was basically descended from those railway builders.

Historically, this was incorrect, since many of the railway builders had returned to India, and many other Indians who had not been involved in that project had migrated into the region in later years. Nevertheless—and what is most interesting for our purposes—the idea that the first major wave of Indian immigration into East Africa consisted of laborers was profoundly proletarian. It converted the Indian presence into a historical phenomenon which had its origins in the indignity of indentured labor. If socialism was an ethic of indignation against exploited labor, the role of helpless Indian laborers in constructing a communications system for an imperial power in a third area of the world, against a background of disease and wild animals, was itself a piece of staggering exploitation.

And yet by the end of their stay in East Africa, the Indians were identified as among the most privileged and affluent. They had passed through a historical process, stretching from the chains of railway construction to the gold bangles of bourgeois affluence. As usual, the actual truth was more complicated than the political myth. Many Asians in East Africa were in fact still laborers, sometimes repairing railway lines, sometimes constructing new buildings; many were also small artisans or clerks in banks and businesses. But on balance, their incomes were considerably higher than the incomes of average black Ugandans.

Clearly, the trans-class ambivalence both of the soldiers, as they now exercised supreme political authority and acted on the prejudices of the peasant, and of the Indians themselves, who were seen as combining proletarian origins with contemporary bourgeois prosperity, was an important factor behind the fate which met them in Uganda under Idi Amin Dada.

Next, there was indeed a low class consciousness in Uganda, both among the Indians themselves and among the soldiers who expelled them. The Indians were neither a coherent community nor a social class. Internally, they were divided by language, religion and caste, as well as by the nuances of class differentiation and the comparative prestige of different occupations. Under challenge, they were likely to rally as an ethnic group rather than in class terms. Their tormentors, the governing soldiers of Uganda, saw themselves either as members of ethnic groups, or as Africans confronting Asians, or as soldiers policing civilians, or as Muslims or Christians. The class factor operated with far less cognition among them.

This low level of class consciousness once again resulted in a high incidence of class masochism. The internal divisions of the Asians themselves contributed at one time to their vulnerability, although by the time Amin came into power it did not make much difference whether the Asians were themselves united or divided. Certain kinds of behavior by the Asians also contributed to their downfall. These ranged from arrogance toward African customers and African employees to the very choice of British citizenship, which could be seen as a credential for the unimpeded exploitation of Uganda.

The soldiers, in turn, displayed similar kinds of class masochism. Idi Amin Dada wanted to create a strong entrepreneurial system, and was keen to ensure that it be in the hands of black Ugandans. He was against socialism and state manipulation of the economy, and strongly in favor of the Africanization of private enterprise in Uganda. But because he was so subject to relatively unsophisticated forms of racist sentiment, and was inclined to take quick action rather than weigh the economic costs and benefits of different strategies, his sudden move to de-Indianize Uganda became an act of considerable class and national masochism. It did result in the speedy enrichment of a number of Africans; but rich men are not necessarily successful capitalists. Amin had wanted to create an indigenous capitalist system, but the specific methods he used simply made it more difficult for Uganda's capitalism to get under way. On the evidence so far, the neighboring state of Kenya has produced a more vigorous and more efficient black bourgeois class, without the sudden expulsion of Asians.

The diffuse ideological orientation manifested by Idi Amin and his government has also been striking. On first attaining power, the soldiers were groping for a sense of direction. In foreign policy, they were inclined to defer to the West and such Western extensions as Israel. But that leaning was not primarily the result of careful ideological consideration; it was mainly a continuation of attitudes developed during the long colonial period. Even the regime's clear preference for an indigenous entrepreneurial system was partly a reaction against Obote's leftist rhetoric and his Move to the Left before the soldiers overthrew him. The capitalist orientation was also shaped in part by a naive belief that wealth could be acquired more quickly by all Africans under such a system than under a socialist strategy.

The Asians were also diffuse in their ideological preferences. Many younger Asians, idealistically inclined and optimistic about their future role in African societies, had supported African nationalism in the last years of colonial rule. But Asian liberalism had received a severe shock from some of the excesses of African nationalism. The more conservative Asians had had no illusions about African liberality, but they had become ideologically confused as they combined external deference and even subservience toward influential Africans, on the one hand, with continuing contempt for African people on the other. This split between thought and behavior increased their vulnerability. Many Africans perceived that some of their Asian benefactors were opportunists, and many Asians became opportunists because they sensed that some African leaders could be bought and sold. A vicious circle was completed, and the tragedy of the Asian exodus was set in motion.

Underlying much of the confrontation between Asians and Africans were the combined primordial forces of differing races and divergent cultures. The groups were identifiable as physically distinct. The colonial experience under the British had strengthened those modes of self-perception between Asians and Africans. The cultural differences, ranging from speech to dress, to methods of work and sexual mores, deepened the great divide. Primordial militancy, our fifth attribute of an underdeveloped class structure, once again made strangers in an African society vulnerable.

Conclusions

Elliott P. Skinner

These essays on strangers in African societies have accomplished two things: they have examined a problem that has long been a source of confusion to both scholars and non-specialists concerned with the ambiguous status of persons who have resided in African societies other than their own for a generation or more, and then found themselves mandated for expatriation to their homeland. They have also contributed to social science theory by viewing the phenomena of strangers in African societies against the backdrop of Georg Simmel's seminal work on this particular social type.

As these essays indicate, Simmel failed to explore many salient features of the complex status and role of the stranger. Perhaps this was inevitable; for he failed to resolve the ambiguity in his treatment of the stranger, in one context, as an individual, and in another, as a member of a social aggregate. Levine, in his chapter in this volume, attempted to clarify this ambiguity by developing a typology of stranger-host relationships, and also a paradigm for the "sociology of the stranger." Nevertheless, what his and other essays demonstrate is that Simmel should never have viewed the stranger as a sociological type, or even a socio-psychological type. Strangers constitute a social category in dynamic relationships with other social categories in human societies. It is only when viewed in this light that the essential sociological characteristics and problems of strangers in African societies or elsewhere can be properly understood.

Central to Simmel's thesis, and explicit in all the essays, is the peculiar social status position of strangers. In Simmel's line of reasoning, this peculiar status naturally follows from strangers not having been involved in the original process of social interaction by which their host societies came into existence, and took their particular form. It logically follows, therefore, that strangers would commonly hold unusual views about their hosts' societies since they are not bound to them by organic ties of kinship, locality and occupation, nor do they share the partisan disposition of their hosts. In Simmel's words, strangers have "a distinctly 'objective' attitude, an attitude that did not signify mere detachment and non-participation, but with a distinct structure composed of remoteness and nearness, indifference and involvement."¹ And Simmel insists that the stranger is "the freer man, practically and theoretically; he examines conditions with less prejudice; he assesses them against standards that are more general and more objective; and his actions are not confined by custom, piety, or precedent."²

The theoretical problem posed by Simmel's strangers, as an ideal type, as well as for strangers in the African societies examined in this volume, is that few human societies willingly tolerate "unsocial" or "objective" persons in their midst. As social persons, strangers participated in the sociological processes that brought their own societies into existence, and they are bound by loyalties to them. And while they may attempt to be "objective" to the social aims of their hosts, they cannot be, at the same time, objective to the aims of their own social group, and the rights, duties, and obligations of membership in it. Therefore, the very social mechanisms which should enable strangers to maintain their personal and social detachment—mechanisms that often give their indigenous group its coherence and permit it to perpetuate itself—create conflicts and contradictions between strangers and their hosts. A simple exchange of goods and services between strangers and their hosts, for instance, generates social bonds and particular attitudes which limit the ability of one group to be absolutely objective in its relation to the other. The more intense the social interaction, and the larger in scale the groups involved, the less objective their attitudes toward one another.

Both Southall and Wilson described how differences in the numbers of strangers in East, Central and South African societies influenced the pattern of interaction with their hosts, how social relations were shaped by the particular political and economic structure of these societies, and how the structure of social relations was altered from one historical period to the next. Certainly, as Shack argued, strangers often have a liminal status, caught betwixt and between those positions normally assigned to "organic members of the society," to use Simmel's words. Assigned a specific status and constrained to play a restricted role, strangers are denied freedom of action. Contrary to Simmel's assertion, strangers are *not free* precisely because they are strangers. And when acting out of ignorance, guile, or assumptions of objectivity, strangers violate the norms of their host society, as several case studies in this volume illustrate, compulsory expatriation often has been the extreme sanction imposed upon them.

The moral indignation expressed by much of the Western world over the expulsion of strangers from African societies coincides with the views of Simmel who, earlier, lamented the propensity of societies to

1. D. S. Levine, ed., *Georg Simmel on Individuality and Social Forms* (Chicago: University of Chicago Press, 1971), p. 145.

2. *Ibid.*, p. 146.

penalize strangers. From the earliest times, Simmel noted, whenever social unrest occured, strangers were made the scapegoat. Apart from the gross injustices inflicted upon strangers, who were not responsible for their plight, as Simmel saw it, the charge that strangers created problems for their hosts "represents an exaggeration of the specific role of the strangers."[3] But neither Simmel nor strangers can have it both ways. If, as he argued, the normal role of strangers leads to their victimization, then the normal role of hosts leads to their aggressiveness toward strangers. In this regard, it is worth noting that in none of the cases discussed in this volume is there evidence that most members of the societies from which strangers were expelled expressed remorse. It can be argued that this apparent lack of concern was due as much to hosts' beliefs about alleged attitudes and practices of strangers, as to salient characteristics of human society itself.

Societies can and do, within limits, tolerate certain differences in the behavior of their members. Beyond that imaginary line of tolerance almost total adherence to the aims and goals of society is imperative. However "irrational" or "religious," in a Durkheimian sense, these aims and goals may be, they are often symbolic of notions concerning cohesion, survival, and the nature of society itself. And when such concerns are deemed to be threatened by the allegedly free and objective strangers whose actions are not confined by custom, piety, and precedent, strangers become the target of criticism. Lack of compliance with the behavioral norms of the hosts is not only resented, but is viewed as having caused or contributed to the problems of the wider society. It is this difference in values and actions that explains why strangers are suspect and deemed dangerous to society even when they are innocent of instigating social unrest. Moreover, since societies tend to exaggerate the gravity of any deviation from normative conduct and expectations of behavior during times of social crises, those persons, like strangers, whose ordinary conduct and behavior are considered "abnormal" must in turn also exaggerate their own conformity, or risk being viewed as "enemies of the people." It is perhaps not accidental that when there are tensions in societies, such as those generated by the decolonization process, that strangers encounter difficulties.

Not all African societies initially had socio-cultural niches for strangers. As Monica Wilson reported, many white foreigners who sojourned in precolonial Africa were assimilated by their hosts. It seems they did not become strangers because they were often too few in number to constitute such a category. Similarly, Christine Obbo described the status of foreigners in the kingdom of Buganda as ranging from pariahs, to assimilated serfs, to veritable strangers in the classic Simmelian sense. No doubt it was the transitional nature of the Buganda society, moving

3. *Ibid.*, p. 145.

from "ranking" to "stratification,"[4] that facilitated the assimilation of various groups of strangers. In West Africa, strangers filled an important economic niche in traditional Ashanti society, though they differed from Simmel's stranger-trader. Here, as Niara Sudarkasa emphasized, Yoruba traders took care to respect both the social and political institutions of their hosts. And perhaps well they did so. It was only with the advent of European colonial rule that African societies of whatever political scale were denied the right to regulate the conduct of non-citizens. Europeans arrogated to themselves the power to transform the cultural, economic and political underpinnings of African societies. The conquerors, therefore, became "estrangers": they alienated the lands, resources, persons, and even psyches of the indigenous populations, who eventually became subordinated to the interests of their conquerors.

European exploitation of colonies under their rule led to the introduction of foreign populations in African societies, or at least facilitated and encouraged their coming. Thus it appears that in colonial Africa, foreigners (other than the estranging Europeans) were a structural part of the dependent societies. This was the case for Asian railroad builders, clerks and traders in East Africa, Lebano-Syrian traders in West Africa, African laborers recruited from neighboring or distant colonies, and Dahomeyan clerks who served throughout French colonial Africa. Of equal importance as the influx of these and other foreigners into colonial African societies was their sociological transformation into strangers. For as Simmel argued, foreigners, as strangers, were not involved in the initial social processes that brought the colonies into being, and produced their forms. Neither were they the conquerors nor the conquered. And even when, as Sudarkasa reported, some African foreigners, for example the Yoruba in Ashanti, helped Europeans conquer the indigenous populations, they were not incorporated into the ranks of the conquerors. Interestingly, those Yoruba and the other Africans who came from areas which had been conquered by Europeans were also not, as a matter of course, merged with the conquered population. They became strangers.

Perhaps another reason for the transformation of foreign populations into strangers was the peculiar nature of colonial societies. Viewing colonial societies from the vantage point of Southeast Asia, Furnivall characterized them as "plural" societies, noting that while the Europeans, the intrusive Asians, and the indigenous populations lived within the same political unit, they did not establish social ties cross-cutting their respective groups. Instead, Furnivall argued, these groups formed a medley, "for they mix but do not combine. Each group holds its own religion, its own culture and language, its own ideas and ways. As individu-

4. Morton H. Fried, *The Evolution of Political Society* (New York: Random House, 1967), pp. 110–226.

als they meet, but only in the market-place, in buying and selling."[5] In this type of society "the economic motive, as the 'highest common factor of the component elements,' came to dominate social life to a far greater extent than in the west."[6] Furnivall insisted that there were no unifying social roles in the plural societies; and in the "absence of any social will," economic progress took precedence over social welfare.

Judging from the importance of economic competition within the societies discussed in this study, and the lack of viable social relations between the estrangers, the strangers, and the indigenous populations, it is tempting to conclude that Furnivall's model of the plural society fits the African case. Nevertheless, it is open to question whether social groups in a plural society, or any other type of society for that matter, do not establish cross-cutting social ties. Like Simmel's strangers, the groups in Furnivall's plural society could not have failed to influence each other socially, if only in market transactions. The case studies for Ghana, Sierra Leone, Uganda, Ivory Coast and Niger have revealed that strangers established social relations with both the conquerors and the conquered. These social relations varied from friendliness to animosity, but they were social relations nonetheless. This is not to suggest, as Gluckman has argued, that conflict necessarily makes for cohesion.[7] Indeed, the fact that overt conflict between strangers and hosts was relatively infrequent in colonial Africa was due primarily to the actual or potential use of military power by the authorities to contain the outbreak of hostilities, and to maintain law and order. True, this latent power was buttressed by mutual understandings that emerged as a function of social interaction even between groups that were structurally separated. Yet these understandings never were sufficient to obviate the need for actual or potential force to maintain law and order in colonial societies.

It is a peculiar irony that social interaction often between mutually exclusive groups within colonial societies, especially in schools, facilitated the rise of nationalism. Small groups of indigenous persons, usually male, were educated in mission and secular schools or trained in America or Europe. In a few instances, Dahomeyan strangers in the Ivory Coast and Niger actually took part in the education of the local people. Through the educational process, the autochthons learned enough about the nature of European power to insist that it devolve upon them.

While the major struggle for independence took place between the colonizers and the colonized, a number of strangers, both as individuals

5. J. S. Furnivall, *Colonial Policy and Practice* (New York: New York University Press, 1956), p. 304.
6. J. S. Furnivall, *Progress and Welfare in Southeast Asia* (New York: Secretariat, Institute of Pacific Relations, 1941), p. 21.
7. M. Gluckman, *Custom and Conflict in Africa* (Oxford: Basil Blackwell, 1963), pp. 150–151.

and as groups, became involved in the contest. Challenor reported that Dahomeyans were among the founders of the Democratic Party of the Ivory Coast, and Eades, Peil, and Sudarkasa also explained that Yoruba and other stranger groups took part in early political movements in Ghana. These examples not only attest to the bonds that developed between the strangers, the estrangers, and the local populations, but also demonstrate that such interaction becomes inevitable when groups operate in the same social-political field.

Perhaps more importantly, in all the studies of contemporary African societies treated in this volume, the strangers encountered grave difficulties during and after the decolonization period. In large measure this was a direct consequence of the changing political structure of the societies in which the strangers found themselves. Political status, rather than social status, became the critical marker distinguishing insiders from outsiders. Concomitant with this political development the status of the colonizing estranger changed to that of expatriate, while the status of the former colonized hosts became transformed into citizenry in the new nation-state. Thus strangers were caught in an ambiguous position: they were neither party to the process by which the colonial society came into being, nor party to the process by which it came to an end. Yet, as Shack suggested, the structural transformation of the colonial society changed the liminal status of the stranger to that of *communitas*, a status enjoyed by their hosts, without which change conflict would ensue. Plainly, many strangers refused to partake in the political and social processes that were obligatory to bring about a change in their status, and similarly, in many instances both colonizers and colonized were ambivalent about permitting them to do so. Under these circumstances strangers were relegated to a new liminal status, that of "aliens."

This kind of structural ambiguity is best illustrated by the Goans in Uganda, described by Kuper. Having identified themselves with Europeans in the colonial period, and labelled by Africans as "Asians," Goans initially rejected the offer of British citizenship, preferring to remain in Uganda. It was only the rising spectre of British racism which threatened to bar immigration to Britain, reinforced by local African opposition, that triggered the exodus of Goans from Uganda. Elsewhere in Africa, Peil, Leighton, Challenor and Sudarkasa described the strategies adopted to adjust to the kind of transition of status that Goans faced in Uganda. Some cast their lot with the traditional authorities who were striving to seize the helm of the emerging nation-states from the new nationalist leaders. Others supported rival factions led by modern political leaders who were the architects of the independence movements, and whose political parties were heavily engaged in struggling over the spoils. Still other strangers, fearing that the prejudices of the past would make normal life impossible in the new nation-states, retreated to the metropoles of England and France. Few delayed passage abroad to witness the symbolic lowering and raising of flags heralding the independence of what, for many, was their birthplace, but not homeland.

Not all leaders of new nation-states opposed granting strangers the rights of citizenship. Indeed, equality and fraternity were popular slogans of the pre-independence political rhetoric. With hindsight, such slogans appear to have been designed to allay the apprehensions of the departing metropolitan powers. Nevertheless, whatever the intentions of new African leaders, their policies toward strangers were shaped by the legacy of colonialism. As Enid Schildkrout showed, stereotypes about strangers die hard, partly because their behavior toward their hosts reinforces the latter's negative attitudes toward them. Ali Mazrui insists that it was the persistence of such primordial sentiments embedded in notions of race and community that led Ugandans to expel Kenyan Africans and Asians, whereas a greater consciousness of social class would have dictated otherwise. Race consciousness most certainly influenced the behavior of certain Asian parents who prevented the marriage of their daughters to prominent Africans, which in turn exacerbated African hostility toward Asians in general.

Ironically, in West Africa the persisting sentiment about the superiority of whites led many Ghanaians to favor European expatriates over African strangers. Nevertheless, the conclusion should not be drawn that it was only these attitudes of race and community, largely generated by the colonial experience, that influenced the behavior of local citizens toward strangers and estrangers. As Eades reported for Ghana, and Challenor for the Ivory Coast, even during the height of the anti-stranger movement some local people aided and protected strangers with whom they were linked by marriage and business interests. When, as it sometimes happened, the expulsion of strangers could not be prevented, they were welcomed back once tensions had eased. Such actions of local citizens in crisis situations attest to the recovery of power lost under colonialism when the local population were involuntary hosts to strangers. It also signified the transformation of the liminal status of strangers which, as Shack would suggest, made them candidates for incorporation into the host's society where the stranger niche was being gradually eradicated.

It was the desire to obliterate the colonial-stranger niche that often led local citizens to prefer expatriates to aliens. Local citizens had far less fear of the estrangers, now transformed into expatriates, than of the strangers, now aliens. In a certain sense the estrangers had lost the game. From their all-powerful position as conquerors, they had surrendered their political power, and while they remained powerful economically and socially, as Morgenthau has shown, they were viewed as persons who could and would readily return to their own homelands if constrained to do so. In fact, expatriates were expected to do so; therefore, they could obtain employment which temporarily could not be performed by local citizens. Those expatriates who chose not to return to their homelands were often viewed with amused toleration. Yet since they made no claims to membership in the local society, they were not viewed as threatening the social order. In contrast, the ritually transformed strangers, as aliens, could not be trusted not to lay permanent claims to status positions which they often occupied in lieu of qualified locals, since most of them had no intention of returning to their homeland. They were not above attempting to retain the privileged status of strangers, even when, as aliens, they opted for local citizenship. Local citizens certainly recognized, though not in terms familiar to social scientists, that when societies are in transition, and where the distinction between *societas* and *civitas* is obscure and very often ambiguous, it is to their advantage to keep strangers at arms' length, until at least their social-legal status has been changed.

It was the differentiation in the treatment of various stranger groups during the decolonization process that led Ruth Morgenthau to suggest that the new African states tended to view the stranger-alien issue in terms of power politics. Unfortunately, and with other authors, she also ignored the distinction between estranger and stranger, treating both statuses as if they were the same, though it is true, as she argues, that each group was accorded differential treatment. Therefore, she rightly concludes that political power, as well as social relations, played an important part in the development, persistence and final demise of the role of strangers in African societies.

Morgenthau's view that the increasingly ubiquitous servant of multi-national corporations is a new type of stranger is provocative particularly in light of her assertion that the colonial system favored one kind of stranger and the post-colonial system another. Indeed, the new multi-nationals do exhibit qualities that are characteristic of Simmel's strangers. Although spawned by the Euro-American nation-states, the multi-nationals and their agents show a considerable lack of sentiment both for their nations of origin and for the societies in which they conduct business. Often displaying a level of objectivity that dismays the governments of their own societies, multi-nationals remain unswerving in their business of integrating the world's economies, and affecting the political and social class systems of nation-states in Africa and elsewhere. Again like the colonial strangers, whose status and role depended upon a pluralistic society, the multi-nationals are involved with pluralistic forces drawing them and their integration into a global economy. This is especially marked in the relatively economically weak African states whose need for capital and advanced technology make them more vulnerable than richer states to the activities of multi-nationals. Morgenthau suggests, and Sudarkasa concurs, that the fledgling African states might have been unduly harsh in their treatment of stranger-aliens, when the greater danger facing them might well be the activities of multi-nationals.

But unless the multi-nationals become the custodians of political power, especially as the purveyors of military force, they may face the same problems of expulsion as all strangers when the societies in which they occupy privileged positions demand adherence to specific social goals. Unless multi-nationals become estrangers, they will be viewed as strangers and thereby become the scapegoats of societies facing critical social problems. In fact, there is some evidence of this already taking place, both in African and non-African states; for example, Lonrho has already been expelled from Zambia, and the Nigerians are demanding that the multinationals boycott South Africa or face expulsion.

It is possible that strangers, both as individuals and in groups, would never find full acceptance in any society. Their status and role seem to generate local hostility that if not initially apparent will inevitably arise when the societies in which they live undergo radical structural change. Greifer's view that the treatment of strangers by a society is an indication of its evolution toward "Western civilization" is too limited, if not altogether Euro-centric. As pointed out in the Introduction and supported by the case studies, there is a close relationship between the development of political and economic institutions and the propensity of societies to harbor strangers. Many traditional African societies had stranger populations; and so did other non-European societies before the advent of colonialism, to say nothing of societies in antiquity. It might be argued that strangers flourished in societies where there was an "absence of any social will," embracing all their members, and where the state, insofar as it existed, concerned itself with other matters.

These essays demonstrate quite clearly, and in contrast to Greifer's view, that as the African societies discussed here evolved toward the stage of "Western civilization,"[8] as characterized by the nation-state, they found it increasingly difficult to harbor strangers. Moreover, it is doubtful whether contemporary African states, or other contemporary societies, for that matter, can create niches for strangers, in the Simmelian sense, as contrasted to toleration of isolated wanderers, sojourners, or social misfits. For the rhetoric, if not the actual commitments of the modern state, is to the welfare of all its citizens or persons residing within its political boundaries. Aliens remain as permanent residents only with the sufferance of the state. Therefore, African leaders, whether democratic or authoritarian, emphasize citizenship over social status. Even when faced with the social reality in which many Africans still express greater loyalties to ethnic groups and local regions than to the nation-state, African leaders have refrained from adopting a politically pluralistic model for their societies. They hold that pluralism is basically divisive since it provides an environment in which social groups, *qua* social groups, attempt to act politically, seeking unequal access to the state's

8. J. L. Greifer, "Attitudes to the Stranger," *American Sociological Review*, vol. 10, no. 6 (1945), pp. 739–745.

resources for their own group at the expense of others. Instead most, if not all, African states have opted for a model which has as its goal the ability of all citizens, unconstrained by ethnic or social ties, to gain equal access to the really limited resources of the society. However, competition over scarce resources between various indigenous ethnic groups might well give rise to a new category of "stranger" in African societies that neither their leaders nor Simmel had ever anticipated.

Bibliography

Addo, N. "Assimilation and Absorption of African Immigrants in Ghana." *Ghana Journal of Sociology*, vol. 3 (1967), pp. 17–32.

———. *Migration and Economic Change in Ghana.* Volume I. Legon: Demographic Unit, Department of Sociology, University of Ghana, 1971.

Alberti, L. *Des Cafres.* Amsterdam: Maaskamp, 1811.

Amin, Samir. *Le Développement du capitalism en Côte d'Ivoire.* Paris: Les Editions du Minuit, 1967.

Arhin, Kwame. "Market Settlements in Northwestern Ashanti: Kintampo." In *Ashanti and the Northwest*, ed. J. Goody and K. Arhin. University of Ghana Institute of African Studies Research Review, supp. no. 1, Legon, Ghana, 1965. Pages 135–151.

———, ed. *Ashanti and the Northeast.* University of Ghana Institute of African Studies Research Review, supp. no. 2, Legon, Ghana, 1970.

———. "Strangers and Hosts: A Study in the Political Organization and History of Atebubu Town." *Transactions of the Historical Society of Ghana*, vol. 12 (1973), pp. 63–82.

Azu, Theo. "Fireworks from Kai-Samba." *Daily Mail* (Freetown), 21 July 1967.

Baran, Paul A. *The Political Economy of Growth.* New York: Monthly Review Press, 1957.

Bascom, W. R. "The Principle of Seniority in the Social Structure of the Yoruba." *American Anthropologist*, vol. 44, no. 1 (January–March 1942), pp. 37–46.

———. "The Esusu: A Credit Institution of the Yoruba." *Journal of the Royal Anthropological Institute*, vol. 82, pt. 1 (1952), pp. 63–69.

Bearnes, Pierre. *Le Moniteur africain*, 12 December 1963.

Becker, H. *Man in Reciprocity.* New York: Praeger, 1950.

Beckingham, C. F., and Huntingford, G. W. B., eds. *The Prester John of the Indies.* 2 vols. Hakluyt Society Series II, vol. cxiv. Cambridge: Cambridge University Press, 1961.

Berg, E. J. "Real Income Trends in West Africa." In *Economic Transition in Africa*, ed. M. J. Herskovits and M. Harwitz. Evanston: Northwestern University Press, 1964. Pages 199–238.

Beyer, William C. "The Civil Service of the Ancient World." *Public Administration Review*, vol. 19, no. 4 (Autumn 1959), pp. 243–249.

Bonacich, E. "A Theory of Middleman Minorities." *American Sociological Review*, vol. 38, no. 5 (October 1973), pp. 583–594.

Boskoff, A. *Theory in American Sociology.* New York: Thomas Y. Crowell, 1969.

Bowdich, T. E. *Mission from Cape Coast Castle to Ashantee.* London: J. Murray, 1819.

———. *An Essay in the Superstitions, Customs, and Arts Common to the Ancient Egyptians, Abyssinians, and Ashantees.* Paris: J. Smith, 1821.

Braudel, Fernand. *The Mediterranean.* Volume II. New York: Harper & Row, 1973.

Busia, K. A. *A Social Survey of Sekondi/Takoradi.* London: Crown Agents, 1950.

Caldwell, J. C. "Migration and Urbanization." In *A Study of Contemporary Ghana: Some Aspects of Social Structure,* ed. W. Birmingham, et al. London: George Allen & Unwin, 1966–1967. Pages 111–140.

Carter, G., and van Reenen, J. *The Wreck of the Grovenor.* Cape Town: van Riebeeck Society, 1927.

Challenor, Herschelle S. "French Speaking West Africa's Dahomeyan Strangers in Colonization and Decolonization." Ph.D. dissertation, Columbia University, 1970.

Chapus, S. "Quatre-Vingt années d'influences européennes en Emerina." *Bulletin de l'Académie Malgache,* nouvelle série, tome VIII (1925), pp. 1–350.

Chronologie politique africaine, vol. 5, no. 6 (1964).

Colson, Elizabeth. "The Alien Diviner and Local Politics Among the Tonga of Zambia." In *Political Anthropology,* ed. M. Swartz, V. Turner, and A. Tuden. Chicago: Aldine, 1966. Pages 221–228.

Cornevin, Robert. *Histoire du Dahomey.* Paris: Editions Berger-Levrault, 1962.

Coser, Lewis A. "The Political Functions of Eunuchism." *American Sociological Review,* vol. 29, no. 6 (December 1964), pp. 880–885.

———. "The Alien as a Servant of Power: Court Jews and Christian Renegades." *American Sociological Review,* vol. 37, no. 5 (October 1972), pp. 574–581.

Crummey, D. *Priests and Politicians: Protestant and Catholic Missions in Orthodox Ethiopia, 1830–1868.* Oxford: Clarendon Press, 1973.

Daily Graphic (Accra), 25 November 1969.

Dakar, Renseignements et Environs Divers en Côte d'Ivoire, no. 59125.17, 1928.

Dakar, *Journal officiel* of Afrique Occidentale Française, 1950. Law no. 50–572, 30 June 1950.

Dakar, *Annuaire statistique,* Afrique Occidentale Française, 1951–1954.

Dakar, *Journal officiel* of Afrique Occidentale Française, 1956. Law no. 56–619, 23 June 1956.

Daniel, A. L. "The Low-caste Stranger in Social Research." In *Ethnics, Politics, and Social Research,* ed. G. Sjoberg. Cambridge, Mass.: Schenkman, 1967. Pages 267–296.

Decraene, Philippe. "Togo: Eviction des prives du secteur minier." *Révue Française d'études politiques africaines,* no. 98 (February 1974), pp. 15–16.

de Gregoris, T. R. *Technology and the Economic Development of the Tropical African Frontier.* Cleveland: Case Western Reserve University Press, 1969.

De la Vaissiere, P. *Histoire de Madagascar, ses habitants et ses missionnaires.* Paris: 1884. 2 vols.

Derricourt, R. M. "Archaeological Survey of the Transkei and Ciskei." Interim Report for 1972, *Fort Hare Papers,* no. 5 (1973), pp. 453–455.

Desai, R. "On Joking Relationships Among Asians in East Africa." Paper read at Puberty and Joking Conference, 1966, Makerere University, Kampala. Cyclostyled.

Desbordes, Jean Gabriel. L'Immigration libano-syrienne en Afrique occidentale française." Ph.D. dissertation, University of Poitiers, Imprimerie Moderne, Renault et Cie, 1938.

Deschamps, Hubert. *Histoire de Madagascar*. Paris: Editions Berger-Levrault, 1965.

de Villiers, Hertha. "Human Skeletal Remains from Cape St. Francis, Cape Province." *South African Archaeological Bulletin*, vol. 29, nos. 115–116 (1974), pp. 89–91.

Dickenson, W. C. *Scotland from the Earliest Times to 1603*. Edinburgh: Nelson & Sons, 1961.

Dinan, C. "Socialization in an Accra Suburb: The Zongo and Its Distinct Subculture." In *Legon Family Research Papers, no. 3: Changing Family Studies*, ed. Christine Oppong. Legon Institute of African Studies, University of Ghana, 1972. Pages 45–62.

Dinwiddy, Bruce. *Promoting African Enterprise*. London: Croom Helm and the Overseas Development Institute, 1974.

Dorjahn, Vernon. "African Traders in Central Sierra Leone." In *Markets in Africa*, ed. Paul Bohannan and George Dalton. Evanston: Northwestern University Press, 1962. Pages 61–88.

Dotson, Floyd, and Dotson, Lillian O. *The Indian Minority of Zambia, Rhodesia, and Malawi*. New Haven: Yale University Press, 1968.

Dupuis, Joseph. *Journal of a Residence in Ashantee*. (London, 1824.) 2nd ed. London: Cass, 1966.

East African Standard (Kenya), 8 October 1970.

Echos d'Afrique noire (Dakar), 3 March 1959.

Economist Intelligence Quarterly, Quarterly Economics, Ivory Coast, Togo, Dahomey, Upper Volta, no. 2, 1974.

Ehrenfels, U. R. "North-South Polarization: A Study in the Typicality of Attitudes." *Centenary Volume*, University of Madras, vol. 28 (1957), pp. 85–103.

Eisenstadt, S. N. *The Political System of Empires: The Rise and Fall of the Historical Bureaucratic Societies*. New York: Free Press, 1969.

Ensslin, Wilhelm. "The Emperor and the Imperial Administration." In *Byzantium: An Introduction to East Roman Civilization*, ed. N. H. Baynes and H. St. L. B. Moss. Oxford: Clarendon Press, 1948. Pages 268–307.

Erikson, E. H. *Insight and Responsibility*. London: Faber & Faber, 1964.

Fallers, L. A., ed. *Immigrants and Associations*. The Hague: Mouton, 1967.

Fiedler, Leslie A. *The Stranger in Shakespeare*. New York: Stein & Day, 1972.

Finnegan, G. A. "Mossi Social Fields." Paper read at Fifteenth Annual Meeting, African Studies Association, 1972, Toronto, Canada.

Forde, Daryll. "A Cultural Map of West Africa: Successive Adaptations to Tropical Forests and Grasslands." *Transactions of the New York Academy of Sciences*, vol. 15, no. 6 (1953), pp. 206–219.

Fordham, P. "Out-groups in East African Society." In *Racial and Communal Tensions in East Africa*. African Contemporary Monographs, no. 3. Nairobi: East African Publishing House, 1966.

Fortes, Meyer. *Kinship and the Social Order*. London: Routledge & Kegan Paul, 1969.

———. "Strangers." In *Studies in African Social Anthropology*, ed. M. Fortes and Sheila Patterson. London: Academic Press, 1975. Pages 230–253.

Fortes, Meyer, and Evans-Pritchard, E. E., eds. *African Political Systems*. London: Oxford University Press for the International African Institute, 1940.

Freud, S. *Group Psychology and the Analysis of the Ego.* Translated by J. Strachey. New York: Liveright, 1949.

Fried, Morton H. *The Evolution of Political Society.* New York: Random House, 1967.

Furnivall, J. S. *Progress and Welfare in Southeast Asia.* New York: Secretariat, Institute of Pacific Relations, 1941.

———. *Colonial Policy and Practice.* Cambridge: Cambridge University Press, 1968.

Fyfe, Christopher. *A History of Sierra Leone.* London: Oxford University Press, 1962.

Fynn, H. F. *The Diary of Henry Francis Fynn.* Edited by J. Stuart and D. McK. Malcolm. Pietermaritzburg: Shuter & Shooter, 1950.

Gaskell, Mrs. Elizabeth. *My Lady Ludlow and Other Tales.* London: Sampson Low, Son & Co., 1861.

Ghai, D. P., and Ghai, Y. P., eds. *Portrait of a Minority: Asians in East Africa.* Rev. ed. Nairobi: Oxford University Press, 1970.

Ghai, Y. P. "The Future Prospects." In *Portrait of a Minority: Asians in East Africa,* ed. D. P. Ghai and Y. P. Ghai. Rev. ed. Nairobi: Oxford University Press, 1970. Pages 176–227.

Ghana, *Kumasi Zongo Affairs,* Ashanti Regional Branch (Kumasi), File no. D–12, 19 January 1923.

Ghana, *Kumasi Zongo Affairs,* Ashanti Regional Branch (Kumasi), File no. D–12/16, 13 June 1928.

Ghana, *Kumasi Zongo Affairs,* Ashanti Regional Branch (Kumasi), File no. D–12/68A, 30 August 1929.

Ghana, *Kumasi Zongo Affairs,* Ashanti Regional Branch (Kumasi), File no. D–12/77, 20 December 1929.

Ghana, *Kumasi Zongo Affairs,* Ashanti Regional Branch (Kumasi), File no. D–12, 5 April 1930.

Ghana, *Kumasi Zongo Affairs,* Ashanti Regional Branch (Kumasi), File no. D–12/264, 3 April 1933.

Ghana, *1960 Population Census of Ghana.* Accra: Government Printing Office, 1964.

Ghana, *Special Report "E": Tribes in Ghana,* by B. Gill, A. F. Aryee and D. K. Ghansah. 1960 Population Census of Ghana. Accra: Government Printing Office, 1964.

Gingyera-Pincywa, A. G. G. "Political Development and Ideological Void." Paper read at the Ninth World Congress of the International Political Science Association, August 1973, Montreal, Canada, and at the Third International Congress of Africanists, December 1973, Addis Ababa, Ethiopia.

Glazer, N., and Moynihan, D. P. *Beyond the Melting Pot.* Cambridge: MIT Press, 1963.

Gluckman, M., ed. *Essays on the Ritual of Social Relations.* Manchester: Manchester University Press, 1962.

———. *Custom and Conflict in Africa.* Oxford: Basil Blackwell, 1963.

———. *Closed Systems and Open Minds: The Limits of Naïvety in Social Anthropology.* Chicago: Aldine, 1964.

Goan Voice (Nairobi), 2 February 1962.

Goddard, T. N. *The Handbook of Sierra Leone*. London: Grant Richards, 1925.

Goody, J. "The Mande and the Akan Hinterland." In *The Historian in Tropical Africa*, ed. J. Vansina, R. Mauny and L. V. Thomas. London: Oxford University Press for the International African Institute, 1964. Pages 193–219.

———. *Technology, Tradition and the State in Africa*. London: Oxford University Press for the International African Institute, 1971.

Goody, J., and Arhin, K., eds. *Ashanti and the Northwest*. University of Ghana Institute of African Studies Research Review, Supplement No. 1, Legon, Ghana, 1965.

Grandidier, Alfred, ed. *Collection des ouvrages anciens concernant Madagascar*. Paris: Comité de Madagascar, 1904.

Gray, John. "A Journey by Land from Tete to Kilwa in 1616." *Tanganyika Notes and Records*, vol. 25 (June 1948), pp. 37–47.

Great Britain, *Anti-Syrian Riots of 1919*, Colonial Office, Co 267/582–7, 1920–1922.

Greifer, J. "Attitudes to the Stranger: A Study of the Attitudes of Primitive Society and Early Hebrew Culture." *American Sociological Review*, vol. 10, no. 6 (December 1945), pp. 739–745.

Grusky, Oscar. "Administrative Succession in Formal Organization." *Social Forces*, vol. 39, no. 2 (December 1960), pp. 105–115.

Gueye, Lamine. *Itinéraire africain*. Paris: Presence Africaine, 1966.

Hall, Martin John. *Through My Spectacles*. London: Church Missionary Society, 1898.

Hamilton-Grierson, P. J. "Strangers." *Encyclopaedia of Religion and Ethics*, ed. J. Hastings. Edinburgh: T. & T. Clark, 1921. Volume XI, pp. 883–896.

Handwerker, W. Penn. "Kinship, Friendship and Business Failure among Market Sellers in Monrovia, Liberia, 1970." *Africa*, vol. 43, no. 4 (October 1973), pp. 288–301.

Hanna, Marwan I. H. "Lebanese Emigrants in West Africa." Ph.D. dissertation, St. Anthony's College, Oxford University, 1959.

Hardy, George. *Histoire sociale de la colonisation française*. Paris: Larose, 1947.

Hart, K. "Informal Income Opportunities and Urban Employment in Ghana." *Journal of Modern African Studies*, vol. 11, no. 1 (March 1973), pp. 61–89.

Hill, Polly. "Landlords and Brokers: A West African Trading System." *Cahiers d'études africaines*, vol. 6, no. 23 (1966), pp. 349–366.

Hodgkin, Thomas, and Ruth Schachter. "French-speaking West Africa in Transition." *Internationale Conciliation*, no. 528 (May 1960), pp. 375–436.

Horowitz, Donald. "Three Dimensions of Ethnic Politics." *World Politics*, vol. 23, no. 2 (January 1971), pp. 232–244.

Hourani, A. *Minorities in the Arab World*. London: Oxford University Press, 1947.

Hughes, E. C. "Social Change and Status Protest: An Essay on the Marginal Man." *Phylon*, vol. 10, no. 1 (First Quarter 1949), pp. 58–65.

Hundsalz, M. "Die Wanderung der Yoruba nach Ghana und Ihre Ruckkehr nach Nigeria." *Erdkunde* (Bonn), band 26 (September 1972), pp. 218–230.

Hunter, Monica. *Reaction to Conquest*. London: Oxford University Press for the International African Institute, 1936.

Inkeles, A. *What is Sociology?* Englewood Cliffs, N.J.: Prentice-Hall, 1964.

Isaacman, Allen F. *Mozambique*. Madison: University of Wisconsin Press, 1972.

Jahoda, G. "The Development of Children's Ideas About Country and Nationality: I." "The Conceptual Frame, II. National Symbols and Themes." *British Journal of Educational Psychology*, vol. 33, nos. 1, 2 (1963), pp. 47–60, 143–153.

Johnson, Marian. *Salaga Papers: I.* Institute of African Studies, University of Ghana, 1966.

Johnson, Willard. *The Cameroon Federation: Political Integration in a Fragmentary Society.* Princeton: Princeton University Press, 1970.

Kadushin, C. "Social Distance Between Client and Professional." *American Journal of Sociology*, vol. 67, no. 5 (March 1962), pp. 517–531.

Kagwa, Sir Apolo. *Ekitabo Kyekika Kye Nsenene.* Kampala: Kagwa Publication, 1904.

———. *Empisa za Baganda.* Kampala: Kagwa Publication, 1911.

———. *Ebika bya Baganda.* Kampala: Kagwa Publication, 1912.

———. *Kagwa Papers.* Makerere University Library, Kampala, 1926.

———. *Basekabaka be Buganda.* Kampala: Uganda Bookshop, 1953.

Kawa, R. T. *I-Bali lama Mfengu.* Lovedale, Cape Province: Lovedale Press, 1929.

Kilson, Martin. *Political Change in a West African State.* Cambridge: Harvard University Press, 1966.

———. "The National Congress of British West Africa, 1918–1953." In *Protest and Power in Black Africa*, ed. Robert I. Rotberg and Ali A. Mazrui. New York: Oxford University Press, 1970. Pages 571–588.

Kiwanuka, M. S. M. Semakula. *A History of Buganda: From the Foundation of the Kingdom to 1900.* London: Longmans, 1971.

Krapf, Rev. Dr. J. L. *Travels, Researches and Missionary Labors, During an Eighteen Year's Residence in Eastern Africa: Together with Journeys to Jagga, Usambara, Ukambani, Shoa, Abessinia, and Khartum; and a Coasting Voyage from Mombaz to Cape Delgado.* Boston: Ticknor & Fields, 1860.

Krige, E. Jensen, and Krige, J. D. *The Realm of a Rain Queen.* London: Oxford University Press for the International African Institute, 1943.

Kuper, Hilda. "'Strangers' in Plural Societies: Asians in South Africa and Uganda." In *Pluralism in Africa*, ed. Leo Kuper and M. G. Smith. Berkeley and Los Angeles: University of California Press, 1969. Pages 247–282.

Kuper, Jessica. "The Goan Community in Kampala, Uganda." Ph.D. dissertation, University of London, 1973.

———. "The Goan Community in Kampala." In *The Expulsion of a Minority: Essays on the Uganda Asians*, ed. M. Twaddle. London: Athlone Press, 1975. Pages 53–69.

Kuper, Leo. *Race, Class and Power.* London: Duckworth, 1974.

La Voix du Dahomey, 13 March 1928.

Legesse, A. *Gada: Three Approaches to the Study of an African Society.* New York: Free Press, 1975.

Leibenstein, H. "Entrepreneurship and Development." *American Economic Review*, vol. 58 (1968), pp. 72–83.

Le Monde, 28–29 September 1958.

Levine, Donald N. *Georg Simmel: On Individuality and Social Forms.* Chicago: University of Chicago Press, 1971.

———. *Greater Ethiopia: The Evolution of a Multiethnic Society.* Chicago: University of Chicago Press, 1974.

Levine, Donald N., Carter, E. B., and Gorman, E. M. "Simmel's Influence on American Sociology." *American Journal of Sociology*, vol. 81, no. 4 (January 1976), pp. 813–845.

LeVine, Robert A., and Campbell, Donald T. *Ethnocentrism: Theories of Conflict, Ethnic Attitudes, and Group Behavior.* New York: John Wiley & Sons, 1972.

Lewis, Arthur W., ed. *Tropical Development, 1880–1913.* Evanston: Northwestern University Press, 1970.

Lloyd, P. C. "The Yoruba Lineage." *Africa*, vol. 25, no. 3 (July 1955), pp. 235–251.

————. *Yoruba Land Law.* Ibadan: Oxford University Press, 1962.

Lofland, L. *A World of Strangers.* New York: Basic Books, 1973.

Lyall, R. *Journal of the Mission of Robert Lyall to Radama I, King of Madagascar (24 October to 8 November, 1827).* London, Department of Manuscripts, British Museum, Add. 34408.

Lybyer, Albert. *The Government of the Ottoman Empire in the Time of Suleiman the Magnificent.* Cambridge: Harvard University Press, 1913.

Mabogunje, A. L. *Regional Mobility and Resource Development in West Africa.* Montreal: McGill-Queen's University Press, 1972.

Mair, Lucy P. *An African People in the Twentieth Century.* London: George Routledge & Sons, 1934.

Mamdani, Mahmood. *From Citizen to Refugee.* London: Pinter, 1972.

Mangat, J. S. *A History of the Asians in East Africa c. 1886–1949.* Oxford: Clarendon Press, 1969.

Marais, J. S. *Maynier and the First Boer Republic.* Cape Town: Maskew Miller, 1944.

Mason, R. J. "First Early Iron Age Settlement in South Africa: Broederstroom 24/73, Brits District, Transvaal." *South African Journal of Science*, no. 69 (November 1973), pp. 324–326.

Mayer, Philip. *Townsmen or Tribesmen.* Cape Town: Oxford University Press, 1961.

Mazrui, Ali A. "Political Superannuation and the Trans-class Man." *International Journal of Comparative Sociology*, vol. 9, no. 2 (June 1968), pp. 81–96.

McFarland, D., and Brown, D. "Social Distance as a Metric: A Systematic Introduction to Smallest Space Analysis." In *Bonds of Pluralism*, ed. E. O. Laumann. New York: Wiley, 1973. Pages 213–253.

McLemore, S. D. "Simmel's 'Stranger': A Critique of the Concept." *Pacific Sociological Review*, vol. 13, no. 2 (Spring 1970), pp. 86–94.

McPhee, Allen. *The Economic Revolution in British West Africa.* London: Routledge, 1926.

Merton, R. K. *Social Theory and Social Structure.* 2nd ed. Glencoe, Ill.: Free Press, 1957.

Michels, Robert. "Materialien zu einer Soziologie des Fremden." *Jahrbuch für Soziologie*, vol. 1 (1925), pp. 296–319.

Middleton, John. "Political Incorporation Among the Lugbara of Uganda." In *From Tribe to Nation: Studies in Incorporation Processes*, ed. Ronald Cohen and John Middleton. Scranton: Chandler Publishing Co., 1970. Pages 55–62.

Mitchell, J. Clyde. *The Kalela Dance*. Rhodes-Livingston Paper no. 27. Manchester: Manchester University Press, 1956.

Mittelman, James H. *Ideology and Politics in Uganda: From Obote to Amin*. Ithaca: Cornell University Press, 1975.

Mondain, G. *Un Siècle de Mission protestante à Madagascar*. Paris: Société des Missions Evangéliques, 1920.

Montemayor, J. S. "A Sociological Analysis of a Goan Village Community." Ph.D. dissertation, University of Delhi, 1970.

Moodie, D. *The Record, 1838–1842*. Volume I. Cape Town and Amsterdam: Balkema, 1960.

Morgan, L. H. *Ancient Society*. New York: Henry Holt, 1877.

Morgenthau, Ruth S. *Political Parties in French-Speaking West Africa*. London: Oxford University Press, 1964.

———. "Multinational Enterprises in Africa," in "Multinational Enterprises and Economic Development." Institute of Policy Study Papers, Yale University, 1974. Mimeographed.

———. "The Developing States of Africa." *Annals of the American Academy of Political and Social Science* (July 1977), pp. 80–95.

Morris, H. S. *The Indians in Uganda*. London: Weidenfeld & Nicolson, 1968.

Mowrer, E. *Disorganization: Personal and Social*. Philadelphia: Lippincott, 1942.

Mukwaya, A. B. *Land Tenure in Buganda*. East African Studies no. 1. Kampala: Eagle Press, 1955.

Nash, Dennison. "The Ethnologist as Stranger." *Southwestern Journal of Anthropology*, vol. 19, no. 1 (Summer 1963), pp. 149–167.

Nash, Dennison, and Wolfe, Alvin W. "The Stranger in Laboratory Culture." *American Sociological Review*, vol. 22, no. 4 (August 1957), pp. 400–405.

Nazareth, P. *In a Brown Mantle*. Nairobi: East African Literature Bureau, 1972.

Nelson, D. "Caste and Club: A Study of Goan Politics in Nairobi." Ph.D. dissertation, University of Nairobi, 1971.

Nsimbi, Michael. *Siwa Muto Lugero*. Kampala: B. C. S. Press, 1948.

———. *Waggumbulizi*. London: Longmans, 1952.

———. *Muddu Awulira*. Kampala: Uganda Bookshop, 1953.

———. *Amanya Amaganda N'Ennono Zaago*. Kampala: Uganda Society, 1956.

O'Brien, Justine. *See* Tandon, Yashpal.

Ogot, B. A. *A History of the Southern Luo*. Volume I. Nairobi: East African Publishing House, 1967.

Oppong-Agyare, J. "Test Case of Credibility." *The Pioneer* (Kumasi), 28 November 1969.

Oyedipe, F. "Some Sociological Aspects of the Yoruba Family." Master's thesis, University of Ghana, Legon, 1967.

Park, R. E. "Human Migration and the Marginal Man." *American Journal of Sociology*, vol. 33, no. 6 (May 1928), pp. 881–893.

Patel, Hasu H. *Indians in Uganda and Rhodesia: Some Comparative Perspectives on a Minority in Africa*. Denver: Center on International Race Relations, University of Denver, 1974.

Peil, M. "The Expulsion of West African Aliens." *Journal of Modern African Studies*, vol. 9, no. 2 (August 1971), pp. 205–229.

———. *The Ghanaian Factory Worker*. Cambridge: Cambridge University Press, 1972.

——. "Ghana's Aliens." *International Migration Review,* vol. 8, no. 3 (Fall 1974), pp. 367–381.

Piaget, S., and Weil, A. "The Development in Children of the Idea of the Homeland and Relations with Other Countries." *International Social Science Bulletin,* vol. 3, (1951), pp. 561–578.

Plamentaz, John. *Man and Society.* 2 vols. London: Longmans, 1963.

——. *Ideology.* London: Macmillan, 1970.

Pocock, D. F. "'Difference' in East Africa: A Study of Caste and Religion in Modern Indian Society." *Southwestern Journal of Anthropology,* vol. 13, no. 4 (Winter 1957), pp. 289–300.

Poku, K. "Traditional Roles and People of Slave Origin in Modern Ashanti—A Few Impressions." *Ghana Journal of Sociology,* vol. 5, no. 1 (1969), pp. 34–38.

Pons, V. G., Xydias, N., and Clement, P. "Social Effects of Urbanization in Stanleyville, Belgian Congo: Preliminary Report of the Field Research Team of the International African Institute." In *Social Implications of Industrialization and Urbanization in Africa South of the Sahara,* ed. Daryll Forde. Paris: UNESCO, 1956. Pages 229–492.

Powesland, P. G. "History of the Migration in Uganda." In *Economic Development and Tribal Change: A Study of Migrant Labor in Buganda,* ed. Audrey I. Richards. Cambridge: W. Heffer & Sons, 1954. Pages 17–51.

Pratt, S. A. J. "The Development of the Sierra Leone Railway." Volume I. Freetown, June 1966. Mimeographed.

Purcell, Victor. *The Chinese in Southeast Asia.* 2nd ed. London: Oxford University Press, 1965.

Ransome, Harry. "The Growth of Moyamba." *The Bulletin* (Freetown: The Journal of the Sierra Leone Geographical Association, no. 9, May 1965), pp. 54–55.

Rattray, R. S. *Ashanti Proverbs.* Oxford: Clarendon Press, 1916.

——. *Religion and Art in Ashanti.* London: Oxford University Press, 1927.

——. *Ashanti Law and Constitution.* London: Oxford University Press, 1929.

Review of T. E. Bowdich, *Mission from Cape Coast Castle to Ashantee, 1819. Journal des Savantes,* 1819.

Richards, Audrey I., ed. *Economic Development and Tribal Change: A Study of Migrant Labor in Buganda.* Cambridge: W. Heffer & Sons, 1954.

Riggs, Fred W. *Administration in Developing Countries.* Boston: Houghton Mifflin, 1964.

Rimmer, Douglas. "The Crisis in the Ghana Economy." *Journal of Modern African Studies,* vol. 4, no. 1 (May 1966), pp. 17–32.

Rochefort, David. "American Policy Toward the Congo Since 1960." Honors Thesis in Politics, Brandeis University, April 1975.

Rolland, Louis, and Lampué, Pierre. *Droit d'outre mer.* 3rd ed. Paris: Dolloz, 1959.

Roscoe, J. "Immigrants and their Influence in the Lake Region of Central Africa." The Frazer Lecture, Cambridge University Press, 1927.

Rose, P. I. "Strangers in Their Midst: Small-town Jews and Their Neighbors." In *The Study of Society,* ed. P. I. Rose. New York: Random House, 1967. Pages 463–479.

Rosenthal, E., and Goodwin, A. J. H. *Cave Artists of South Africa.* Cape Town: Balkema, 1953.

Rouch, Jean. "Migration in the Gold Coast." Accra, 1954. Mimeographed.

————. *Migrations au Ghana.* Paris: Centre National de Recherche Scientifique, 1956.

————. "Second Generation Migrants in Ivory Coast." In *Social Change in Modern Africa,* ed. Aidan W. Southall. London: Oxford University Press for the International African Institute, 1961. Pages 300–304.

Rowe, John A. "Myth, Memoir, and Moral Admonition: Luganda Historical Writing, 1893–1969." *Uganda Journal,* vol. 33, pt. 1 (1969), pp. 17–40.

————. "Myth, Memoir, and Moral Admonition: Luganda Historical Writing, 1893–1969." *Uganda Journal,* vol. 33, pt. 2 (1969), pp. 217–219.

Runciman, W. G. "Status Consistency, Relative Deprivation, and Attitudes to Immigrants." In *Sociology in Its Place,* ed. W. G. Runciman. Cambridge: Cambridge University Press, 1970. Pages 176–194.

Ryan, Selwyn. "Economic Nationalism and Socialism in Uganda." *Journal of Commonwealth Political Studies,* vol, 11, no. 2 (July 1973), pp. 140–158.

Saylor, Ralph G. *The Economic System of Sierra Leone.* Durham: Duke University Press, 1967.

Schapera, I. *A Handbook of Tswana Law and Custom.* London: Oxford University Press for the International African Institute, 1938.

————. *The Ethnic Composition of Tswana Tribes.* London: London School of Economics and Political Science, Monographs on Social Anthropology, no. 11, 1952.

————. *Government and Politics in Tribal Societies.* London: C. A. Watts, 1956.

Schildkrout, E. "Strangers and Local Government in Kumasi." *Journal of Modern African Studies,* vol. 8, no. 2 (July 1970), pp. 251–269.

————. "Government and Chiefs in Kumasi Zongo." In *West African Chiefs: Their Changing Status Under Colonial Rule and Independence,* ed. M. Crowder and O. Ikeme. Ile-Ife: University of Ife Press, 1970. Pages 370–393.

————. "Ethnicity and Generational Differences Among Urban Immigrants in Ghana." In *Urban Ethnicity.* Association of Social Anthropologists Monograph no. 12. Edited by A. Cohen. London: Tavistock, 1974. Pages 187–222.

————. "Islam and Politics in Ghana: An Analysis of Disputes Over the Kumasi Central Mosque." *Anthropological Papers of the American Museum of Natural History* (New York), vol. 52, no. 2 (1974), pp. 113–137.

————. *People of the Zongo: The Transformation of Ethnic Identities in Ghana.* Cambridge: Cambridge University Press, 1978.

Schutz, Alfred. "The Homecomer." *American Journal of Sociology,* vol. 50, no. 5 (March 1945), pp. 369–376.

Schweitzer, F. R. "Archaeological Evidence for Sheep at the Cape." *South African Archaeological Bulletin,* vol. 29, nos. 115–116 (1974), pp. 75–82.

Scott, James C. "The Analysis of Corruption in Developing Nations." *Comparative Studies in Society and History,* vol. 2, no. 3 (June 1969), pp. 315–349.

Shack, W. A. *The Central Ethiopians: Amhara, Tigrinya and Related Peoples.* Ethnographic Survey of Northeastern Africa, Part IV. London: International African Institute, 1974.

————. "Ethiopia and Afro-Americans: Some Historical Notes, 1920–1970." *Phylon,* vol. 35, no. 2 (June 1974), pp. 142–155.

———. "Religious Strangers in the Kingdom of Ethiopia." *Journal of Modern African Studies*, vol. 13, no. 2 (June 1975), pp. 361–366.

Shaw, William. *The Story of My Mission in South-Eastern Africa.* London: Hamilton, Adams & Co., 1860.

Sierra Leone, *Legislative Council Debates*, Colony of Sierra Leone, CO 270/41, 21 September 1905, pp. 519–526.

Sierra Leone, *Chief's Courts*, Commissioner, Southeastern Province, File P/9/4, 25 September 1941.

Sierra Leone, *Protectorate Assembly*, Proceedings of the Eleventh Meeting. Freetown: Government Printing Department, 1955.

Sierra Leone, Public Notices, no. 78, *Constitution*, 1961.

Sierra Leone, *Report of the Mines Department.* Freetown: Government Printer, 1962.

Sierra Leone, *The Report of the Commission Appointed to Enquire into and Report on the Matters Contained in the Director of Audit's Report on the Account of Sierra Leone for the Year 1960-61 and the Government Statement thereon.* (Cole Commission) Mr. Justice C. O. E. Cole, Chairman. Freetown: Government Printer, 1963.

Sierra Leone, *Restriction of Retail Trade Act No. 30*, 1965.

Sierra Leone, *Annual Reports*, Sierra Leone Produce Marketing Board. Freetown: Government Printer, 1967.

Sierra Leone, National Reformation Council, *Report of the Forster Commission of Inquiry on Assets of Ex-Ministers and Ex-Deputy Ministers*, 1967.

Simmel, G. *Soziologie.* Leipzig: Duncker & Humblot, 1908. Translated by R. E. Park and E. W. Burgess as *Introduction to the Science of Society.* Chicago: University of Chicago Press, 1921.

———. "The Stranger." In *The Sociology of Georg Simmel.* Translated and edited by K. H. Wolff. New York: Free Press, 1950. Pages 402–408.

———. *Conflict and the Web of Group Affiliation.* Translated by K. H. Wolff and R. Bendix. Glencoe, Ill.: Free Press, 1955.

Siu, P. C. P. "The Sojourner." *American Journal of Sociology*, vol. 58, no. 1 (July 1952), pp. 34–44.

Skinner, E. P. "Strangers in West African Societies." *Africa*, vol. 33, no. 4 (October 1963), pp. 307–320.

———. "West African Economic Systems." In *Economic Transition in Africa*, ed. M. J. Herskovits and M. Harwitz. Evanston, Northwestern University Press, 1964. Pages 77–97.

———. "Theoretical Perspectives on the Stranger." Paper presented at the Conference on Strangers in Africa, 16–19 October 1974, Smithsonian Conference Center, Belmont, Maryland.

Sklar, Richard. *Corporate Power in an African State.* Berkeley: University of California Press, 1975.

Smith, Robert. "West African Economic Cooperation—Problems and Prospects." *Foreign Service Journal* (Washington, D.C.), April 1974.

Soga, J. H. *The South-Eastern Bantu.* Johannesburg: Witwatersrand University Press, 1930.

———. *The Ama-Xosa, Life and Customs.* Lovedale, Cape Province: Lovedale Press, 1931.

Soga, T. B. *Intlalo ka-Xosa*. Lovedale, Cape Province: Lovedale Press, n.d.

Southall, Aidan W. "Padhola: Comparative Social Structure." Conference Paper, East African Institute of Social Research, 1957.

———. "Population Movements in East Africa." In *Essays on African Population*, ed. K. M. Barbour and R. M. Prothero. London: Routledge & Kegan Paul, 1961. Pages 157–192.

———. *Alur Society*. Cambridge: W. Heffer & Sons, 1963.

———. "Incorporation Among the Alur." In *From Tribe to Nation in Africa: Studies in Incorporation Processes*, ed. Ronald Cohen and John Middleton. Scranton, Pa.: Chandler, 1970. Pages 71–82.

———. "General Amin and the Coup: Great Man or Historical Inevitability?" *Journal of Modern African Studies*, vol. 13, no. 1 (March 1975), pp. 85–105.

Speke, John H. *Journal of the Discovery of the Source of the Nile*. Edinburgh and London: William Blackwood & Sons, 1863.

Standard (Tanzania), 7 October 1970.

Staniland, S. *The Lions of Dagbon*. Cambridge: Cambridge University Press, 1975.

Stanley, Richard, and Neame, Alan, eds. *The Exploration Diaries of H. M. Stanley*. London: William Kimber, 1961.

Stonequist, E. *The Marginal Man*. New York: Scribner's, 1937.

Sudarkasa, Niara. *Where Women Work*. Ann Arbor: University of Michigan Museum of Anthropology, 1973.

———. "Commercial Migration in West Africa, with Special Reference to the Yoruba in Ghana." *African Urban Notes*, ser. B, no. 1 (Winter 1974–75), pp. 61–103.

———. "The Economic Status of the Yorubas in Ghana Before 1970." *Nigerian Journal of Economic and Social Studies*, vol. 17, no. 1 (1975).

Suret-Canale, Jean. *Afrique noire occidentale et centrale*. Paris: Editions Sociale, 1958.

Tandon, Yashpal, [O'Brien, Justine]. *Brown Britons: The Crisis of the Uganda Asians*. London: Runnymede Trust Publications, 1972.

The Pioneer (Kumasi, Ghana), 19 November 1969.

The Pioneer (Kumasi, Ghana), 24 November 1969.

The Sunday Times (London), 23 May 1976.

Theal, G. M. *Records of South Eastern Africa*, 9 vols. Cape Town: Government of the Cape Colony, 1898.

Thompson, G. *Travels and Adventures in Southern Africa*. London: Colburn, 1827.

Thompson, L. A., and Ferguson, J., eds. *Africa in Classical Antiquity*. Ibadan: Ibadan University Press, 1969.

Tiryakian, E. A. "Sociological Perspectives on the Stranger." *Sounding* (Spring 1973), pp. 45–58.

———. "Perspectives on the Stranger." In *The Rediscovery of Ethnicity*, ed. S. TeSelle. New York: Harper & Row, 1973. Pages 45–58.

Trumbull, H. C. *The Threshold Covenant*. New York: Scribner's Sons, 1896.

Turner, Victor. *The Ritual Process*. Chicago: Aldine, 1969.

Twaddle, Michael, ed. *Expulsion of a Minority: Essays on Uganda Asians*. London: Athlone Press, University of London for the Institute of Commonwealth Studies, 1975.

Uganda, *A Report of the Census of the Non-Native Population of Uganda Protectorate.* Entebbe: East African Statistical Department, 1955.

University of Natal, Research Team. *The Dunn Reserve.* Natal: University of Natal Press, 1963.

Van den Berghe, P. L. "Asians in East and South Africa: A Comparison." In *Portrait of a Minority: Asians in East Africa,* ed. D. P. Ghai and Y. P. Ghai. Rev. ed. Nairobi: Oxford University Press, 1970. Pages 151–175.

Van der Laan, H. L. *The Sierra Leone Diamonds.* London: Oxford University Press, 1965.

van Gennep, A. *The Rites of Passage.* Translated by M. Vizedom and G. Caffee. London: Routledge & Kegan Paul, 1960.

Verger, Pierre. "Les Afro-américains." *Mémoires de l'Ifan,* no. 27. Dakar: Imprimerie Nationale, 1953.

Vernon, Raymond. *Sovereignty at Bay.* New York: Basic Books, 1971.

West Africa (London), 20 December 1969.

West Africa (London), 18 February 1974.

West Africa (London), 27 May 1974.

West Africa (London), 16 June 1975.

Westie, Frank. "A Technique for the Measurement of Race Attitudes." *American Sociological Review,* vol. 18, no. 1 (February 1953), pp. 73–78.

Wilks, I. "The Position of Muslims in Metropolitan Ashanti in the Early Nineteenth Century." In *Islam in Tropical Africa,* ed. I. M. Lewis. London: Oxford University Press for the International African Institute, 1966. Pages 318–341.

———. "Ashanti Government." In *West African Kingdoms in the Nineteenth Century,* ed. Daryll Forde and P. M. Kaberry. London: Oxford University Press for the International African Institute, 1967. Pages 206–238.

———. "Asante Policy Towards the Hausa Trade in the Nineteenth Century." In *The Development of Indigenous Trade and Markets in West Africa,* ed. C. Meillassoux. London: Oxford University Press for the International African Institute, 1971. Pages 124–141.

———. *Asante in the Nineteenth Century.* African Studies Series no. 13. Cambridge: Cambridge University Press, 1975.

Williams, R. M., Jr. *Strangers Next Door: Ethnic Relations in American Communities.* Englewood Cliffs, N.J.: Prentice-Hall, 1964.

Wilson, G. M. "The Luo Homestead and Family." Mimeographed. 1955.

Wilson, Monica. *Good Company.* London: Oxford University Press for the International African Institute, 1951.

———. *Peoples of the Nyasa-Tanganyika Corridor.* Cape Town: University of Cape Town, 1958.

———. *Communal Rituals of the Nyakyusa.* London: Oxford University Press for the International African Institute, 1959.

———. "The Interpreters." Third Dugmore Memorial Lecture. Grahamstown, South Africa, 1972.

Wilson, Monica, Kaplan, S., Maki, T., and Walton, E. M. *Social Structure,* Keiskammahoek Rural Survey, III. Pietermaritzburg; Shuter and Shooter, 1952.

Wilson, Monica, and Thompson, Leonard, eds. *The Oxford History of South Africa.* 2 vols. Oxford: The Clarendon Press, 1969 and 1971.

Wood, M. M. *The Stranger: A Study in Social Relationships.* New York: Columbia University Press, 1934.

Wriggins, Howard. *Ceylon: Dilemmas of a New Nation.* Princeton: Princeton University Press, 1960.

Zajonc, Robert. "Aggressive Attitudes of the 'Stranger' as a Function of Conformity Pressures." *Human Relations,* vol. 5, no. 2 (May 1952), pp. 205–216.

Zartman, William I. *International Relations in the New Africa.* Englewood Cliffs, N.J.: Prentice-Hall, 1966.

Index

abeLungu clan, origins of, 54
Abidjan, Ivory Coast, 75, 78
Aboabo, 153, 160, 161
Abomey, 80
Absorption. *See* Assimilation of strangers
Abyssinia, status of strangers in, 10, 42–43, 109. *See also* Ethiopia
Accra, Ghana, 124, 125, 138
Acholi, 233
Addo, N. O., 128n, 136
Adhola, 233
Adultery, 59
African Democratic Rally Party: formation of, 76; strangers in, 80
African nation-states: accommodation of strangers in, 14–15, 287; citizenship emphasized over social status in, 287–288; colonial institutions in, 163–164; defined, 37n; disparity between rich and poor, 116; economic barriers among, 106, 107, 117, 266–267; formation of influenced by multinational enterprises, 133–115, 286; and "open" or "closed" social systems relative to strangers, 37, 41, 43, 45, 46; peaceful settlements of conflicts between, 81–82; political relations changed by multinational enterprises in, 115–117; regional regrouping of, 116; "reliminalized" status of strangers in, 42, 46; right to expel non-nationals from, 6–7, 82, 100, 166–167; ritual process of stranger relations in, 42, 45, 46–47; social interaction influenced by regional economic inequality in, 184, 194–195, 198, 205–206, 207; status of strangers altered in, 6–7, 35, 42, 45, 46–47, 99–103, 106–108, 116–117, 131, 139, 193–195, 254, 287–288
African political leaders: affluence of, 110; colonial rule changes relations between strangers and, 5–6, 146–152, 162–166, 193; historical cleavages exploited by, 65; ideological diffuseness of, 272–274, 277–278; integration policies of, 117–118; relations between multinational enterprises and, 111–115, 119; rivals among, 114–115
African strangers: in the economic development of the Ivory Coast, 6, 74–78; expelled from Ghana, 47, 123, 132–143 *passim*, 162–165; expelled from Uganda,

261, 262–267, 271; favorable attitudes toward in Ghana, 123–129; free migration of across territorial boundaries in pre-colonial Africa, 8, 39–40, 51, 270–271; in Ganda villages, 227–241; and regional identity, 185–207; nationalism promotes expulsion of, 105–108; ritual incorporation of during pre-colonial era, 38–41, 45; Simmel's concept of the stranger applied to, 5, 143–145; transformed from sojourners to aliens, 129–139. *See also* Ganda; Luo laborers from Kenya; Yoruba stranger communities in Ghana
African trade, clandestine vs. official, 106–107
African traders: expelled from Ghana, 132–133, 137; effects of indigenization on, 105–108; kinship system promotes success of, 169–182; sexual roles among, 132–133, 169–170, 194n; social distance maintained by, 133; and Simmel's concept of the stranger, 23, 38, 40, 133
Africanization of commerce: African traders influenced by, 105–108; in the diamond trade, 92–93; economic constraints and limitations of, 108; economic and political effects in Sierra Leone, 99, 100; in Ghana, 107, 108, 131; of private enterprise in Uganda, 277; and racial identity, 254–255, 259; stimulated by restrictive legislation against strangers, 100–101
Age, 191; and assimilation of aliens, 135, 136
Agents, 86; colonial, 220–222; use of modern currency accelerated by, 90
Agricultural laborers, foreign, 68; on cash-crop farms in Buganda, 227, 234, 235, 236, 237; imported to the Ivory Coast, 74, 78; slaves as, 188; in southern Ghana, 136, 187, 193, 194
Agricultural trade, controlled by Lebanese traders in Sierra Leone, 88–89, 90, 91
Agriculture: effect of multinational enterprises on, 111; and urban growth, 118–119
Ahomodegbe, President, 83
Akan, 189; assimilation of migrants by, 123, 124; term for stranger, 185–186
Alao, A. H., 157n
Alberti, L., 56

Design: Dave Comstock
Compositor: Freedman's Organization
Printer: Thomson-Shore
Binder: Thomson-Shore
Text: Compugraphic Paladium
Display: Compugraphic Paladium
Cloth: Roxite B Vellum
Paper: 50lb. P&S Offset Vellum B32